5,000 QUOTATIONS
FOR TEACHERS AND PREACHERS

5,000 Quotations

for

Teachers and Preachers

Compiled by
ROBERT BACKHOUSE

*This book
belongs to
Revd David Durie*

KINGSWAY PUBLICATIONS
EASTBOURNE

ISBN 0 85476 403 8

Produced by Bookprint Creative Services
P.O. Box 827, BN21 3YJ, England, for
KINGSWAY PUBLICATIONS LTD
Lottbridge Drove, Eastbourne, E Sussex BN23 6NT.
Printed in Finland.

Contents

Introduction   vii
List of Entries   xi
The Quotations   1
Index of Sources   241

Introduction

Sources of quotations

The sources of the quotations in this book can be classified under three headings: quotations by non-Christian writers, quotations by Christian writers and biblical quotations.

Secular quotations

There are a number of quotations in this book spoken and written by agnostics and atheists. Such quotations are valuable because they help the Christian to understand the worldview of the non-Christian. Quotations from atheists help the Christian to see how to apply the good news about Jesus Christ to those who are not used to thinking in a Christian way. It is necessary to see and feel what it is like to live a meaningless life today before one starts talking about how Christ can and does give meaning to life.

Christian quotations

Quotations from Christian sources make up the vast majority of the quotations in this book. Christian quotations from the first century onwards have been culled from sermons, prayers, letters, books, hymns, diaries, journals, confessions of faith and speeches.

Particular care has been taken to include quotations from the early church fathers, the so-called 'Christian mystics' and some of the most important theologians – thinkers such as Augustine, Luther and Calvin.

Biblical quotations

Quotations from the Bible are also included. They give the teaching of God on the wide variety of subjects covered in this book, and are a yardstick by which quotations from other people, be they Seneca, Voltaire, Robert Louis Stevenson or Tolstoy, can be judged. It is interesting to see how relevant and pertinent God's word is on issues which are of crucial importance to today's world.

Types of quotations

Memorable quotations

Proverbs make memorable quotations, and this book includes a number of well-known Latin, Greek and English proverbs as well as German, Spanish and Italian proverbs which are not usually found in other books of quotations. A number of telling proverbs from the biblical book of Proverbs are also included.

Important quotations

Care has been taken to include quotations which may be termed important, even if they were not phrased in a memorable or vivid way. Martin Luther's quotation about his conscience being captive to the word of God may not be considered in itself to be particularly memorable. However, it is included because it reflects one of the pivotal moments in the history of the Christian church: the debate about the authority of human reason, church tradition and the Bible.

Other quotations may appear at first sight to be rather pedestrian but nevertheless they may encapsulate the conclusion of hundreds of years of years of controversial theological debate. An example of this is the quotation about the divinity and humanity of Jesus Christ from the Council of Chalcedon: 'We all with one voice teach that it should be confessed that our Lord Jesus Christ is one and the same Son, the same perfect in Godhead, the same perfect in manhood, truly God and truly man.'

Use of quotations

For fun

Some people read books of quotations in the way others engage in the pursuit of solving crossword puzzles: for fun, leisure, relaxation and mental stimulus. They revel in either dipping into or reading right through books of quotations.

For understanding

Winston Churchill recommended the uneducated to read right through a book of quotations. Frank Tibolt advocates that a book of quotations should be permanently kept on the kitchen table. He says he cannot overemphasise the potential value of a book of quotations. A single quotation can completely revolutionise a person's life with undreamed-of beneficial results.

For teaching

Many Christians spend part of their lives teaching or preaching the Christian faith, leading Bible study groups or attempting to be of assistance to individuals. They are dedicated to building up other Christians in their faith. These quotations have been placed under carefully selected headings so that they can be easily located and used in talks, addresses and sermons.

Repetition

Sometimes similar quotations by various people are included under the same heading. It is interesting to see how different people from different ages say the same thing. It is a teaching method which the prophet Isaiah would have approved: 'The Lord is going to teach you letter by letter, line by line, lesson by lesson' (Is 28:13).

Jesus' use of quotations

Our Lord Jesus Christ was fond of using quotations. Many of his were from the Old Testament, but he used other sources as well. Sometimes he would deliberately set up a quotation as an Aunt Sally so that he could knock it down. For example, in the Sermon on the Mount, Jesus says, 'You have heard that it was said, "Love your friends and hate your enemies."' (Mt 5:43). Contrary to what is often thought this is not a quotation from the Old Testament but comes from the Jewish teachers. Jesus used this quotation to teach the opposite, that is 'love your enemies' (Mt 5:44).

The battle for the mind

Every time anybody teaches the Christian faith in any way, formally or informally, the battle for the truth is being fought. All age groups, but perhaps young people in particular, are crying out for understandable, relevant teaching about the Saviour of the world. This book of quotations is presented in the hope that it may be of real use in this battle. The last words of Jesus recorded in Matthew's Gospel are our inspiration: 'Go . . . to all peoples everywhere and make them my disciples . . . *teach* them to obey everything I have commanded you.'

Robert Backhouse
Norwich, 1994

List of Entries

Abandonment
Abiding in God
Ability
Abortion
Abstinence
Abundance
Abuse
Acceptance
Accepting God
Accidents
Accusation, False
Achievement
Action
  *and the present
    moment*
  and trust
  and words
Adam and Eve
Adoration
Adultery
Adventure
Adversity
Advice
Affection
Ages of man
Agnosticism
Agreement
Aid
AIDS
Ambassadors
Ambition
  *Warnings
    against*
Angels
Anger
  Positive views of
  Righteous
Anglican Church
Animals

Annunciation
Anxiety
Apologies
Apostolic doctrine
Apostolic
        succession
Appearances
Appreciation
Architecture
Argument
Arrogance
Art
Ascension
Assurance
Astrology
Atheism
Atonement
Attack
Attitude
Authority
Automation
Awareness of God

Backsliding
Bankers
Baptism
  and salvation
Beatitudes
Beauty
  Spiritual
Beginning
Behaviour
Being
Belief
  in self
Belonging
Bereavement
  *Individuals'
    reactions to*

Bible
  and Reason
  and Society
  *as the Word of
    God*
  Authority of
  Christ in the
  Criticism of
  Early scholars of
  Early witness to
  Inspiration of
  Interpretation of
  Obedience to
  Reading the
  Sufficiency of
  Translation of
  *Trustworthiness
    of*
  Uniqueness of
  and science
Biography
Birth control
Birthdays
Bishops
Blessings
Blindness
Blood
Blushing
Boasting
Body, The
Brevity
Bribery
Broken-hearted-
        ness
Brotherhood
Burden-sharing
Business
Busybodies
Busyness

Call
Calvinism v.
        Arminian-
          ism
Careers
Caring
Causes, Righteous
Caution
Celibacy
Challenge
Chance
Change
Character
Charity
Cheerfulness
Child evangelism
Children
  Advice to
  and Jesus
  of God
  Upbringing
Christ
  as King
  as Mediator
  *as our
    Righteousness*
  *as our
      Sin-bearer*
  as Shepherd
  Baptism of
  Birth of
  Divinity of
  Early witnesses
  Humanity of
  Knocking
  Life of
  Mission of
  Power of
  Sinlessness of

Christ (continued)
  Strength of
  Verdict of non-
    Christians on
Christian life
  as conflict
  as following
    Jesus
Christian message
Christian unity
Christian
  upbringing
Christian writing
Christianity
  Historicity of
  Message of
  Spread of
  Verdict of non-
    Christians
    on
Christians
  Early
  and the State
Christlike
  behaviour
Christmas
Church
  as Mother
  Leaving the
    True
  buildings
  government
  invisible
  membership
  services
  visible
Churchgoing
Circumstances
Cities
Civilisation
Clairvoyance
Cleanliness
Closeness to God
Comfort
Commandments
Committees
Common sense
Communal living
Communism
Commuters
Compassion
Conceit
Concentration
Condemnation
Confession
Conscience

Conscientiousness
Consecration
Consequences of
  evil
Conservation
Consistency
Contemplation
Contentment
Convents
Conversation
Conversion
  Holy Spirit's
    work in
  of Barnardo
  of Booth
  of Bunyan
  of children
  of colliers at
    Kingswood
  of Early
    Christians
  of Edwards
  of Luther
  of Moody
  of Patrick
  of Whitefield
Conversions,
  Preachers'
    work for
Conviction
Co-operation
Correction
Counselling
Courage
Courtesy
Courtship
Covenant
Covetousness
Creation
Creativity
Creeds
Crises
Criticism
Cross
  Personal
    response to
Crucifixion
Cruelty
Curiosity
Custom
Cynics

Daily help from
  God
Dance
Danger

Darkness
Dead, Christian
Death
  as leveller
  destroyed by
    God's
    power
  in the midst of
    life
  Inevitability of
  Non-Christian
    views of
  of a child
  Readiness for
Debate
Debt
  to God
Deceit
Decision for Christ
Decisions
Decline
Delay
Delegation
Democracy
Denominations,
  Christian
Dependence on
  God
Depression
Desire
Despair
Despising
Destiny
Detachment
Details
Determination
Devil
  Existence of
  Fighting the
Dictators
Difficult people
Difficulties in life
Difficulties in
    science
Diffidence
Dignity
Diplomacy
Disability
Disappointments
Disaster
Discipleship,
  Secret
Discipline
Discoveries
Discretion
Divorce

Doctors
Doctrine
Dogma
Doubt
Dreams
Dress
Drink
Duty

Economists
Education
Effort
Egotism
Egypt
Election, Divine
Elections,
    Govern-
    ment
Emotions
Employers
Emptiness
Encouragement
Endurance
Enemies
England
Enjoyment
Enlightenment
Enoch
Enthusiasm
Environment
Envy
Ephesians, Paul's
    letter to the
Epitaphs
Equality
Error
Essentials
Eternal life
Eternity
Europe
Evangelism
Eve
Evening
Evidences for
    Christianity
Evil
Evolution
Examinations
Example
Excellence
Excess
Excuses
Expectations
Experience
Exploitation
Extravagance

Faces
Facts
Failure
Faith
  Definitions of
  Power of
  and action
  and fear
  and obedience
  and prayer
  and reason
  and suffering
  required
Faithfulness
Fall, The
Falling away
Fame
Families
Family, The
        Christian
Fanaticism
Farming
Fashion
Fasting
Fathers
Fathers in God
Faults
Fear
Fear of God
Feelings
Fellowship
  with God
Festivals
Flattery
Flippancy
Follow-up
Food
Foolishness
Foreigners
Forgiveness
Forgiving others
Formalism
Fortune
Free will
Freedom
  Christian
French people
Fretting
Friars
Friends of God
Friendship
  Acquiring
  and sincerity
  in times of need
  Learning from
  Value of

Friendship (cont.)
  Spiritual
Fulfilment
Fun
Fund-raising
Funerals
Future

Gambling
Garden of
        Geth-
        semane
Gardens
Garrulity
Genius
Gentlemen
Gentleness
Gifts
Giving
  and getting
  willingly
Gloating
Gluttony
Goals
  Absence of
  Examples of
God
  and mankind
  as Creator
  as Father
  as Friend
  as last resort
  as Refuge
  as Shepherd
  as Sustainer
  Belief in
  Greater than
        mankind
  Understanding
Godliness
God's actions
God's care
God's existence
God's faithfulness
God's gifts
God's goodness
God's grace
God's holiness
God's image
God's invitation
God's judgement
God's law
God's love
  Abundance of
  Adversity and
  Desire for

God's love (cont.)
  Judgement and
  Response to
  inescapable
  more important
        than any-
        thing else
God's mercy
God's names
God's nature
God's power
God's presence
  amid everyday
        activities
  and the
        believer's
        response
  in gardens
  in prison
  in the believer's
        heart
  when there is no
        other help
God's protection
God's provision
God's will
God's word
God's work
God's wrath
Good and evil
Good deeds
  Motive of
Good news
Gospel
Gossip
Government
Grace
  and human will
  and its effect on
        the believer
  and nature
  defined
Grace (prayer)
Graces
Gratitude
  and adversity
  and friendship
  and ingratitude
  and trust
Greatness
Greed
Grief
Growing up
Growth, Personal
Growth, Spiritual
Grumbling

Guidance
Guilt

Habits
  Overcoming
Happiness
  Effects of
  Lack of
  Sources of
Hard times
Hate
Healing
Health
Hearts
Heaven
  Nature of
  Ways to
Hebrews 11
Hell
  Nature of
  Ways to
Heresy
History
  and Jesus Christ
Holiness
Holy Spirit
  Fruit of the
  Gifts of the
  Indwelling of the
  and free will
  and the Bible
  and the Church
  and work
Home
Honesty
Honour
Hope
Hopelessness
Hospitality
Human rights
Humility
  Examples of
  Exhortations to
  False
  Importance of in
        Christianity
  Learning
  Nature of
  Rewards of
Humour
Hunger
Husbands
Hypocrisy

Ideals
Ideas

Idleness
Sacred
Idols
defined
Ignorance
Illness
Imagination
Imitation of God
Immortality
Incarnation
Indecision
Indifference
Individuals
Indulgences
Infallibility
Infant baptism
Inner life
Insight
Inspiration
Institutions
Instruction
Insults
Integrity
Intolerance
Invitations

Jealousy
Job, Book of
John 3:16
Joy
Judaism
Judgement
Judging others
Justice
Justification by
faith

Kindness
Response to
Kingdom of God
Kingdom of
heaven
Knowledge
Means to
Warnings
concerning
Knowledge of God
Limits of
Means of
Possibility of

Language
Last words
Laughter
Law
of God

Leadership
Learning
after un-
promising
beginnings
from all sources
throughout life
Leisure
Leprosy
Letter-writing
Lies
Life
Spiritual
after death
in Jesus
Light
Listening
Little things
Liturgy
Living
Day by day
God's help for
Purpose of
and dying
and human re-
lationships
for God
Loneliness
Longevity
Longing for God
Lord's Prayer
Lord's Supper
Physical
elements in
ineffective by
itself
to be received
worthily
Lordship of Christ
Lost souls
Love
Christian
Consistency of
Lack of
Learning
Platonic
Purity of
Response to
Sexual
and actions
and anger
and error
and fear
and giving
and God's
nature

Love (continued)
and humility
and prayer
and self
and suffering
and the faults of
the beloved
for Christians
for enemies
for God
Loyalty
Lukewarmness
Luxury

Mankind
Christ's
redemption
of
compared with
animals
Depravity of
Exalted
estimates of
Inhumanity to
man
Insignificance of
Middle state of
Nature of
Potential with
God
Social aspects of
Manners
Marriage
Christian
and celibacy
and faithfulness
and heaven
and love
Martyrdom
Effects of
welcomed
Marxism
Mary
Mass
Maturity
Meaning of life
Meaninglessness
Meditation
Melancholy
Mercy
Methodism
Millionaires
Mind
Ministers of religion
Authority of
Choice of

Miracles
of Jesus
Misery
Mission
Missionaries
Missionary call
Mistakes
Mobs
Mockery
Moderation
Modesty
Money
Dissatifaction
with
Limits to the
usefulness
of
Love of
Spending
and the service
of God
Monks
Monuments
Morality
Motherhood
Mothers-in-law
Motivation
Motives
Mottoes
coporate
personal and
family
Mourning
Murder
Murphy's law
Music
Effects of
and the devil
in church
services
Mystery
Mysticism

Name of Jesus
Nations
Nature
Redeemed
and the praise of
God
as revealing God
Need of God
Neighbour, Love
for
and love for God
and the 'Golden
Rule'

Neighbours
New creation
New Testament
New Year
Nicknames
Non-violence
Novelty

Obedience
Offence, Giving
Old age
*Respect for
and action
and maturing*
Old Testament
Opinions, Other
people's
Opportunity
Opposition
Optimism
Order
Original sin
Originality

Pain
Parenthood
Parents, Respect
for
Parley
Passion
Patience
Paul, The apostle
Peace
Peace
*False
and its source in
the self
and truth
of God
and the death
of Jesus
desired
foretold
of mind*
Peacemaking
Pentecost
People
Perfection
in the church
Persecution
*in the early
church*
Perseverance
*in politics
to the end*
Personality

Persuasion
Philosophy
Pagan
Pilgrimage
Pioneers
Plagiarism
Pleasing God
Pleasure
Poetry
Politeness
Politics
Polygamy
Pope, The
Positive thinking
Possessions
Potential
Poverty
*Relief of
Spiritual
Understanding*
Power
Spiritual
Practice
Praise
*of God
of others
of self*
Prayer
*and faith
and the devil
and the heart's
desire
and the will of
God
Definitions of
Effects of on
person
praying
Extempore
Intercessory
Lack of
Length of
Method of
Occasions and
times of
People of
Persistence in
Power of
Prevailing*
Preaching
*Manner of
Open-air
Purpose of
Simplicity in
Skill in
and love*

Preaching (cont.)
*and practice
and the gospel
message
and the Holy
Spirit
by God's
command*
Predestination
Prejudice
Preoccupation
Preparation
Pride
*and its correction
and its source
and what it leads
to*
Principles
Prison
Procrastination
Progress
Promises
of God
Prophecy
Prophets
Propitiation
Prosperity
Proverbs
Providence of God
Prudence
Psychoanalysis
Public opinion
Punctuality
Punishment
Purgatory
Purity

Quakers
Questions
Quietness
Quotation

Race
Rainbows
Reading
Devotional
Reality
Reason
Limitations of
Rebuke
Redemption
Reform
Reformation
*Church
Personal*
Reformers

Refreshment,
Spiritual
Regeneration
Rejection
Rejoicing
Relationships
Religion
Hostile views of
Religions, Non-
Christian
Religious
fanaticism
Religious practice
Remembering
Remuneration
Renunciation
Renewal
Repentance
Reputation
Respect
of persons
Responsibility
Rest
Restoration
Results
Resurrection
*appearances
of Jesus
Evidence for
of the body*
Retirement
Retreat
Revelations
Revenge
Reverence for
God
Revival
Revolutions
Reward
Ridicule
Ridiculousness
Righteousness
from God
Roman Catholic
Church
Romans, Paul's
letter to
the
Rush

Sabbath
Sacraments
Saints
Salvation
*as experienced
by Bilney*

Salvation (cont.)
  as experienced
    by Wesley
  as God's gift
  Mankind's need
    of
Sanctification
Saving
Saviour
Scandal
Science
  and Christianity
Searching for God
  in one's
    emptiness
  in one's interior
Second coming of
    Christ
Secrets
Security
Self
  Death of
  Value of
Self-confidence
Self-control
Self-deception
Self-denial
Self-discipline
Self-examination
Self-knowledge
Self-righteousness
Self-sacrifice
Selfishness
Sensuality
Service
  Prayers
    dedicating
    the self to
  and God's plans
  and humility
  and love for God
  in small things
Sex
Sexual intercourse
Shame
Sharing
Sickness
Sight
  Spiritual
Silence
  Reprehensible
  in society
Simplicity
Sin
  Awareness of
  Dealing with

Sin (continued)
  Defeat of
  Definition of
  Effects of
  Seriousness of
  Unforgivable
  and sins
    forsaken
Singing
Singleness of mind
Sisters
Slander
Slavery
Smiling
Smoking
Social action
Social reform
Social sin
Society
  and the
    Christian
Solitude
Sorrow
  Remedies for
Soul
Sowing
Specialists
Speech
  Godly
  Thoughtless
  Unkind
  and action
  and listening
  and observation
  and self-control
Spiritual coolness
Spiritual guides
Spirituality
Statistics
Stewardship
Stillness
Stoicism
Strangers
Stubbornness
Study
Sumbling-blocks
Stupidity
Success
Suffering
  Causes of
  Learning from
  Patience in
  Peace in
  and prayer
Sunday
Superstition

Surrender
Swearing
Symbolism
Sympathy
Systematic
    theology

Tact
Talents
Taxes
Teachers
Teamwork
Tears
Technology
Temperance
Temptation
  Purpose of
  Resisting
  Ways to escape
Ten Command-
    ments
Testimonies to
    Christ
Thanksgiving
Theology
Thief on the cross
Thinking
  Avoiding
  Buddhist view of
  Humility in
  Maturity in
  Resting from
  and action
  and character
  and happiness
  and speech
  deeply
Thrift
Time
Tiredness
Toleration
Tongues
Tradition
Training
Transformation
Travel
Tribulations
Trinity
Trouble
Trust
Trust in God
  among wild
    animals
  and God's
    promises
  at life's end

Trust in God (cont.)
  at sea
  because of his
    past mercies
  in battle
  for the church
  for the future
  when daunted
    by work
  when deserted
  when we seem
    abandoned
    by him
Truth
  Absolute
  and error
  and God
  and Jesus Christ
  and mankind
  and martyrdom
  and novelty
  and the church
  and the devil
  and the dying
  examined
  in relation-
    ships
  triumphant
  wherever it is
    found
Tyranny

Understanding
Unhappiness
Union with God
Unity
Usefulness

Vanity
Variety
Vices
Victory
Vigilance
Violence
Virgin birth
Virtue
Vision

War
Weakness
Wealth
  and happiness
  and its use
  and pride
  and slavery
Weariness

Weddings
Wholeheartedness
Will
Will-power
Wills
Wisdom
  and happiness
  and humility
  and knowledge
  and riches
Wise people
Wise sayings
Wishful thinking
Wit
Witchcraft

Witness
  through
          behaviour
  through
          speaking
Wives
Women
  Education of
  Inferiority of
  Leadership of
  Superiority of
  Wisdom of
  and religion
  and the fall of
          man
  and the home

Women's rights
Wonder
Word of God
Words
  and deeds
Work
  Limitations of
  Need for
  Perfection in
  Reluctance to
  and overwork
  at ordinary
          things
  for God's sake
Working class

World
  Concern for
  Love of
Worldliness
Worry
Worship
Worth
Writing

Yawning
Young people
Youth

Zeal
  Thoughtless

The Quotations

The Quotations

A

Abandonment

My God, my God, why have you abandoned me?

The Bible, Psalm 22:1

My father and mother may abandon me,
but the Lord will take care of me.

The Bible, Psalm 27:10

'Abba' see GOD, AS FATHER

Abiding in God

No human tongue could describe the passionate love with which Francis burned for Christ, his spouse; he seemed to be completely absorbed by the fire of divine love like a glowing coal.

An early biographer of Francis of Assisi

You have nothing to do in life except to live in union with me [Christ].

Rufus Mosely

If in everything you seek Jesus, you will doubtless find him. But if you seek yourself, you will indeed find yourself, to your own ruin. For you do yourself more harm by not seeking Jesus than the whole world and all your enemies could do to you.

Thomas à Kempis, The Imitation of Christ

Abide in me [says Jesus]. Cling to me. Stick fast to me. Live the life of close and intimate communion with me. Get nearer to me. Roll every burden on me. Cast your whole weight on me. Never let go your hold on me for a moment. Be, as it were, rooted and planted in me. Do this and I will never fail you. I will ever abide in you.

J.C. Ryle

Hold thou thy cross
before my closing eyes;
Shine through the gloom,
and point me to the skies;
Heaven's morning breaks,
and earth's vain shadows flee;
In life, in death, O Lord,
abide with me.

Henry Francis Lyte

Oh! for a closer walk with God,
A calm and heavenly frame;
A light to shine upon the road
That leads me to the Lamb!

So shall my walk be close with God,
Calm and serene my frame;
So purer light shall mark the road
That leads me to the Lamb.

William Cowper

Watch against lip religion. Above all abide in Christ and he will abide in you.

Robert Murray M'Cheyne

Ability

There is great ability in knowing how to conceal ability.

La Rochefoucauld

There is something rarer than ability. It is the ability to recognise ability.

Elbert Hubbard

Abortion

Abortion leads to an appalling trivialisation of the art of procreation.
Donald Coggan, speech to the
Shaftesbury Society, 2 October
1973

We are fighting abortion by adoption. We have sent word to the clinics, to the hospitals, to the police stations. 'Please do not destroy the child. We will take the child.'
Mother Teresa of Calcutta, Nobel
Peace Prize lecture, 1979

Abstinence

Abstinence without charity is useless.
Gildas

Total abstinence is easier for me than perfect moderation.
Augustine of Hippo

Abundance

My cup runneth over.
The Bible, Psalm 23:5 (AV).

Abuse   see also ADVERSITY

Iron, when heated in the flames and pounded, becomes a fine sword. Wise men and saints are tested by abuse.
Nichiren Daishonin, Letter from
Sado

Acceptance

Just as I am, thou wilt receive,
Wilt welcome, pardon, cleanse, relieve:
Because thy promise I believe,
O Lamb of God, I come.
Charlotte Elliott

Accepting God   see also
CONSECRATION; CONVERSION

Come, whoever is thirsty; accept the water of life as a gift, whoever wants it.
The Bible, Revelation 22:17

I take God the Father to be my God;
I take God the Son to be my Saviour;
I take the Holy Ghost to be my Sanctifier;
I take the Word of God to be my rule;
I take the people of God to be my people;
And I do hereby dedicate and yield my whole self to the Lord:
And I do this deliberately, freely, and for ever. Amen.
Act of commitment taught to
Matthew Henry by his father

Batter my heart, three-person'd God; for, you
As yet but knock, breathe, shine, and seek to mend;
That I may rise, and stand, o'erthrow me, and bend
Your force, to break, blow, burn and make me new.
I, like an usurp'd town, to another due,
Labour to admit you, but Oh, to no end,
Reason your viceroy in me, me should defend,
But is captiv'd, and proves weak or untrue.
Yet dearly I love you, and would be loved fain,
But am betroth'd unto your enemy:
Divorce me, untie, or break that knot again,
Take me to you, imprison me, for I
Except you enthral me, never shall be free,
Nor ever chaste, except you ravish me.
John Donne

Accidents

The most important events are often the results of accidents.
Polybius

Accidents will occur in the best-regulated families.
Charles Dickens, Mr Micawber in
David Copperfield

Accusation, False

When a man is accused falsely, the reproach does not go farther than his ears.
Æschines

Achievement

Yard by yard, all tasks are hard.
Inch by inch, they're all a cinch.
Author unknown

Nothing great was ever achieved without enthusiasm.
Ralph Waldo Emerson, Essays,
Circles

Life affords no greater pleasure than overcoming obstacles.
Author unknown

To leave footprints on the sands of time, wear work shoes.
Author unknown

Those who believe that they are exclusively in the right are generally those who achieve something.
Aldous Huxley

Action   see also BEGINNING; FAITH AND
ACTION; IDLENESS

He who desires but acts not, breeds
pestilence.

William Blake

There is no such thing as a great talent
without great will-power.

*Honoré de Balzac, La Muse du
Département*

Nothing will ever be attempted, if all
possible objections must be first overcome.

Samuel Johnson, Rasselas

Whatever you do, do cautiously, and
look to the end.

Gesta Romanorum

How vain it is to sit down and write
when you have not stood up to live!

Henry David Thoreau

No man has a right to lead such a life of
contemplation as to forget in his own
ease the service due to his neighbour;
nor has any man a right to be so
immersed in active life as to neglect
the contemplation of God.

Augustine of Hippo

For purposes of action nothing is more
useful than narrowness of thought
combined with energy of will.

Henri Frédéric Amiel

He does not believe, that does not live
according to his belief.

Proverb

'He means well' is useless unless he
does well.

Plautus

You will give yourself relief if you do
every act of your life as if it were the
last.

Marcus Aurelius

I am never better than when I am on
the full stretch for God.

George Whitefield

The great end of life is not knowledge
but action.

T.H. Huxley

Help yourself, and heaven will help
you.

La Fontaine

He does much who loves much.

Thomas à Kempis

He who deliberates fully before taking
a step will spend his entire life on one
leg.

Chinese proverb

Our nature consists in motion; complete inaction is death.

Blaise Pascal, Pensées

The ancestor of every action is a
thought.

Ralph Waldo Emerson

Nobody makes a greater mistake than
he who does nothing because he could
only do a little.

Edmund Burke

Little strokes fell great oaks.

Proverb

Whatever is worth doing at all is worth
doing well.

*Lord Chesterfield, Letters, 10
March 1746*

This only is charity, to do all, all that
we can.

John Donne

Love's secret is always to be doing
things for God, and not to mind
because they are such very little ones.

F.W. Faber

Action and the present moment

Our grand business is not to see what
lies dimly at a distance, but to do what
lies clearly at hand.

Thomas Carlyle

Act well at the moment, and you have
performed a good action to all eternity.

Johann Kaspar Lavater

Love cannot be practised right unless
we first exercise it the moment God
gives the opportunity.

*John Wesley, A Plain Man's
Guide to Holiness*

No one notices what is at his feet; we
all gaze at the stars.

*Quintus Ennius, Iphigenia,
quoted in Cicero, De Divinatione,
II.13*

Action and trust

Leave nothing to chance, and then
leave everything to God.

Author unknown

Action and words

Well-done is better than well-said.

Benjamin Franklin

Men will not attend to what we say,
but examine into what we do; and will
say, 'First obey your own words, and
then exhort others.' This is the great
battle, this is the unanswerable

demonstration, which is made by our acts.

John Chrysostom

Deeds, and not fine speeches, are the proof of love.

Spanish proverb

The shortest answer is doing.

Herbert

Actions speak louder than words.

Proverb

Adam and Eve   see also EVE

And the man said, The woman thou gavest to be with me, she gave me of the tree, and I did eat.

The Bible, Genesis 3:12 (AV)

As in Adam all die, even so in Christ shall all be made alive.

The Bible, The apostle Paul,
1 Corinthians 15:22 (AV)

They sewed fig leaves together, and made themselves breeches.

The Bible, Genesis 3:7 (Geneva
version, 1560)

Adoration

The most fundamental need, duty, honour and happiness of mankind is not petition, nor even contrition, nor again even thanksgiving – these three kinds of prayer which, indeed, must never disappear out of our spiritual lives – but adoration.

Friedrich von Hügel

Adultery

The lips of another man's wife may be as sweet as honey and her kisses as smooth as olive-oil, but when it is all over, she leaves you nothing but bitterness and pain.

The Bible, Proverbs 5:4–5

A man can hire a prostitute for the price of a loaf of bread, but adultery will cost him all he has.

The Bible, Proverbs 6:26

Adultery is a trap.

The Bible, Proverbs 22:14

Anyone who looks at a woman and wants to possess her is guilty of committing adultery with her in his heart.

The Bible, Jesus Christ, Matthew
5:28

Every Jew must die before he will commit idolatry, murder or adultery.

Rabbinic saying

Adventure

Adventure is the champagne of life.

G.K. Chesterton

Adversity   see also DIFFICULTIES; TRIBULATIONS

Though the Lord give you the bread of adversity, and the water of affliction, yet shall not thy teachers be removed into a corner any more, but thine eyes shall see thy teachers.

The Bible, Isaiah 30:20 (AV)

They gave our Master a crown of thorns. Why do we hope for a crown of roses?

Martin Luther

Adversity makes a man wise, not rich.

John Ray, A Collection of English
Proverbs

Adversity reveals genius, prosperity conceals it.

Horace

Prosperity doth best discover vice; but adversity doth best discover virtue.

Francis Bacon

As sure as ever God puts his children in the furnace he will be in the furnace with them.

C.H. Spurgeon

When the storm passes over, the grass will stand up again.

Kikuyu proverb

Afflictions are but the shadow of God's wings.

George Macdonald

Prosperity is not without many fears and distastes; and adversity is not without comforts and hopes. . . . Prosperity is the blessing of the Old Testament; adversity is the blessing of the New.

Francis Bacon

It has done me good to be somewhat parched by the heat and drenched by the rain of life.

Henry Wadsworth Longfellow

It is the crushed grape that yields the wine.

Author unknown

In all trouble you should seek God. You shoud not set him over againbst your troubles, but within them. God can only relieve your troubles if youi in your anxiety cling to him. Trouble should not really be thought of as this thing or that in particular, for our

whole life on earth involves trouble; and through the troubles of our earthly pilgrimage we find God.
Augustine of Hippo, Discourses on the Psalms

Whenever I find myself in the cellar of affliction, I always look about for the wine.
Samuel Rutherford

Grace grows best in the winter.
Samuel Rutherford

The person who bears and suffers evils with meekness and silence, is the sum of a Christian man.
John Wesley, A Plain Man's Guide to Holiness

Advice see also CRITICISM

Your instructions give me pleasure: they are my advisers.
The Bible, Psalm 119:24

Stupid people always think they are right. Wise people listen to advice.
The Bible, Proverbs 12:15

A word spoken in due season, how good it is!
The Bible, Proverbs 15:23 (AV)

An intelligent person learns more from one rebuke than a fool learns from being beaten a hundred times.
The Bible, Proverbs 15:22

Advice is like snow. The softer it falls, the easier it's absorbed, the deeper it sinks, and the longer it lasts.
Author unknown

He who can take advice is sometimes superior to him who can give it.
Karl von Knebel

No gift is more precious than good advice.
Erasmus

A woman seldom asks advice before she has bought her wedding clothes.
Joseph Addison, The Spectator, no 475

Let no man give advice to others that he has not first given himself.
Seneca

Affection

Most people would rather get than give affection.
Aristotle, Nicomachean Ethics

Affection hides three times as many virtues as charity does sins.
Horace Mann

Affection has no price.
Jerome, Letters, 3

Affliction see ADVERSITY; DIFFICULTIES; SUFFERING

Ages of man

Youth is a blunder; manhood a struggle; old age a regret.
Benjamin Disraeli, Coningsby, Bk. 3, Ch. 1

Youth is made rich by its dreams of the future; age is made poor by its regrets for the past.
Rochepèdre

Forty is the old age of youth; fifty the youth of old age.
Victor Hugo

When, as a child, I laughed and wept,
    Time crept.
When, as a youth, I dreamed and talked,
    Time walked.
When I became a full-grown man,
    Time ran.
And later, as I older grew,
    Time flew.
Soon I shall find, while travelling on,
    Time gone.
Will Christ have saved my soul by then?
    Amen.
Inscription on clock in Chester Cathedral

Agnosticism

The agnostic's prayer: 'O God, if there is a god, save my soul, if I have a soul.'
Ernest Renan

Agreement

When you say that you agree to a thing in principle you mean that you have not the slightest intention of carrying it out in practice.
Bismarck

'My idea of an agreeable person,' said Hugo Bohun, 'is a person who agrees with me.'
Benjamin Disraeli, Lothair

Aid

Charity is injurious unless it helps the recipient to become independent of it.
John D. Rockefeller

The present social order is the most abject failure the world has ever seen . . . Governments have never learned yet how to so legislate as to distribute the fruits of industry of their people. The countries of the earth produce enough to support all, and if the earnings of each was fairly distributed it would make all men toil some, but no man toil too much. This great civilisation of ours has not learned so to distribute the product of human toil so that it shall be equitably held. Therefore, the government breaks down.
C.I. Scofield, Bible Notes, 1903

Charity degrades those who receive it and hardens those who dispense it.
George Sand, Consuelo

The race of mankind would perish did they cease to aid each other. We cannot exist without mutual help. All therefore that need aid have a right to ask it of their fellow-men; and no one who has the power of granting can refuse it without guilt.
Walter Scott

AIDS

Men are not punished for their sins, but by them.
Elbert Hubbard

Ambassadors

[An ambassador is] an honest man sent to lie abroad for the good of his country.
Henry Wotton

Ambition

Every French soldier carries in his cartridge-pouch the baton of a marshal of France.
Napoleon

Try not to become a man of success but rather try to become a man of value.
Albert Einstein

The longer I live, the stronger becomes my conviction that the truest difference between the success and the failure, between the strong and the weak, between the big and the small man, that separates the boys from the men, is nothing but a powerful aim in life, a purpose once fixed and then death or victory. And no perfect speech or manners, no culture or education, no pull or influence, can make a two-legged creature a man without it.
Thomas Buxton

The wish is father to the thought.
Latin proverb

The crowd, the world, and sometimes even the grave, step aside for the man who knows where he's going, but pushes the aimless drifter aside.
Latin proverb

Seek first God's kingdom and his righteousness, and all these things will be given to you as well.
*The Bible, Jesus Christ,
Matthew 6:33*

Hitch your wagon to a star.
*Ralph Waldo Emerson, Society
and Solitude, Civilisation*

May I know thee more clearly,
Love thee more dearly,
And follow thee more nearly,
For ever and ever.
Richard of Chichester

Failure to plan is knowingly planning to fail.
Author unknown

Love's the frailty of the mind,
When 'tis not with ambition join'd.
*William Congreve, The Way of the
World, III.xii*

To reach the height of our ambition is like trying to reach the rainbow; as we advance it recedes.
Edmund Burke

Ambition, Warnings against

Ambition can creep as well as soar.
Edmund Burke

Ambition destroys its possessor.
The Talmud

Ambition often puts men upon doing the meanest offices: so climbing is performed in the same posture with creeping.
Jonathan Swift

There is no peace in ambition.
Mme de Pompadour

Love and meekness, lord,
Become a churchman better than ambition.
*William Shakespeare, Henry VIII,
V.iii*

Who soars too near the sun
    with golden wings,

Melts them; to ruin his own
fortune brings.

William Shakespeare

Accurst ambition,
How dearly I have bought you.

John Dryden

Oh, beware! Do not seek to be something! Let me be nothing, and Christ be all in all.

John Wesley

Cromwell, I charge thee, fling away ambition:
By that sin fell the angels. How can man then,
The image of his maker, hope to win by it?

*William Shakespeare, Henry VIII,
III.2*

Angels

Remember the angels who did not stay within the limits of their proper authority, but abandoned their own dwelling place: they are bound with eternal chains in the darkness below, where God is keeping them for that great Day on which they will be condemned.

The Bible, Jude 6

An angel is a spiritual being created by God without a body, for the service of Christendom and the church.

Martin Luther, Table Talk

Angels are bright still, though the brightest fell.

*William Shakespeare, Macbeth,
IV.iii.*

They are not Angles but angels.

*Pope Gregory I, on seeing some
young English slaves in Rome*

Anger

If you stay calm, you are wise, but if you have a hot temper, you only show how stupid you are.

The Bible, Proverbs 14:29

He who angers you, conquers you.

Proverb

No form of vice, not worldliness, not greed of gold, not drunkenness itself, does more to un-Christianise society than evil temper. For embittering life, for breaking up communities, for destroying the most sacred relationships, for devastating homes, for withering up men and women, for taking the bloom off childhood; in short, for sheer gratuitous misery-producing power, this influence stands alone.

Henry Drummond

Never forget what a man says to you when he is angry.

Henry Ward Beecher

As long as anger lives, she continues to be the fruitful mother of many unhappy children.

John Climacus, Climax

Anger is never without an argument, but seldom with a good one.

Lord Halifax

Everything a man does in anger will in the end be found to have been done wrong.

Menander

The best is not to be angry; the next is not to show in words or countenance your anger.

*Thomas Lupset, An Exhortation
to Yonge Men, 1534*

No matter how just your words may be, you ruin everything when you speak with anger.

*John Chrysostom, Commentary
on Acts*

The best remedy for anger is a little time for thought.

Seneca

Anger is a short madness.

Horace, Epistles

To seek to extinguish anger utterly is but a bravery of the Stoics. We have better oracles: 'Be angry, but sin not.' 'Let not the sun go down upon your wrath.'

Francis Bacon

He that is slow to anger is better than the mighty; and he that ruleth his spirit than he that taketh a city.

The Bible, Proverbs 16:32 (AV)

Anger begins in folly, and ends in repentance.

Pythagoras

Never answer an angry word with an angry word. It's always the second remark that starts the trouble.

Author unknown

Anger blows out the lamp of the mind. It's a child's reaction to an adult situation.

Author unknown

Anger is only one letter, and one second, away from danger.

Author unknown

He that overcomes his anger conquers his greatest enemy.
Latin proverb

Anger is the fever and frenzy of the soul.
Thomas Fuller, Gnomologia

Anger is short-lived in a good man.
Thomas Fuller, Gnomologia

Anger, Positive views of

Anybody can become angry – that is easy; but to be angry with the right person, and to the right degree, and at the right time, and for the right purpose, and in the right way – that is not within everybody's power and it is not easy.
Aristotle

A man is as big as the things that make him angry.
Winston Churchill

Anger is one of the sinews of the soul. He who lacks it hath a maimed mind.
Thomas Fuller, Gnomologia

The dove loves when it quarrels; the wolf hates when it flatters.
Augustine of Hippo, Sermons

Anger, Righteous

A man that does not know how to be angry does not know how to be good. A man that does not know how to be shaken to his heart's core with indignation over things evil is either a fungus or a wicked man.
Henry Ward Beecher, Proverbs from a Plymouth Pulpit

Anglican Church

The merit claimed for the Anglican Church is, that if you let it alone, it will let you alone.
Ralph Waldo Emerson

Animals

A good man takes care of his animals, but wicked men are cruel to theirs.
The Bible, Proverbs 12:10

A dog starv'd at his master's gate
Predicts the ruin of the State,
A horse misus'd upon the road
Calls to Heaven for human blood.
Each outcry of the hunted hare
A fibre from the brain does tear,
A skylark wounded in the wing,
A cherubim does cease to sing.
William Blake, Auguries of Innocence

He who shall hurt the little wren
Shall never be belov'd by men.
He who the ox to wrath has mov'd
Shall never be by woman lov'd.
William Blake, Auguries of Innocence

Animals are such agreeable friends – they ask no questions, they pass no criticisms.
George Eliot, Scenes of Clerical Life, Mr Gilfil's Love Story, ch. 7

Nobody is truly a Christian unless his cat or dog is the better off for it.
Rowland Hill

A man of kindness to his beast is kind,
But brutal actions show a brutal mind.
Remember, he who made thee made the brute;
Who gave thee speech and reason, formed him mute.
He can't complain, but God's all-seeing eye
Beholds thy cruelty – he hears his cry.
Author unknown

A Robin Redbreast in a cage
Puts all Heaven in a rage.
William Blake

Annunciation

The feast we call the Annunciation of the Virgin Mary, when the angel came to Mary and brought her the message from God, may be fitly called the Feast of Christ's Humanity; for then began our deliverance.
Martin Luther

Anxiety

Anxiety does not empty tomorrow of its sorrows, but only empties today of its strength.
C.H. Spurgeon

Anxiety is the greatest evil that can befall us except sin; for just as revolt and sedition in a country cause havoc and sap its resistance to a foreign invasion, so we, when troubled and worried, are unable to preserve the virtues we have already acquired, or resist the temptations of the devil, who then diligently fishes, as they say, in troubled waters.
Francis de Sales

Apologies

A stiff apology is a second insult.
G.K. Chesterton

Apostolic doctrine

We are in communion with the apostolic churches because there is no difference of doctrine. This is our guarantee of truth.

Tertullian, De Praescriptione Haereticorum

I do not, as Peter and Paul, issue commandments to you. They were apostles; I am just a condemned man.

Ignatius of Antioch, Epistle to the Romans, c. A.D. 110

Apostolic succession

I must believe in the Apostolic Succession, there being no other way of accounting for the descent of the Bishop of Exeter from Judas Iscariot.

Sydney Smith

Appearances

Judge not according to the appearance.

The Bible, Jesus Christ, John 7:24 (AV)

The Lord said to him, '. . . I do not judge as man judges. Man looks at the outward appearance, but I look at the heart.'

The Bible, 1 Samuel 16:7

Don't rely too much on labels,
For too often they are fables.

C.H. Spurgeon

All that glitters is not gold.

Proverb

Appreciation

Appreciation is a wonderful thing: it makes what is excellent in others belong to us as well.

Voltaire

Architecture

No person who is not a great sculptor or painter can be an architect. If he is not a sculptor or painter, he can only be a builder.

John Ruskin

Argument

The start of an argument is like the first break in a dam; stop it before it goes any further.

The Bible, Proverbs 17:14

It is useless for us to reason a man out of a thing he has never been reasoned into.

Jonathan Swift

Argument is the worst sort of conversation.

Jonathan Swift

Arrogance

The Lord hates everyone who is arrogant; he will never let them escape punishment.

The Bible, Proverbs 16:5

Art

All art is quite useless.

Oscar Wilde

If [the artist] sees nothing within him, then he should also refrain from painting what he sees before him.

Caspar David Friedrich

Life without industry is guilt, and industry without art is brutality.

John Ruskin, Lectures on Art, The Relation of Art to Morals

Art for art's sake.

Victor Cousin, Lecture at Sorbonne, 1818

Art is not the bread, but the wine of life.

Jean Paul Richter

Art is I; Science is We.

Claude Bernard

Art takes nature as its model.

Aristotle

All art is but imitation of nature.

Seneca, Epistles

The aim of art is to represent not the outward appearance of things, but their inward significance.

Aristotle

A man paints with his brains and not with his hands.

Michelangelo

The artist doesn't see things as they are, but as he is.

Author unknown

Art is not a thing; it is a way.

Elbert Hubbard

Ascension

When [Christ] returned to heaven, he withdrew his physical presence from our sight. He didn't stop being with the disciples but by the ascension fulfilled his promise to be with us to the end of the world. As his body was raised to heaven, so his power and reign have spread to the uttermost parts.

John Calvin, The Institutes of Christian Religion, 2.16.14

Godhead here in hiding, whom I do
    adore
Masked by these bare shadows, shape
    and nothing more,
See, Lord, at thy service low lies here
    a heart
Lost, all lost in wonder at the God
    thou art.
*Thomas Aquinas, translated by
Gerard Manley Hopkins*

Hail the day that sees him rise
To his throne above the skies;
Christ, a while to mortals given,
Re-ascends his native heaven.
Charles Wesley

Assurance

Repose in the blood of Christ; a firm
confidence in God, and persuasion of
his favour; the highest tranquillity,
serenity, and peace of mind, with a
deliverance from every fleshly desire,
and a cessation of all, even inward sins.
*Arvid Gradin, defining the 'full
assurance of faith' (Hebrews
10:22) for John Wesley*

Speculations I have none. I'm resting
on certainties. 'For I know whom I
have believed, and am persuaded that
he is able to keep that which I have
committed unto him against that day.'
*Michael Faraday, nearing death,
quoting from the Bible, The
apostle Paul, 2 Timothy 1:12 (AV)*

Astrology

Esau and Jacob were born of the same
father and mother, at the same time,
and under the same planets, but their
nature was wholly different. You
would persuade me that astrology is a
true science!
Martin Luther

Atheism   see also GOD, BELIEF IN

The fool hath said in his heart, There is
no God.
The Bible, Psalm 14:1 (AV)

An atheist is a man who has no invisible means of support.
John Buchan

The religion of the atheist has a God-
shaped blank at its heart.
H.G. Wells

The worst moment for the atheist is
when he is really thankful and has
nobody to thank.
Dante Gabriel Rossetti

Atheism turns out to be too simple. If
the whole universe has no meaning,
we should have never found out that it
has no meaning.
C.S. Lewis, Mere Christianity

I can see how it might be possible for a
man to look down upon the earth and
be an atheist, but I cannot conceive
how he could look up into the heavens
and say there is no God.
Abraham Lincoln

He has denied the faith, and is worse
than an unbeliever.
*The Bible, The apostle Paul,
1 Timothy 5:8*

An atheist is a man who believes himself an accident.
Francis Thompson

Atonement

Behold the Lamb of God, which
taketh away the sins of the world.
*The Bible, John the Baptist,
John 1:29 (AV)*

The blood of Jesus, his Son, purifies us
from every sin.
*The Bible, The apostle John,
1 John 1:7*

If there had been no sin, the Son of
God would not have had to become a
lamb, nor would he have had to
become incarnate and be put to
death.
Origen, Sermons on Numbers

Attack

Oh, he is mad, is he? Then I wish he
would bite some other of my generals.
George II, of General Wolfe

Attitude

Our attitude to all men would be
Christian if we regarded them as
though they were dying, and determined our relation to them in the light
of death, both of their death and of our
own.
Nicolas Berdyaev

Authority

He [Jesus Christ] wasn't like the
teachers of the Law; instead, he taught
with authority.
The Bible, Matthew 7:29

I, too, am a man under the authority of
superior officers, and I have soldiers
under me. I order this one, 'Go!' and
he goes; and I order that one, 'Come!'

and he comes; and I order my slave, 'Do this!' and he does it.

The Bible, a Roman officer,
Matthew 8:9

This man [Jesus Christ] has authority to give orders to the evil spirits, and they obey him!

The Bible, Mark 1:27

Automation

It is questionable if all the mechanical inventions yet made have lightened the day's toil of any human being.

John Stuart Mill

Avarice   see GREED

Awareness of God

It is beyond dispute that some awareness of God exists in the human mind by natural instinct, since God himself has given everyone some idea of him so that no one can plead ignorance.

John Calvin, The Institutes of
Christian Religion, 1.3.1

It is so easy to deny the nobility of something just because it mingles with our earthly clay.

George Macdonald

B

Backsliding

The backslider in heart shall be filled with his own ways: and a good man shall be satisfied from himself.

The Bible, Proverbs 14:14 (AV)

Bankers

A banker is a fellow who lends his umbrella when the sun is shining and wants it back again the minute it begins to rain.

Mark Twain

Baptism   see also INFANT BAPTISM

Christians are made, not born.

Jerome

This is how we dedicate ourselves to God after being newly created through Christ. . . . We bring them to somewhere where there is water, where they are regenerated as we were, for they then wash themselves in the water in the name of God the Father and

Lord of all, and of our Saviour Jesus Christ and of Holy Spirit.

Justin Martyr, Apologia

Those who are going to be baptised must pray repeatedly, fasting and kneeling and in vigils, and confess all their past sins.

Tertullian, Baptism

Baptism signifies that the old Adam in us is to be drowned by daily sorrow and repentance, and perish with all sins and evil lusts; and that the new man should daily come before God in righteousness and purity for ever.

Martin Luther

Baptism is the sign of initiation by which we are admitted to the fellowship of the church.

John Calvin, The Institutes of
Christian Religion, 4.15.1

Those who see baptism only as confession of our faith have missed the main point. Baptism is tied to the promise of forgiveness. 'Whoever believes and is baptised will be saved' (Mark 16:16).

John Calvin, The Institutes of
Christian Religion, 4.15.1

True believers when troubled by sin can always remember their baptism, and so be assured of eternal washing in the blood of Christ.

John Calvin, The Institutes of
Christian Religion, 4.15.4

Baptism and salvation

Not everyone is washed to receive salvation. We who have received the grace of baptism in the name of Christ have been washed; but I do not know which of us has been washed to salvation.

Origen, Sermons on Ezekiel

Beatitudes

The Beatitudes: Beautiful Attitudes.

Author unknown

Happy are those who know they are
    spiritually poor;
    the Kingdom of heaven belongs to
    them!
Happy are those who mourn;
    God will comfort them!
Happy are those who are humble;
    they will receive what God has
    promised!
Happy are those whose greatest desire
    is to do what God requires;

God will satisfy them fully!
Happy are those who are merciful to
    others;
    God will be merciful to them!
Happy are the pure in heart;
    they will see God!
Happy are those who work for peace;
    God will call them his children!
The Bible, Jesus Christ,
Matthew 5:3–9

Beauty

Beauty in a woman without good
judgement is like a gold ring in a pig's
snout.
The Bible, Proverbs 11:22

Charm is deceptive and beauty disap-
pears, but a woman who honours the
Lord should be praised.
The Bible, Proverbs 31:30

Beauty is but skin-deep.
Author unknown

Though we travel the world over to
find the beautiful, we must carry it
with us or we find it not.
Ralph Waldo Emerson

Beauty unadorned, adorned the most.
Proverb

If you get simple beauty and nought
else, you get about the best thing God
invents.
Robert Browning

Beauty is a flower, fame a breath.
Latin proverb

Beauty is the gift of God.
Aristotle

Beauty is like a rich stone, best plain
set.
Francis Bacon, Essays, Of Beauty

God passes through the thicket of the
world, and wherever his glance falls he
turns all things to beauty.
John of the Cross, The Spiritual
Canticle

Beauty is God's handwriting. Welcome it in every fair face, every fair
day, every fair flower.
Charles Kingsley

Ask the earth and the sea, the plains
and the mountains, the sky and the
clouds, the stars and the sun, the fish
and animals, and all of them will say,
'We are beautiful because God made
us.' This beauty is their testimony to
God. Ask men and women, too, and
they know that their beauty comes

from God. Yet what is it that sees the
beauty? What is it that can be en-
raptured by the loveliness of God's
creation? It is the soul which appreci-
ates beauty. Indeed, God made men's
souls so that they could appreciate the
beauty of his handiwork.
Augustine of Hippo, Sermons

Beauty is indeed a good gift of God;
but that the good may not think it a
great good, God dispenses it even to
the wicked.
Augustine of Hippo

Glory be to God for dappled things –
    For skies of couple-colour as a
        brinded cow;
        For rose-moles all in stipple upon
        trout that swim;
Fresh-firecoal chestnut-falls; finches'
    wings;
    Landscape plotted and pieced –
        fold, fallow, and plough;
        And all trades, their gear and
        tackle and trim.
All things counter, original, spare,
    strange;
    Whatever is fickle, freckled (who
        knows how?)
    With swift, slow; sweet, sour;
        adazzle, dim;
He fathers-forth whose beauty is past
    change:
        Praise him.
Gerard Manley Hopkins, Pied
Beauty

A thing of beauty is a joy for ever:
Its loveliness increases; it will never
Pass into nothingness.
John Keats, Endymion, I.1

Beauty, Spiritual

Each conception of spiritual beauty is
a glimpse of God.
Moses Mendelssohn

Your beauty should consist of your
true inner self, the ageless beauty of a
gentle and quiet spirit.
The Bible, The apostle Peter,
1 Peter 3:4

The being of all things is derived from
the divine beauty.
Thomas Aquinas

I pray, O God, that I may be beautiful
within.
Socrates

How goodness heightens beauty!
Hannah More

God's fingers can touch nothing but to mould it into loveliness.
George Macdonald

Becoming a Christian   see ACCEPTING GOD; CONVERSION

Beginning

The beginning is the half of the whole.
Hesiod

A journey of a thousand miles must begin with a single step.
Lao Tzu

It is only the first step that costs.
Mme du Deffand, on the distance St Denis is reputed to have walked carrying his head

Well begun is half done.
English proverb

What you can do, or dream you can, begin it.
Boldness has genius, power and magic in it.
Only engage, and then the mind grows heated;
Begin it and the task will be completed.
Goethe

It came to me that as they lay brick on brick, so I could still lay word on word, sentence on sentence.
Thomas Carlyle, facing the prospect of having to rewrite his entire book on the French Revolution after the only manuscript had been destroyed

Begin; to have begun makes the work half done. Half still remains; again begin this, and you will complete the task.
Ausonius

Be slow to undertake a work, but once undertaken, go through with it.
Bias

Behaviour   see also ANGER; CHARITY; KINDNESS; MOTTOES; PRAISE; RELATIONSHIPS

Whoever does good belongs to God; whoever does what is bad has not seen God.
The Bible, 3 John 11

Love, and do what you wish.
Augustine of Hippo

He who knows others is wise; he who knows himself is enlightened.
Lao Tzu

I have no secret. You haven't learned life's lesson very well if you haven't noticed that you can give the tone or colour, or decide the reaction you want of people in advance. It's unbelievably simple. If you want them to smile, smile first. If you want them to take an interest in you, take an interest in them first. If you want to make them nervous, become nervous yourself. If you want them to shout and raise their voices, raise yours and shout. If you want them to strike you, strike first. It's as simple as that. People will treat you like you treat them. It's no secret. Look about you. You can prove it with the next person you meet.
Winston Churchill

I firmly believe people have hitherto been a great deal too much taken up about *doctrine* and far too little about practice. The word 'doctrine', as used in the Bible, means teaching of duty, not theory.
George Macdonald

Throughout our life, our worst weaknesses and meannesses are usually committed for the sake of the people whom we most despise.
Charles Dickens, Great Expectations

Behave to your inferiors as you would wish your betters to behave to you.
Seneca, Epistles

If you do not shun small defects, bit by bit you will fall into greater ones.
Thomas à Kempis, The Imitation of Christ

Now is the time for doing, and now is the time to fight; now is the proper time to amend my life.
Thomas à Kempis, The Imitation of Christ

The end justifies the means.
Hermann Busenbaum, Medulla Theologiae Moralis, 1650

Do as you would be done by is the surest method that I know of pleasing.
Chesterfield, Letters, 16 October 1747

He who makes a beast of himself gets rid of the pain of being a man.
Samuel Johnson

If a man be gracious and courteous to strangers, it shows he is a citizen of the world.
Francis Bacon, Essays, Of Goodness

Learn to overrule minor interests in favour of great ones, and generously to do all the good the heart prompts; a man is never injured by acting virtuously.

Vauvenargues

Give up money, give up fame, give up science, give up the earth itself and all it contains, rather than do an immoral act.

Thomas Jefferson

You will rest from vain fancies if you perform every act in life as though it were your last.

Marcus Aurelius, Meditations

Do all the good you can
By all the means you can
In all the ways you can
In all the places you can
To all the people you can
As long as ever you can.

John Wesley

Civility costs nothing.

Author unknown

When in Rome, live as the Romans do; when elsewhere, live as they live elsewhere.

Ambrose, giving advice to Augustine

Anyone can carry his burden for one day. Anyone can be pleasant, courteous, and friendly for one day. And that continued is all there is to life.

Author unknown

Rudeness, yelling, anger, and swearing are a weak man's imitation of strength.

Author unknown

Being

The way to do is to be.

Lao Tzu

One must not always think so much about what one should do, but rather what one should be. Our works do not ennoble us; but we must ennoble our works.

Meister Eckhart

What you are thunders so loud that I cannot hear what you say.

Ralph Waldo Emerson

Belief   see also FAITH

Verily, verily, I say unto you, He that believeth on me hath everlasting life.

The Bible, Jesus Christ, John 6:47 (AV)

Never allow what you do know to be disturbed by what you do not know.

Richard Whateley

Be not faithless, but believing.

The Bible, Jesus Christ, John 20:27 (AV)

[To Margaret Fuller's 'I accept the universe':] Gad! She'd better!

Thomas Carlyle

The ox and the ass understood more of the first Christmas than the high priests in Jerusalem. And it is the same today.

Thomas Merton

Men's ears are less reliable than their eyes.

Herodotus

Credulity is the man's weakness, but the child's strength.

Charles Lamb

Belief is a wise wager. Granted that faith cannot be proved, what harm will come to you if you gamble on its truth and it proves false? . . . If you gain, you gain all; if you lose, you lose nothing. Wager, then, without hesitation, that [God] exists.

Blaise Pascal

If we let ourselves believe that man began with divine grace, that he forfeited this by sin, and that he can be redeemed only by divine grace through the crucified Christ then we shall find a peace of mind never granted to philosophers.

Blaise Pascal

The point of having an open mind, like having an open mouth, is to close it on something solid.

G.K. Chesterton

Seeing is believing.

Proverb

It is not as a child that I believe and confess Christ. My hosanna is born of a furnace of doubt.

Fyodor Dostoevsky

All things are possible to him that believeth.

The Bible, Jesus Christ, Mark 9:23 (AV)

Belief in self

For they can conquer who believe they can.

Virgil

Belonging

The deepest principle in human nature is the craving to be appreciated.
William James

The strongest want in human nature is the desire to be great.
Sigmund Freud

The first and prime want in human nature is the desire to be important.
John Dewey

More than anything else, people want to be noticed, recognised.
Goethe

Bereavement   see also DEATH OF A CHILD; GRIEF

No man is an island, entire of itself; every man is a piece of the continent, a part of the main. . . . Any man's death diminishes me, because I am involved in mankind; and therefore never send to know for whom the bell tolls; it tolls for thee.
John Donne, Devotions

Sometimes God sends his love-letters in black-edged envelopes.
C.H. Spurgeon

The bitterest tears shed over graves are for words left unsaid and deeds left undone.
Harriet Beecher Stowe, Little Foxes

Grief drives men into the habits of serious reflection, sharpens the understanding and softens the heart.
John Adams, letter to Thomas Jefferson, 6 May 1816

Grief should be the instructor of the wise.

Sorrow is knowledge: they who know the most
Must mourn the deepest.
Lord Byron, Manfred

Bereavement, Individuals' reactions to

I subdue my grief as well as I can, but you know how tender, or rather soft, my mind is. Had not strong self-control been given me I could not have borne up so long.
John Calvin, after the death of his wife

My little daughter Elizabeth is dead. She has left me wonderfully sick at heart and almost womanish, I am so moved by pity for her. I could never

have believed a father's heart could be so tender for his child. Pray to God for me.
Martin Luther

Bible   see also NEW TESTAMENT; OLD TESTAMENT

The Bible applied to the heart by the Holy Ghost, is the chief means by which men are built up and stablished in the faith, after their conversion.
J.C. Ryle, Practical Religion

Give me a candle and a Bible, and shut me up in a dark dungeon, and I will tell you what the whole world is doing.
Author unknown

We search the world for truth; we cull
The good, the pure, the beautiful
From graven stone and written scroll,
From all old flower-fields of the soul;
And, weary seekers of the best
We come back laden from the quest
To find that all the sages said
Is in the Book our mothers read.
John Greenleaf Whittier

The holy scriptures are that divine instrument by which we are taught what to believe, concerning God ourselves, and all things, and how to please God unto eternal life.
John Robinson

We present you with this Book, the most valuable thing that this world affords. Here is wisdom; this is the royal Law; these are the lively Oracles of God.
Accession service for English monarchs

Here is the secret of England's greatness.
Queen Victoria, to an African prince, with the gift of a Bible

A thorough knowledge of the Bible is worth more than a college education.
Theodore Roosevelt

Nobody ever outgrows scripture; the book widens and deepens with our years.
C.H. Spurgeon

My ever dear delight;
And still new beauties may I see
And still increasing light.
Anne Steele

The scriptures teach us the best way of living, the noblest way of suffering, and the most comfortable way of dying.

John Flavel

In all my perplexities and distresses the Bible has never failed to give me light and strength.

Robert E. Lee

The devil can cite scripture for his purpose.

William Shakespeare, Antonio in
The Merchant of Venice

There is a medicine in the Bible for every sin-sick soul, but every soul does not need the same medicine.

R.A. Torrey

Unless a man accepts with clear conscience the Bible and its great message he cannot hope for salvation. For myself I glory in the Bible.

Haile Selassie

I am a creature of a day, passing through life as an arrow through the air. I am a spirit, coming from God, and returning to God; just hovering over the great gulf; a few months hence I am no more seen; I drop into an unchangeable eternity! I want to know one thing – the way to heaven. . . . God himself has condescended to teach the way. He hath written it down in a book. O give me that book! At any price, give me that book!

John Wesley

Bible, and Reason

Scripture is above our natural reason, understanding, and comprehension.

Justin Martyr

Bible, and Society

The Bible is the Magna Charta of the human soul.

Woodrow Wilson, in a public
speech in 1911

I ask of every man and woman in this audience that from this night on they will realise that part of the destiny of America lies in their daily perusal of this great book of revelations – that if they would see America free and pure they will make their own spirits free and pure by this baptism of the holy scripture.

Woodrow Wilson

Bible, as the Word of God

When you have read the Bible you will know that it is the Word of God, because you will have found it the key to your own heart, your own happiness, your own duty.

Woodrow Wilson

The best proof that this book is the word of God is that it warms and lights my soul.

C.H. Spurgeon

Lord, thy word abideth,
And our footsteps guideth;
Who its truth believeth
Light and joy receiveth.

Henry W. Baker

The soul can do nothing without the word of God, and the soul can manage without anything except the word of God.

Martin Luther

Bible, Authority of

We cannot rely on the doctrine of Scripture until we are absolutely convinced that God is its author.

John Calvin, The Institutes of
Christian Religion, 1.7.4

The Bible is no mere book, but a Living Creature, with a power that conquers all that oppose it.

Napoleon

Defend the Bible? I would as soon defend a lion! Unchain it and it will defend itself!

C.H. Spurgeon

So long as your mind entertains any doubts as to the truth of the Word, its authority will be weak and doubtful. Or rather, it will have no authority at all. It is not enough to believe that God is true and cannot lie or deceive, unless you feel firmly convinced that every word which proceeds from him is sacred, absolute truth.

John Calvin, The Institutes of
Christian Religion, 3.2.6

Bible, Christ in the

Some people say, 'Unless I find it in the scriptures I will not believe it in the gospel.' And when I tell them it *is* in the scriptures, they say, 'That remains to be proved.' But as far as I am concerned, Jesus Christ *is* the scriptures: you cannot alter his cross, death and resurrection, and faith through him.

Ignatius of Antioch, To the
Philadelphians

We have the most striking and unmistakable likeness of a man portrayed, not by one, but by twenty or twenty-five artists, none of whom had ever seen the man they were painting. The man was Jesus Christ. The painters were the Bible writers. The canvas is the Bible. Beginning with faint touches in the books of Moses, Christ's whole career is described, the pictures becoming more and more precise as the time of fulfilment draws near. And what makes these announcements so immeasurably more astounding and marvellous is the fact that they are not made by one person nor at one time, nor in one place, but partly by one person, and partly by another, and in many different places, and at totally different periods, yet all fit into one another, like the pieces of a child's puzzle, and together make up a perfect image of Jesus Christ.

Vaughan, Concerning the Holy Bible

Read all the prophetic books without seeing Christ in them, and what will you find so insipid and flat? See Christ there, and what you read becomes fragrant.

John Chrysostom

The whole of scripture deals with Christ throughout.

Martin Luther, The Epistle to the Romans

Every word of the Bible rings with Christ.

Martin Luther, The Epistle to the Romans

Knowledge of scripture is knowledge of Christ and ignorance of them is ignorance of him.

Jerome

Bible, Criticism of

Have we gone too far in saying that modern thought has grown impatient with the Bible, the gospel, and the cross? Let us see. What part of the Bible has it not assailed? The Pentateuch it has long ago swept from the canon as unauthentic. What we read about the creation and the flood is branded as fable. . . . [We are told that] Paul was a fanatic who wrote unthinkingly, and that much of what bears his name was never written by

him at all. Thus is the Bible rubbed through the tribulum of criticism from Genesis to Revelation, until, in the faith of the age in which we live, as represented by its so-called leaders, there are but a few inspired fragments here and there remaining.

Arthur Mursell

Bible, Early scholars of

The fourth century supplies a catalogue of fourteen writers who expended their labours upon the books of the New Testament, and whose works or names are come down to our times: Eusebius, A.D. 315; Juvencus, Spain, 330; Theodore, Thrace, 334; Hilary, Poitiers, 354; Fortunatus, 340; Apollinarius of Laodicea, 362; Damasus, Rome, 366; Gregory, Nyssa, 371; Didimus of Alexandria, 370; Ambrose of Milan, 374; Diodore of Tarsus, 378; Gaudentius of Brescia, 387; Theodore of Cilica, 349; Jerome, 392; Chrysostom, 398.

William Paley, Evidences of Christianity

Bible, Early witness to

I trust that you are well exercised in the holy scriptures, as in these scriptures it is said, 'Be ye angry and sin not, and let not the sun go down upon your wrath.'

Polycarp, less than 130 years after Christ's death

Bible, Inspiration of

All Scripture is inspired by God and is useful for teaching the truth, rebuking error, correcting faults, and giving instruction for right living.

The Bible, The apostle Paul, 2 Timothy 3:16

Their task [that of the writers of the Bible] was but to surrender themselves wholly to the working of the Spirit of God, that the divine plectrum descending from heaven might make use of holy men as of a harp or lyre, in order to reveal to us the knowledge of divine and heavenly things.

Justin Martyr

The sacred books are pervaded by the fulness of the Spirit. There is nothing either in the prophets, or in the law, or in the gospels, or in the epistles, which does not spring from the fulness of the divine majesty.

Origen

Bible, Interpretation of

God let Jonah be swallowed by a whale, not so that he should die but so that he should be brought up and be more obedient to God and glorify him more because of this unexpected deliverance, and so that he should bring the Ninevites to sincere repentance. . . . In the same way, God let man be swallowed by a great whale, namely the author of man's sin, not so that he should die but because he had planned and prepared a scheme of salvation for him.

Irenaeus, Against Heresies, 3.21.1

No public man in these islands ever believes that the Bible means what it says; he is always convinced that it says what he means.

George Bernard Shaw

The scriptures were written by the agency of God's Spirit. They have not only the meaning which is clear on the surface but also another meaning which is hidden from most people, by which the narrative presents types of certain mysteries and pictures of divine matters.

Origen, On First Principles

The right way of interpreting scripture is to take it as we find it, without any attempt to force it into any particular system.

Cecil

I hold it for a most infallible rule in the exposition of scripture, that when a literal construction will stand, the furthest from the literal is commonly the worst.

Richard Hooker

In expounding the Bible if one were always to confine oneself to the unadorned grammatical meaning, one might fall into error. Not only contradictions and propositions far from true might thus be made to appear in the Bible, but even grave heresies and follies. Thus it would be necessary to assign to God feet, hands and eyes.

Galileo

Let us know, then, that the true meaning of scripture is the natural and obvi-ous meaning; and let us embrace and abide by it resolutely. Let us not only neglect as doubtful, but boldly set aside as deadly corruptions, those pretended expositions which lead us away from the natural meaning.

John Calvin, Commentary on Galatians

[To Mary Queen of Scots' question, 'Ye interpret the scriptures in one manner, and they in another; whom shall I believe, and who shall judge?':] Believe God, that plainly speaketh in his word: and further than the word teacheth you, ye shall neither believe the one nor the other. The word of God is plain in itself; and if there appear any obscurity in one place, the Holy Ghost, which is never contrarious to himself, explains the same more clearly in other places.

John Knox, The History of the Reformation of the Church of Scotland

The Bible without the Holy Spirit is a sun-dial by moonlight.

Dwight L. Moody

Bible, Obedience to

Most people are bothered by those passages of scripture which they cannot understand; but as for me, I have always noticed that the passages in scripture which trouble me most are those which I do understand.

Mark Twain

A man may be said to depart from the living God when he departs from his word, which is living and makes all things live. In fact, the word is God himself. Therefore, when men depart from the word, they die. He who does not believe is dead.

Martin Luther, The Epistle to the Hebrews

Whoever seems to himself to have understood the divine scriptures in such a way that he does not build up that double love of God and neighbour has not yet understood.

Augustine of Hippo

Back to the Bible, or back to the jungle.

Luis Palau

Bible, Reading the

Open my eyes, so that I may see
the wonderful truths in your law.

The Bible, Psalm 119:18

Straightaway a flame was kindled in my soul, and a love of the prophets and of those men who are friends of Christ, possessed me.

Justin Martyr, Dialogue

Our reading of the gospel story can be and should be an act of personal communion with the living Lord.

William Temple

Next to praying there is nothing so important in practical religion as Bible-reading.

J.C. Ryle, Practical Religion

We come together to recollect the divine scriptures; we nourish our faith, raise our hope, confirm our trust, by the sacred word.

Tertullian

O Lord, heavenly Father, in whom is the fullness of light and wisdom, enlighten our minds by your Holy Spirit, and give us grace to receive your Word with reverence and humility, without which no one can understand your truth. For Christ's sake, Amen.

John Calvin

We come to a cradle in order to see the baby, so we come to the Bible to see Christ.

Martin Luther

Bible laid open, millions of surprises.

George Herbert, The Temple

I began to read the holy scriptures upon my knees, laying aside all other books, and praying over, if possible, every line and word. This proved meat indeed and drink indeed to my soul. I daily received fresh life, light and power from above.

George Whitefield, Journal

If God drew up his Bible to heaven and sent me down another, it would not be newer to me.

William Grimshaw, quoted in J.C. Ryle, Five Christian Leaders of the Eighteenth Century

I do not sit down to the perusal of scripture in order to impose a sense on the inspired writers, but to receive one, as they give it me. I pretend not to teach them, I wish like a child to be taught by them.

Charles Simeon

There is nothing in the whole universe to be compared with the scriptures of truth, nothing that will so enrich the mind, nothing that will so benefit the soul. To treasure them up in our minds should be our daily and most delightful employment. Not a day should pass without adding to their blessed store, and not only in memory and mind, but in heart and soul.

Charles Simeon, Sermon 2187

The vigour of our spiritual life will be in exact proportion to the place held by the Bible in our life and thoughts.

George Müller

I never saw a useful Christian who was not a student of the Bible. If a person neglects the Bible there is not much for the Holy Spirit to work with. We must have the word.

Dwight L. Moody

Apply yourself wholly to the scriptures, and apply the scriptures wholly to yourself.

Bengel

It is a great thing, this reading of the scriptures! For it is not possible ever to exhaust the mind of the scriptures. It is a well that has no bottom.

John Chrysostom

If you believe what you like in the gospel, and reject what you like, it is not the gospel you believe, but yourself.

Augustine of Hippo

After all my troubles and toilings in the world, I find that my private life in the country has afforded me more contentment than ever I met with in all my public employments. I have lately applied myself to the study of the Bible, wherein all wisdom, and the greatest delights are to be found. I therefore counsel you [the English ambassador] to make the study and practice of the Word of God your chief contentment and delight; as indeed it will be to every soul that favours the truths of God, which infinitely excel all worldly things.

Oxenstiern

Bible, Sufficiency of

Holy scripture containeth all things necessary to salvation: so that whatsoever is not read therein, nor may be proved thereby, is not to be required of any man, that it should be believed as an article of the faith, or be thought requisite or necessary to salvation.

Book of Common Prayer, Article 6

The Bible and the Bible only is the religion of Protestants.

William Chillingworth, The Religion of Protestants, 1637

Here is knowledge enough for me. Let me be a man of one Book.

John Wesley

From the year 1725, and very definitely from 1730, I began to be *homo unius libri* (man of *one* book), regarding no other book as equal to the Bible.

John Wesley, A Plain Man's Guide to Holiness

Bible, Translation of

If God spare my life, ere many years I will cause a boy who drives the plough to know more of the scriptures than you do.

William Tyndale, in argument with a scholar

I would to God that a ploughman would sing a text of the scripture at his plough and that the weaver would hum them to the tune of his shuttle.

Erasmus

Whereas some men think many translations make divisions in the faith, that is not so, for it was never better with the congregation of God than when every church almost had a sundry translation. Would to God it had never been left off after the time of St Augustine, then we should never have come into such blindness and ignorance, such errors and delusions.

Miles Coverdale

What enterprise can there be more worthy of singular commendation than the building of the Lord's Temple, the church of Christ?

Geneva Bible (1560), Dedication

Bible, Trustworthiness of

I set out to look for truth on the border-land where Greece and Asia meet, and found it there. You may press the words of Luke in a degree beyond any other historian's and they stand the keenest scrutiny and the hardest treatment.

William Ramsay

Bible, Uniqueness of

The English Bible, a book which, if everything else in our language should perish, would alone suffice to show the whole extent of its beauty and power.

Lord Macaulay, Edinburgh Review essay on John Dryden

I believe that the Bible is the best gift that God has ever given to man. All the good from the saviour of the world is communicated to us through this book. I have been driven many times to my knees by the overwhelming conviction that I had nowhere else to go.

Abraham Lincoln

How petty are the books of the philosophers with all their pomp, compared with the gospels!

Jean Jacques Rousseau

Some books are copper, some are silver, and some few are gold; but the Bible alone is like a book all made up of bank notes.

John Newton

There is no book upon which we can rest in a dying moment but the Bible.

John Selden

Bible and science

There can be no doubt that the Bible . . . became a stumbling-block in the path of progress, scientific, social and even moral. It was quoted against Copernicus as it was against Darwin.

Preserved Smith

Biography

Read no history: nothing but biography, for that is life without theory.

Benjamin Disraeli, Contarini Fleming

The record of a great and pure personality is the best bequest of time.

F.W.H. Meyers

I would rather have written a great biography than a great book of any other sort, as I would rather have painted a great portrait than any other kind of picture.

Phillips Brooks

Birth control

Any use whatsoever of matrimony exercised in such a way that the act is deliberately frustrated in its natural power to generate life is an offence against the law of God and of nature, and those who indulge in such are branded with the guilt of a grave sin.

Pope Pius XI

Birthdays

FOR HIS WIFE, ON HER BIRTHDAY

Come away to the skies,
My beloved arise,
And rejoice on the day thou wast
    born,
On the festival day
Come exulting away,
To thy heavenly country return.

Charles Wesley

Bishops

Let no one apart from the bishop do anything to do with the church. A valid eucharist should be one under the bishop or someone he has appointed. Wherever the bishop appears, let the people be, just as wherever Christ Jesus may be, there is the universal church.

Ignatius of Antioch, To the Smyrnaeans

When a certain bishop was complaining to the king of Mr Whitefield's great and eccentric labours, and advising him what steps were best to be taken to put a stop to his preaching, his Majesty very shrewdly replied, 'My Lord, I can see no other way but for us to make a bishop of him. This will stand a good chance of stopping his wild career.'

David Simpson, A Plea for Religion and the Sacred Writings

Blessings

The Lord bless thee, and keep thee:
The Lord make his face shine upon thee, and be gracious unto thee:
The Lord lift up his countenance upon thee, and give thee peace.

The Bible, Numbers 6:24–26 (AV)

Blindness

The very limit of human blindness is to glory in being blind.

Augustine of Hippo

Blood

Blood is always mentioned whenever Scripture explains the way of salvation. The shedding of Christ's blood was not only for propitiation but for the cleansing of sin.

John Calvin, The Institutes of Christian Religion, 2.16.6

Blushing

Every man who can blush has, methinks, some honesty in him.

Menander

Man is the only animal that blushes. Or needs to.

Mark Twain, Following the Equator

Boasting

The horseshoe that clatters needs a nail.

Spanish proverb

The fly sat on the axle-tree of the chariot-wheel and said, What a dust do I raise!

Francis Bacon

You beat your pate, and fancy wit will come;
Knock as you please, there's nobody at home.

Alexander Pope

One ought not to swagger about being the fellow citizen of Shakespeare; rather one ought to feel that Shakespeare might have had a better fellow citizen.

G.K. Chesterton

He who boasts achieves nothing.

Lao Tzu, Tao Te Ching

Body, The

Use your bodies for God's glory.

The Bible, The apostle Paul, 1 Corinthians 6:20

No one hates his body.

Augustine of Hippo

Books   see WRITING

Born again experience   see
CONVERSION; REGENERATION

Brevity

The Lord's Prayer has 56 words. Psalm 23 has 118 words. The Gettysburg Address has 226 words. The Ten Commandments have 297 words. The American Declaration of Independence has 300 words. The US Department of Agriculture order on the price of cabbage has 15,629 words. The European Economic Community Directive on the export of duck eggs has 26,911 words.

Various sources

Bribery

Don't take bribes and you will live longer.

The Bible, Proverbs 15:27

If you take a bribe, you ruin your character.

The Bible, Ecclesiastes 7:7

Fight with silver spears, and you will conquer everywhere.

The Delphic oracle's advice to Philip of Macedon, who then boasted he could capture any town if he could bribe its citizens

Broken-heartedness

He [God] heals the broken-hearted and bandages their wounds.

The Bible, Psalm 147:3

Brotherhood

Until you have become really in actual fact a brother of everyone, brotherhood will not come to pass. Only by brotherhood will liberty be saved.

Fyodor Dostoevsky

Burden-sharing

Let us help one another to bear the burdens of life.

Voltaire

Business

Give something to gain something; you must spend to earn.

Prodicus

Cast thy bread upon the waters: for thou shalt find it after many days.

The Bible, Ecclesiastes 11:1 (AV)

Busybodies

'If everybody minded their own business,' the Duchess said in a hoarse growl, 'the world would go round a deal faster than it does.'

Lewis Carroll, Alice in Wonderland

Busyness   see also RUSH

A pure, simple, and steadfast spirit is not distracted by the number of things to be done, because it performs them all to the honour of God, and endeavours to be at rest from self-seeking.

Thomas à Kempis, The Imitation of Christ

Lord, thou knowest how busy I must be this day. If I forget thee, do not thou forget me.

Jacob Astley, before commanding soldiers in the battle of Edgehill

Extreme busyness, whether at school or college, kirk or market, is a symptom of deficient vitality.

Robert Louis Stevenson

C

Call   see also MISSIONARY CALL

Jesus said to them, 'Come with me, and I will teach you to catch men.' At once they left their nets and went with him.

The Bible, Matthew 4:19–20

The awareness of a need and the capacity to meet that need: this constitutes a call.

John R. Mott

Calvinism v. Arminianism

When I come to a text which speaks of election, I delight myself in the doctrine of election. When the apostles exhort me to repentance and obedience, and indicate my freedom of choice and action, I give myself up to that side of the question.

Charles Simeon

Where God has begun a real work of grace, incidental mistakes will be lessened by time and experience; where he has not, it is of little signification what sentiments people hold, or whether they call themselves Arminians or Calvinists.

John Newton, Cardiphonia

Careers

All rising to great place is by a winding stair.

Francis Bacon, Essays, Of Great Place

To choose a career on selfish grounds is probably the greatest single sin that any young person can commit, for it is the deliberate withdrawal from allegiance to God of the greatest part of time and strength.

William Temple

Blessed is he who has found his work; let him ask no other blessedness.

Thomas Carlyle

Don't put your daughter on the stage, Mrs Worthington.

Noel Coward song title

Today a king, tomorrow nothing.
French proverb

Today a man, tomorrow a mouse.
English proverb

I would rather be Head of the Ragged Schools than have the command of armies.
Lord Shaftesbury

Caring   see also CHARITY; KINDNESS; SERVICE

Christianity has taught us to care. Caring is the greatest thing, caring matters most.
Friedrich von Hügel, Letters from Baron von Hügel to his Niece

It is our care for the helpless, our practice of lovingkindness, that brands us in the eyes of many of our opponents. 'Look!' they say. 'How they love one another! Look how they are prepared to die for one another.'
Tertullian

I was eyes for the blind,
    and feet for the lame.
The Bible, Job, Job 29:15

He who sustains God's creatures is as though he had created them.
Tanhuma

It is a kingly task, believe me, to help the afflicted.
Ovid

You find people ready enough to do the Samaritan, without the oil and twopence.
Sydney Smith

We should help others by deeds, not words.
Latin proverb

Assuredly nobody will care for him who cares for nobody.
Thomas Jefferson

Causes, righteous

In a righteous cause the weak overcomes the strong.
Sophocles

Noble spirits ally themselves to great causes even when there is no hope of ultimate success.

Caution   see also PRUDENCE
The desire for safety stands against every great and noble enterprise.
Tacitus

Accountability: the mother of caution.
Ambrose Bierce, The Devil's Dictionary

The frontiers of the kingdom of God were never advanced by men and women of caution.
Mrs H.W.K. Mowll, Archbishop Mowll

Celebration   see FESTIVALS

Celibacy

Marriage has many pains, but celibacy has no pleasures.
Samuel Johnson

Challenge

Soldiers, all our efforts against superior forces have been unavailing. I have nothing to offer you but hunger and thirst, hardship and death; but I call on all who love their country to join with me.
Garibaldi, after the siege of Rome in 1849

I have nothing to offer but blood, toil, tears, and sweat.
Winston Churchill, May 1940

Chance

If a man does not believe that all the world is God's family, where nothing happens by chance but is all guided and directed by the care and providence of a being that is all love and goodness to all of his creatures; if a man does not believe this from his heart, he cannot truly be said to believe in God.
William Law

I shall never believe that God plays dice with the world.
Albert Einstein

Change   see also TRADITION

I pity the man who, proud of his system, says, 'My ideas have not changed for thirty years; I am what I was; I love what I loved.' The ridiculous man is he who never changes.
Barthélemy

The man who never alters his opinion is like standing water, and breeds reptiles of the mind.
William Blake

All things flow; nothing abides.
Heraclitus, quoted in Plato, Cratylus, 402a

Earth changes, but thy soul and God stand sure.

Robert Browning

We must all obey the great law of change. It is the most powerful law of nature.

Edmund Burke

A state without the means of some change is without the means of its conservation.

Edmund Burke, Reflections on the Revolution in France, 1790

Everyone thinks of changing humanity and no one ever thinks of changing himself.

Leo Tolstoy

The seven last words of many churches: 'We never did it this way before.'

Owen Hendrix

There are two great dangers facing the church: ritualism and rutualism. Rutualism is far the most dangerous.

Elderly Presbyterian minister

The wise man changes his mind, the fool never.

Spanish proverb

Love slays what we have been that we may be what we were not.

Augustine of Hippo

Those who never retract their opinions love themselves more than they love truth.

Joseph Joubert, Pensées

Character

Bad companions ruin good character.

The Bible, The apostle Paul, 1 Corinthians 15:33

Reputation is what men and women think of us. Character is what God and the angels know of us.

Thomas Paine

In war, three-quarters turns on personal character and relations; the balance of manpower and materials counts only for the remaining quarter.

Napoleon

If I keep my good character, I shall be rich enough.

Platonicus

Character is destiny.

Heraclitus

You cannot carve rotten wood.

Chinese proverb

Character is better than ancestry, and personal conduct is of more importance than the highest parentage.

Thomas Barnardo

Sow a thought, reap a word;
sow a word, reap a deed;
sow a deed, reap a habit;
sow a habit, reap a character;
sow a character, reap a destiny.

Author unknown

Men best show their character in trifles, where they are not on their guard. It is in insignificant matters, and in the simplest habits, that we often see the boundless egotism which pays no regard to the feelings of others, and denies nothing to itself.

Arthur Schopenhauer

Authority will prove a man.

Bias

Character is what you are in the dark.

Dwight L. Moody, Sermons

Charity   see also AID; CARING

The living need charity more than the dead.

George Arnold, The Jolly Old Pedagogue

Charity begins at home.

Proverb

He that bestows his goods upon the poor,
Shall have as much again, and ten times more.

John Bunyan, The Pilgrim's Progress

Charity is, indeed, a great thing, and a gift of God, and when it is rightly ordered likens us to God himself, as far as that is possible; for it is charity which makes the man.

John Chrysostom, True Almsgiving

Charity means nothing else but to love God for himself above all creatures, and to love one's fellow men for God's sake as one loves oneself.

Author unknown, The Cloud of Unknowing

Though I speak with the tongues of men and of angels, and have not charity, I am become as sounding brass, or a tinkling cymbal.

The Bible, The apostle Paul, 1 Corinthians 13:1 (AV)

Feel for others – in your pocket.

C.H. Spurgeon, Salt Cellars

All our doings without charity are
nothing worth.
> Book of Common Prayer, Collect
> for Quinquagesima

In charity there is no excess.
> Francis Bacon, Essays, Of
> Goodness

Cheerfulness

A merry heart maketh a cheerful
countenance.
> The Bible, Proverbs 15:13 (AV)

Being cheerful keeps you healthy. It is
slow death to be gloomy all the time.
> The Bible, Proverbs 17:22

Child evangelism

Give me the children until they are
seven and anyone may have them
afterwards.
> Francis Xavier

Childlikeness

The great man is he who does not lose
his child's heart.
> Mencius

Children

Children are a gift from the Lord;
  they are a real blessing.
> The Bible, Psalm 127:1

The greatest respect is due to a child.
> Juvenal

Suffer the little children to come unto
me, and forbid them not: for of such is
the kingdom of God.
> The Bible, Jesus Christ, Mark
> 10:14 (AV)

Better a late mulberry than an almond
tree in flower.
> Spanish proverb, referring to the
> almond's susceptibility to blight
> because of its early flowering, and
> hence meaning that slow
> developers are better than
> precocious children who do not
> fulfil their early promise

Children, advice to

Love God.
Thrust down pride.
Forgive gladly.
Be sober of meat and drink.
Use honest company.
Reverence thine elders.
Trust in God's mercy.
Be always well occupied.
Lose no time.
Falling down, despair not.
Ever take a fresh, new, good purpose.
Persevere constantly.
Wash clean.
Be no sluggard.
Awake quickly.
Enrich thee with virtue.
Learn diligently.
Teach what thou hast learned lovingly.
> John Colet, catechism for children

Children, and Jesus

Jesus' selection of a little child as an
example to his apostles; and [his wel-
coming little children] support the
view that Jesus may be justly
acclaimed as the lover of little children.
> H.D.A. Major, The Mission and
> Message of Jesus

Children, Upbringing see also
CHRISTIAN UPBRINGING

If a child lives with criticism,
  he learns to condemn.
If a child lives with hostility,
  he learns to fight.
If a child lives with fear,
  he learns to be apprehensive.
If a child lives with pity,
  he learns to feel sorry for himself.
If a child lives with jealousy,
  he learns to feel guilty.
If a child lives with encouragement,
  he learns to be self-confident.
If a child lives with tolerance,
  he learns to be patient.
If a child lives with praise,
  he learns to be appreciative.
If a child lives with acceptance,
  he learns to love.
If a child lives with approval,
  he learns to like himself.
If a child lives with recognition,
  he learns to have a goal.
If a child lives with fairness,
  he learns what justice is.
If a child lives with honesty,
  he learns what truth is.
If a child lives with sincerity,
  he learns to have faith in himself and
  those around him.
If a child lives with love,
  he learns that the world is
  a wonderful place to live in.
> Author unknown

Why do you turn and scrape every
stone to gather wealth and take so

little care of your children to whom one day you must relinquish all?

Socrates

Children of God

Everyone who does what is right is God's child.

The Bible, 1 John 2:29

Choice see DECISIONS

Christ see also ASCENSION; ATONEMENT; BLOOD; CROSS; INCARNATION; LORDSHIP OF CHRIST; NAME OF JESUS; RESURRECTION; SAVIOUR; SECOND COMING; TESTIMONIES TO CHRIST; VIRGIN BIRTH

I believe in . . . Jesus Christ, his only Son, our Lord, who was conceived by the Holy Spirit, born of the Virgin Mary, suffered under Pontius Pilate, was crucified, dead and buried; the third day he rose again from the dead; he ascended into heaven and sitteth on the right hand of God the Father Almighty; from thence he shall come to judge the living and the dead.

Apostles' Creed

Jesus Christ is the same yesterday, today, and for ever.

The Bible, Hebrews 13:8

In the gospel Jesus is *autobasileia*, the kingdom himself.

Origen

Nature forms us, sin deforms us, school informs us, Christ transforms us.

Author unknown

God had one son on earth without sin, but never one without suffering.

Augustine of Hippo

If Jesus Christ is a man
     And only a man – I say
That of all mankind I cleave to him
     And to him will I cleave alway.

If Jesus Christ is a god –
     And the only God – I swear
I will follow him through heaven and
     hell,
     The earth, the sea, and the air!

Author unknown

Jesus is a God whom we can approach without pride and before whom we can humble ourselves without despair.

Blaise Pascal

We all with one voice teach that it should be confessed that our Lord Jesus Christ is one and the same Son, the same perfect in Godhead, the same perfect in manhood, truly God and truly man.

Council of Chalcedon

We believe him to be the Christ, and the Son of God, because he healed the lame and the blind; and we are the more confirmed in this persuasion by what is written in the prophecies. . . . But that he also raised the dead, and that it is not a fiction of those who wrote the gospels, is evident from this, that if it had been a fiction there would have been many recorded as being raised up who had been long in their graves; but because it was not a fiction, few have been recorded.

Origen

In his life Christ is an example,
     showing us how to live;
In his death he is a sacrifice,
     satisfying for our sins;
In his resurrection, a conqueror;
In his ascension, a king;
In his intercession, a high priest.

Martin Luther

Jesus Christ is the centre of all, and the goal to which all tends.

Blaise Pascal

Apart from Christ we know neither what our life nor our death is; we do not know what God is nor what we ourselves are.

Blaise Pascal, Pensées

Beyond that which is found in Jesus Christ, the human race has not and never will progress.

Coleridge

No apostle, no New Testament writer, ever *remembered* Christ. . . . The Christian religion depends not on what Christ was, merely, but on what he is; not simply on what he did, but on what he does.

James Denney

Jesus does not give recipes that show the way to God as other teachers of religion do. He is himself the way.

Karl Barth

Christ's character was more wonderful than the greatest miracle.

Alfred, Lord Tennyson

It would take a Jesus to forge a Jesus.
Author unknown

I am far within the mark when I say
that all the armies that ever marched,
and all the navies that ever sailed, and
all the parliaments that ever sat, and
all the kings that ever reigned, put
together have not affected the life of
man upon earth as has that One Solitary Life.
Author unknown

Pythagoras, Epicurus, Socrates,
Plato, these are the torches of the
world; Christ is the light of day.
Victor Hugo

Christ is not valued at all unless he is
valued above all.
Augustine of Hippo

I read about Napoleon and am edified.
I read about Jesus and am profoundly
disturbed.
Carnegie Simpson

We know God only through Jesus
Christ.
Pascal

Christ, as King

The capital of heaven is the heart in
which Jesus Christ is enthroned as
king.
Sundar Singh

Christ, as Mediator

I am the way, the truth, and the life: no
man cometh unto the Father, but by
me.
The Bible, Jesus Christ,
John 14:6 (AV)

Christ's work as Mediator was unique:
it was to restore us to divine favour and
to make us sons of God, instead of
sons of men; heirs of a heavenly kingdom instead of heirs of hell.
John Calvin, The Institutes of
Christian Religion, 2.12.2

The knowledge of God without the
knowledge of our wretchedness
creates pride. The knowledge of our
wretchedness without the knowledge
of God creates despair. The knowledge of Jesus Christ is the middle way,
because in him we find both God and
our wretchedness.
Blaise Pascal

The Son of God could only become
our Mediator by becoming the Son of
man. He so received what is ours as to

transfer to us what is his. What is his by
nature can become ours by grace.
John Calvin, The Institutes of
Christian Religion, 2.12.2

We only know God by Jesus Christ.
Without this mediator all communion
with God is taken away; through Jesus
Christ we know God.
Blaise Pascal

Christ, as our Righteousness

Methought I saw, with the eyes of my
soul, Jesus Christ at God's right hand;
there I say, was my righteousness; so
that wherever I was, or whatever I was
doing, God could not say of me, he
wants my righteousness, for that was
just before Him. I saw also, moreover,
that it was not my good frame of heart
that made my righteousness better, nor
yet my bad frame of that made my righteousness worse; for my righteousness
was Jesus Christ Himself, 'the same
yesterday, and today and for ever.' Now
did the chains fall off my legs indeed.
John Bunyan, Grace Abounding

Christ, as our Sin-bearer

He is not like Moses who only shows sin,
but rather like Aaron who bears sin.
Martin Luther, The Epistle to the
Hebrews

Unutterable exchange! The sinless One
is condemned, the guilty go free. The
Blessed bears the curse, the cursed bear
the blessing. The Life dies and the dead
live. The glory is covered with shame,
and the shame covered with glory.
Lefèvre

Our acquittal lies in this: that the guilt
which made us liable to punishment
was transferred to the head of the Son
of God. It is really important to
remember that he has taken our place,
so that we may not spend all our lives in
trepidation and anxiety, as if the
punishment we deserve, but which the
Son of God took to himself, was still
hanging over us.
John Calvin, The Institutes of
Christian Religion, 2.16.5

Christ, as Shepherd see also GOD, AS SHEPHERD

I am the good shepherd: the good
shepherd giveth his life for the sheep.
The Bible, Jesus Christ,
John 10:11 (AV)

Christ, Baptism of

As soon as Jesus was baptised, he came up out of the water. Then heaven was opened to him, and he saw the Spirit coming down like a dove and alighting on him. Then a voice said from heaven, 'This is my own dear Son, with whom I am pleased.'

The Bible, Matthew 3:16–17

Christ, Birth of   see also CHRISTMAS

She [Mary] will have a son, and you will name him Jesus – because he will save his people from their sins.

*The Bible, An angel speaking to
Joseph, Matthew 1:21*

The angel said to [the shepherds], 'Don't be afraid! I am here with good news for you, which will bring great joy to all the people. This very day in David's town your Saviour was born – Christ the Lord!'

The Bible, Dr Luke, Luke 2:10–11

Christ, Divinity of

I have come down from heaven.

The Bible, Jesus Christ, John 6:38

The Father and I are one.

The Bible, Jesus Christ, John 10:30

I did come from the Father, and I came into the world; and now I am leaving the world and going to the Father.

The Bible, Jesus Christ, John 16:28

Take hold of Jesus as a man and you will discover that he is God.

Martin Luther

Brethren, we ought so to think of Jesus Christ as of God.

*2 Clement (the oldest extant
Christian sermon after those in the
New Testament)*

You believed on him who raised our Lord Jesus Christ from the dead and gave him glory and a throne on his right hand; to whom everything in heaven and on earth were made subject; whom every living creature serves; who comes as judge of living and dead; whose blood God will require of those who are disobedient to him.

*Polycarp, letter to the church at
Philippi, c. A.D. 110*

Jesus is either God, or he is not good.

Anselm

Gentlemen, I know men, and Jesus Christ was more than a man.

*Napoleon, on hearing a group of
sceptics discussing Jesus*

Had the doctrine of the deity of Christ been lost, Christianity would have vanished like a dream.

Thomas Carlyle

He that cried in the manger, that sucked the paps of a woman, that hath exposed himself to poverty, and a world of inconveniences, is the Son of the living God, of the same substance with his Father, begotten before all ages, before the morning-stars; he is God eternal.

Jeremy Taylor

Christ either deceived mankind by conscious fraud, or he was himself deluded, or he was divine. There is no getting out of this trilemma.

George Duncan

Christ, Early witnesses to   see also
CHRISTIANITY, HISTORICITY OF

He healed those who had been blind, and deaf, and lame, from their birth; causing, by his word, one to leap, another to hear, and a third to see: and by raising the dead and making them to live he induced, by his works, the men of that age to know him.

*Justin Martyr, c. 130 years after
Christ's death*

Nero punished with the utmost refinement of cruelty, a class hated for their abominations, who were commonly called Christians. Chrestus, from whom their name is derived, was executed at the hands of the Procurator Pontius Pilate in the reign of Tiberius.

*Tacitus, second-century Roman
historian*

That person whom the Jews had vainly imagined, from the meanness of his appearance, to be a mere man, they afterwards, in consequence of the power he exerted, considered as a magician, when he, with one word, ejected devils out of the bodies of men, gave sight to the blind, cleansed the leprous, strengthened the nerves of those that had the palsy, and, lastly, with one command, restored the dead to life; when he, I say, made the very elements obey him, assuaged the storms, walked upon the seas, demonstrating himself to be the Word of God.

*Tertullian, c. 180 years after
Christ's death*

Christ, Humanity of

Do not listen to anyone who avoids saying that Jesus Christ was descended from David, born of Mary, was truly born, ate and drank; was truly persecuted under Pontius Pilate, truly crucified and died while those in heaven, on earth, and under the earth watched; who also was truly raised from the dead.

Ignatius of Antioch, To the Trallians

He ate, drank, slept, walked, was weary, sorrowful, rejoicing, he wept and laughed; he knew hunger and thirst and sweat; he talked, he toiled, he prayed . . . so that there was no difference between him and other men, save only this, that he was God and had no sin.

Martin Luther

Christ, Knocking

Listen! I stand at the door and knock; if anyone hears my voice and opens the door, I will come into his house and eat with him, and he will eat with me.

The Bible, Revelation 3:20

Christ, Life of

The life of Jesus Christ is more wonderful than the greatest miracle.

Alfred, Lord Tennyson

Jesus' life began in a borrowed stable and ended in a borrowed tomb.

Alfred Plummer, Exegetical Commentary on the Gospel According to Saint Matthew

[Joseph] made his home in a town called Nazareth. And so what the prophets had said came true: 'He will be called a Nazarene.'

The Bible, Matthew 2:23

Christ, Mission of

I am not come to call the righteous, but sinners to repentance.

The Bible, Jesus Christ, Matthew 9:13 (AV)

I am come in order that you might have life – life in all its fulness.

The Bible, Jesus Christ, John 10:10

He became what we are that he might make us what he is.

Athanasius of Alexandria

To put the matter at its simplest, Jesus Christ came to make bad men good.

James Denney

Christ, Power of

Christ is the power of God and the wisdom of God.

The Bible, The apostle Paul, 1 Corinthians 1:31

'My grace is all you need, for my power is greatest when you are weak.' I am most happy, then, to be proud of my weaknesses, in order to feel the protection of Christ's power over me.

The Bible, The apostle Paul, 2 Corinthians 12:9

Will-power does not change men. Time does not change men. Christ does.

Henry Drummond

Christ, Sinlessness of

He committed no sin, and no one ever heard a lie come from his lips.

The Bible, 1 Peter 2:22

In him [Christ] is no sin.

The Bible, 1 John 3:5

Christ, Strength of

I can do all things through Christ which strengtheneth me.

The Bible, The apostle Paul, Philippians 4:13 (AV)

Christ, Verdict of non-Christians on

Jesus Christ was a virtuous and an amiable man; the morality which he preached and practised was of the most benevolent kind.

Thomas Paine

Christ's system of morals and religion as he left them to us is the best the world has seen or is likely to see.

Benjamin Franklin

It would have been a greater miracle to invent such a life as Christ's than to be it.

Jean-Jacques Rousseau

If the life and death of Socrates are those of a sage, the life and death of Jesus Christ are those of a God.

Jean-Jacques Rousseau

An historian like myself, with no theological bias whatever, cannot portray the progress of humanity honestly without giving Jesus of Nazareth foremost place.

H.G. Wells

He is the incomparable man to whom the universal conscience has decreed the title of Son of God, and that with justice.

Ernest Renan

Christian life

We are not ashamed of Christ, for we rejoice to be his disciples and in his name to suffer.
Tertullian

When Christ calls a man he bids him come and die.
Dietrich Bonhoeffer, The Cost of Discipleship

Jesus promised his disciples three things – that they would be completely fearless, absurdly happy and in constant trouble.
G.K. Chesterton

The trivial round, the common task,
Would furnish all we ought to ask;
Room to deny ourselves; a road
To bring us, daily, nearer God.
John Keble

A man who has faith must be prepared not only to be a martyr, but to be a fool.
G.K. Chesterton, Heretics

The true Christian practises being God.
Clement of Alexandria

No man is awake to the peril of the ungodly, who has not trembled under the sense of personal danger. No man forms a correct estimate of the value of the atonement, who has not had the blood of Christ sprinkled on his own conscience.
John Smith

We die daily. Happy those who daily come to life as well.
George Macdonald

A Christian is nothing but a sinful man who has put himself to school to Christ for the honest purpose of becoming better.
Henry Ward Beecher

The life of God in the soul of man.
Title of a book by Henry Scougal, and John Wesley's definition of a Christian

If a man cannot be a Christian where he is, he cannot be a Christian anywhere.
Henry Ward Beecher

The wilderness is the way to Canaan.
C.H. Spurgeon

Those whom the Lord has chosen and honoured with his friendship must be prepared for a hard, strenuous and testing life, full of many different troubles.
John Calvin, The Institutes of Christian Religion, 3.8.1

Bear the cross cheerfully and it will bear you. . . . If you bear it unwillingly, you make it a burden for yourself.
Thomas à Kempis, The Imitation of Christ

If you reject one cross, without doubt you will find another, and perhaps a heavier.
Thomas à Kempis, The Imitation of Christ

A Christian man is the most free lord of all, and subject to none; a Christian man is the most dutiful servant of all, and subject to everyone.
Martin Luther

Christian life consists of faith and charity.
Martin Luther

The entrance fee into the kingdom of heaven is nothing: the annual subscription is everything.
Henry Drummond

Beware of thinking, 'Because I am filled with love, I need not have so much holiness. Because I pray always, therefore I need no set time for private prayer. Because I watch always, therefore I need no particular self-examination.'
John Wesley, A Plain Man's Guide to Holiness

If men are to know that we are disciples of Christ by so loving one another according to his new example of love, then it is certain that if we are empty of this love we make it clear that we are not his disciples.
William Law

To be a Christian or not to be, is not a matter of being a somewhat better man, or a man perhaps not quite so good. It is a matter of life or death.
James Denney

My great concern is not whether God is on our side, my great concern is to be on God's side.
Abraham Lincoln

Expect great things from God,
Attempt great things for God.
William Carey

Whatever you desire or fear, seek or shun, whatever you think, speak, or do, let it be in order for your happiness in God, the sole end, as well as source, of your being.
John Wesley

Christian life as conflict

You are but a poor soldier of Christ if you think you can overcome without fighting, and suppose you can have the crown without the conflict.

John Chrysostom

Every true Christian is a Soldier of Christ – a hero par excellence! Braver than the bravest – scorning the soft seductions of peace and her oft-repeated warnings against hardship, disease, danger, and death, whom he counts among his bosom friends.

C.T. Studd

Christian life as following Jesus

Let us always follow Jesus and never falter, for if we follow him we never fail because he gives his strength to his followers. The nearer you are to this strength, the stronger you will be.

Ambrose of Milan

When Christ calls a man he bids him come and die.

Dietrich Bonhoeffer

In simple trust like theirs who heard
Beside the Syrian sea
The gracious calling of the Lord,
Let us, like them, without a word,
Rise up and follow thee.

John Greenleaf Whittier

A better priest I trow that nowhere
none is;
He waited after no pomp and
reverence,
Ne maked him a spicèd conscience,
But Christès lore, and his Apostles
twelve,
He taughte, but first he followed it
himself.

*Geoffrey Chaucer, Canterbury
Tales, Prologue*

I am not worthy to follow in the steps of my Lord, but, like him, I want no home, no possessions. Like him I will belong to the road, sharing the suffering of my people, eating with those who will give me shelter, and telling all men of the love of God.

Sundar Singh

Christian message

While I was with you, I made up my mind to forget everything except Jesus Christ and especially his death on the cross.

*The Bible, The apostle Paul,
1 Corinthians 2:2*

Christian perfection   see PERFECTION

Christian unity   see also CHURCH,
LEAVING THE

There is one Lord, one faith, one baptism; there is one God and Father of all mankind, who is Lord of all, works through all, and is in all.

*The Bible, The apostle Paul,
Ephesians 4:5–6*

Unity in things necessary, liberty in things doubtful, charity in everything.

Augustine of Hippo

Above all, do not divide into sects and groups, each quarrelling with the others. When we are split into sects our attention is drawn away from inward grace to outward works, each sect trying to prove it is better than the others. Sects arise when people wrongly set themselves up as presbyters and prophets, winning allegiance not by the truth of their teaching but by their charm. Such people will always be present, ready to foster dissension, and it is for all of us to discern their falsehood and guard against them.

Martin Luther

Matters non-essential should not be the basis of argument among Christians.

*John Calvin, The Institutes of
Christian Religion, 4.1.12*

Christian upbringing

Parents, do not treat your children in such a way as to make them angry. Instead, bring them up with Christian discipline and instruction.

*The Bible, The apostle Paul,
Ephesians 6:4*

I cannot help taking notice of your remarks upon the advantage of an early education in the principles of religion, because I have myself most happily experienced it; since I owe to the early care of a most excellent woman, my mother, that bent and bias to religion, which, with the co-operating grace of God, hath at length brought me back to those paths of peace from when I might otherwise have been in danger of deviating for ever!

*Gilbert West, who had planned to
write a book against religion but
was converted by reading the Bible
in preparation for it*

I learned more about Christianity from my mother than from all the theologians of England.
John Wesley

No man is poor who has a godly mother.
Abraham Lincoln

Christian writing

The author . . . would wish his work to be brought to this test – does it uniformly tend

TO HUMBLE THE SINNER?

TO EXALT THE SAVIOUR?

TO PROMOTE HOLINESS?

If in any one instance it loses sight of any of these points, let it be condemned without mercy.
Charles Simeon, Horae Homileticae, Preface

Christianity

[Question (by a teacher of comparative religion):] What have you found in Christianity that you did not find in your old religion?
[The Sadhu's answer:] I found the dear Lord Jesus.
Yes, but what principle or doctrine or ethic or understanding did you find?
I found the dear Lord Jesus.
Sundar Singh

The Christian ideal has not been tried and found wanting. It has been found difficult; and left untried.
G.K. Chesterton

Christianity is that power which can make bad men good.
James Denney

No religion is genuine that is not in accordance with truth.
Lactantius

Christianity is not the conclusion of a philosophical debate on the origins of the universe: it is a catastrophic historical event following on the long spiritual preparation of humanity.
C.S. Lewis, The Problem of Pain

Pure and true religion is confidence in God coupled with genuine fear.
John Calvin, The Institutes of Christian Religion, 1.2.2

I reject Christianity because it is Jewish, because it is international and because, in cowardly fashion, it preaches peace on earth.
Erich Ludendorff

Give me a religion that will stand by me at all seasons, in prosperity and adversity, in sickness and health, in time and eternity. I would not give a rush for a religion which will only serve my turn when the sunshine of worldly favour illumines my steps, and fail me when I stand in the greatest need of its supports.
David Simpson, A Plea for Religion and the Sacred Writings

Provided that meetings, pamphlets, policies, movements, causes and crusades, matter more to him than prayers and sacraments and charity, he is ours – and the more 'religious' (on those terms) the more securely ours. I'd show you a pretty cageful down here. – Your affectionate uncle, Screwtape.
C.S. Lewis, The Screwtape Letters

Christianity is rational and sublime in its doctrines, humane and beneficent in its precepts, pure and simple in its worship.
William Robertson

No religion ever appeared in the world whose natural tendency was so much directed to promote the peace and happiness of mankind than Christianity.
Bolingbroke

Christianity promises to make men free; it never promises to make them independent.
W.R. Inge

Christianity, Historicity of

At that time lived Jesus, a wise man, if he may be called a man, for he performed many wonderful works. He was a teacher of such men as received the truth with pleasure. He drew over to him many Jews and Gentiles. This was the Christ; and when Pilate, at the instigation of the chief men among us, had condemned him to the cross, they who before had conceived an affection for him, did not cease to adhere to him; for, on the third day, he appeared to them alive again, the divine prophets having foretold these and many wonderful things concerning him. And the sect of the Christians, so called from him, subsists to this time.
Josephus, Antiquities of the Jews

The apostles have preached to us from our Lord Jesus Christ from God, for, having received their command, and being thoroughly assured by the resurrection of our Lord Jesus Christ, they went abroad, publishing that the kingdom of God was at hand.

Clement

Christianity, Message of

If you want to understand the Christian message you must start with the wounds of Christ.

Martin Luther

Judaism proclaimed, indeed, that God forgave sin, but Christianity proclaimed that God redeemed sinners.

James Parkes, The Conflict of the Church and the Synagogue

Had the doctrines of Jesus been preached always as pure as they came from his lips, the whole civilised world would not have been Christian.

Thomas Jefferson

Christianity, Spread of

We were but of yesterday, and we have filled your cities, islands, towns, and boroughs, the camp, the senate, and the forum. They [the heathen adversaries of Christianity] lament that every sex, age and condition, and persons of every rank also, are converts to that name.

Tertullian

While that great body [the Roman empire] was invaded by open violence or undermined by slow decay, a pure and humble religion gently insinuated itself into the minds of men, grew up in silence and obscurity, derived new vigour from opposition, and finally erected the triumphant banner of the cross on the ruins of the Capitol.

Edward Gibbon, The Decline and Fall of the Roman Empire

The philosophers were confined to Greece, and to their particular retainers; but the doctrine of the Master of Christianity did not remain in Judea, as philosophy did in Greece, but is spread throughout the whole world, in every nation, and village, and city, both of Greeks and barbarians, converting both whole houses and separate individuals, having already brought over to the truth not a few of the philosophers themselves. If the Greek philosophy be prohibited, it immediately vanishes; whereas, from the first preaching of our doctrine, kings and tyrants, governors and presidents, with their whole train, and with the populace on their side, have endeavoured with their whole might to exterminate it, yet it flourishes more and more.

Clement of Alexandria

Throughout all Greece, and in all other nations, there are innumerable and immense multitudes who, having left the laws of their country, and those whom they esteemed gods, have given themselves up to the law of Moses, and the religion of Christ: and this not without the bitterest resentment from the idolaters, by whom they were frequently put to torture, and sometimes to death: and it is wonderful to observe how, in so short a time, the religion has increased, amidst punishment and death, and every kind of torture.

Origen, 3rd-century Christian scholar

The Christian religion has so flourished and increased continually, that it is now preached freely and without molestation, although there were a thousand obstacles to the spreading of the doctrine of Jesus in the world.

Origen

The Indians, Persians, Goths and Egyptians philosophise and firmly believe the immortality of the soul and future recompenses which, before, the greatest philosophers had denied or doubted of, or perplexed with their disputes. The fierceness of Thracians and Scythians is now softened by the gentle sound of the gospel; and everywhere Christ is all in all.

Jerome, late 4th/early 5th century

Christianity, Verdict of non-Christians on

He who shall introduce into public affairs the principle of primitive Christianity will change the face of the world.

Benjamin Franklin, Letter to the French Ministry, March 1778

I call Christianity the one great curse, the one enormous and innermost perversion, the one great instinct of revenge, for which no means are too venomous, too underhand, too underground and too petty – I call it the one immortal blemish of mankind.

Friedrich Nietzsche

Christians

Surely you know that you are God's temple and that God's Spirit lives in you!

The Bible, The apostle Paul,
1 Corinthians 3:16

Christian: One who believes that the New Testament is a divinely inspired book admirably suited to the spiritual needs of his neighbour.

Ambrose Bierce

An honest and religious man is a wall to a whole city, a sea to a whole island.

Ambrose of Milan

The saint is a saint because he received the Holy Spirit, who took up his abode with him and inwardly married himself to the soul.

Abraham Kuyper, The Work of
the Holy Spirit

Christians, Early

The disciples were first called Christians at Antioch.

The Bible, Dr Luke, Acts of the
Apostles 11:29

They walk in all humility and kindness, and falsehood is not found among them, and they love one another. They do not despise the widow, or grieve the orphan. He who has, distributes liberally to him who has not. If they see a stranger, they bring him under their roof, and rejoice over him, as it were their own brother.

Aristides (AD 125)

Among us you will find uneducated people, and artisans, and old women who, if they are unable to prove in words the benefit of our doctrine, yet by their deeds they show the benefit which comes from their being convinced of its truth. They do not rehearse speeches, but exhibit good works; when struck, they do not strike again; when robbed, they do not go to law; they give to those that ask of them, and they love their neighbours as themselves.

Athenagoras, Embassy for
Christians

Christians and the State

We are subject to the men who rule over us, but subject only in the Lord. If they command anything against him, let us not pay the least regard to it.

John Calvin

For the sake of the Lord submit to every human authority.

The Bible, 1 Peter 2:13

Christlike behaviour

To be like Christ is to be a Christian.

William Penn

It's not great talents that God blesses, but great likeness to Jesus.

Robert Murray M'Cheyne

Christmas

Behold, a virgin shall conceive, and bear a son, and shall call his name Immanuel.

The Bible, Isaiah 7:14 (AV)

The people that walked in darkness have seen a great light: they that dwell in the land of the shadow of death, upon them hath the light shined.

The Bible, Isaiah 9:2 (AV)

For unto us a child is born, unto us a son is given: and the government shall be upon his shoulder: and his name shall be called Wonderful, Counsellor, The mighty God, The everlasting Father, The Prince of Peace. Of the increase of his government there shall be no end.

The Bible, Isaiah 9:6–7 (AV)

She gave birth to her first son, wrapped him in strips of cloth and laid him in a manger – there was no room for them to stay in the inn.

The Bible, Luke 2:7

Joy to the world! the Lord is come;
　Let earth receive her King.
Let ev'ry heart prepare Him room,
　And heav'n and nature sing.

Isaac Watts, after The Bible,
Psalm 98

The only person in history who was able to choose where he was to be born, chose a stable.

Author unknown

Thou didst leave thy throne
　And thy kingly crown
When thou camest to earth for
　me. . . .

O come to my heart, Lord Jesus!
There is room in my heart for thee.
Emily E.S. Elliott

What can I give him
  Poor as I am?
If I were a shepherd
  I would bring a lamb;
If I were a wise man
  I would do my part;
Yet what I can I give him –
  Give my heart.
Christina Rossetti

Since we are not yet ready for the banquet of our Father, let us grow familiar
with the manger of our Lord Jesus
Christ.
Augustine of Hippo

Some say that ever 'gainst that season
  comes
Wherein our Saviour's birth is
  celebrated,
The bird of dawning singeth all night
  long,
And then, they say, no spirit dare stir
  abroad,
The nights are wholesome, then no
  planets strike,
No fairy takes, nor witch hath power
  to charm:
So hallowed and so gracious is that
  time.
William Shakespeare

This is the Month and this the happy
  morn
Wherein the Son of Heav'ns eternal
  King,
Of wedded Maid and Virgin Mother
  born,
Our great Redemption from above did
  bring;
For so the holy Sages once did sing,
That he our deadly forfeit should
  release,
And with his Father work us a
  perpetual peace.
John Milton

God all-bounteous, all-creative,
  Whom no ills from good dissuade,
Is incarnate, and a native
  Of the very world he made.
Christopher Smart

Church see also CLERGYMEN;
DENOMINATIONS; CHRISTIANITY, SPREAD
OF; CHRISTIANS, EARLY

Thou art Peter, and upon this rock I
will build my church; and the gates of
hell shall not prevail against it.
The Bible, Jesus Christ,
Matthew 16:18 (AV)

Before Christ comes it is useless to
expect to see a perfect church.
J.C. Ryle, Practical Religion

If anyone wants to be saved . . . let
him come to this house where the
blood of Christ is a sign of redemption.
Origen, Sermons on Joshua

Let no one persuade himself or
deceive himself: outside this house,
that is, outside the church, no one is
saved.
Origen, Sermons on Joshua

There is no salvation outside the
church.
Augustine of Hippo

No man ever went to heaven alone; he
must either find friends or make them.
John Wesley

Nobody worries about Christ as long
as he can be kept shut up in churches.
He is quite safe inside. But there is
always trouble if you try and let him
out.
G.A. Studdert-Kennedy

The day we find the perfect church, it
becomes imperfect the moment we
join it.
C.H. Spurgeon

I cherish and follow the church in all
things. I resist only those who in the
name of the Church of Rome try to
erect a Babylon for us . . . as if holy
scripture no longer existed.
Martin Luther, justification before
Cajetan

The nearer to church, the farther from
God.
Lancelot Andrewes

And of all plagues with which mankind
  are curst,
Ecclesiastic tyranny's the worst.
Daniel Defoe, The True-Born
Englishman, 2.299

Upon this rock which you have confessed – upon myself, the Son of the
living God – I will build my church. I
will build you on myself, and not
myself on you.
Augustine of Hippo, On the
Words of the Lord, Sermon 13

There are many sheep without, many wolves within.

Augustine of Hippo

The church exists for the sake of those outside it.

William Temple

Wherever we see the Word of God purely preached and heard, there a church of God exists, even if it swarms with many faults.

John Calvin

Church, as Mother

For those to whom God is a Father, the Church must also be a mother.

John Calvin, The Institutes of Christian Religion, 4.1.1

The Church [is] the gathering of God's children, where they can be helped and fed like babies and then, guided by her motherly care, grow up to manhood in maturity of faith.

John Calvin, The Institutes of Christian Religion, 4.1.1

He cannot have God for his Father who has not the Church for his mother.

Cyprian, De Unitate Ecclesiae

The title, Mother, underlines how essential it is to know about the visible Church. There is no other way of entering into life unless we are conceived in her womb, brought to birth and then given her milk.

John Calvin, The Institutes of Christian Religion, 4.1.4

The church is the daughter born of the Word, not the Word's mother.

Martin Luther

Church, Leaving the   see also
CHRISTIAN UNITY

Those in the forefront of inciting defection from the Church only want to demonstrate their own superiority by despising others.

John Calvin, The Institutes of Christian Religion, 4.1.16

God has chosen that the fellowship of his Church should be maintained in human society, and anyone who breaks its bonds, through hatred of the ungodly, embarks on a slippery slope, where there is great danger of cutting oneself off from the communion of saints.

John Calvin, The Institutes of Christian Religion, 4.1.16

Church, True

When we say that the pure ministry of the Word and pure celebration of the sacraments are sufficient signs by which to recognise a Church, we mean that we should not write it off as long as these exist, even though it may be riddled with other faults. There may even be shortcomings in the administration of the Word and sacraments, but this should not cut us off from fellowship.

John Calvin, The Institutes of Christian Religion, 4.1.12

Church buildings

I never weary of great churches. It is my favourite kind of mountain scenery. Mankind was never so happily inspired as when it made a cathedral.

Robert Louis Stevenson, An Inland Voyage

Church government   see also
CHRISTIAN UNITY

Be zealous to do all things in harmony with God, with the bishop presiding in the place of God and the presbyters in the place of the Council of the Apostles, and the deacons, who are most dear to me, entrusted with the service of Jesus Christ.

Ignatius of Antioch

The Church of England shall be free.

Magna Carta

Church invisible

Of course we believe in the invisible Church, evident to God's eye alone, but we are also told to accept the visible Church and remain in communion with it.

John Calvin, The Institutes of Christian Religion, 4.1.7

Church membership

God's fatherly love and the evidence of spiritual life are restricted to his own people. So abandoning the Church is always fatal.

John Calvin, The Institutes of Christian Religion, 4.1.4

I am more of a flying buttress: I support it from the outside.

Winston Churchill, when asked if he were a pillar of the church

Church of England   see ANGLICAN CHURCH

Church services see also MUSIC IN
CHURCH SERVICES
Hatch, match and despatch.
Author unknown

Church visible

In regard to the secret predestination
of God, there are very many sheep
outside, and very many wolves inside.
Augustine of Hippo

Churchgoing

As some to church repair,
Not for the doctrine, but the music
there.
*Alexander Pope, Essay on
Criticism*

Circumstances

Circumstances! I make circumstances!
Napoleon

Man is not the creature of circumstances. Circumstances are the creatures of men.
Benjamin Disraeli, Vivian Grey

Cities

City life: Millions of people being
lonesome together.
Henry David Thoreau

Civilisation

Civilisation is a limitless multiplication
of unnecessary necessities.
Mark Twain

Civilisation is the slow process of
learning to be kind.
Author unknown

The true test of a civilisation is not the
census, nor the size of cities, nor the
crops – no, but the kind of man the
country turns out.
*Ralph Waldo Emerson, Society
and Solitude*

The world gets more civilised – so I am
told, though, when I read the news-
papers, I am not quite sure that it is so.
C.H. Spurgeon

Clairvoyance

Clairvoyant: A person, commonly a
woman, who has the power of seeing
that which is invisible to her patron –
namely, that he is a blockhead.
Ambrose Bierce

Cleanliness

Let it be observed, that slovenliness is
no part of religion; that neither this

nor any text of scripture, condemns
neatness of apparel. Certainly this is a
duty, not a sin. 'Cleanliness is, indeed,
next to godliness.'
John Wesley, Sermons, On Dress

Clergymen see MINISTERS OF RELIGION

Closeness to God

Any flea as it is in God is nobler than
the highest of angels in himself.
Meister Eckhart

Comfort see also SERVICE

Singing to a person who is depressed is
like taking off his clothes on a cold day
or like rubbing salt in a wound.
The Bible, Proverbs 25:20

Comfort ye, comfort ye my people,
saith your God. Speak ye comfortably
to Jerusalem, and cry unto her, that
her warfare is accomplished.
The Bible, Isaiah 40:1 (AV)

He helps us in all our troubles, so that
we are able to help others who have all
kinds of troubles, using the same help
that we ourselves have received from
God.
*The Bible, The apostle Paul,
2 Corinthians 1:4*

By what believers feel in themselves
they learn by degrees how to warn,
pity, and bear with others. A soft,
patient, and compassionate spirit, and
a readiness and skill in comforting
those who are cast down, is not
perhaps attainable in any other way.
John Newton, Cardiphonia

God does not comfort us to make us
comfortable, but to make us comforters.
J.H. Jowett

His masterpiece was in comforting
wounded consciences.
*Thomas Fuller, Church History of
Britain, writing of the puritan
minister Richard Greenham*

A trifle consoles us because a trifle
upsets us.
Blaise Pascal, Pensées

Sometimes a light surprises
The Christian while he sings:
It is the Lord who rises
With healing in his wings;
When comforts are declining,
He grants the soul again
A season of clear shining
To cheer it after rain.
William Cowper

In a picture I want to say something comforting.

Vincent Van Gogh

We all have enough strength to bear the misfortunes of others.

La Rochefoucauld

I never knew any man in my life who could not bear another's misfortunes perfectly like a Christian.

Alexander Pope

Commandments   see also TEN COMMANDMENTS

The eleventh commandment: Thou shalt not be found out.

George Whyte-Melville

Committees

A committee is a thing which takes a week to do what one good man can do in an hour.

Elbert Hubbard

Common sense

Common sense is not so common.

Voltaire

Nothing astonishes men so much as common sense and plain dealing.

Ralph Waldo Emerson

Common sense in an uncommon degree is what the world calls wisdom.

Samuel Taylor Coleridge

Communal living

And all that believed were together, and had all things common.

The Bible, Dr Luke, Acts 2:44 (AV)

Communication

The medium is the message.

Marshall McLuhan,
Understanding Media, 1964

Communism   see also MARXISM

From each according to his abilities, to each according to his needs.

Karl Marx

What is a communist? One who has yearnings
For equal division of unequal earnings.

Author unknown

The contradictions in the Communist society have their cause in the inability to make a selfless man.

Nikita Khrushchev

Commuters

Their doors are shut in the evening;
And they know no songs.

G.K. Chesterton

Compassion

Jesus wept.

The Bible, John 11:35

When a man suffers himself, it is called misery; when he suffers in the suffering of another, it is called pity.

Augustine of Hippo

When a man has pity on all living creatures then only is he noble.

Buddha

Compassion is the basis of all morality.

Arthur Schopenhauer

The wretched have no compassion.

Samuel Johnson

Compassion will cure more sins than condemnation.

Henry Ward Beecher

Pity melts the mind to love.

John Dryden

Conceit

A self-made man? Yes – and worships his creator.

William Cowper

I've never any pity for conceited people, because I think they carry their comfort with them.

George Eliot

It is a curious fact that of all the illusions that beset mankind none is quite so curious as that tendency to suppose that we are mentally and morally superior to those who differ from us in opinion.

Elbert Hubbard

Concentration

To be great, concentrate. Most people remain ordinary because they scatter their energies.

Author unknown

Condemnation

No believer ever performed a single deed which, if tested by God's strict justice, could escape condemnation. Even if he could, because the deed is tainted by his sins it is stripped of all merit.

John Calvin, The Institutes of
Christian Religion, 3.14.11

Confession

You will never succeed in life if you try to hide your sins. Confess them and give them up; then God will show mercy to you.

The Bible, Proverbs 28:13

Confession is good for the soul.

Scottish proverb

If you wish to be good, first consider that you are wicked.

Epictetus

By the confession of sins and by the confession of praise, let your whole life confess him!

Bernard of Clairvaux

A petition for pardon is in itself a full confession, because he who begs for pardon fully admits his guilt.

Tertullian, On Prayer

Conscience

In the night my conscience warns me.

The Bible, Psalm 16:7

When my conscience won't come down to brass-tacks but will only vaguely accuse or vaguely approve, we must say to it, like Herbert, 'Peace, prattler' – and get on.

C.S. Lewis, Letters to Malcolm Chiefly on Prayer

My conscience is captive to the Word of God.

Martin Luther

Conscience is a god to all mortals.

Menander, Monostikoi

A good conscience is a soft pillow.

German proverb

A clear conscience can bear any trouble.

Thomas Fuller, Gnomologia

Let us look to our own consciences as we do to our own hands, to see if they be dirty.

Florence Nightingale

A good conscience is wont to speak out openly and fearlessly.

Pausanias

Conscience is the voice of the soul.

Jean-Jacques Rousseau

God breathes, not speaks, his verdicts.

Robert Browning

Labour to keep alive in your breast that little spark of celestial fire, conscience.

George Washington

A heart unspotted is not easily daunted.

William Shakespeare

Thus conscience does make cowards of us all.

William Shakespeare, Hamlet, III.i.

And I will place within them as a guide
My Umpire Conscience, whom if they will hear,
Light after light well used they shall attain,
And to the end persisting, safe arrive.

John Milton

A good conscience is a continual Christmas.

Benjamin Franklin

Conscientiousness   see also
FAITHFULNESS; LITTLE THINGS

A little neglect may breed mischief, . . . for want of a nail, the shoe was lost; for want of a shoe the horse was lost; and for want of a horse the rider was lost.

Benjamin Franklin, Poor Richard's Almanac, 1858

Consecration

The world has yet to see what God will do with a man fully consecrated to him.

Author unknown

Your religion, if it is real, and given by the Holy Ghost, must be in your *heart*. It must occupy the citadel. It must hold the reins. It must sway the affections. It must lead the will. It must direct the tastes. It must influence the choices and decisions. It must fill the deepest, lowest, inmost seat in your soul.

J.C. Ryle, Practical Religion

All these things had become as nothing to my brother. He only cared about the Bible and the Lord Jesus Christ; and God taught me the same lesson.

C.T. Studd

And if you will here stop and ask yourself, why you are not as pious as the primitive Christians were, your own heart will tell you, that it is neither through ignorance, nor inability, but purely because you never thoroughly intended it.

William Law

God made man's soul so like himself that nothing else in earth or heaven resembles God so closely as the human soul. God wants this temple cleared of everything but himself.

Meister Eckhart

Intend to live in continual mortification, and never to expect or desire any worldly ease or pleasure.
Jonathan Edwards, Diary, 1723

When I left Springfield, I asked the people to pray for me; I was not a Christian. When I buried my son – the severest trial of my life – I was not a Christian. But when I went to Gettysburg, and saw the graves of thousands of our soldiers, I then and there consecrated myself to Christ.
Abraham Lincoln

My heaven is to please God and glorify him, and to give all to him, and to be wholly devoted to his glory; that is the heaven I long for.
David Brainerd

Devotion means a life given, or devoted, to God.
William Law

Just as I am – thy love unknown
Has broken every barrier down –
Now to be thine, yea, thine alone,
   O Lamb of God, I come!
Charlotte Elliott

Consequences of evil

People who set traps for others get caught themselves. People who start landslides get crushed.
The Bible, Proverbs 26:27

Conservation

Whoever could make two ears of corn . . . grow upon a spot of ground where only one grew before, would deserve better of mankind . . . than the whole race of politicians put together.
Jonathan Swift

Consistency

The silent power of a consistent life.
Florence Nightingale

Contemplation   see also MEDITATION

Contemplation is nothing else but a secret, peaceful, and loving infusion of God, which, if admitted, will set the soul on fire with the spirit of love.
John of the Cross, The Dark Night of the Soul

Contentment   see also GREED; GRUMBLING; PEACE OF MIND

I know what it is to be in need and what it is to have more than enough. I have learnt this secret, so that anywhere, at any time, I am content, whether I am full or hungry, whether I have too much or too little.
The Bible, The apostle Paul, Philippians 4:12

Have mercy on me, O Beneficent One, for I was angry that I had no shoes – and then I met a man who had no feet.
Chinese proverb

I am content with what I have,
   Little be it, or much:
And, Lord, contentment still I crave,
   Because thou savest such.
John Bunyan, The Pilgrim's Progress

He who doesn't find a little enough, will find nothing enough.
Epicurus

Let the man who has enough for his wants, desire nothing more.
Horace

Contentment is riches enough.
Quintilian

Enough is as good as a feast.
Proverb

But if I'm content with a little,
Enough is as good as a feast.
Isaac Bickerstaffe, Love in a Village, III.i.

The camel, desiring horns, lost its ears as well.
Latin proverb

Better a little with contentment than a lot with contention.
Benjamin Franklin

To be content, look backward on those who possess less than yourself, not forward on those who possess more.
Benjamin Franklin, Poor Richard's Almanac

For people who give themselves to God and diligently seek to do his will, whatever God may send will be the best . . . and therefore, since you know it to be God's will, you ought to rejoice in it.
Meister Eckhart

Convents

Convent: A place of retirement for women who wish for leisure to meditate upon the sin of idleness.
Ambrose Bierce

Conversation   see also SPEECH

The character of man is known from his conversation.

Menander

Conversion   see also REGENERATION

Except ye be converted, and become as little children, ye shall not enter into the kingdom of heaven.

The Bible, Jesus Christ,
Matthew 18:3 (AV)

Allowances must be made for our natural temperaments, for conversion does not entirely rule out our natural dispositions; for those sins toward which a man is naturally inclined before his conversion will still be the ones that he is apt to fall into.

Jonathan Edwards, Treatise
Concerning the Religious
Affections

You will never be happy till you are converted.

J.C. Ryle, Practical Religion

Preach faith until you have it.

Peter Bohler's advice to the young
John Wesley

Just because you were born in a garage it doesn't mean to say that you are a car.

Author unknown

I had supposed that conversion was due to the operation of the Holy Spirit – a change wrought without the co-operation, almost without the know-ledge, of the subject of it. Now I found that the pressure of divine grace on all human hearts is constant; God's will to save is always there; Christ stands at the door of every one and knocks; but the decisive point is where the will awakes, opens the door and lets him in, responds to the infinite and universal love of God, yields to the steady though gentle insistence of redeeming grace.

R.F. Horton

If you want to work for the kingdom of God, and to enter into it, there is just one condition to be first accepted. You must enter it as children, or not at all.

John Ruskin

When I came to see that Jesus Christ had died for me, it didn't seem hard to give up all for him. It seemed just common, ordinary honesty.

C.T. Studd

Conversion is committing all of me to all I know of Christ.

Author unknown

You can't tell the exact moment when night becomes day, but you know when it is daytime.

Author unknown

There is one, even Christ Jesus, that can speak to thy condition.

George Fox, describing the joyful
truth he had found after seeking

Just because you go to church it doesn't mean to say that you are a born again Christian.

Billy Graham

Between the stirrup and the ground
I mercy ask'd, I mercy found.

Camden's Remains. Epitaph on a
wicked man killed by falling from
a horse

I've lived all my life for the devil up 'til now, and from here on I'm going to live it for the Lord.

Author unknown

Conversion, Holy Spirit's work in

I believe that I cannot in my own understanding and strength believe in or come to Jesus Christ, but that the Holy Spirit has called me.

Martin Luther

The work of conversion itself, and in especial the act of believing, or faith itself, is expressly said to be of God, to be wrought in us by him, to be given unto us from him. The scripture says [that God gives us] faith, repentance, and conversion.

John Owen, The Nature, Causes,
and Means of Regeneration

Before the conversion of man there are but two efficient causes found, namely, the Holy Spirit, and the Word of God as the instrument of the Holy Spirit, through which he effects con-version, and which man is to hear; he cannot, however, give credence to it and accept it through his own powers, but exclusively through the grace and operation of God the Holy Spirit.

Concorde Formulae

We are so dead, so blind, so perverse, that neither can we feel when we are pricked, see the light when it shines, nor assent to the will of God when it is revealed, except the Spirit of the Lord Jesus quicken that which is dead, remove the darkness from our minds, and bow our stubborn wills to the obedience of the blessed gospel.

Scottish Confession, Article 12

Conversion of Barnardo

I was brought to Christ in the year 1862. A Dr Hunt, of Harcourt Street, Dublin, had been the means in God's hands of awakening inquiry in the mind of my brother George. I actually found Christ without any human intervention when alone, some days after a special interview with my brother Fred and Dr Hunt.

Thomas Barnardo

Conversion of Booth

I remember as if it were but yesterday . . . the rolling away from my heart of the guilty burden . . . and the going forth to serve my God and my generation from that hour.

William Booth

Conversion of Bunyan

I began to give place to the word, which with power did over and over make this joyful sound within my Soul: 'Thou art my Love, thou art my Love; and nothing shall separate thee from my love;' and 'Nor height nor depth nor any other creature shall be able to separate us from the love of God, which is in Christ Jesus our Lord' (Romans 8:39, AV) came into my mind. Now was my heart filled full of comfort and hope, and now I could believe that my sins would be forgiven; indeed, I was now so taken with the love and mercy of God that I remember I did not know how to contain myself till I got home; I thought I could have spoken of his love, and of his mercy to me, even to the crows that sat upon the ploughed land in front of me, if they had been able to understand; so I said to my soul with much gladness, 'Well, I wish I had a pen and ink here: I would write this down before I go any further, for surely I will not forget this forty years from now'; but alas, within less than forty days I began to question everything again.

John Bunyan, Grace Abounding

Conversion of children   see also CHILD EVANGELISM

The following Christian leaders gave their hearts to Christ Jesus in childhood: Polycarp was converted at 9 years. Matthew Henry, at 11 years. President Edwards, at 7 years. Isaac Watts, at 9 years.

Henry Clark, The Faith and the Book

Conversion of colliers at Kingswood

The first discovery of their being afffected was to see the white gutters made by their tears which plentifully fell down their black cheeks. . . . Hundreds and hundreds of them were soon brought under deep convictions, which, as the event proved, happily ended in a sound and thorough conversion.

George Whitefield

Conversion of Early Christians

We who formerly delighted in fornication now embrace chastity alone; we who formerly used magical arts dedicate ourselves to the good and unbegotten God; we who valued above all things the acquisition of wealth and possessions now bring what we have into a common stock and share with everyone who is in need.

Justin Martyr, First Apology

Conversion of Edwards

On January 12th 1723, I made a solemn dedication of myself to God and wrote it down; giving up myself and all that I had to God; to be for the future in no respect my own.

Jonathan Edwards

Conversion of Luther

I felt myself absolutely born again. The gates of paradise had been flung open and I had entered. There and then the whole of scripture took on another look to me.

Martin Luther

Conversion of Moody

The old sun shone a good deal brighter than it ever had before. I thought that it was just smiling upon me; and as I walked out upon Boston Common and heard the birds singing in the trees, I thought they were all singing a song to me. . . . I had not a bitter feeling against any man, and I was ready to take all men to my heart.

Dwight L. Moody, describing the morning after his conversion

Conversion of Patrick

I was like a stone lying in deep mud but he that is mighty lifted me up and placed me on top of the wall.

Patrick

Conversion of Whitefield

I was delivered from the burden that had so heavily suppressed me. The spirit of mourning was taken from me, and I knew what it was to truly rejoice in God my saviour.

George Whitefield

Conversions, Preachers' work for

He was infinitely and insatiably greedy of the conversion of souls.

Said of Joseph Alleine, by a friend

When he landed, in 1848, there were no Christians.
When he left, in 1872, there were no heathen.

Memorial to John Geddie in Aneityum

Conviction

My conscience is taken captive by God's word; I cannot and will not recant anything. On this I take my stand. I can do no other. So help me God.

Martin Luther

Bear in mind that when you face death or persecution, I cannot be with you, or you with me. Every man must fight for himself.

Martin Luther

Co-operation   see also TEAMWORK

Many hands make light work.

Proverb

Two heads are better than one.

Proverb

Correction   see also DISCIPLINE

People who listen when they are corrected will live, but those who will not admit that they are wrong are in danger.

The Bible, Proverbs 10:17

Better to correct someone openly than to let him think you don't care for him at all.

The Bible, Proverbs 27:5

If you get more stubborn every time you are corrected, one day you will be crushed and never recover.

The Bible, Proverbs 28:13

It is better to have wise people reprimand you than to have stupid people sing your praises.

The Bible, Ecclesiastes 7:5

Counselling

The leader should be a near neighbour to everyone in sympathy, and yet exalted above all in contemplation. . . . The same eye of the heart, which in his elevation he lifts to the invisible, he bends in his compassion upon the secrets of those who are subject to infirmity.

Gregory the Great

A word fitly spoken is like apples of gold in pictures.

The Bible, Proverbs 25:11 (AV)

Who are you to question my wisdom with your ignorant, empty words?

The Bible, God to Job, Job 38:2

Courage

Courage is resistance to fear, mastery of fear, not absence of fear.

Mark Twain

Always look a mob in the face.

John Wesley

Courage is the thing. All goes if courage goes.

J.M. Barrie, The Admirable Crichton

As I stood at the table, and just before I opened my mouth, the words of God came forcibly to my mind, 'Only be strong and of good courage.'

Lord Shaftesbury, recalling the day he introduced to the Commons a Bill to control child labour

The secret of happiness is freedom, and the secret of freedom, courage.

Thucydides

Without courage there cannot be truth: and without truth there can be no other virtue.

Walter Scott

Fortune follows courage.

Latin proverb

Courage is reckoned the greatest of all virtues, because unless a man has that virtue he has no security for preserving any other.

Samuel Johnson

Life without the courage for death is slavery.

Seneca, Letters to Lucilius

Courage is fear that has said its prayers.

Proverb

Even if there were as many devils in Worms as there are tiles on the roofs, I would enter anyway.

Martin Luther, having been summoned to defend his beliefs before the emperor and many enemies at the Diet of Worms

A great deal of talent is lost to the world for want of a little courage.

Sydney Smith

Courtesy

Of courtesy it is much less
Than courage of heart or holiness,
Yet in my walks it seems to me
That the grace of God is in courtesy.

Hilaire Belloc

Courtship

DURING HIS COURTSHIP
Keep from me thy loveliest Creature,
  Till I prove
JESUS' Love
Infinitely sweeter.

Charles Wesley

Covenant

I am putting my bow in the clouds. It will be the sign of my covenant with the world. Whenever I cover the sky with clouds and the rainbow appears, I will remember my promise to you and to all the animals.

The Bible, Genesis 9:13–15

Covetousness

'Take heed and beware of covetousness.' . . . 'Take heed and beware of covetousness.' . . . 'Take heed and beware of covetousness.' . . . What if I should say nothing else these three or four hours?

Hugh Latimer, in a sermon before Edward VI

Creation   see also GOD AS CREATOR; NATURE

In the beginning God created the heaven and the earth. And the earth was without form, and void; and darkness was upon the face of the deep. And the Spirit of God moved upon the face of the water. And God said, Let there be light: and there was light.

The Bible, Genesis 1:1 (AV)

And God said, Let us make man in our image, after our likeness.

The Bible, Genesis 1:26 (AV)

In the beginning was the Word, and the Word was with God, and the Word was God.

The Bible, John 1:1 (AV)

When considering the creation, the how and the when does not matter so much as the why and the wherefore.

R. de Campoamor

Had I been present at the creation, I would have given some useful hints for the better ordering of the universe.

Alfonso the Wise (after studying Ptolemy's theory of the universe)

Creativity

There *is* a fountain of youth. It is your mind, your talents, the creativity you bring in your life and the lives of people you love. . . . Today, women are doing things that their mothers would never have dreamed of doing. I consider myself very fortunate to be living in a time when there is always a future for a woman, no matter what her age.

Sophia Loren

If my hand slacked,
I should rob God – since he is fullest good,
Leaving a blank instead of violins.
He could not make Antonio
  Stradivari's violins
Without Antonio.

George Eliot, from a poem in which Antonio Stradivari, the maker of the famous Stradivarius violins, is the speaker

Cynics do not create.

Calvin Coolidge

Creeds

The unbeliever's creed: I believe that there is no God, but that matter is God, and God is matter; and that it is no matter whether there is any God or no. I believe also, that the world was not made; that the world made itself; that it had no beginning; that it will last for ever, world without end. I believe that a man is a beast, that the soul is the body, and the body is the soul; and that after death there is neither body nor soul. I believe there is no religion; that natural religion is the only religion; and that all religion is unnatural. I believe not in Moses; I believe in the first philosophy: I believe not the Evangelists; I believe in Chubb,

Collins, Toland, Tindal, Morgan, Mandeville, Woolston, Hobbes, Shaftesbury; I believe in Lord Bolingbroke; I believe not St Paul. I believe not revelation; I believe in tradition; I believe in the Talmud; I believe in the Alcoran; I believe not the Bible; I believe in Socrates; I believe in Confucius; I believe in Sanconiathan; I believe in Mahomet; I believe not in Christ. Lastly, I believe in all unbelief.

> *The author of The Connoisseur, quoted by David Simpson, A Plea for Religion and the Sacred Writings*

Crises

If you are weak in a crisis, you are weak indeed.

> *The Bible, Proverbs 24:10*

Criticism see also ADVICE; JUDGING OTHERS; REBUKE

Someone who holds back the truth causes trouble, but one who openly criticises works for peace.

> *The Bible, Proverbs 10:10*

Criticism comes easier than craftsmanship.

> *Zeuxis, quoted in Pliny the Elder, Natural History*

Most of us would rather be ruined by praise than helped by criticism.

> *Author unknown*

The man who is asked by another what he thinks of his work, is put to the torture and is not obliged to speak the truth.

> *Samuel Johnson*

Cross see also CRUCIFIXION; THIEF ON THE CROSS

He was wounded for our transgressions, he was bruised for our iniquities: the chastisement of our peace was upon him; and with his stripes we are healed. All we like sheep have gone astray; we have turned every one to his own way; and the Lord hath laid on him the iniquity of us all. He was oppressed, and he was afflicted, yet he opened not his mouth.

> *The Bible, Isaiah 53:5–7 (AV)*

Eli, Eli, lama sabachthani? . . . My God, my God, why hast thou forsaken me?

> *The Bible, Jesus Christ, Matthew 27:46 (AV)*

It is finished!

> *The Bible, Jesus Christ, John 19:30*

Christ himself carried our sins in his body to the cross.

> *The Bible, 1 Peter 2:24*

Christ died for sins once and for all, a good man on behalf of sinners, in order to lead you to God.

> *The Bible, 1 Peter 3:18*

By his [Jesus Christ's] sacrificial death he has freed us from our sins.

> *The Bible, Revelation 1:5*

For you were killed, and by your sacrificial death you bought for God people from every tribe, language, nation, and race.

> *The Bible, Revelation 5:9*

Through a conquered man humanity went to death; so through a conqueror we ascend to life.

> *Irenaeus, Against Heresies, 5.3.1*

Through a tree we were made debtors to God; so through a tree we have our debt cancelled.

> *Irenaeus, Against Heresies, 5.17.3*

Christ was sent to die, and so he had to be born in order to be able to die, for it is the rule that only what is born dies. Birth and mortality are connected by a mutual bond.

> *Tertullian, On the Body of Christ*

Christ would have lived, and taught, and preached, and prophesied, and wrought miracles in vain, if he had not *crowned all by dying for our sins as our substitute*! His death was our life. His death was the payment of our debt to God. Without his death we should have been of all creatures most miserable.

> *J.C. Ryle, Practical Religion*

At Calvary God at least took his own medicine.

> *Dorothy Sayers*

Jesus became the greatest liar, perjurer, thief, adulterer and murderer that mankind has ever known – not because he committed these sins but because he was actually made sin for us.

> *Martin Luther*

There are some sciences that may be learned by the head, but the science of Christ crucified can only be learned by the heart.

> *C.H. Spurgeon*

By the cross we know the gravity of sin and the greatness of God's love towards us.

John Chrysostom

God gives the cross, and the cross gives us God.

Madame Guyon, A Short and Easy Method of Prayer

And, sitting down, they watched him
    there,
The soldiers did;
There, while they played with dice,
He made his sacrifice,
And died upon the cross to rid
God's world of sin.
He was a gambler too, my Christ,
He took his life and threw
It for a world redeemed.
And ere his agony was done,
Before the westering sun went down,
Crowning that day with its crimson
    crown,
He knew that he had won.

G.A. Studdert-Kennedy

In Christ crucified is the true theology and the knowledge of God. 'No man comes to the Father except through me.' 'I am the door.' While a man does not know Christ, he does not know God hidden in sufferings. Such a man prefers works to sufferings, and glory to a cross.

Martin Luther at the Heidelberg Disputation

It pleased God to make Christ the perfect author of salvation and he used suffering as a way to fulfil this work.

Martin Luther, The Epistle to the Hebrews

That terrible tree, which is the death of God and the life of man.

G.K. Chesterton

His death was *sufficient* for all: it was *efficient* in the case of many.

John Calvin

The way of the cross is the way of light.

Medieval proverb

The memory of Christ Jesus crucified was ever present in the depths of his heart like a bundle of myrrh.

Bonaventure, Life of St Francis

Lovely was the death
Of him whose life was love.

Samuel Taylor Coleridge

That cross is a tree set on fire with invisible flame, that illumineth all the world. The flame is love.

Thomas Traherne, Centuries of Meditations

There is no health of soul, nor hope of eternal life, except in the cross.

Thomas à Kempis, The Imitation of Christ

There is a green hill far away,
Without a city wall,
Where the dear Lord was crucified,
Who died to save us all.

Mrs C.F. Alexander

Cross, Personal response to

O sacred head, sore wounded,
    Defiled and put to scorn;
O kingly head, surrounded
    With mocking crown of thorn:
What sorrow mars thy grandeur?
    Can death thy bloom deflower?
O countenance whose splendour
    The hosts of heaven adore!

P. Gerhardt, based on a 13th-century hymn; paraphrased for the Yattendon Hymnal

Man of Sorrows! What a name
For the Son of God, who came
Ruined sinners to reclaim!
    Alleluia! What a Saviour!

Philipp Bliss

And in the garden secretly,
    And on the cross on high,
Should teach his brethren, and inspire
    To suffer and to die.

John Henry Newman, The Dream of Gerontius

When I survey the wondrous Cross
Where the young Prince of Glory died,
My richest gain I count but loss,
And pour contempt on all my pride.

Forbid it, Lord, that I should boast
Save in the death of Christ, my God;
All the vain things that charm me
    most,
I sacrifice them to his blood.

See from his head, his hands, his feet,
Sorrow and love flow mingled down;
Did e'er such love and sorrow meet?
Or thorns compose so rich a crown?

His dying crimson like a robe
Spreads o'er his body on the Tree,
Then am I dead to all the globe,
And all the globe is dead to me.

Were the whole realm of nature mine,
That were a present far too small;
Love so amazing, so divine,
Demands my soul, my life, my all.
Isaac Watts

Crucifixion   see also CROSS

First the upright wood was planted in
the ground. It was not high, and probably the feet of the sufferer were not
above one or two feet from the
ground. Thus could the communication described in the Gospels take
place between him and others; thus
also might his sacred lips be moistened
with the sponge attached to a short
stalk of hyssop. Next the transverse
wood (antenna) was placed on the
ground and the sufferer laid upon it,
when his arms were extended, drawn
up and bound to it. Then (this not in
Egypt, but in Carthage and in Rome) a
strong sharp nail was driven first into
the right, then into the left hand (the
clavi trabales). Next the sufferer was
drawn up by means of ropes, perhaps
ladders; the transverse either bound or
nailed to the upright and a rest or support for the body (the cornu or sedile)
fastened on it. Lastly, the feet were
extended and either one nail hammered into each or a larger piece of
iron through the two. And so might
the crucified hang for hours, even
days, in the unutterable anguish of suffering till consciousness at last failed.
Alfred Edersheim, Life and Times
of Jesus the Messiah

It is a crime for a Roman citizen to be
bound; it is a worse crime to be killed;
what am I to say if he be killed on a
cross? A nefarious action such as that
is incapable of description by any word,
for there is none fit to describe it.
Cicero

Cruelty

At seven went to school – a very large
one at Chiswick. Nothing could have
surpassed it for filth, bullying, neglect
and hard treatment of every sort; nor
had it in any respect any one compen-
sating advantage, except perhaps, it
may have given me an early horror of
oppression and cruelty.
Lord Shaftesbury

All cruelty springs from weakness.
Seneca

Cruelty to animals   see ANIMALS

Crying   see MOURNING; TEARS

Curiosity

Curiosity: An objectionable quality of
the female mind. The desire to know
whether or not a woman is cursed with
curiosity is one of the most active and in-
satiable passions of the masculine soul.
Ambrose Bierce

Custom

Custom without reason is but ancient
error.
Thomas Fuller, Gnomologia

It is superstitious to put one's faith in
conventions; but it is arrogance not to
submit to them.
Blaise Pascal

Custom reconciles us to everything.
Edmund Burke

Cynics

Cynic: A blackguard whose faulty
vision sees things as they are, not as
they ought to be.
Ambrose Bierce

D

Daily help from God

He who gives you the day will give you
also the things necessary for the day.
Gregory of Nyssa, The Lord's
Prayer, Sermon 4

I do not ask to see
The distant scene, – one step enough
for me.
J.H. Newman

Dance

David, wearing only a linen cloth
round his waist, danced with all his
might to honour the Lord.
The Bible, 2 Samuel 6:14

Danger

Danger, the spur of all great minds.
George Chapman, Revenge of
Bussy D'Ambois, V.i

Darkness

Reconcile yourself to wait in this darkness as long as is necessary, but still go

on longing after him whom you love.
For if you are to feel him in this life, it
must always be in this cloud in this
darkness.
Author unknown, The Cloud of
Unknowing

I await my excommunication from
Rome any day now, so I have set all my
affairs in order, so that when they
come I shall be ready for them with
loins girded. I shall be like Abraham
not knowing where I am going. Yet I
am most certain where I am going, for
God is everywhere.
Martin Luther

If I stoop
Into a dark tremendous sea of cloud,
It is but for a time; I press God's lamp
Close to my breast; its splendour, soon
    or late,
Will pierce the gloom: I shall emerge
    one day.
Robert Browning, Paracelsus

Dead, Christian

Write this: Happy are those who from
now on die in the service of the Lord!
The Bible, Revelation 14:13

Death   see also BEREAVEMENT;
CRUCIFIXION; FUNERALS; LIFE AFTER
DEATH; SACRIFICE

But at my back I always hear
Time's wingèd chariot hurrying near:
And yonder all before us lie
Deserts of vast Eternity.
Andrew Marvell, To His Coy
Mistress

Everyone must die once.
The Bible, Hebrews 9:27

The reports of my death are greatly
exaggerated.
Mark Twain

Because I could not stop for Death,
He kindly stopped for me;
The carriage held but just ourselves
And Immortality.
Emily Dickinson

They shall not grow old, as we that are
    left grow old:
Age shall not weary them, nor the
    years condemn.
At the going down of the sun and in the
    morning
We will remember them.
Lawrence Binyon, For the Fallen
(1914–1918)

I must not think it strange if God takes
in youth those whom I would have
kept on earth until they were older.
God is peopling eternity, and I must
not restrict him to old men and
women.
Jim Elliot

A single death is a tragedy; a million
deaths is a statistic.
Josef Stalin

I came from God, and I'm going back
to God, and I won't have any gaps of
death in the middle of my life.
George Macdonald

To go back is nothing but death: to go
forward is fear of death, and life everlasting beyond it. I will yet go forward.
John Bunyan

Death is the gate of life.
Latin proverb

Believe me, life lived in earnest does
not die; it goes on for ever.
Edward Thring

No coward soul is mine,
No trembler in the world's
    storm-troubled sphere:
I see Heaven's glories shine,
And Faith shines equal, arming me
    from fear.

O God within my breast,
Almighty, ever-present Deity!
Life—that in me has rest,
As I—undying Life—have power in
    Thee!

Vain are the thousand creeds
That move men's hearts: unutterably
    vain;
Worthless as withered weeds,
Or idlest froth amid the boundless
    main,

To waken doubt in one
Holding so fast by Thine infinity;
So surely anchored on
The steadiest rock of immortality

With wide-embracing love
Thy Spirit animates eternal years,
Pervades and broods above,
Changes, sustains, dissolves, creates,
    and rears.

Though earth and man were gone,
And suns and universes ceased to be,
And Thou were left alone,
Every existence would exist in Thee.

There is not room for Death,
Nor atom that his might could render
    void:
Thou—THOU art Being and Breath,
And what THOU art may never be
    destroyed.

Emily Brontë

And to the faithful, death the gate of
life.

John Milton, Paradise Lost

Die, my dear doctor, that's the last
thing I shall do!

Viscount Palmerston

The paths of glory lead but to the
grave.

*Thomas Gray, Elegy Written in a
Country Churchyard*

Man that is born of woman hath but a
short time to live, and is full of misery.

*Book of Common Prayer, Burial
service, quoting the Bible, Job 14:1*

Death, as leveller

Death is a mighty leveller. He spares
none, he waits for none, and stands on
no ceremony. He will not tarry till you
are ready.

J.C. Ryle, Practical Religion

The bodies of those that made such a
noise and tumult when alive, when
dead, lie as quietly among the graves
of their neighbours as any others.

*Jonathan Edwards,
Procrastination*

When we quit this world and are
placed in the earth, the prince walks
along as narrow a path as the journey-
man.

Cervantes

What did we bring into the world?
Nothing! What can we take out of the
world? Nothing!

*The Bible, The apostle Paul,
1 Timothy 6:7*

Death destroyed by God's power

The Sovereign Lord will destroy death
for ever! He will wipe away the tears
from everyone's eyes.

The Bible, Isaiah 25:8

The last enemy that shall be destroyed
is death.

*The Bible, The apostle Paul,
1 Corinthians 15:26 (AV)*

I am the living one! I was dead, but
now I am alive for ever and ever. I

have authority over death and the
world of the dead.

The Bible, Revelation 1:18

Death, be not proud, though some
    have callèd thee
Mighty and dreadful, for thou art not so:
For those whom thou think'st thou
    dost overthrow
Die not, poor Death; nor yet canst
    thou kill me.
From Rest and Sleep, which but thy
    picture be,
Much pleasure, then from thee much
    more must flow;
And soonest our best men with thee do
    go—
Rest of their bones and souls' delivery!
Thou'rt slave to fate, chance, kings,
    and desperate men,
And dost with poison, war, and
    sickness dwell;
And poppy or charms can make us
    sleep as well
And better than thy stroke. Why
    swell'st thou then?
One short sleep past, we wake
    eternally,
And Death shall be no more: Death,
    thou shalt die!

John Donne

Death in the midst of life

In the midst of life we are in death.

*Book of Common Prayer, Burial
service*

The hour which gives us life begins to
take it away.

Seneca, Hercules Furens

Death, Inevitability of

Old and young, we are all on our last
cruise.

*Robert Louis Stevenson,
Virginibus Puerisque*

In this world nothing can be said to be
certain, except death and taxes.

*Benjamin Franklin, letter to Jean
Baptiste Le Roy, 1789*

There is a remedy for all things but
death.

Proverb

Heaven knows its time; the bullet has
its billet.

Walter Scott, Count Robert of Paris

Death, Non-Christian views of

Once a man dies there is no resurrection.

Aeschylus

There is hope for those who are alive, but those who have died are without hope.
Theocritus

When once our brief light sets, there is one perpetual night through which we must sleep.
Catullus

I was not; I became; I am not; I care not.
Classical epitaph

Isn't my life almost over? Leave me alone!
Let me enjoy the time I have left.
I am going soon and will never come back –
going to a land that is dark and gloomy,
a land of darkness, shadows, and confusion,
where the light itself is darkness.
The Bible, Job, Job 10:20–22

Here's Death plucking my ear. 'Live,' says he, 'for I'm coming!'
Virgil

This day, which thou fearest as thy last, is the birthday of eternity.
Seneca, Letters to Lucilius

Death is the utmost boundary of wealth and power.
Horace

Death of a child

I'm so glad Elisabeth is with the Lord, and not in that box.
Mrs R.A. Torrey, at the funeral of her twelve-year-old daughter

IN MEMORY OF MY DEAR GRANDCHILD
ELIZABETH BRADSTREET,
WHO DECEASED AUGUST, 1665,
BEING A YEAR AND A HALF OLD
Blest babe, why should I once bewail thy fate,
Or sigh thy days so soon were terminate,
Sith thou art settled in an Everlasting state?
Anne Bradstreet

ON THE DEATH OF HIS SON
Dead! dead! the Child I lov'd so well!
Transported to the world above!
I need no more my heart conceal.
I never dar'd indulge my love;
But may I not indulge my grief,
And seek in tears a sad relief?
Charles Wesley

Death of Christ see CROSS

Death, Readiness for

To a mind which misliketh this world, nothing can come so welcome as death, because it takes him out of the world.
Richard Greenham

No man should be afraid to die, who hath understood what it is to live.
Thomas Fuller, Gnolomogia, 1732

We therefore commit his body to the ground; earth to earth, ashes to ashes, dust to dust; in sure and certain hope of the resurrection to eternal life, through our Lord, Jesus Christ.
Book of Common Prayer, Burial service

GASCOIGNE'S GOOD-NIGHT
My bones shall in this bed remain,
my soul in God shall trust,
By whom I hope to rise again
from death and earthly dust.
George Gascoigne

THE DYING CHRISTIAN TO HIS SOUL
The world recedes; it disappears!
Heaven opens on my eyes! my ears
With sounds seraphic ring!
Lend, lend your wings! I mount! I fly!
O Grave! where is thy victory?
O Death! where is thy sting?
Alexander Pope

It is not darkness you are going to, for God is Light. It is not lonely, for Christ is with you. It is not unknown country, for Christ is there.
Charles Kingsley

Mr Valiant-for-Truth said, 'I am going to my Father's; and though with great difficulty I have got hither, yet now I do not repent me of all the trouble I have been at to arrive where I am. . . . My marks and scars I carry with me, to be a witness for me that I have fought his battles, who now will be my re-warder.' When the day that he must go hence was come, many accompanied him to the river-side; into which, as he went, he said, 'Death, where is thy sting?' And as he went deeper he said, 'Grave, where is thy victory?' So he passed over, and all the trumpets sounded for him on the other side.
John Bunyan, The Pilgrim's Progress

Lord, if any have to die this day, let it be me, for I am ready.

Billy Bray

The approach of death is very dreadful. I am afraid to think on that which I know I cannot avoid. It is vain to look round and round for that help which cannot be had. Yet we hope and hope, and fancy that he who has lived today may live tomorrow.

Samuel Johnson, who however found when his death actually approached that his fears 'were calmed and absorbed by the prevalence of his faith, and his trust in the merits and propitiation of Jesus Christ'

I am ready to meet my maker. Whether my maker is prepared for the ordeal of meeting me is another matter.

Winston Churchill, on his seventy-fifth birthday

Debate

When you have no basis for an argument, abuse the plaintiff.

Cicero

An honest man speaks the truth, though it may give offence; a vain man, in order that it may.

William Hazlitt

The rule is perfect: in all matters of opinion our adversaries are insane.

Mark Twain

Debt

To accept a kindness is to sell one's freedom.

Publius Syrus

Debt makes slaves of free men.

Menander

He goes a-sorrowing
   who goes a-borrowing.

English proverb

Out of debt, out of danger.

Proverb

Debt to God

While a man lives, there is not a single hour, day or night, when he is not a debtor.

Origen

Deceit   see also LIES; WISHFUL THINKING

If a man deceived me once, shame on him. If he deceived me twice, shame on me.

Italian proverb

The heart is deceitful above all things, and desperately wicked.

The Bible, Jeremiah, Jeremiah 17:9 (AV)

O what a tangled web we weave
When first we practise to deceive.

Walter Scott, Marmion

Do all things like a man,
   not sneakingly:
Think the king sees thee still;
   for his King does.

George Herbert, The Temple

Decision for Christ   see also CONVERSION

Wilt thou leave thy sins and go to heaven, or wilt thou have thy sins and go to hell?

The voice John Bunyan heard

Decisions   see also INDECISION

I am now giving you the choice between life and death, between God's blessing and God's curse, and I call heaven and earth to witness the choice you make. Choose life.

The Bible, Moses, Deuteronomy 30:19

How much longer will it take you to make up your minds?

The Bible, Elijah, asking the people to decide between God and Baal, 1 Kings 18:21

The peace that Christ gives is to guide you in the decisions you make.

The Bible, The apostle Paul, Colossians 3:15

To every man there openeth
A way and ways and a way;
And the high soul treads the high way,
And the low soul gropes the low;
And in between on the misty flats
The rest drift to and fro;
But to every man there openeth
A high way and a low;
And every man decideth
The way his soul shall go.

John Oxenham

Every time you make a choice you are turning the central part of you, the part that chooses, into something a little different from what it was before.

C.S. Lewis, Mere Christianity

Decline

[Some people] harm their souls . . . without being exposed to great temptations. They simply let their souls wither. They allow themselves to be dulled by the joys and worries and distractions of life, not realising that thoughts which earlier meant a great deal to them in their youth turned into meaningless sounds.

Albert Schweitzer

Dedication   see CONSECRATION

Delay

Delay is preferable to error.
Thomas Jefferson, letter to George Washington, 1792

Delegation

Our company never really expanded until I realised, through a nervous breakdown, that I couldn't do everything myself. So I learned to work through others and our business boomed.

F.W. Woolworth

Democracy

Democracy is the severest form of despotism.
Aristotle

Democracy becomes a government of bullies tempered by editors.
Ralph Waldo Emerson

Denominations, Christian   see also ANGLICAN CHURCH; METHODISM; QUAKERS; ROMAN CATHOLIC CHURCH

Do not call yourselves Lutherans, call yourselves Christians. Has Luther been crucified for the world?
Martin Luther

Dependence on God

Dear Lord, Although I am sure of my position, I am unable to sustain it without you. Help me or I am lost.
Martin Luther

Depression   see also DESPAIR

No matter how low you feel, if you count your blessings, you'll always show a profit.
Author unknown

Before any great achievement, some measure of depression is very usual.
C.H. Spurgeon

All mental work tends to weary and depress, for much study is a weariness of the flesh. But ours [the work of pastors] is more than mental work; it is *heart* work – the labour of the inmost

soul. How often on Lord's Day evenings do we feel as if life were completely washed out of us!
C.H. Spurgeon

When you come to the bottom, you find God.
Neville Talbot

O weary days, O evenings that never end! For how many long years I have watched that drawing-room clock and thought it would never reach the ten! . . . In my thirty-first year I see nothing desirable but death.
Florence Nightingale, four years before going to the Crimea

I am now the most miserable man living. If what I feel were equally distributed to the whole human family, there would not be one cheerful face on earth. Whether I shall ever be better I cannot tell; I awfully forebode I shall not. To remain as I am is impossible.
Abraham Lincoln, during his attack of depression in 1841, when it was said that 'melancholy dripped from him as he walked'

Desire

Desire is half of life. Indifference is half of death.
Author unknown

He who is without affection either for good or evil is firmly fixed in perfect knowledge.
Bhagavad Gita

Despair   see also DEPRESSION

Trust in the Lord.
  Have faith, do not despair.
Trust in the Lord.
The Bible, Psalm 27:14

We need not despair of any man as long as he lives.
Augustine of Hippo

Despair is the conclusion of fools.
Benjamin Disraeli

I have plumbed the depths of despair and have found them not bottomless.
Thomas Hardy

I grew more wretched, and you, God, grew nearer.
Augustine of Hippo

To live without hope is to cease to live.
Fyodor Dostoevsky

Remember that despair belongs only to passionate fools or villains, such as were Ahitophel and Judas, or else to devils and damned persons; and as the hope of salvation is a good disposition towards it, so is despair a certain consignment to eternal ruin. A man may be damned for despairing to be saved. Despair is the proper passion of damnation.

Jeremy Taylor

Despair can be the Gate of Dawn
And Death itself but Heaven's Door.

Author unknown

Despising

Blessed are those who heal us of our self-despisings.

Mark Rutherford

Destiny   see also PREDESTINATION

He that is born to be hanged shall never be drowned.

Proverb

Detachment

The soul has a private door into divine nature at the point where for her all things come to nothing.

Augustine of Hippo

Keep yourself detached from all mankind; keep yourself devoid of all incoming images; emancipate yourself from everything which entails addition, attachment or encumbrance, and focus your mind at all times on the saving contemplation of God. Carry him within your heart as the fixed object from which your eyes never waver.

Meister Eckhart

Details   see also LITTLE THINGS

Men too involved in details usually become unable to deal with great matters.

La Rochefoucauld, Maxims

Determination

We shall fight on the beaches, we shall fight on the landing grounds . . . we shall fight in the hills; we shall never surrender.

Winston Churchill

If you are so resolutely determined to make a lawyer of yourself, the thing is more than half done already. Always bear in mind that your resolution to succeed is more important than any other thing.

Abraham Lincoln, to an aspiring lawyer who had asked for advice

We haven't failed. We now know a thousand things that won't work, so we're that much closer to finding what will.

Thomas Edison, after many abortive experiments trying to produce a light bulb

Devil

Be alert, be on the watch! Your enemy, the Devil, roams round like a roaring lion, looking for someone to devour.

The Bible, 1 Peter 5:8

The Devil has come down to you, and he is filled with rage, because he knows that he has only a little time left.

The Bible, Revelation 12:12

The devil can counterfeit all the saving operations and graces of the Spirit of God.

Jonathan Edwards, Treatise Concerning the Religious Affections

The devil . . . the proud spirit . . . cannot endure to be mocked.

Thomas More

Satan hasn't a single salaried helper; the Opposition employs a million.

Mark Twain

The devil hath power to assume a pleasing shape.

William Shakespeare

I am a great enemy to flies; when I have a good book, they flock upon it and parade up and down it, and soil it. It is just the same with the devil. When our hearts are purest, he comes and soils them.

Martin Luther

Who is the most diligent bishop and prelate in England? I will tell you. It is the devil. He is never out of his diocese. The devil is diligent at his plough.

Hugh Latimer, Sermon on the Ploughers

Where God built a church, there the devil would also build a chapel. Thus the devil is always God's ape.

Martin Luther, Table Talk

Wherever God erects a house of prayer,
The Devil always builds a chapel there;
And 'twill be found, upon examination,
The latter has the largest congregation.

Daniel Defoe, The True-Born Englishman, i.1

The devil can cite scripture for his purpose.

William Shakespeare, Merchant of
Venice, I.iii

Devil, Existence of

The existence of the devil is so clearly taught in the Bible . . . that to doubt it is to doubt the Bible itself.

Archibald G. Brown, Selah

There is nothing that Satan more desires than that we should believe that he does not exist and that there is no such a place as hell.

Bishop Wordsworth, Sermons on
Future Rewards and Punishments

In all ages of the church, unbelief in [the existence of the devil] has been marked by a corresponding unbelief in the scriptures.

Archibald G. Brown, Selah

Devil, Fighting the

Put on all the armour that God gives you, so that you will be able to stand up against the devil's evil tricks.

The Bible, The apostle Paul,
Ephesians 6:11

The best way to drive out the devil, if he will not yield to texts of scripture, is to jeer and flout him, for he cannot bear scorn.

Martin Luther

Dictators see also TYRANNY

The triumph of demagogies is passing. But the ruins are eternal. Order, and order alone, definitively makes liberty. Disorder makes servitude. Only demagogues have an interest in trying to make us believe the contrary.

Charles Péguy, Basic Verities

Difficult people

It is no great matter to associate with the good and gentle, for this is naturally pleasing to all, and everyone happily enjoys peace, and loves those which do not agree with him. But to be able to live in peace with hard and perverse persons is a great grace, and a most commendable thing.

Thomas à Kempis

Difficulties in life see also ADVERSITY; DOUBT; PERSISTENCE

Being aware of the absolute importance and arduous nature of the service in which he is engaged, the true Christian sets about his task with vigour and diligence. He is prepared to meet difficulties and is not discouraged when they occur.

William Wilberforce

There are three stages in the work of God: Impossible; Difficult; Done.

Hudson Taylor

Never let life's hardships disturb you. After all, no one can avoid problems, not even saints or sages.

Nichiren Daishonin, Happiness in
the World

God delights to increase the faith of his children. We ought, instead of wanting no trials before victory, no exercise for patience, to be willing to take them from God's hand as a means. I say – and say it deliberately – trials, obstacles, difficulties, and sometimes defeats, are the very food of faith.

George Müller

Take courage, and turn your troubles, which are without remedy, into material for spiritual progress. Often turn to our Lord, who is watching you, poor frail little being as you are, amid your labours and distractions.

Francis de Sales

Diligence overcomes difficulties, sloth makes them.

Benjamin Franklin, Poor
Richard's Almanac

Difficulties in science

We must not expect to be able . . . to resolve all difficulties, and answer all objections, since we can never directly answer those which require for their solution a perfect comprehension of what is infinite.

Robert Boyle

Diffidence

Now Giant Despair had a wife, and her name was Diffidence.

John Bunyan

Dignity

It is only people of small moral stature who have to stand on their dignity.

Arnold Bennett

No race can prosper till it learns that there is as much dignity in tilling a field as in writing a poem.

Booker T. Washington, Up from
Slavery

Diplomacy

Diplomacy: the patriotic art of lying for one's country.

Ambrose Bierce, The Devil's Dictionary

Disability

Let there be a law that no deformed child shall be reared.

Aristotle, Politics 7.14.10

Mad dogs we knock on the head; the fierce and savage ox we slay; sickly sheep we put to the knife to keep them from infecting the flock; unnatural progeny we destroy; we drown even children who at birth are weakly and abnormal. It is not anger but reason which separates the harmful from the sound.

Seneca, On Anger, 1.15.2

Disappointments

There are no disappointments to those whose wills are buried in the will of God.

F.W. Faber

[May I accept God's will] not with dumb resignation, but with holy joy; not only with the absence of murmur, but with a song of praise.

George Matheson, who became blind and was disappointed in love

Disaster

There is great value in disaster. All our mistakes are burned up. Thank God we can start anew.

Thomas Edison, after fire had destroyed two million dollars' worth of his equipment

A host is like a general: calamities often reveal his genius.

Horace

Discipleship   see CHRISTIAN LIFE

Discipleship, Secret

Either the secrecy kills the discipleship, or the discipleship kills the secrecy.

Author unknown

Discipline   see also WILL-POWER

The Lord corrects those he loves.

The Bible, Proverbs 3:12

Discipline your children while they are young enough to learn. If you don't, you are helping them to destroy themselves.

The Bible, Proverbs 19:18

Correction and discipline are good for children. If a child has his own way, he will make his mother ashamed of him.

The Bible, Proverbs 29:15

It is natural for us to wish that God had designed for us a less glorious and less arduous destiny; but then we are wishing not for more love but for less.

C.S. Lewis, The Problem of Pain

If you have but one gift to give your children, let it be discipline.

H. Ross Perot

Discipline is the hidden ingredient that turns nobodies into somebodies.

Author unknown

To be a money master, you must first be a self master.

J. Pierpont Morgan

It was by strict method, by stern discipline, by rigid attention to detail, by ceaseless labour, by the fixed determination of an indomitable will. Beneath her cool and calm demeanour, there lurked fierce and passionate fires.

Lytton Strachey, on Florence Nightingale's achievements in British army hospitals

There is but one philosophy: fortitude, self mastery.

Socrates

Thank God every morning you get up and find you have something to do that must be done, whether you feel like doing it or not. This builds character.

Ralph Waldo Emerson

Discipline is the midwife of Liberty.

Author unknown

Discouragement   see ADVERSITY; DEPRESSION; DIFFICULTIES

Discoveries

What hath God wrought!

(from the Bible, Numbers 23:23 [AV]) Samuel Morse in the first message by electric telegraph in 1844

The process of scientific discovery is, in effect, a continual flight from wonder.

Albert Einstein

Mr Creator, why did you make the peanut?

George Washington Carver, when faced with an apparently unsaleable product grown for the sake of the soil – and the question which led him to discover 300 marketable products from the peanut

I do not know what I may appear to the world; but to myself I seem to have been only a boy playing on the seashore, and diverting myself in now and then finding a smoother pebble or a prettier shell than ordinary whilst the great ocean of truth lay all undiscovered before me.

Isaac Newton

Discretion

Discretion is the better part of valour.

Proverb

Divorce

If a man divorces his wife, for any cause other than her unfaithfulness, then he is guilty of making her commit adultery if she marries again; and the man who marries her commits adultery also.

The Bible, Jesus Christ,
Matthew 5:32

Women were married to be divorced and divorced to be married.

Seneca

I should like to add an eighth sacrament to those of the Roman church – the sacrament of divorce.

Samuel Butler, Notebooks

It is the *one* exception that gives prominence to the illegitimacy of every other reason. Preoccupation with the one exception should never be permitted to obscure the force of the negation of all others.

John Murray, Divorce;
commenting on Matthew 5:32 and
Matthew 19:9

Doctors

The best doctors in the world are Doctor Diet, Doctor Quiet and Doctor Merryman.

Jonathan Swift

Cultivate the physician in accordance with the need of him,
For him also hath God ordained.
It is from God that the physician getteth wisdom,
And from the king that he receiveth gifts.

The Book of Sirach, 38:1–15

Doctrine see also HERESY

False doctrine does not necessarily make a man a heretic, but an evil heart can make any doctrine heretical.

Samuel Taylor Coleridge

Doctrine is not a matter of talk but of life. It is not grasped by intellect alone, like other branches of learning. It is received only when it fills the soul and finds a home in the inmost recesses of the heart.

John Calvin, The Institutes of
Christian Religion, 3.6.4

You may be as orthodox as the devil, and as wicked.

John Wesley

Dogma

The difference between orthodoxy or my-doxy and heterodoxy or thy-doxy.

Thomas Carlyle

Doubt

Doubt is not a pleasant mental state, but certainty is a ridiculous one.

Voltaire

Faith which does not doubt is dead faith.

Miguel de Unamuno

Our doubts are traitors
And make us lose the good we oft might win
By fearing to attempt.

William Shakespeare, Measure for
Measure

The doubting mind sees many ghosts.

Chinese proverb

The centipede was happy quite,
Until the toad in fun
Said 'Pray, which leg goes after which?'
Which worked her mind to such a pitch,
She lay distracted in a ditch,
Considering how to run.

Author unknown

With great doubts comes great understanding; with little doubts comes little understanding.

Chinese proverb

To deny, to believe, and to doubt well are to a man as the race is to a horse.

Blaise Pascal

There lives more faith in honest doubt, Believe me, than in half the creeds.

Alfred, Lord Tennyson, In
Memoriam

Ten thousand difficulties do not make one doubt.

J.H. Newman

One must know when it is right to doubt, to affirm, to submit. Anyone who does otherwise does not understand the force of reason.

Blaise Pascal

I doubt, therefore truth is.
Augustine of Hippo

He fought his doubts and gather'd
strength,
He would not make his judgement
blind,
He faced the spectres of the mind
And laid them: thus he came at length
To find a stronger faith his own.
Alfred, Lord Tennyson, In
Memoriam

The art of doubting is easy, for it is an
ability that is born with us.
Martin Luther

Doubt sees the obstacles,
Faith sees the way;
Doubt sees the blackest night,
Faith sees the day;
Doubt dreads to take step,
Faith soars on high;
Doubt questions, 'Who believes?'
Faith answers, 'I!'
Author unknown

Who knows nothing, doubts nothing.
French proverb

The wise are prone to doubt.
Greek proverb

If a man will begin with certainties, he
shall end in doubts; but if he will be
content to begin with doubts, he shall
end in certainties.
Francis Bacon, The Advancement
of Learning

Dreams see also VISIONS

Dreams are sent by God.
Homer

Dress

Gold, silver, jewelry, and both silken
and sumptuous clothing are either laid
aside or sold and the proceeds distributed to the poor.
Huldrych Zwingli, letter to Blarer,
1528

Drink

Drinking too much makes you loud
and foolish. It's stupid to get drunk.
The Bible, Proverbs 20:1

Show me someone who drinks too
much, who has to try out some new
drink, and I will show you someone
miserable and sorry for himself,
always causing trouble and always
complaining.
The Bible, Proverbs 23:29–30

Do not get drunk with wine, which will
only ruin you; instead, be filled with
the Spirit.
The Bible, The apostle Paul,
Ephesians 5:18

Liquor can destroy success faster than
genius can rebuild it.
Author unknown

When the wine is in the wit is out.
Thomas Becon, Catechism

Let us drink, for we must die.
Seneca

The dipsomaniac and the abstainer are
not only both mistaken, but they both
make the same mistake. They both
regard wine as a drug and not as a
drink.
G.K. Chesterton

What soberness conceals drunkenness
reveals.
Latin proverb

Duty

The right, practical divinity is this:
Believe in Christ, and do your duty in
that state of life to which God has
called you.
Martin Luther

The path of duty lies in what is near,
and man seeks for it in what is remote.
Mencius

Fear God, and keep his commandments: for this is the whole duty of
man.
The Bible, Ecclesiastes 12:13 (AV)

No, the Lord has told us what is good.
What he requires of us is this: to do
what is just, to show constant love, and
to live in humble fellowship with our
God.
The Bible, Micah 6:8

Do your duty and leave the rest to
Providence.
Stonewall Jackson

I fancy that it is just as hard to do your
duty when men are sneering at you as
when they are shooting at you.
Woodrow Wilson

Let us have faith that right makes
might; and in that faith let us to the end
dare to do our duty as we understand
it.
Abraham Lincoln

The consciousness of a duty performed gives us music at midnight.
George Herbert

The whole duty of man is summed up in obedience to God's will.
George Washington

A scholar profanes the Name of God if he does not pay the butcher at once.
The Talmud

Duty is the sublimest word in our language. Do your duty in all things. You cannot do more. You should never wish to do less.
Robert E. Lee

The reward of one duty done is the power to fulfil another.
George Eliot

Dying   see DEATH; LAST WORDS

Dying to self   see SELF, DEATH OF

E

Eating   see FOOD; GLUTTONY

Economists

If all economists were laid end to end, they would not reach a conclusion.
George Bernard Shaw

Education

To neglect the wise sayings of great thinkers is to deny ourselves our truest education.
William James

Religious education must, I think, become the watchword of our church before we can expect abiding fruit on our labours. God forbid that I should limit the Holy One of Israel, but still I think that in the ordinary course of things education is our only hope.
Andrew Murray, 1859

They know enough who know how to learn.
Henry Adams, The Education of Henry Adams

The secret of education is respecting the pupil.
Ralph Waldo Emerson

A school should not be a preparation for life. A school should be life.
Elbert Hubbard

All who have meditated on the art of governing mankind have been convinced that the fate of empires depends on the education of youth.
Aristotle

A man who has never gone to school may steal from a freight car; but if he has a university education, he may steal the whole railroad.
Theodore Roosevelt

You can do anything with children if you only play with them.
Bismarck

I never let my schooling interfere with my education.
Mark Twain

Let me teach for a generation, and I will become ruler of the state.
Napoleon

Education is a weapon whose effect depends upon who holds it in his hands and at whom it is aimed.
Josef Stalin

True education doesn't merely bring us learning, but love of learning; not merely work but love of work.
Author unknown

If a man's education is finished, he is finished.
E.A. Filene

Educate men without religion and you make them but clever devils.
Duke of Wellington

Effort   see also GENIUS; PERSEVERANCE

Forced effort tires us three times as fast as enthusiastic effort. One of life's richest blessings is doing what comes naturally.
Author unknown

Egotism

Egotist: a person of low taste, more interested in himself than in me.
Ambrose Bierce, The Devil's Dictionary

Egypt

Ten measures of sorcery descended into the world; Egypt received nine, the rest of the world one.
Talmud

Election, Divine

If we are searching for God's fatherly love and grace, we must look to Christ, in whom alone the Father is well pleased. If we are searching for salvation, life and immortality, we must turn to him again, since he alone is the fountain of life, the anchor of salvation and the heir of the kingdom. The purpose of election is no more than that, when we are adopted as sons by the heavenly Father, we will inherit salvation and eternal life through his favour.

John Calvin, The Institutes of Christian Religion, 3.24.5

When God elects us it is not because of our beautiful eyes.

John Calvin

Faith depends not on election, but election on faith. God's grace is universal and some are not predestined to salvation more than others.

Hermes Bolsec

As many as are called by the gospel are unfeignedly called: for God hath most earnestly and truly declared in his word what will be acceptable to him – namely, that all who are called should comply with the invitation.

Canons of the Synod of Dort, Article 8

Elections, Government

The ballot is stronger than the bullet.

Abraham Lincoln, speech on 19 May 1856

Emotions

God has not created man to be a stock or stone but has given him five senses and a heart of flesh, so that he loves his friends, is angry with his enemies, and commiserates with his dear friends in adversity.

Martin Luther

Employers

Know that it is thy duty so to behave thyself to thy servant, that thy service may not only be for thy good, but for the good of thy servant, and that both in body and soul.

John Bunyan, Christian Behaviour

Emptiness

[The world is suffering] a neurosis of emptiness.

Carl Jung

Encouragement

The really great man is the man who makes every man feel great.

G.K. Chesterton

Encouragement after censure is as the sun after a shower.

Goethe

Endurance   see also PERSISTENCE

Who would wish for hardship and difficulty? You command us to endure these troubles, not to love them. No one loves what he endures even though he may be glad to endure it.

Augustine of Hippo

Because of envy and strife, Paul gave an example of the prize of endurance: he was put in prison seven times, was exiled and stoned; he preached in the East and the West, and won fame for his faith. He taught righteousness to the whole world and went to the western edge of the world. He witnessed to rulers, and then left the world and went on to the holy place, having shown that he himself was the greatest example of endurance.

Clement of Rome, Epistle to the Corinthians

Nothing great was ever done without much enduring.

Catherine of Siena

Let nothing disturb you,
     nothing frighten you;
All things are passing;
     God never changes;
Patient endurance
Attains all things;
Whoever possesses God
Lacks nothing;
God alone suffices.

Teresa of Avila

Enemies

Wise men often learn from their enemies.

Aristophanes

Love your enemies, for they tell you your faults.

Benjamin Franklin, Poor Richard's Almanac, 1756

A courageous foe is better than a cowardly friend.

Thomas Fuller, Gnomologia

England

You are fortunate indeed, and now more blessed than any land since you were the first to see Constantine as emperor. Nature endows you with every benefit, winters not too cold, summers not too hot, cornfields so productive that they assure you of the gifts not only of Ceres but of liberality too. No terrible beasts shelter in your woods, no noxious snakes infest your earth. Far from it, your domestic herds are innumerable, their udders bulge with milk and their backs are laden with wool. To make life more pleasant, days are long and no night goes by without some light.

An orator congratulating
Constantine on becoming emperor
at York

Enjoyment

Let's get rid of the inhuman philosophy which only allows necessities. Not only does it wrongly deprive us of legitimate enjoyment of God's generosity, but it cannot be effected without depriving man of all his senses, reducing him to a block.

John Calvin, The Institutes of
Christian Religion, 3.10.3

Enlightenment

Knowing others is wisdom. Knowing the self is enlightenment.

Lao Tzu, Tao Te Ching

Enoch

Enoch walked with God: and he was not, for God took him.

The Bible, Genesis 5:24 (AV)

Enthusiasm

Enthusiasm is the invisible magnet that draws others to our view.

Author unknown

Every great movement in the annals of history is the triumph of enthusiasm.

Ralph Waldo Emerson

Nothing great was ever achieved without enthusiasm.

Ralph Waldo Emerson, Essays,
Circles

Environment

He plants trees that another generation may benefit.

Caecilius Statius, Synephebi,
quoted in Cicero, De Senectute, 7

He that plants trees loves others besides himself.

Thomas Fuller, Gnomologia, 1732

A man does not plant a tree for himself; he plants it for posterity.

Alexander Smith, Dreamthorp

Small is beautiful: a study of economics as if people mattered.

E.F. Schumacher, book title

We are united with all life that is in nature. Man can no longer live his life for himself alone.

Albert Schweitzer

Envy

Envy dwells at the bottom of the human heart as a viper dwells in its hole.

Honoré de Balzac

Envy slays itself by its own arrows.

The Greek Anthology

Envy is the greatest of all diseases among men.

Euripides

Nothing sharpens sight like envy.

Thomas Fuller, Gnomologia

Ephesians, Paul's letter to the

The divinest composition of man.

Samuel Taylor Coleridge

Epitaphs

A tomb now suffices him for whom the whole world was not sufficient.

for Alexander the Great

Here lie the earthly remains of John Berridge, late vicar of Everton, and an itinerant servant of Jesus Christ, who loved his Master and his work, and after running on his errands many years was called to wait on him above. Reader, art thou born again? No salvation without new birth! I was born in sin, February 1716. Remained ignorant of my fallen state till 1730. Lived proudly on faith and works for salvation till 1754. Was admitted to Everton Vicarage, 1755. Fled to Jesus alone for refuge, 1756.

for (and written by) John Berridge

He could have added fortune to fame, but caring for neither, he found happiness and honour in being helpful to the world.

for George Washington Carver

That we spent, we had:
That we gave, we have:
That we left, we lost.

for the Earl of Devonshire, quoted
by Spenser, The Shepherd's
Calendar

He touched nothing which he did not adorn.

for Oliver Goldsmith

Free at last, free at last
Thank God A'mighty I'm free at last.

for Martin Luther King

John Newton, Clerk,
Once an infidel and libertine,
A servant of slaves in Africa:
Was by the rich mercy of our Lord and
    Saviour,
Jesus Christ,
Preserved, restored, pardoned,
And appointed to preach the Faith
He had long laboured to destroy.
Near sixteen years at Olney in Bucks:
And twenty-seven years in this Church.
for John Newton

Equality

The world is meant to be like a household in which all the servants receive
equal allowances, for all men are
equal, since they are brothers.
John Chrysostom

There is nothing that so strikes men
with fear as saying that they are all the
sons of God.
G.K. Chesterton

The defect of equality is that we only
desire it with our superiors.
Henri Becque

All animals are equal, but some animals are more equal than others.
George Orwell

Error   see also MISTAKES; TRUTH

The wisest of the wise may err.
Aeschylus, Fragments

To err is human, to persist in error is
devilish.
Augustine of Hippo, Sermons

People gave ear to an upstart
astrologer [i.e., Copernicus] who
strove to show that the earth revolves,
not the heavens or the firmament, the
sun and the moon . . . but sacred scripture tells us that Joshua commanded
the sun to stand still, and not the earth.
Martin Luther

Essentials

Cling only to what is necessary.
*Gregory of Nyssa, The Lord's
Prayer, Sermon 4*

Eternal life   see also LIFE AFTER DEATH

God's free gift is eternal life in union
with Christ Jesus our Lord.
*The Bible, The apostle Paul,
Romans 6:23*

This is what Christ himself promised to
give us – eternal life.
The Bible, 1 John 2:25

God has given us eternal life, and this
life has its source in his Son. Whoever
has the Son has this life; whoever does
not have the Son of God does not have
life.
The Bible, 1 John 5:11–12

For a small living, men run a great
way; for eternal life, many will scarce
move a single foot.
Thomas à Kempis

I entered into my inward self, with you
my guide. . . . And I saw with the eye
of my soul, above my mind, the
unchangeable light. It was not this
ordinary light which all flesh may look
upon, but it were a greater of the same
kind. . . . He who knows the truth
knows that light, and he who knows it
knows eternity.
Augustine of Hippo, Confessions

Eternity

He that would live well, let him make
his dying day his company-keeper.
John Bunyan

What we weave in time we wear in
eternity.
J.C. Ryle

God hath given to man a short time
here upon earth, and yet upon this
short time eternity depends.
Jeremy Taylor

Europe

We are part of the community of
Europe, and we must do our duty as
such.
*William Ewart Gladstone, speech
at Caernarvon, 10 April 1888*

Evangelism   see also CHILD
EVANGELISM; FOLLOW-UP; MISSION;
PREACHING

The gospel does not fall from the
clouds like rain by accident, but is
brought by the hands of men to whom
God has sent it.
John Calvin

I exhort you, press on in your course,
and exhort all men that they may be
saved.
Polycarp

God scattered Israel among the
nations for the sole end that proselytes
should wax numerous among them.
Rabbi Eleazar

Every time in history that man has tried to turn crucified truth into coercive truth he has betrayed the fundamental principle of Christianity.

Nicholas Berdyaev, Dostoevsky

Religion is caught, not taught.

W.R. Inge

I look upon this world as a wrecked vessel. God has given me a lifeboat and said to me: 'Moody, save all you can.'

Dwight L. Moody

Even if I were utterly selfish, and had no care for anything but my own happiness, I would choose, if I might, under God, to be a soul-winner; for never did I know perfect, overflowing, unutterable happiness of the purest and most ennobling order till I first heard of one who had sought and found the Saviour through my means. No young mother ever so rejoiced over her first born child, no warrior was so exultant over a hard won victory.

C.H. Spurgeon

My studies were . . . sadly interrupted by the more practical business of saving souls.

William Booth

Young man, if I thought I could win one more soul for Christ by standing on my head and beating a tambourine with my feet I would learn how to do it.

William Booth, to Rudyard Kipling, who had expressed his dislike of tambourines

Christ sent me to preach the gospel and he will look after results.

Mary Slessor

Some want to live within the sound
 Of Church or Chapel bell;
I want to run a rescue shop
 Within a yard of hell.

C.T. Studd

When the power of reclaiming the lost dies out of the church, it ceases to be the church.

John Seeley

I look upon all the world as my parish.

John Wesley, Journal

The church has nothing to do but to save souls; therefore spend and be spent in this work.

John Wesley

Eve

Eve was not taken from the feet of Adam to be his slave, nor from his head to be his lord, but from his side to be his partner.

Peter Lombard, Sentences

[Eve was] not made out of his [Adam's] head to top him, nor out of his feet to be trampled upon by him, but out of his side to be equal with him, under his arm to be protected, and near his heart to be beloved.

Matthew Henry

Evening

The curfew tolls the knell of parting day,
The lowing herd winds slowly o'er the lea,
The ploughman homeward plods his weary way,
And leaves the world to darkness and to me.

Thomas Gray

It is a beauteous evening, calm and free,
Thy holy time is quiet as a Nun
Breathless with adoration; the broad sun
Is sinking down in its tranquillity;
The gentleness of heaven broods o'er the Sea:
Listen! the mighty Being is awake,
And doth with his eternal motion make
A sound like thunder – everlastingly.

William Wordsworth

Evidences for Christianity

There is not a nation, either of Greek or Barbarian, or of any other name, even of those who wander in tribes, and live in tents, amongst whom prayers and thanksgivings are not offered to the Father and creator of the universe by the name of the crucified Jesus.

Justin Martyr

Evil   see also CONSEQUENCES OF EVIL

To honour the Lord is to hate evil.

The Bible, Proverbs 8:13

Wicked people love the taste of evil.

The Bible, Proverbs 19:28

Woe unto them that call evil good, and good evil.

The Bible, Isaiah 5:20

Be not overcome of evil, but overcome evil with good.

The Bible, The apostle Paul,
Romans 12:21 (AV)

He who passively accepts evil is as much involved in it as he who helps to perpetuate it.

Martin Luther King, Strides
Towards Freedom

The Lord God is subtle, but malicious he is not.

Albert Einstein

I would far rather be ignorant than knowledgeable of evils.

Aeschylus, The Suppliants

There is no devil like a white devil.

Puritan proverb

Nine times out of ten, the coarse word is the word that condemns an evil and the refined word the word that excuses it.

G.K. Chesterton

God knows evil under the form of good.

Dionysius the Areopagite

Evil, once manfully fronted, ceases to be evil; there is generous battle-hope in place of dead, passive misery.

Thomas Carlyle

God's mind perceives all sin and evil in the idea of the corresponding good, not in the form of sin; for instance, he knows lying in the idea of truth.

Meister Eckhart

Men never do evil so fully and so happily as when they do it for conscience' sake.

Blaise Pascal

Evil is easy, and has infinite forms.

Blaise Pascal, Pensées

Evolution

The mystery of the beginning of all things is insoluble by us; and I for one must be content to remain an agnostic.

Charles Darwin

Examinations

Examinations are formidable even to the best prepared, for the greatest fool may ask more than the wisest man can answer.

C.C. Colton, Lacon

I am to be examined. I hope to have got it pretty perfect. I have spared no pains to get it. Therefore I trust that God will support me!

George Whitefield, diary

Example

You must follow the example of good men and live a righteous life.

The Bible, Proverbs 2:20

Example is not the main thing in influencing others – it is the only thing.

Albert Schweitzer

People will not attend to what we say, but examine what we do; and will say, 'First obey your own words, and then exhort others.' This is the great battle, this is the unanswerable demonstration which is made by our acts.

John Chrysostom

Example is better than precept.

Proverb

A good example is the best sermon.

Benjamin Franklin, Poor
Richard's Almanac, 1747

When I saw that unwearied patience, that unflagging zeal, those enlightened sons of Africa, I became a Christian at his side, though he never spoke to me about it.

H.M. Stanley, having observed
David Livingstone's patience and
sympathy for the Africans

Excellence

The best is the enemy of the good.

Voltaire

Excess

Nothing in excess.

Cleobulus, written on the temple at
Delphi

All things in excess are contrary to nature.

Hippocrates

The best things carried to excess are wrong.

Charles Churchill, The Rosciad

Excuses

He that excuses himself, accuses himself.

Proverb

Expectations

Blessed is he who expects nothing, for he shall never be disappointed.

Alexander Pope, letter, 1727

The basic things expected by our people of their political and economic systems are simple. They are: Equality of opportunity for youth and for others. Jobs for those who can work. Security for those who need it. The ending of special privilege for the few. The preservation of civil liberties for all. The enjoyment of the fruits of scientific progress in a wider and constantly rising standard of living. These are the simple, the basic things that must never be lost sight of in the turmoil and unbelievable complexity of our modern world.

Franklin Delano Roosevelt,
speech to Congress, 1941

Experience

Learn all you can from others. The school of experience takes so long that the graduates are too old to go to work.

Henry Ford

We should be careful to get out of an experience only the wisdom that is in it – and stop there; lest we be like the cat that sits down on a hot stove-lid. She will never sit down on a hot stove-lid again – and that is well; but also she will never sit down on a cold one any more.

Mark Twain

All experience is an arch to build upon.

Henry Adams, The Education of Henry Adams

Life is a series of experiences, each one of which makes us bigger, even though sometimes it is hard to realise this.

Henry Ford

Experience is the best of schoolmasters, only the school fees are heavy.

Thomas Carlyle

Experience is the comb that nature gives us when we are bald.

Belgian proverb

Exploitation

Those who occupy the fields and extract the wealth of the land. Can anyone be more wicked than these men? If you look how they treat the brave but miserable labourers, you will see that they are more cruel than the barbarians. They make cruel and unbearable demands on those who are wracked with hunger and spend their lives working, and force them to do the hardest work. They treat them like asses or mules, or rather like a stone, and allow them not a moment's rest.

John Chrysostom

Extravagance

The curse of extravagance kills more opportunities than taxes, sickness, and hard times.

Author unknown

Extravagance takes from us ten times as much as Congress.

Author unknown

Faces

The face is the index of the mind.

Latin proverb

Facts

Facts are stubborn things.

Ebenezer Elliott, Field Husbandry

Comment is free but facts are sacred.

C.P. Scott, Manchester Guardian,
1926

Failure

It's nobler to try something and fail than to try nothing and succeed. The result may be the same, but you won't be. We always grow more through defeats than victories.

Author unknown

I would sooner fail than not be among the greatest.

John Keats, letter to James Hessey,
1818

A fall is not a signal to lie wallowing, but to rise.

Christina Rossetti

Our greatest glory is, not in never failing, but in rising every time we fall.

Confucius

Success has many fathers, but failure is an orphan; no one wants to claim it.

John F. Kennedy

There is no failure except in no longer trying.

Elbert Hubbard

Failure doesn't mean you are a failure;
it *does* mean you haven't yet
   succeeded.
Failure doesn't mean you have
   accomplished nothing;
it *does* mean you have learned
   something.

Failure doesn't mean that you have
been a fool;
it *does* mean you have a lot of faith.
Failure doesn't mean you have been
disgraced;
it *does* mean you were willing to try.
Failure doesn't mean you don't have it;
it *does* mean you have to do something
in a different way.
Failure doesn't mean you are inferior;
it *does* mean you are not perfect.
Failure doesn't mean you've wasted
your life;
it *does* mean you have a reason to start
afresh.
Failure doesn't mean you should give up;
it *does* mean you must try harder.
Failure doesn't mean you will never
make it;
it *does* mean it will take a little longer.
Failure doesn't mean God has
abandoned you;
it *does* mean God has a better way.

Author unknown

Most failures are caused by not realising the power of momentum – getting
started.

Author unknown

Failure is the line of least persistence.

Author unknown

There's hope for every failure, as long
as he doesn't blame others for his fate.

Author unknown

No one ever fails. They just quit trying. Many of our greatest men tried
and failed so often they decided to quit
– but tried once more – and won.

Author unknown

Learn by failures.

Proverb

We are told by all spiritual writers that
one important point to bear in mind,
as we seek to attain humility, is not to
be surprised by our own faults and failures.

*François Fénelon, Christian
Perfection, letter to a lady*

Faith

The just shall live by faith.

*The Bible, The apostle Paul,
Romans 1:17 (AV)*

Faith comes from hearing the message,
and the message comes through
preaching Christ.

*The Bible, The apostle Paul,
Romans 10:17*

Faith is never identical with piety.

Karl Barth

My imprisonment might end on the
gallows for ought that I could tell. . . .
Methought I was ashamed to die with a
pale face and tottering knees for such a
cause as this. . . . Wherefore, thought
I, I am for going on and venturing my
eternal state with Christ whether I
have comfort here or no; if God doth
not come in, thought I, I will leap off
the ladder even blindfold into eternity,
sink or swim, come heaven, come hell;
Lord Jesus, if thou wilt catch me, do; if
not, I will venture for thy name.

*John Bunyan, as he waited in
prison not knowing what the future
might hold*

Faith expects from God what is
beyond all expectation.

Andrew Murray

'Let's consider your age to begin with –
how old are you?'
'I'm seven and a half exactly.'
'You needn't say "exactly",' the
Queen remarked: 'I can believe it
without that. Now I'll give *you* something to believe. I'm just one hundred
and one, five months and a day.'
'I can't believe *that*!' said Alice.
'Can't you?' the Queen said in a pity-
ing tone. 'Try again: draw a long
breath, and shut your eyes.'
Alice laughed. 'There's no use trying,'
she said: 'one *can't* believe impossible
things.'
'I daresay you haven't had much practice,' said the Queen. 'When I was
your age, I always did it for half an
hour a day. Why, sometimes I've
believed as many as six impossible
things before breakfast.'

*Lewis Carroll, Through the
Looking Glass*

Faith is under the left nipple.

Martin Luther

When we have an atom of faith in our
hearts, we can see God's face, gentle,
serene and approving.

*John Calvin, The Institutes of
Christian Religion, 3.2.19*

The complete atheist stands on the
penultimate step to most perfect faith
(he may or may not take a further
step), but the indifferent person has no
faith whatever except a bad fear, and

that but rarely, and only if he is sensitive.

Fyodor Dostoevsky

One article, the only solid rock, rules
in my heart, namely, faith in Christ;
out of which, and to which all my
theological opinions ebb and flow, day
and night.

*Martin Luther, Commentary on
the Epistle to the Galatians*

All the works mentioned throughout
the Bible are written up as works of
faith.

*Martin Luther, The Epistle to the
Hebrews*

Faith, by which I mean the life of a
Christian man, is more God's work
than ours.

*Martin Luther, The Epistle to the
Hebrews*

The Holy Spirit is not a sceptic.

Martin Luther

Faith declares what the senses do not
see, but not the contrary of what they
see.

Blaise Pascal

There is no love without hope, no
hope without love, and neither hope
nor love without faith.

Augustine of Hippo

I do not want merely to possess a faith,
I want a faith that possesses me.

Charles Kingsley

Though the fig-tree does not bud
and there are no grapes on the vines,
though the olive crop fails
and fields produce no food,
though there are no sheep in the pen
and no cattle in the stalls,
yet I will rejoice in the Lord,
I will be joyful in God my Saviour.

The Bible, Habakkuk 3:17–18

When I cannot enjoy the faith of assurance, I live by the faith of adherence.

Matthew Henry

Console yourself, you would not seek
me if you had not already found me.

Blaise Pascal, Pensées

The God of the infinite is the God of
the infinitesimal.

Author unknown

Faith, Definitions of

To have faith is to be sure of the things
we hope for, to be certain of the things
we cannot see.

The Bible, Hebrews 11:1

Faith: Belief without evidence in what
is told by one who speaks, without
knowledge, of things without parallel.

Ambrose Bierce

Faith is a living, daring confidence in
God's grace. It is so sure and certain
that a man could stake his life on it a
thousand times.

Martin Luther

Faith is nothing but believing what
God promises or says. . . . Whatever
remarkable thing we read of happening in the Old or New Testament, we
read that it was done by faith – not by
works, not by a general faith, but by
faith directed to the matter in hand.

*Martin Luther, justification before
Cajetan*

Flouting
Appearances
I
Trust in
Him.

Author unknown

Faith is a living and unshakeable confidence, a belief in the grace of God so
assured that a man would die a
thousand deaths for its sake.

*Martin Luther, in the preface to his
translation of St Paul's letter to the
Romans*

Faith
Asks
Impossible
Things
Humbly.

Author unknown

Feeling
Afraid
I
Trust
Him

Author unknown

Forsaking
All
I
Take
Him.

Author unknown

Faith is not belief without proof, but
trust without reservations.

Elton Trueblood

Faith, Power of

Faith, mighty faith, the promise sees
And looks to that alone,

Laughs at impossibilities
And cries: It shall be done.
Charles Wesley

Everything is possible for the person who has faith.
The Bible, Jesus Christ, Mark 9:23

Little faith will bring your souls to heaven but great faith will bring heaven to your souls.
C.H. Spurgeon

The world was never conquered by intrigue; it was conquered by faith.
Benjamin Disraeli, Tancred

If ye have faith as a grain of mustard seed, ye shall say unto this mountain, Remove hence to yonder place; and it shall remove; and nothing shall be impossible unto you.
The Bible, Jesus Christ, Matthew 17:20 (AV)

Faith and action

Faith without works is dead.
The Bible, The apostle James, James 2:20 (AV)

It is by his actions that a person is put right with God, and not by his faith alone.
The Bible, James 2:24

Faith is sometimes spelled R – I – S – K.
Author unknown

Trust God and keep your powder dry.
Oliver Cromwell

Deeds, not creeds, are the true measure of a man.
Author unknown

Faith and fear

The right fear comes from faith, false fear from doubt. . . . Some fear to lose him, others to find him.
Blaise Pascal

Lead, kindly light, amid the encircling gloom;
   Lead thou me on;
The night is dark, and I am far from home;
   Lead thou me on.
Keep thou my feet; I do not ask to see
The distant scene; one step enough for me.
J.H. Newman

Fear imprisons, faith liberates;
fear paralyses, faith empowers;
fear disheartens, faith encourages;
fear sickens, faith heals;

fear makes useless, faith makes serviceable;
most of all, fear puts hopelessness at the heart of life,
while faith rejoices in its God.
Harry Emerson Fosdick

Faith and obedience

Faith and obedience are bound up in the same bundle; he that obeys God, trusts God and he that trusts God, obeys God. He that is without faith, is without works and he that is without works, is without faith.
C.H. Spurgeon

Obedience is the fruit of faith; patience, the bloom on the fruit.
Christina Rossetti

Faith and prayer

Faith is to prayer what the feather is to the arrow: without faith it will not hit the mark.
J.C. Ryle

Faith and reason

The seat of faith is not in the brain, but in the heart, and the head is not the place to keep the promises of God, but the heart is the chest to lay them up in.
Richard Greenham

It is the heart which is conscious of God, not the reason. This then is faith: God sensible to the heart, not to the reason.
Blaise Pascal

If faith did not exist apart from intellect, clever people would have a better hope of salvation than stupid people.
R.H. Benson

Faith is the first step to understanding; understanding is the reward of faith.
Augustine of Hippo, Sermons

Reason is our soul's left hand,
   Faith her right,
By these we reach divinity.
John Donne

If the work of God could be comprehended by reason, it would be no longer wonderful, and faith would have no merit if reason provided proof.
Gregory the Great

Faith must trample under foot all reason, sense, and understanding.
Martin Luther

Faith and suffering

The only way to learn strong faith is to endure great trials. I have learned my faith by standing firm amid severe testings.

George Müller

Faith required

Faith is required of you, and a sincere life, not loftiness of intellect, nor deepness in the mysteries of God.

Thomas à Kempis, The Imitation of Christ

Ask a Christian by what work he is made worthy of the name of Christian and he can give no answer but hearing the word of God, which is faith. So the ears alone are the organs of a Christian man, because is he justified and judged as a Christian not by the works of any other part but by faith.

Martin Luther, The Epistle to the Hebrews

God does not keep an extra supply of goodness that is higher than faith, and there is no help at all in anything that is below it. *Within* faith is where the Lord wants us to stay.

Julian of Norwich, Revelations of Divine Love

Faithfulness   see also GOD'S
FAITHFULNESS; LITTLE THINGS

To every person who has something, even more will be given, and he will have more than enough; but the person who has nothing, even the little that he has will be taken away from him.

The Bible, Jesus Christ, Matthew 25:29

O Lord my God, give me understanding to know you, diligence to seek you, wisdom to find you, and a faithfulness that may finally embrace you.

Thomas Aquinas

Be content with doing with calmness the little which depends on yourself and let all else be to you as if it were not.

François Fénelon

Faithfulness in carrying out our present duties is the best preparation for the future.

François Fénelon, Christian Perfection

Faithful found
Among the faithless, faithful only he;

Among innumerable false, unmoved,
Unshaken, unseduced, unterrified,
His loyalty he kept, his love, his zeal;
Nor number, nor example, with him wrought
To swerve from truth, or change his constant mind
Though single.

John Milton, Paradise Lost, Book 5

He is invited to do great things who receives small things greatly.

Cassiodorus

It is, however, only by fidelity in little things that a true and constant love of God can be distinguished from a passing fervour of spirit.

François Fénelon, Letters and Reflections

He does most in God's great world who does his best in his own little world.

Thomas Jefferson

The evangelist Dwight L. Moody led to God a man called Mordecai Ham; Mordecai was a faithful, though not a great evangelist, but he led to God Billy Graham, who led thousands to God.

Fall, The

To the question, 'What is meant by the fall?' I could answer with complete sincerity, 'That whatever I am, I am not myself.'

G.K. Chesterton

Falling away

Whoever thinks he is standing firm had better be careful that he does not fall.

The Bible, The apostle Paul, 1 Corinthians 10:12

You do not love me now as you did at first.

The Bible, Revelation 2:4

Those who fall away have never been thoroughly imbued with the knowledge of Christ but only had a slight and passing taste of it.

John Calvin

Where is the blessedness I knew when first I saw the Lord?

William Cowper

Fame

He rose like a rocket, he fell like a stick.

Thomas Paine, speaking of Edmund Burke

Families   see also CHRISTIAN
UPBRINGING; HUSBANDS; MARRIAGE

Do not think that I have come to bring
peace to the world. No, I did not come
to bring peace, but a sword. I came to
set sons against their fathers,
daughters against their mothers,
daughters-in-law against their
mothers-in-law; a man's worst
enemies will be the members of his
own family.

Whoever loves his father or mother
more than me, is not fit to be my disciple; whoever loves his son or daughter more than me is not fit to be my disciple.
*The Bible, Jesus Christ,
Matthew 10:34–37*

The best training a father can give his
children is to love their mother.
Author unknown

It is an evident truth, that most of the
mischiefs that now infest or seize upon
mankind throughout the earth, consist
in, or are caused by the disorders and
ill-governedness of families.
*Richard Baxter, Christian
Directory, 1673*

He that loves not his wife and children
feeds a lioness at home and broods a
nest of sorrows.
*Jeremy Taylor, Sermons, Married
Love*

All happy families resemble one
another, each unhappy family is
unhappy in its own way.
Leo Tolstoy, Anna Karenina

I don't know who my grandfather was;
I am much more concerned to know
what his grandson will be.
Abraham Lincoln

God is the first object of our love: Its
next office is to bear the defects of
others. And we should begin the practice of this amid our own household.
*John Wesley, A Plain Man's
Guide to Holiness*

The mind of Christ is to be learned in
the family. Strength of character may
be acquired at work, but beauty of
character is learned at home. There
the affections are trained.
Henry Drummond

A saint abroad, and a devil at home.
*John Bunyan, The Pilgrim's
Progress*

I wish I were half as great as my infant
thinks I am, and only half as stupid as
my teenager thinks I am.
Unknown father

By the time a son realises his father is
usually right, he has a son who thinks
his father is usually wrong.
Author unknown

Family, The Christian

Whoever does what my Father in
heaven wants him to do is my brother,
my sister, and my mother.
*The Bible, Jesus Christ,
Matthew 12:50*

A godly parentage is a costly boon. Its
blessing not only rests upon the children of the first family, but has often
been traced in many successive generations.
Andrew Murray

There is no such thing as an atmosphere of belief. It is equally true that
there is an atmosphere in which young
men may best arrive at life decisions,
and that atmosphere can best be gen-
erated in genuinely Christian homes.
Unconsciously, in most cases, the
child fulfils the desire of the parent's
heart.
John R. Mott

Fanaticism   see also RELIGIOUS
FANATICISM

Fanaticism, the false fire of an over-
heated mind.
William Cowper

A fanatic is one who can't change his
mind and won't change the subject.
Winston Churchill

Farming

Unused fields could yield plenty of
food for the poor, but unjust men keep
them from being farmed.
The Bible, Proverbs 13:23

Fashion

The fashion wears out more apparel
than the man.
William Shakespeare

Fashion: A despot whom the wise
ridicule and obey.
*Ambrose Bierce, The Devil's
Dictionary*

Fasting

When you fast, do not put on a sad face as the hypocrites do . . . so that others cannot know that you are fasting – only your Father, who is unseen, will know.

The Bible, Jesus Christ, Matthew 6:16, 18

Whoso will pray, he must fast and be clean,
And fat his soul and make his body lean.

Geoffrey Chaucer, Canterbury Tales, Summoner's Tale

Fathers

One father is more than a hundred schoolmasters.

Proverb

Fathers in God

In your life in union with Christ Jesus I have become your father by bringing the Good News to you.

The Bible, The apostle Paul, 1 Corinthians 4:15

Faults   see also CONFESSION; MISTAKES; PERFECTION

A fault confessed is half redressed.

Author unknown

Who never admits wrong loves pride more than facts.

Proverb

Only great men have great defects.

La Rochefoucauld

He is lifeless that is faultless.

J. Heywood, A Dialogue containing . . . the Proverbs in the English Tongue

Not in committing, but in prolonging acts of folly is the shame.

Horace

A fault, once denied, is twice committed.

Thomas Fuller, Gnomologia

It is right that someone who asks pardon for his own faults should be willing to pardon others.

Horace

Search others for their virtues, yourself for your faults.

Author unknown

Do not be discouraged at your faults; bear with yourself in correcting them, as you would with your neighbour. Lay aside this ardour of mind, which exhausts your body, and leads you to commit errors. Accustom yourself gradually to carry prayer into all your daily occupations. Speak, move, work, in peace, as if you were in prayer, as indeed you ought to be.

François Fénelon

Fear

There is no fear in love; perfect love drives out all fear.

The Bible, 1 John 4:18

Whoever listens to me will have security. He will be safe, with no reason to be afraid.

The Bible, Proverbs 1:33

If I could hear Christ praying for me in the next room, I would not fear a million enemies. Yet distance makes no difference. He *is* praying for me.

Robert Murray M'Cheyne

Jesus came treading the waves; and so he puts all the swelling tumults of life under his feet. Christians – why afraid?

Augustine of Hippo

He [John Knox] feared God so much that he never feared the face of any man.

Author unknown

Yea, though I walk through the valley of the shadow of death, I will fear no evil.

The Bible, Psalm 23:4 (AV)

The only thing we have to fear is fear itself.

Franklin Delano Roosevelt

Nothing is so much to be feared as fear.

Henry David Thoreau

Courage faces fear and thereby masters it. Cowardice represses fear and is thereby mastered by it.

Martin Luther King

Nothing is terrible except fear itself.

Francis Bacon

The only thing I am afraid of is fear.

Duke of Wellington

He has not learnt a lesson of life, who does not every day surmount a fear. Do the thing you fear, and the death of fear is certain.

Ralph Waldo Emerson

Fear closes the ears of the mind.

Sallust

71

No passion so effectually robs the mind of all its powers of acting and reasoning as fear.

Edmund Burke

Fear of God

The fear of God furthers every enterprise that governments undertake.

Macchiavelli

I fear God, yet I am not afraid of him.

Thomas Browne

Feelings

Luther was once asked, 'Do you feel that you are a child of God this morning?' and he answered, 'I cannot say that I do, but I know that I am.'

Believe God's word and power more than you believe your own feelings and experiences. Your rock is Christ, and it is not the rock which ebbs and flows, but your sea.

Samuel Rutherford

It is as necessary for the heart to feel as for the body to be fed.

Napoleon, Political Aphorisms

Fellowship

Be eager for more frequent gatherings for thanksgiving [*eucharist*] to God and for his glory. For when you meet frequently the forces of Satan are annulled and his destructive power is cancelled in the concord of your faith.

Ignatius of Antioch, To the Ephesians

Behind every saint stands another saint.

Friedrich von Hügel, The Mystical Element in Religion

Help us to help each other, Lord,
  Each other's cross to bear,
Let each his friendly aid afford,
  And feel his brother's care.

Charles Wesley

Fellowship with God   see also HOLINESS; LIFE IN JESUS

All the doors that lead inward, to the sacred place of the Most High, are doors outward – out of self, out of smallness, out of wrong.

George Macdonald

Festivals   see also SUNDAY

The life without festival is a long road without an inn.

Democritus of Abdera

Flattery

Among all the diseases of the mind there is not one more epidemical or more pernicious than the love of flattery.

Richard Steel, The Spectator, 238

Flattery corrupts both the receiver and giver.

Edmund Burke

Flattery is a false coinage, which our vanity puts into circulation.

La Rochefoucauld

A man's body is remarkably sensitive. Pat him on the back and his head swells.

Author unknown

I can't be your friend, and your flatterer too.

Thomas Fuller, Gnomologia

What really flatters a man is that you think him worth flattering.

George Bernard Shaw

Flippancy

If prolonged, the habit of Flippancy builds up around a man the finest armour-plating against the Enemy [i.e., God] that I know, and it is quite free from the dangers inherent in the other sources of laughter. It is a thousand miles away from joy: it deadens, instead of sharpening, the intellect; and it excites no affection between those who practise it.

C.S. Lewis, The Screwtape Letters

Follow-up

I determined by the grace of God not to strike one blow in any place where I cannot follow the blow.

John Wesley, Journal

My brother Wesley acted more wisely than I. The souls that were awakened under his ministry he joined together in classes, and so preserved the fruit of his labours. I failed to do this, and as a result my people are a rope of sand.

George Whitefield

If everyone who worked for the conversion of others was to introduce them immediately to prayer and to the interior life and made it their main aim to win over their hearts, innumerable, permanent conversions would definitely take place.

Madame Guyon, A Short and Easy Method of Prayer

Following God   see CHRISTIAN LIFE

Food   see also GLUTTONY

Whatever you do, whether you eat or
drink, do it all for God's glory.
The Bible, The apostle Paul,
1 Corinthians 10:31

For a long life, breakfast like a king;
lunch moderately and dine like a
pauper.
Author unknown

Tell me what you eat, and I will tell
you what manner of man you are.
Brillat Savarin

Man is what he eats.
German proverb

One eats in holiness and the table
becomes an altar.
Martin Buber

Three good meals a day is bad living.
Benjamin Franklin, Poor
Richard's Almanac, 1737

He that never eats too much, will
never be lazy.
Benjamin Franklin, Poor
Richard's Almanac, 1756

A fat paunch breeds no fine thoughts.
Greek proverb

A full belly makes a dull brain.
Benjamin Franklin, Poor
Richard's Almanac, 1758

Foolishness

Fools say to themselves,
    'There is no God.'
The Bible, Psalm 53:1

Don't try to talk sense to a fool; he
can't appreciate it.
The Bible, Proverbs 23:9

The greatest lesson in life is to know
that even fools are right sometimes.
Winston Churchill

No one is a fool always, everyone
sometimes.
Author unknown

Fools and wise folk are alike harmless.
It is the half-wise, and the half-foolish,
who are most dangerous.
Goethe

Wise men learn more from fools than
fools from wise men.
Cato

A fool always finds a bigger fool to
admire him.
Boileau, L'Art Poétique

Foreigners

Modern man . . . is educated to understand foreign languages and misunder-
stand foreigners.
G.K. Chesterton

Forgiveness

As far as the east is from the west,
    so far does he remove our sins from
    us.
The Bible, Psalm 103:12

Though your sins be as scarlet, they
shall be as white as snow.
The Bible, Isaiah 1:18 (AV)

If you forgive others the wrongs they
have done to you, your Father in
heaven will also forgive you. But if you
do not forgive others, then your
Father will not forgive the wrongs you
have done.
The Bible, Jesus Christ,
Matthew 6:14–15

God forgave us all our sins.
The Bible, The apostle Paul,
Colossians 2:13

Only one petition in the Lord's Prayer
has any condition attached to it: it is
the petition for forgiveness.
William Temple, Personal
Religion and the Life of Fellowship

Only a Person can forgive.
C.S. Lewis, Mere Christianity

I can pardon everyone's mistakes but
my own.
Cato

Dear Lord and Father of mankind,
    Forgive our foolish ways!
Reclothe us in our rightful mind,
In purer lives thy service find,
    In deeper reverence, praise.
John Greenleaf Whittier

Rock of Ages, cleft for me,
Let me hide myself in Thee!
Let the water and the blood
From Thy riv'n side which flow'd,
Be of sin the double cure,
Cleanse me from its guilt and power.
Augustus Montague Toplady

Forgiveness proceeds from a generous
soul.
Macchiavelli

When Christ's hands were nailed to
the cross, he also nailed your sins to
the cross.
Bernard of Clairvaux, The Song of
Songs

Forgive others often, thyself never.
Latin proverb

I will love you, O Lord, and thank you, and confess to your name, because you have forgiven me my evil and nefarious deeds. I impute it to your grace and mercy that you have made my sins melt away like ice. . . . Who is there who, considering his own weakness, dare ascribe his chastity or innocence to his own strength, that he may love you less, as though your mercy were less necessary to him, whereby you forgive the sins of those who are converted to you?
Augustine of Hippo, Confessions

Forgiveness of sins is the very heart of Christianity, and yet it is a very dangerous thing to preach.
Martin Luther

The sinner of today is the saint of tomorrow. Wherefore, unmindful of the sins and shortcomings of our neighbours, let us look to our own imperfections, surely forgetting what God has forgotten: sins truly repented, which God has forgotten, we have no business to remember.
Meister Eckhart

Write across that list in red ink, 'The blood of Jesus Christ, his Son, cleanses us from all sin.'
Martin Luther's reply to the devil's list of sins Luther had committed

Humanity is never so beautiful as when praying for forgiveness or else forgiving another.
Jean Paul Richter

[To General Oglethorpe's saying 'I never forgive.'] Then, sir, I hope that you never sin.
John Wesley

To err is human, to forgive divine.
Alexander Pope, Essay on Criticism

Long my imprisoned spirit lay . . .
I woke, the dungeon flamed with light:
My chains fell off, my heart was free,
I rose, went forth, and followed thee.
Charles Wesley

Forgiving others

If you want people to like you, forgive them when they wrong you.
The Bible, Proverbs 17:9

'Lord, if my brother keeps on sinning against me, how many times do I have to forgive him? Seven times?'
'No, not seven times,' answered Jesus, 'but seventy times seven.'
The Bible, Matthew 18:21–22

Father, forgive them: for they know not what they do.
The Bible, Jesus Christ, Luke 23:34 (AV)

You must forgive one another just as the Lord has forgiven you.
The Bible, The apostle Paul, Colossians 3:13

Lo, here is a token that I forgive thee.
George Wishart, as he kissed his hesitant executioner

The offender never pardons.
George Herbert

Two works of mercy set a man free: forgive and you will be forgiven, and give and you will receive.
Augustine of Hippo, Sermons

'I can forgive, but I cannot forget' is only another way of saying, 'I cannot forgive.'
Henry Ward Beecher

Doing an injury puts you below your enemy;
Revenging one makes you but even with him;
Forgiving it sets you above him.
Benjamin Franklin

He that cannot forgive others breaks the bridge over which he must pass himself; for every man has need to be forgiven.
Thomas Fuller

To be wronged is nothing unless you continue to remember it.
Confucius

The noblest vengeance is to forgive.
Proverb

Formalism

Formality, formality, formality is the great sin of England at this day, under which the land groans. – There is more light than there was, but less life; more shadow, but less substance; more profession, but less sanctification.
Thomas Hall, 1658

He that hath but a form is a hypocrite; but he that hath not a form is an atheist.
Joseph Hall

There is no devil so dangerous as Evangelical formalism.

J.C. Ryle, Practical Religion

Fortune

Once more I declare this to be most true, and every page of history confirms my words, that men can assist Fortune, but they cannot resist her; they may weave her webs, but they cannot break them.

Macchiavelli

There is a tide in the affairs of men,
Which, taken at the flood, leads on to fortune.

William Shakespeare

Free will

God, having placed good and evil in our power, has given us full freedom of choice; he does not keep back the unwilling, but embraces the willing.

John Chrysostom

Without free will, how shall God judge the world? Without grace, how shall God save the world?

Author unknown

Concerning free will it is taught that to some extent man has freedom of will to lead a just and honourable life, to choose between things which reason comprehends; but without grace, assistance, and the operation of the Holy Spirit he is unable to become pleasing to God, or to fear God in heart, or to believe in him, or to cast out of his heart the innate evil propensity; but *these things are effected through the Holy Spirit*, which is given through the word of God.

Augsburg Confession, Article 17

You will notice that scripture just sails over the problem [of the whole puzzle about grace and free will]. 'Work out your own salvation in fear and trembling' – pure Pelagianism. But why? 'For it is God who worketh in you' – pure Augustinianism. It is presumably only our presuppositions that make this appear nonsensical.

C.S. Lewis, Letters to Malcolm Chiefly on Prayer

In divine and spiritual things we have no free will, but only in name.

Martin Luther

He who created us without our help will not save us without our consent.

Augustine of Hippo

God wants only one thing in the whole world – to find the innermost part of the spirit of man clean and ready for him to accomplish the divine purpose therein. He has all power in heaven and earth, but the power to do his work in man against man's will he has not got.

John Tauler

Freedom

Man is born free, and everywhere he is in chains.

Jean-Jacques Rousseau, The Social Contract

There are two freedoms – the false, where a man is free to do what he likes; the true, where a man is free to do what he ought.

Charles Kingsley

If negro freedom is taken away, or that of any minority group, the freedom of all the people is taken away.

Paul Robeson

I have freed my soul.

Bernard of Clairvaux

O Lord my God, I have hoped in thee,
O dear Jesus, set me free.
Though hard the chains that fasten me,
And sore my lot, yet I long for thee
I languish and groaning bend my knee,
Adoring, imploring, O set me free.

Mary Queen of Scots

If liberty is to be saved, it will not be by the doubters, the men of science or the materialists; it will be by religious conviction, by the faith of individuals, who believe that God wills man to be free but also pure.

Samuel Taylor Coleridge

But what is Freedom? Rightly understood,
A universal licence to be good.

Hartley Coleridge, Freedom

Freedom is participation in power.

Cicero

Those who deny freedom to others deserve it not for themselves.

Abraham Lincoln

Liberty is the power that we have over ourselves.

Hugo Grotius

Freedom is that faculty which enlarges the usefulness of all other faculties.
Immanuel Kant

When people are free to do as they please, they usually imitate each other.
E. Hoffer

If the sea were ink, and the earth parchment, it would never serve to describe the praises of liberty.
Rabbinical saying

Freedom, Christian

Live as free people; do not, however, use your freedom to cover up any evil, but live as God's slaves.
The Bible, 1 Peter 2:16

The author of peace and lover of concord, in knowledge of whom standeth our eternal life, whose service is perfect freedom.
The Book of Common Prayer: Second Collect, for Peace

Christian freedom is a spiritual matter. Its whole purpose is to give peace to trembling consciences, whether they are anxious about forgiveness of sins, imperfect actions or the exercise of choice.
John Calvin, The Institutes of Christian Religion, 3.19.9

French people

The French are the eldest sons of antiquity; they have the intelligence of the Romans, and the disposition of the Greeks.
Chateaubriand

Fretting see also ANXIETY

I feel and grieve, but, by the grace of God, I fret at nothing.
John Wesley

Friars

Live in obedience, in chastity, and without property, following the teaching and footsteps of our Lord Jesus Christ.
Franciscan Rule of 1221

Friends of God

Henceforth I call you not servants; for the servant knoweth not what his lord doeth; but I have called you friends; for all things that I have heard of my Father I have made known unto you.
The Bible, Jesus Christ, John 15:15 (AV)

We were God's enemies, but he made us his friends through the death of his Son.
The Bible, The apostle Paul, Romans 5:10

Abraham was called God's friend.
The Bible, James 2:23

Friendship

Friendly is as friendly does.
Proverb

This belonged to the best friend I ever had.
Lord Shaftesbury, when showing people the gold watch which he had had from the family housekeeper who had taught him about Jesus

I had a friend.
Charles Kingsley, referring to his friend F.D. Maurice, when asked the secret of his own life

It [friendship] redoubleth joys, and cutteth griefs in halves.
Francis Bacon, Essays, Of Friendship

Love is rarer than genius itself. And friendship is rarer than love.
Charles Péguy, Basic Verities

Life goes headlong. . . . But if suddenly we encounter a friend, we pause.
Ralph Waldo Emerson

Do not use a hatchet to remove a fly from your friend's forehead.
Chinese proverb

Blessed is the influence of one true, loving soul on another.
George Eliot

The language of friendship is not words but meanings.
Henry David Thoreau

Instead of loving your enemies, treat your friends a little better.
Ed Howe

Love desires the body, friendship the soul.
R. de Campoamor

Bad company is a disease;
Who lies with dogs, shall rise with fleas.
Rowland Watkyns, Flamma Sine Fumo

Friendship is always a sweet responsibility, never an opportunity.
Kahlil Gibran

As gold is tried in the furnace, so friends are tried in adversity.
Menander

Neither armies, nor treasures, but friends, are the surest protection of a king.
Sallust

A friend is a second self.
Latin proverb

A faithful friend is an image of God.
French proverb

The more we love, the better we are, and the greater our friendships are, the dearer we are to God.
Jeremy Taylor

Ships that pass in the night, and speak
    each other in passing,
Only a signal shown and a distant voice
    in the darkness;
So on the ocean of life we pass and
    speak one another,
Only a look and a voice, then darkness
    again and a silence.
Henry Wadsworth Longfellow,
Tales of a Wayside Inn, 3

Tell me what company you keep, and I'll tell you what you are.
Cervantes, Don Quixote, II.23

Friendship, Acquiring

We often choose a friend as we do a mistress – for no particular excellence in themselves, but merely from some circumstance that flatters our self-love.
William Hazlitt, Characteristics

A friend may well be reckoned the masterpiece of Nature. . . . The only reward of virtue is virtue; the only way to have a friend is to be one.
Ralph Waldo Emerson, Essays,
Friendship

You'll make more friends in ten minutes by taking an interest in others than in a month trying to get others interested in you.
Author unknown

I look upon every day to be lost, in which I do not make a new acquaintance.
Samuel Johnson

Friendship is like money, easier made than kept.
Samuel Butler, Note Books

Friendship, and sincerity

True friendship ought never to conceal what it thinks.
Jerome

Love comes from blindness, friendship from knowledge.
Bussy-Rabutin, Histoire
Amoureuse des Gaules

A judicious friend, into whose bosom we may pour out our souls, and tell our corruptions as well as our comforts, is a very great privilege.
George Whitefield

A friend is a person with whom I may be sincere. Before him I may think aloud.
Ralph Waldo Emerson

Friendship, in times of need

A friend loveth at all times, and a brother is born for adversity.
The Bible, Proverbs 17:17 (AV)

A friend ought to be like the blood, which runs quickly to the wound without waiting to be called.
A. Perez

A friend in need is a friend indeed.
Proverb

Some friends are more loyal than brothers.
The Bible, Proverbs 18:24

Rare is the faithful friend who is constant in all his friends' distresses.
Thomas à Kempis, The Imitation
of Christ

There is nothing more friendly than a friend in need.
Plautus, Epidicus III.iii

Friendship, Learning from

God send me a friend that will tell me of my faults.
Thomas Fuller, Gnomologia

By associating with wise people you will become wise yourself.
Menander

There is no man so friendless but what he can find a friend sincere enough to tell him disagreeable truths.
Edward Bulwer-Lytton

A friend means well, even when he hurts you.
The Bible, Proverbs 27:6

People learn from one another, just as iron sharpens iron.
The Bible, Proverbs 27:17

The best mirror is an old friend.
George Herbert, Jacula
Prudentum

Friendship, Value of

So long as we love, we serve; so long as we are loved by others I would almost say that we are indispensable; and no man is useless while he has a friend.
Robert Louis Stevenson

Life has no pleasure higher or nobler than that of friendship.
Samuel Johnson

The greatest blessing is a pleasant friend.
Horace

To lose a friend is the greatest of all losses.
Latin proverb

Those who possess good friends are truly rich.
Spanish proverb

A true friend is the most precious of all possessions and the one we take least thought about acquiring.
La Rochefoucauld, Maxims

Life is not worth living for the man who has not even one good friend.
Democritus of Abdera

No one is rich enough to be without friends. Make new friends but keep the old. New are silver; old are gold.
Author unknown

Fruit, Spiritual

It is no use to anybody for a tree to bud and blossom if the blossom does not develop into fruit. Many are the folk who perish in blossom. . . . A man's existence is always in a state of non-being, becoming, and being. . . . He is always in sin, in justification, in righteousness. Always a sinner, always penitent, always justified.
Martin Luther, The Epistle to the Romans

Fulfilment

Find your satisfaction in him who made you, and only then find satisfaction in yourself as part of his creation.
Augustine of Hippo, Discourses on the Psalms

Desire only God, and your heart will be satisfied.
Augustine of Hippo, Discourses on the Psalms

The desire of man is like a sieve or pierced vessel which he ever tries to, and can never, fill.
Plato

It is better to be Socrates dissatisfied than a pig satisfied.
John Stuart Mill

Fun   see also HUMOUR

A good and wholesome thing is a little harmless fun in this world; it tones a body up and keeps him human and prevents him from souring.
Mark Twain

Seek the kind of fun that doesn't make you ashamed the next day.
Author unknown

Fund-raising

Depend on it! God's work done in God's way will never lack God's supply.
Hudson Taylor

Funerals   see also BEREAVEMENT

Ah, why should we wear black for the guests of God?
John Ruskin

Here lies he who neither feared nor flattered any flesh.
At the burial of John Knox in 1572

Future

You, Lord, are all I have,
and you give me all I need;
my future is in your hands.
The Bible, Psalm 16:5

I know not what the future hath
Of marvel or surprise;
Assured of this, that life and death
His mercy underlies.
John Greenleaf Whittier

Tomorrow has two handles: the handle of fear and the handle of faith. You can take hold of it by either handle.
Author unknown

G

Gambling

A wager is a fool's argument.
French proverb

There are two times in a man's life when he should not speculate; when he can't afford it, and when he can.
Mark Twain

The worst thing that can happen to a man who gambles is to win.
C.H. Spurgeon

Garden of Eden   see ADAM AND EVE

Garden of Gethsemane

Jesus was in a garden, not of delight as
the first Adam, in which he destroyed
himself and the whole human race, but
in one of agony, in which he saved
himself and the whole human race.

Blaise Pascal, Pensées

Gardens

God Almighty first planted a garden.
And indeed it is the purest of human
pleasures.

*Francis Bacon, Essays, Of
Gardens*

Garrulity

The more you talk, the more likely you
are to sin. If you are wise, you will
keep quiet.

The Bible, Proverbs 10:19

There are few wild beasts more to be
dreaded than a talking man having
nothing to say.

Jonathan Swift

They talk most who have the least to
say.

Matthew Prior

Generosity   see GIVING

Genius

Genius is one per cent inspiration and
99 per cent perspiration.

Thomas Edison

Genius develops in quiet places,
character out in the full current of
human life.

Goethe

It is the great triumph of genius to
make the common appear novel.

Goethe

Works of genius are the first things in
the world.

John Keats

Genius is nothing but a great aptitude
for being patient.

Buffon

True genius resides in the capacity for
evaluation of uncertain, hazardous,
and conflicting information.

Winston Churchill

The principal mark of genius is not
perfection but originality, the opening
of new frontiers.

Arthur Koestler

The essence of genius is knowing what
to overlook.

William James

Genius is an infinite capacity for taking
pains.

Author unknown

Genius usually starts great things; only
labour and drudgery finish them.

Author unknown

[Queen Victoria: 'Mr Paderewski, you
are a genius.'] 'That may be, Ma'am, but
before I was a genius, I was a drudge.'

*Paderewski, who might practise
the same phrase on his violin fifty
times to perfect it*

I can make nobles and great lords
when I please, but God alone can
make such a man as this whom we are
about to lose.

*François I (said to have been his
comment at Leonardo da Vinci's
death-bed, when some courtiers
thought the king honoured the
great artist too highly)*

Gentlemen

A gentleman is a man who can disagree without being disagreeable.

Author unknown

Gentleness

Show a gentle attitude towards everyone.

*The Bible, The apostle Paul,
Philippians 4:5*

He who is gentle remembers good
rather than evil, the good one has
received rather than the good one has
done.

Aristotle

Be mild at their anger, humble at their
boastings, to their blasphemies return
your prayers, to their error your
firmness in the faith; when they are
cruel, be gentle; not endeavouring to
imitate their ways, let us be their
brethren in all kindness and moderation: but let us be followers of the
Lord; for who was ever more unjustly
used, more destitute, more despised?

Ignatius of Antioch

A gentle answer quietens anger.

The Bible, Proverbs 15:1

Gentleness does more than violence.

La Fontaine

Nothing is so strong as gentleness,
nothing so gentle as real strength.

Francis de Sales

It is the spirit which rectifies and red-
resses the injustices of justice.
R.C. Trench

Gifts

They brought out their gifts of gold,
frankincense, and myrrh, and presented them to him.
The Bible, Matthew 2:11

Giving

Honour the Lord by making him an
offering from the best of all that your
land produces.
The Bible, Proverbs 3:9

When thou doest alms, let not thy left
hand know what thy right hand doeth.
That thine alms may be in secret: and
thy Father which seeth in secret himself shall reward you openly.
*The Bible, Jesus Christ,
Matthew 6:3–4 (AV)*

Every Sunday each of you must put
aside some money, in proportion to
what he has earned.
*The Bible, The apostle Paul,
1 Corinthians 16:2*

We make a living by what we get, but
we make a life by what we give.
Winston Churchill

She would rather put her money in the
stomachs of the needy than in a purse.
Jerome, Letters

Any Christian who takes for himself
anything more than the plain neces-
saries of life lives in an open, habitual
denial of the Lord. He has gained
riches and hell-fire!
John Wesley

If I leave behind me £10, you and all
mankind bear witness against me that I
lived and died a thief and a robber.
John Wesley

Only one life, 'twill soon be past.
Only what's done for others will last.
Proverb

No purchase is as good as a gift.
French proverb

Do not give, as many rich men do, like a
hen that lays an egg, and then cackles.
*Henry Ward Beecher, Proverbs
from a Plymouth Pulpit*

Giving and getting

It is more blessed to give than to
receive.
*The Bible, Jesus Christ,
Acts 20:35 (AV)*

When a man dies he clutches in his
hands only that which he has given
away during his lifetime.
Jean-Jacques Rousseau

Nothing is really ours until we share it.
C.S. Lewis

The hand that gives, gathers.
Proverb

A man there was,
    though some did count him mad,
The more he cast away,
    the more he had.
*John Bunyan, The Pilgrim's
Progress*

Who shuts his hand has lost his gold
Who opens it hath it twice told.
George Herbert

Spend and God will send.
Proverb

Give according to your income, lest
God make your income according to
your giving.
Author unknown

He who takes but never gives,
may last for years but never lives.
Proverb

Abundant giving brings abundant
living.
Proverb

Be generous, and you will be prosper-
ous. Help others, and you will be
helped.
The Bible, Proverbs 11:25

When you give to the poor, it is like
lending to the Lord, and the Lord will
pay you back.
The Bible, Proverbs 19:17

Giving willingly

He gives nothing but worthless gold
Who gives from a sense of duty.
*James Russell Lowell, The Vision
of Sir Launfal*

He gives twice who gives quickly.
Latin proverb

God loves a cheerful giver.
*The Bible, The apostle Paul,
2 Corinthians 9:7 (AV)*

Gloating

Don't be glad when your enemy meets
disaster, and don't rejoice when he
stumbles. The Lord will know if you
are gloating, and he will not like it.
The Bible, Proverbs 24:17–18

Gluttony

Gluttony kills more than the sword.
Latin proverb

We ought to eat in order to live, not live in order to eat.
Cicero

More people die from overeating than from undernourishment.
The Talmud

There are more gluttons than drunkards in hell.
Author unknown

In general, mankind, since the improvement of cookery, eats twice as much as nature requires.
Benjamin Franklin

Goals   see also AMBITION

Plan carefully what you do, and whatever you do will turn out right.
The Bible, Proverbs 4:26

Will a person gain anything if he wins the whole world but loses his life? Of course not! There is nothing he can give to regain his life.
The Bible, Jesus Christ, Matthew 16:26

When goal goes, meaning goes; when meaning goes, purpose goes; when purpose goes, life goes dead on our hands.
Carl Jung

To have succeeded is to have finished one's business on earth, like the male spider who is killed by the female the moment he has succeeded in his courtship. I like a state of continual becoming, with a goal in front and not behind.
George Bernard Shaw

People are like buttons, unattached, useless. Attached, indispensable. People, unattached to a goal, useless. Attached, men with missions.
Author unknown

There is always room at the top.
Daniel Webster

First build a proper goal. That proper goal will make it easy, almost automatic, to build a proper You.
Goethe

Now all our trouble and disquiet are built on the desire for something or other. If we want to find the true cause of it all we should just find out the cause of our wants.
William Law

The rational questions:
1. Where am I?
2. Where do I want to be?
3. How do I know I am getting there?
Author unknown

The fool wanders: the wise man travels.
Thomas Fuller, Gnomologia

Before you score, you must have a goal.
Author unknown

A written down goal, in some way no one yet understands, tends to attract every ingredient it needs to realise it.
Author unknown

Goals, Absence of

The poorest of all men is not the one without gold, but without a goal. Life for him has no meaning – no reason for living.
Author unknown

Ninety-five per cent of working American males have no goals in their life.
Owen Hendrix

Many are stubborn in pursuit of the path they have chosen, few in pursuit of the goal.
Friedrich Nietzsche

If you aim at nothing, you hit it.
Author unknown

No one can be making much of his life who has not a very definite conception of what he is living for.
Henry Drummond

That carpenter is not the best
Who makes more chips than all the rest.
A. Guiterman

Goals, Examples of

Give me grace always to desire and to will what is most acceptable to you and most pleasing in your sight.
Thomas à Kempis

I have found my destiny. I must take the gospel to the people of the East End.
William Booth

If I had a thousand lives, I would give them all for the women of China.
Lottie Moon

God   see also CHRIST; HOLY SPIRIT; TRINITY

God and mankind

God is no respecter of persons.
*The Bible, The apostle Peter, Acts
10:34 (AV)*

Man is man's A.B.C. There is none
that can
Read God aright, unless he first spell
Man.
Francis Quarles

Without God, we cannot. Without us,
God will not.
Augustine of Hippo

Where there is no God, there is no
man.
Nicholas Berdyaev

God is the country of the soul.
Augustine of Hippo

The relationship between God and a
man is more private and intimate than
any possible relation between two fellow creatures.
*C.S. Lewis, Letters to Malcolm
Chiefly on Prayer*

God, as Creator

This is the creator: by his love, our
Father; by his power, our Lord; by his
wisdom, our maker and designer.
Irenaeus, Against Heresies, 5.16.3

Everything is good when it leaves the
Creator's hands; everything degener-
ates in the hands of man.
*Jean-Jacques Rousseau, The
Social Contract*

The world forgets you, its creator, and
falls in love with what you have
created instead of with you.
Augustine of Hippo

Out of him we have all come, in him
we are all enfolded and towards him
we are all journeying.
*Julian of Norwich, Revelations of
Divine Love*

God creates out of nothing. Therefore, until a man is nothing God can
make nothing out of him.
Martin Luther

I praise thee; for I am fearfully and
wonderfully made: marvellous are thy
works; and that my soul knoweth right
well. My substance was not hid from
thee, when I was made in secret, and
curiously wrought in the lowest parts
of the earth.
The Bible, Psalm 139:14–15 (AV)

The end of God's creating the world
was to prepare a kingdom for his Son.
Jonathan Edwards

No rain, no mushrooms. No God, no
world.
African proverb

I cannot forgive Descartes; in all his
philosophy he did his best to dispense
with God. But he could not avoid making him set the world in motion with a
flip of his thumb; after that he had no
more use for God.
Blaise Pascal, Pensées

God, as Father

'Abba' is only a little word, and yet
contains everything. It is not the
mouth but heart's affection which
speaks like this. Even if I am oppressed
with anguish and terror on every side,
and seem to be forsaken and utterly
cast away from your presence, yet am I
your child, and you are my Father. For
Christ's sake: I am loved because of
the Beloved. So this little word, Abba,
Father, deeply felt in the heart, sur-
passes all the eloquence of Demosthenes, Cicero, and the most eloquent
speakers that ever lived. This matter is
not expressed with words, but with
groanings, and these groanings cannot
be uttered with any words of eloquence, for no tongue can express
them.
Martin Luther

Before I had children of my own, I
used to think, 'God will not forget me';
but when I became a father I learned
something more – God *cannot* forget
me.
Martin Luther

God, as Friend

John Chrysostom was threatened with
banishment by the Emperor. He
replied, 'You cannot banish me, for
the world is my Father's house.'
'Then I will kill you,' stormed the
Emperor.
'But you cannot, for my life is hidden
with Christ in God,' replied the saint.
'Your wealth will be confiscated.'
'That cannot be, for my wealth is in
heaven, as my heart is there.'
'But I will drive you away from people
and you will have no friends left.'
'That you cannot do either, for I have

a Friend in heaven who has said, "I will never leave you nor forsake you."'

God, as last resort

We regard God as an airman regards his parachute; it's there for emergencies but he hopes he'll never have to use it.

Author unknown, quoted in C.S. Lewis, The Problem of Pain

God, as Refuge

The eternal God is thy refuge, and underneath are the everlasting arms.
The Bible, Deuteronomy 33:27 (AV)

God is our refuge and strength, a very present help in trouble.
The Bible, Psalm 46:1 (AV)

God, as Shepherd

The Lord is my shepherd; I shall not want.
The Bible, Psalm 23:1 (AV)

He will take care of his flock like a shepherd;
he will gather the lambs together and carry them in his arms;
he will gently lead their mothers.
The Bible, Isaiah 40:11

Wherever he may guide me,
No want shall turn me back;
My shepherd is beside me,
And nothing can I lack.
A.L. Waring

God, as Sustainer

In him we live, and move, and have our being.
The Bible, The apostle Paul, Acts 17:28 (AV)

God is love who, by his love, provides all creatures with their life and being, preserving them in his love. Just as the colour of cloth is preserved in the cloth, so creatures are preserved in existence by love, that is, from God.
Meister Eckhart

In this Revelation he showed me something else, a tiny thing, no bigger than a hazelnut, lying in the palm of the hand, and as round as a ball. I looked at it, puzzled, and thought, 'What is it?'
The answer came: 'It is everything that is made.'
I wondered how it could survive. It was so small that I expected it to

shrivel up and disappear.
Then I was answered, 'It exists now and always because God loves it.'
Thus I understood that everything exists through the love of God.
In this small thing I saw three truths: first God made it, second God loves it, and third God looks after it. But what he really means to me as Maker, Keeper and Lover, I cannot tell.
Julian of Norwich, Revelations of Divine Love

God, Belief in

A little philosophy inclineth man's mind to atheism; but depth in philosophy bringeth men's minds about to religion.
Francis Bacon, Essays, Of Atheism

He who works in man both to will and to do, and indeed all things in all, produces both the will to believe and the act of believing also.
Canons of the Synod of Dort, Article 14

What thinking man is there who still requires the hypothesis of a God?
Friedrich Nietzsche

I have never been able to conceive mankind without him.
Fyodor Dostoevsky

I had rather believe all the fables in the legends and the Talmud and the Alcoran, than that this universe is without a mind.
Francis Bacon

Denial of the Infinite leads straight to nihilism: all creation becomes merely 'a conception of the mind'. Discussion is not possible with nihilism, for no way is opened to the mind by a philosophy which meets every opinion with a 'No'. To 'No' there is but one reply – 'Yes!'
Victor Hugo

To believe in God for me is to feel that there is a God, not a dead one, or a stuffed one, but a living one, who with irresistible force urges us towards more loving.
Vincent Van Gogh

God, Greater than mankind

'My thoughts,' says the Lord, 'are not like yours,
and my ways are different from yours.

As high as the heavens are above the earth,
so high are my ways and thoughts above yours.'

The Bible, Isaiah 55:8–9

God, Understanding

A comprehended God is no God.

John Chrysostom

Godliness see also HOLINESS

Godliness with contentment is great gain.

The Bible, The apostle Paul,
1 Timothy 6:6 (AV)

Would to God that we might spend a single day really well!

Thomas à Kempis, The Imitation
of Christ

We cannot learn fear of God and the basic principles of godliness, unless we are pierced by the sword of the Spirit and destroyed. It is as if God were saying that to rank among his sons our ordinary natures must be wiped out.

John Calvin, The Institutes of
Christian Religion, 3.3.8

God's actions

I know that everything God does will last for ever. You can't add anything to it or take anything away from it.

The Bible, Ecclesiastes 3:14

God's care

You will support us both when little and even to grey hairs.

Augustine of Hippo

Are not five sparrows sold for two farthings, and not one of them is forgotten before God?

The Bible, Jesus Christ,
Luke 12:6 (AV)

God's existence

God is that, nothing greater than which can be conceived.

Anselm, Proslogion, 3

At bottom God is nothing more than an exalted father.

Sigmund Freud, Totem and Taboo

If God did not exist, it would be necessary to invent him.

Voltaire, Épîtres, xcvi. A l'Auteur
du Livre des Trois Imposteurs

The evidence for God lies primarily in inner personal experience.

William James

God's faithfulness

The work which his goodness began
The arm of his strength will complete.

Augustus Toplady

God's gifts see also GOD'S

PROVIDENCE; HOLY SPIRIT, GIFTS OF

God's gifts put man's best dreams to shame.

Elizabeth Barrett Browning

God often gives in one brief moment that which he has for a long time denied.

Thomas à Kempis

I have experienced that the habit of taking out of the hand of our Lord every little blessing and brightness on our path, confirms us, in an especial manner, in communion with his love.

M.A. Schimmeleninck

God's goodness

Just as the body wears clothes and the flesh skin, and the bones flesh, and the heart the chest, so we, soul and body are clothed and enfolded in the goodness of God.

Julian of Norwich, Revelations of
Divine Love

Our heavenly Father never takes anything from his children unless he means to give them something better.

George Müller

God's grace see GRACE

God's holiness

Holy, holy, holy, is the Lord of hosts: the whole earth is full of his glory.

The Bible, Isaiah 6:3 (AV)

A true love of God must begin with a delight in his holiness, and not with a delight in any other attribute; for no other attribute is truly lovely without this.

Jonathan Edwards, A Treatise
Concerning Religious Affections

God's image

Christ is the visible likeness of the invisible God.

The Bible, The apostle Paul,
Colossians 1:15

The image of God is worth more than all substances, and we give it for colours, for dreams, for shadows.

John Donne

God's invitation

Ho, every one that thirsteth, come ye to the waters, and he that hath no money; come ye, buy, and eat; yea, come, buy wine and milk without money and without price. Wherefore do ye spend money for that which is not bread? and your labour for that which satisfieth not?

The Bible, Isaiah 55:1–2 (AV)

God's judgement

'I have set a time for judgement,'
    says God,
    'and I will judge every living
    creature with fairness.'

The Bible, Psalm 75:2

For all of us must appear before Christ, to be judged by him. Each one will receive what he deserves, according to everything he has done, good or bad, in his bodily life.

The Bible, The apostle Paul, 2 Corinthians 5:10

I saw the dead, great and small alike, standing before the throne. Books were opened, and then another book was opened, the book of the living. The dead were judged according to what they had done, as recorded in the books.

The Bible, Revelation 20:12

When the elect are all converted, then Christ will come to judgement.

Thomas Watson

It is a hard subject to handle lovingly.

Robert Murray M'Cheyne

God's law   see LAW OF GOD

God's love   see also MOTHERHOOD

The Lord is good;
    his love is eternal
    and his faithfulness lasts for ever.

The Bible, Psalm 100:5

For the Lord is full of compassion and mercy, long-suffering, and very pitiful, and forgiveth sins, and saveth in time of affliction.

The Bible (Apocrypha), Ecclesiasticus 2:11 (AV)

God loves each of us as if there were only one of us to love.

Augustine of Hippo

I drew them to me with affection and love.

I picked them up and held them to my cheek;
I bent down to them and fed them.

The Bible, God, Hosea 11:4

None of us ever desired anything more ardently than God desires to bring men to a knowledge of himself.

John Tauler

For the love of God is broader
    Than the measures of man's mind;
And the heart of the Eternal
    Is most wonderfully kind.

F.W. Faber

Some of us believe that God is almighty and may do everything, and that he is all-wisdom and can do everything; but that he is all-love and wishes to do everything – there we stop short. It is this ignorance, it seems to me, that hinders most of God's lovers.

Julian of Norwich

It was not after we were reconciled by the blood of his Son that God began to love us, but before the foundation of the world.

John Calvin

Grievous is it not to love, and grievous too to love; but far more grievous is it to love and love in vain.

Anacreon

The Lord is not slow to do what he has promised, as some think. Instead, he is patient with you, because he does not want anyone to be destroyed, but wants all to turn away from their sins.

The Bible, 2 Peter 3:9

Do you want to know what our Lord meant in all this? Learn it well: love was what he meant. Who showed it to you? Love. What did he show you? Love. Why did he show it? Out of love. . . . So I was taught that love was what our Lord meant.

Julian of Norwich, Revelations of Divine Love

God's love, Abundance of

The love of God is like the Amazon river flowing down to water one daisy.

Author unknown

God's love, Adversity and

His love in times past
    Forbids me to think
He'll leave me at last
    In trouble to sink;

Each sweet Ebenezer
  I have in review,
Confirms his good pleasure
  To help me quite through.
John Newton

I do not know whether he has any lover on earth whom he always keeps from falling: this was not revealed to me. But what was revealed was that when we fall and when we rise again we are very precious to him and are protected by the same love.
Julian of Norwich, Revelations of
Divine Love

Do you know the Apostles' Creed? ['Of course,' replies the peasant, depressed because he has lost everything in a fire.] Then say it. [He repeats the Creed. Luther asks him to say it again. He does so.] Now, if you really believe what you have just said, surely you cannot doubt that your loving, almighty God will look after your needs?
Martin Luther

God's love, Desire for

I am nothing, I have nothing, I desire nothing but the love of Jesus in Jerusalem.
Walter Hilton, The Scale of
Perfection

Love Divine, all loves excelling,
  Joy of heaven, to earth come down,
Fix in us thy humble dwelling,
  All thy faithful mercies crown.
Charles Wesley

God's love, Judgement and

When the evening of life comes, we shall be judged by God's love.
John of the Cross

God's love, Response to

We love because God first loved us.
The Bible, 1 John 4:19

One second can change your life. You can't stop God from loving you. You can lie, steal, cheat, commit arson or murder. But God will still love you. You have a standing invitation to rejoin him. Refuse a thousand times and the offer still holds. Whatever your problem he can solve it in a second. Accept him and you can rise from your chair and be a new person. 'Be ye transformed by the renewing of your mind.'

Change your thoughts and you change your life.
Author unknown, quoting the
Bible, The apostle Paul,
Romans 12:2 (av)

A man receives God in the soul as often as for love of God he abstains from a fault, be it only a word or an idle glance.
Albert

And can it be, that I should gain
  An interest in the Saviour's blood?
Died he for me, who caused his pain,
  For me, who him to death pursued?
Amazing Love! How can it be
That thou, my God, shouldst die for
  me?
Charles Wesley

God, Thou art love! I build my faith on
  that . . .
I know Thee who has kept my path and
  made
Light for me in the darkness,
  tempering sorrow
So that it reached me like a solemn
  joy.
It were too strange that I should doubt
  Thy love.
Robert Browning

Jesus, lover of my soul,
  Let me to thy bosom fly,
While the nearer waters roll,
  While the tempest still is high;
Hide me, O my Saviour, hide,
  Till the storm of life past;
Safe into the haven glide,
  O receive my soul at last.
Charles Wesley, Hymns and
Sacred Poems, 1740

O love that wilt not let me go,
I rest my weary soul in thee,
I give thee back the life I owe,
That in thine ocean depths its flow
May richer, fuller, be.
George Matheson

Give me the faith which can remove
And sink the mountain to a plain;
Give me the childlike, praying love,
Which longs to build thy house again;
Thy love, let it my heart o'erpower,
Let it my ransomed soul devour.
Charles Wesley

Love bade me welcome: yet my soul
  drew back,
  Guilty of dust and sin.
George Herbert

God's love, inescapable

I know not where his islands lift
  Their fronded palms in air.
I only know I cannot drift
  Beyond his love and care.

John Greenleaf Whittier

To stop God loving me would be to rob him of his Godhood, for God is love no less than he is truth.

Meister Eckhart

God's love, more important than anything else

Human love is capable of great things. What then must be the depth and height and intensity of divine love. Know nothing, think of nothing but Jesus Christ and him crucified.

Lord Shaftesbury, to his schoolboy son who was mortally ill

If you'd ever really got inside the mind of Jesus, ever had a single taste of his burning love, considerations of your own loss or gain would mean nothing to you.

Thomas à Kempis

Painting and sculpture will lose their appeal for the soul turned to that divine love which opened its arms upon the cross to welcome us.

Michelangelo

God's mercy   see also MERCY

Among the attributes of God, although they are all equal, mercy shines with even more brilliance than justice.

Miguel de Cervantes

God's mercy may be found between bridge and stream.

Augustine of Hippo

There's a wideness in God's mercy,
  Like the wideness of the sea;
There's a kindness in his justice,
  Which is more than liberty.

F.W. Faber

God's names   see also NAME OF JESUS

Let not the reader wonder if he find one and the same to be the Prince and Priest, the Bullock, Ram, and Lamb; for in the scripture, on variety of causes, we find him called Lord, God, and Man, the Prophet, a Rod, and the Root, the Flower, Prince, Judge, and Righteous King; Righteousness, the Apostle and Bishop, the Arm and Servant of God, the Angel, the Shepherd, the Son, the Only-begotten, the First-begotten, the Door, the Way, the Arrow, the Wisdom, and sundry other things.

Jerome, Commentary on Ezekiel

The name of God is anything whereby God maketh himself known.

Westminster Shorter Catechism

God's nature

I, the Lord, am a God who is full of compassion and pity, who is not easily angered, and who shows great love and faithfulness. I keep my promise for thousands of generations and forgive evil and sin; but I will not fail to punish children and grandchildren to the third and fourth generation for the sins of their parents.

The Bible, Exodus 34:6–7

The Father of all . . . is all understanding, all spirit, all thought, all hearing, all seeing, all light, and the whole source of everything good.

Irenaeus, Against Heresies, 2.13.3

The more God is in all things, the more he is outside them. The more he is within, the more without.

Meister Eckhart

God, to keep us sober, speaks sparingly of his essence.

John Calvin

God is always active, always quiet.

Augustine of Hippo

God is a Spirit: and they that worship him must worship him in spirit and in truth.

*The Bible, Jesus Christ,
John 4:24 (AV)*

God is a Spirit, infinite, eternal, and unchangeable, in his being, wisdom, power, holiness, justice, goodness and truth.

Shorter Catechism

God is the denial of denials.

Meister Eckhart

God is not in need of anything, but all things are in need of him.

Marcus Aristides

The God of the universe has need of nothing.

Clement of Rome

God's power

One man with God is always in the majority.

Inscription on the Reformation Monument in Geneva

No Goliath is bigger than God.

Author unknown

The greatest single distinguishing feature of the omnipotence of God is that our imagination gets lost thinking about it.

Blaise Pascal, Pensées

God's presence see also HOLY SPIRIT

Remember that I have commanded you to be determined and confident! Don't be afraid or discouraged, for I, the Lord your God, am with you wherever you go.

The Bible, Joshua 1:9

God has said, 'I will never leave you; I will never abandon you.'

The Bible, Hebrews 13:5

[God] is not far away from us. . . . Rather he awaits us every instant in our action, in the work of the moment. There is a sense in which he is at the tip of my pen, my spade, my brush, my needle.

Pierre Teilhard de Chardin

I am always aware of the Lord's presence;
he is near, and nothing can shake me. . . .
You will show me the path that leads to life;
your presence fills me with joy and brings me pleasure for ever.

The Bible, Psalm 16:8, 11

I am certain that nothing can separate us from his love: neither death nor life, neither angels nor other heavenly rulers or powers, neither the present nor the future, neither the world above nor the world below – there is nothing in all creation that will ever be able to separate us from the love of God which is ours through Christ Jesus our Lord.

The Bible, The apostle Paul, Romans 8:38–39

And warm, sweet, tender, even yet
A present help is he;
And faith has still its Olivet,
And love its Galilee.

John Greenleaf Whittier

Be thou a bright flame before me,
Be thou a guiding star above me,
Be thou a smooth path below me,
Be thou a kindly shepherd behind me,
Today – tonight – and for ever.

Columba of Iona

When Jesus is present, all is well, and nothing seems difficult.

Thomas à Kempis, The Imitation of Christ

My living faith was raised, that I saw all was done by Christ the life, and my belief was in him. When at any time my condition was veiled, my secret belief was stayed firm, and hope underneath held me, as an anchor in the bottom of the sea, and anchored my immortal soul.

George Fox, Journal

Breathe through the heats of our desire
Thy coolness and thy balm;
Let sense be dumb, let flesh retire;
Speak through the earthquake, wind, and fire,
O still small voice of calm!

John Greenleaf Whittier

What our Lord did was done with this intent, and this alone, that he might be with us and we with him.

Meister Eckhart

God's presence amid everyday activities

The time of business does not with me differ from the time of prayer; and in the noise and clatter of my kitchen, while several persons are at the same time calling for different things, I possess God in as great tranquillity as if I were upon my knees.

Brother Lawrence

Know that even when you are in the kitchen, our Lord moves amidst the pots and pans.

Teresa of Avila

God's presence and the believer's response

Take no account of who is for you or against you, but let it be your business and care that God be with you in everything you do.

Thomas à Kempis, The Imitation of Christ

Christ has been too long locked up in the mass or in the Book: let him be your prophet, priest and king. Obey him.

George Fox

Having found in many books different methods of going to God, and diverse practices of the spiritual life, I thought this would serve rather to puzzle me than facilitate what I sought after, which was nothing but how to become wholly God's. I began to live as though there was none but he and I in the world. I worshipped him as often as I could, keeping my mind in his holy presence.

Brother Lawrence

Do not forget him, but think on him often, adore him continually, live and die with him; this is the glorious employment of a Christian; in a word, this is our profession; if we do not know it we must learn it. I will endeavour to help you with my prayers.

Brother Lawrence

God's presence in gardens

A garden is a lovesome thing, God wot!
   Rose plot,
   Fringed pool,
Fern'd grot –
   The veriest school
   Of peace; and yet the fool
Contends that God is not –
Not God! In gardens! when the eve is
   cool?
   Nay, but I have a sign;
'Tis very sure God walks in mine.

Thomas Edward Brown

God's presence in prison

Jesus Christ came into my prison cell last night, and every stone flashed like a ruby.

Samuel Rutherford

God's presence in the believer's heart

He departed from our eyes that we should return to our hearts and find him there.

Augustine of Hippo

The Lord showed me, so that I did see clearly, that he did not dwell in these temples which men had commanded and set up, but in people's hearts . . . his people were his temple, and he dwelt in them.

George Fox, Journal

God is nearer to us than our soul, for he is the ground on whom our soul depends.

Julian of Norwich, Revelations of Divine Love

'Who are you,' said Trajan, 'you wretch of a devil, that you are so ready to transgress our orders, whilst seducing others also, that they may come to a bad end?'
Ignatius said, 'No one calls somebody who bears God a wretch of a devil; for the devils stand aloof from the servants of God.'
Trajan said: 'And who is he who bears God?'
Ignatius answered: 'He who has Christ in his breast.'
Trajan said, 'Do you not think then that we too have gods in our heart, seeing that we employ them as allies against our enemies?'
Ignatius said: 'You are deceived, when you call the devils of the nations god. For there is one God who made the heaven and the earth and the sea and all things that are in them, and one Christ Jesus is his only-begotten Son, whose friendship I want to enjoy.'
Trajan said: 'Are you speaking of him who was crucified under Pontius Pilate?'
Ignatius said, 'I speak of him that nailed on the cross sin and its author, and sentenced every malice of the devils to be trampled under foot of those that carry him in their heart.'
Trajan said: 'Do you then carry Christ within yourself?'
Ignatius said: 'Yes, for it is written, "I will dwell in them and will walk about in them".'
Trajan gave sentence: 'It is our order that Ignatius who says he bears about the crucified in himself shall be put to chains by the soldiers and taken to mighty Rome there to be made food for wild beasts, as a spectacle and a diversion for the people.'

The Martyrdom of St Ignatius

I have heard a grave divine say, that God has two dwellings, one in heaven, and the other in the meek and thankful heart.

Izaak Walton

God's presence when there is no other help

Would you like me to tell you what supported me through all the years of exile among a people whose language I could not understand, and whose attitude toward me was always uncertain and often hostile? It was this, 'Lo, I am with you alway, even unto the end of the world.' On these words I staked everything, and they never failed.

David Livingstone

Abide with me, fast falls the eventide;
The darkness deepens; Lord, with me abide:
When other helpers fail, and comforts flee,
Help of the helpless, oh abide with me.

Henry Francis Lyte

God's promises   see PROMISES OF GOD

God's protection

In the shadow of your wings I find protection.

The Bible, Psalm 57:1

Our God is a strong tower.

Martin Luther, after the Bible, Psalm 144:2

When we have once asked for God's protection against evil and have obtained it, then against everything which the devil and the world can do against us, we stand secure and safe. For what fear is there in this life to the man whose guardian in this life is God?

Cyprian, The Lord's Prayer

God be with you till we meet again;
When life's perils thick confound you,
Put his arm unfailing round you:
God be with you till we meet again.

J.E. Rankin

God's provision

What a wonderful experience mine has been during these thirty-nine years! What inexhaustible supplies have been vouchsafed to the work in my hands. How amazing to mere unaided human reason have been the answers to prayer, even when faith has almost failed and our timidity has begotten distrust instead of love and hope! And God has not failed us once!

Thomas Barnardo

Providence has at all times been my only dependence, for all other resources seem to have failed us.

George Washington

The best things are nearest: breath in your nostrils, light in your eyes, flowers at your feet, duties at your hand, the path of God just before you.

Robert Louis Stevenson

God's will

Not everyone who calls me 'Lord, Lord' will enter the Kingdom of heaven, but only those who do what my Father in heaven wants them to do.

The Bible, Jesus Christ, Matthew 7:21

When I vacillated about my decision to serve the Lord my God, it was I who willed, and I who willed not, and nobody else. I was fighting against myself. . . . All you asked was that I cease to want what I willed, and begin to want what you willed.

Augustine of Hippo

I have trained myself not merely to obey God, but to agree with his decisions. I follow him because my soul wills it, and not because I must.

Seneca, Letters, 96.2

The end of life is not to deny self, nor to be true, nor to keep the Ten Commandments – it is simply to do God's will.

Henry Drummond

You are to think of yourself as only existing in this world to do God's will. To think that you are your own is as absurd as to think you are self-created. It is an obvious first principle that you belong completely to God.

William Law

Give what you command, and command what you will. You impose continency upon us.

Augustine of Hippo, Confessions, X.29

Use me from now on for whatever you wish. I am yours; I crave exemption from nothing that seems good in your sight; lead me wherever you will; clothe me in whatever you will.

Epictetus, Discourses 2.16.42

I have submitted my freedom of choice to God. He wants me to have fever; it is my wish too. He wants me to get something; it is my wish too. He does not want it; I do not want it.

Epictetus, Discourses 4.1.89

In doing [God's] will we find our peace.

Dante

A man's heart is right when he wills what God wills.

Thomas Aquinas

God's word

I simply taught, preached, wrote God's word: otherwise I did nothing. And then, while I slept, or drank Wittenberg beer with my friend Philip or my friend Amsdorf, the word so greatly weakened the papacy that no prince or emperor ever inflicted such damage upon it. I did nothing. The word did it all. Had I wished to foment trouble, I could have brought great bloodshed upon Germany. Indeed, I could have started such a game at Worms that the emperor would not have been safe. But what would it have been? A fool's game. I left it to the word.

Martin Luther

God's work

God buries his workmen, but carries on his work.

Proverb quoted by Charles Wesley in one of his letters

God's wrath

Love can forbear, and Love can forgive . . . but Love can never be reconciled to an unlovely object. He can never therefore be reconciled to your sin, because sin itself is incapable of being altered; but he may be reconciled to your person, because that may be restored.

Thomas Traherne

Sometimes when I went on and on discussing silly sins with my confessor, he said, 'You are a fool. God is not incensed against you, but you are incensed against God. God is not angry with you, but you are angry with God.'

Martin Luther

A study of the concordance will show that there are more references in scripture to the anger, fury, and wrath of

God, than there are to his love and tenderness.

A.W. Pink, The Attributes of God

A sentimental and hedonist generation tries to eliminate 'wrath' from its conception of God. Of course, if 'anger' and 'wrath' are taken to mean the emotional reaction of an irritated self-concern, there is no such thing in God. But if God is holy love, and I am in any degree given to uncleanness or selfishness, then there is, in that degree, stark antagonism in God against me.

William Temple, Readings in St John's Gospel

[God's wrath is] identical with the consuming fire of inexorable divine love in relation to our sins.

D.M. Baillie

Good and evil

You call evil good and good evil. You turn darkness into light and light into darkness. You make what is bitter sweet, and what is sweet you make bitter.

The Bible, Isaiah 5:20

Good deeds

The Lord is righteous and loves good deeds; those who do them will live in his presence.

The Bible, Psalm 11:7

Whenever you possibly can, do good to those who need it.

The Bible, Proverbs 3:27

Do not forget to do good and to help one another, because these are the sacrifices that please God.

The Bible, Hebrews 13:16

If a rich person sees his brother in need, yet closes his heart against his brother, how can he claim that he loves God? My children, our love should not be just words and talk; it must be true love, which shows itself in action.

The Bible, 1 John 3:17–18

When you do a good deed, give the credit not to yourself but to God.

Bias

We make a ladder out of our vices if we trample them underfoot.

Augustine of Hippo, Sermons

The greatest pleasure I have known is to do a good action by stealth, and to have it found out by accident.
Charles Lamb, Table Talk

When the day of judgement comes, we shall not be asked what we have read, but what we have done.
Thomas à Kempis, The Imitation of Christ

We have a call to do good, as often as we have the power and the occasion.
William Penn

England! awake! awake! awake!
Jerusalem thy sister calls!
Why wilt thou sleep the sleep of death
And close her from thy ancient walls?
William Blake, Jerusalem

I read somewhere that this young man, Jesus Christ, went about doing good. But I just go about.
Toyohiko Kagawa

To fear God is never to pass over any good thing that ought to be done.
Gregory the Great

Faith is a living, busy, active, powerful thing; it is impossible for it not to do us good continually. It never asks whether good works are to be done, but has done them before there is time to ask the question, and it is always doing them.
Martin Luther

We can do noble acts without ruling earth and sea.
Aristotle

Good deeds, Motive of

The love of God is the principle and end of all our good works.
John Wesley, A Plain Man's Guide to Holiness

Our Lord does not care so much for the importance of our works as for the love with which they are done.
Teresa of Avila

A Christian should always remember that the value of his good works is not based on their number and excellence, but on the love of God which prompts him to do these things.
John of the Cross

We are not made righteous by doing righteous deeds; but when we have been made righteous we do righteous deeds.
Martin Luther, Thesis 40

Good deeds that are done silently and for a good motive, are the dead that live even in the grave; they are flowers that withstand the storm; they are stars that know no setting.
Claudius

No people do so much harm as those who go about doing good.
Mandell Creighton

Do what good you can, and do it solely for God's glory, as free from it yourself as though you did not exist. Ask nothing whatever in return. Done in this way, your works are spiritual and godly.
Meister Eckhart

Good news

As cold waters to a thirsty soul, so is good news from a far country.
The Bible, Proverbs 25:25 (AV)

Gospel

The Sovereign Lord has filled me with
  his spirit.
He has chosen me and sent me
To bring good news to the poor,
To heal the broken-hearted,
To announce release to captives
And freedom to those in prison.
He has sent me to comfort all who
  mourn.
The Bible, Isaiah 61:1–2

The beginning of the gospel is nothing but the whole Old Testament.
Origen, Commentary on John

Gossip

A man who hides his hatred is a liar. Anyone who spreads gossip is a fool.
The Bible, Proverbs 10:18

Gossip is so tasty – how we love to swallow it!
The Bible, Proverbs 18:8

Without wood, a fire goes out; without gossip, quarrelling stops.
The Bible, Proverbs 26:20

Whoever gossips to you will gossip of you.
Spanish proverb

Gossip is mischievous, light and easy to raise, but grievous to bear and hard to get rid of. No gossip ever dies away entirely, if many people voice it: it too is a kind of divinity.
Hesiod, Works and Days

Never listen to accounts of the frailties of others; and if anyone should complain to you of another, humbly ask him not to speak of him at all.

John of the Cross

I lay it down as a fact of life that if all men knew what others say of them, there would not be four friends left in the world.

Blaise Pascal

In scandal as in robbery, the receiver is always thought as bad as the thief.

Lord Chesterfield

Gossip is vice enjoyed vicariously.

Elbert Hubbard

Why do dogs have so many friends? Because they wag their tails and not their tongues!

Author unknown

The only time people dislike gossip is when you gossip about them.

Will Rogers

Gossip is a sort of smoke that comes from the dirty tobacco-pipes of those who diffuse it; it proves nothing but the bad taste of the smoker.

George Eliot, Daniel Deronda

Confidant, confidante: One entrusted by A with the secrets of B confided to himself by C.

Ambrose Bierce, The Devil's Dictionary

Government   see also CHRISTIANS AND THE STATE; DEMOCRACY; POLITICS

You can fool some of the people all the time and all the people some of the time; but you can't fool all the people all of the time.

Abraham Lincoln

When you see the orb set under the cross, remember that the whole world is subject to the power and empire of Christ our Redeemer.

Coronation service for English monarchs, as the sovereign is presented with the golden orb surmounted by a cross

In the field of world policy I would dedicate this nation to the policy of the good neighbour.

Franklin Delano Roosevelt, first inaugural address, 1933

Where some people are very wealthy and others have nothing, the result be

either extreme democracy or absolute oligarchy, or despotism will come from either of those two excesses.

Aristotle, Politics

No man ruleth safely but he that is willingly ruled.

Thomas à Kempis

It is impossible to rightly govern the world without God and the Bible.

George Washington

We here resolve that the dead shall not have died in vain, that this nation, under God, shall have a new birth of freedom; and that government of the people, by the people, and for the people, shall not perish from the earth.

Abraham Lincoln, Gettysburg address

The Bible is for the government of the people, by the people, and for the people.

John Wycliffe

Men must choose to be governed by God, or they condemn themselves to be ruled by tyrants.

William Penn

Grace

Where sin abounded, grace did much more abound.

The Bible, The apostle Paul, Romans 5:20 (AV)

God's mercy is so abundant, and his love for us is so great, that while we were spiritually dead in our disobedience he brought us to life with Christ. It is by God's grace that you have been saved.

The Bible, The apostle Paul, Ephesians 2:4–5

Neither doth a man begin to be converted or changed from evil to good by the beginnings of faith, unless the free and undeserved mercy of God work it in him. Let the grace of God, therefore, be so accounted of, that from the beginnings of his conversion to the end of his perfection, he that glorieth should glory in the Lord. Because, as none can begin a good work without the Lord, so none can perfect it without the Lord.

Augustine of Hippo

There is nothing but God's grace. We walk upon it; we breathe it; we live and die by it; it makes the nails and axles of the universe.

Robert Louis Stevenson

He rides pleasantly enough whom the grace of God carries.

Thomas à Kempis, The Imitation of Christ

The Law works fear and wrath; grace works hope and mercy.

Martin Luther at the Heidelberg Disputation

In thy word, Lord, is my trust,
To thy mercies fast I fly;
Though I am but clay and dust,
Yet thy grace can lift me high.

Thomas Campion

Grace and human will   see also FREE WILL

I reject and condemn as erroneous every doctrine which extols our free will, and fights against the assistance and grace of our Saviour Jesus Christ; because without Christ death and sin rule over us, and the devil is the god and prince of the unconverted world.

Martin Luther

It is certain that we will when we will, but he causes us to will who works in us to will.

Augustine of Hippo

Grace and its effect on the believer

If grace doth not change human nature, I do not know what grace doth.

John Owen

Grace is given to heal the spiritually sick, not to decorate spiritual heroes.

Martin Luther at the Heidelberg Disputation

There, but for the grace of God, goes John Bradford.

John Bradford, as he saw criminals being led away to execution

We have not received the Spirit of God because we believe, but that we may believe.

Fulgentius

By God's grace I am what I am, and the grace that he gave me was not without effect.

The Bible, The apostle Paul, 1 Corinthians 15:10

Grace and nature

Grace does not abolish nature but perfects it.

Thomas Aquinas

Grace is sometimes so weak and feeble that it looks like nature. Nature is sometimes so plausible and well-dressed, that it looks like grace.

J.C. Ryle, Practical Religion

Simply to will comes from man's nature; to will wickedly comes from corrupt nature; to will well, from supernatural grace.

Bernard of Clairvaux

Grace defined

Grace is but glory begun, and glory is but grace perfected.

Jonathan Edwards

Grace is the free, undeserved goodness and favour of God to mankind.

Matthew Henry

Grace (prayer)

I own that I am disposed to say grace upon twenty other occasions in the course of the day besides my dinner. I want a form for setting out upon a pleasant walk, for a moonlight ramble, for a friendly meeting, or a solved problem. Why have we none for books, those spiritual repasts – a grace before Milton – a grace before Shakespeare – a devotional exercise proper to be said before reading the Faerie Queene?

Charles Lamb

Graces

Come Lord Jesus, be our guest,
And may our meal by you be blessed.
Amen.

Martin Luther

Praise God from whom all blessings flow,
Praise him, all creatures here below,
Praise him above, angelic host,
Praise Father, Son and Holy Ghost.

Thomas Ken

Gratitude

The person who has stopped being thankful has fallen asleep in life.

Robert Louis Stevenson

It is the highest and holiest of the paradoxes that the man who really knows he cannot pay his debt will be forever paying it.

G.K. Chesterton

Oh Lord! that lends me life,
Lend me a heart replete with
   thankfulness!

William Shakespeare, Henry in 2 Henry VI, I.i

See that you do not forget what you were before, lest you take for granted the grace and mercy you received from God and forget to express your gratitude each day.
Martin Luther

Gratitude is the heart's memory.
Massieu

Thou that hast given so much to me,
Give one thing more – a grateful heart;
Not thankful when it pleaseth me,
As if thy blessings had spare days;
But such a heart, whose pulse may be
Thy praise.
George Herbert

The children of Israel did not find in the manna all the sweetness and strength they might have found in it – not because the manna did not contain them, but because they longed for other food.
John of the Cross

Gratitude is heaven itself.
William Blake

Count your many blessings,
Name them one by one.
Author unknown

Would you know who is the greatest saint in the world? It is not he who prays most or fasts most, it is not he who lives most, but it is he who is always thankful to God, who receives everything as an instance of God's goodness and has a heart always ready to praise God for it.
William Law

Gratitude and adversity

If I could tell you the shortest, surest way to all happiness and all perfection, it would be to make a rule for yourself to thank and praise God for everything that happens to you. For it is certain that whatever seeming calamity may happen to you, if you thank and praise God for it you turn it into a blessing. If you could work miracles, you would not do more for yourself than to have this wonderful spirit, for it heals by just a word and turns all that it touches into happiness.
William Law

Gratitude and friendship

Gratitude preserves old friendship, and procures new.
Thomas Fuller, Gnomologia

Gratitude and ingratitude

Ingratitude is the sepulchre of love.
Portuguese proverb

Blow, blow, thou winter wind,
Thou art not so unkind
    As man's ingratitude.
William Shakespeare, As You Like It, II.vii.174

Gratitude is the least of virtues, but ingratitude is the worst of vices.
Thomas Fuller, Gnomologia

The earth produces nothing viler than an ungrateful man.
Horace

Ingratitude sickens the heart, chills and thickens goodwill's lifeblood.
William Wilberforce, A Practical View

I believe the best definition of man is the ungrateful biped.
Fyodor Dostoevsky

Gratitude and trust

Let gratitude for the past inspire us with trust for the future.
François Fénelon

Greatness

Greatness lies not in being strong but in the right use of strength.
Henry Ward Beecher

Be not afraid of greatness: some are born great, some achieve greatness and some have greatness thrust upon 'em.
William Shakespeare, Twelfth Night, II.v

To be great is to be misunderstood.
Ralph Waldo Emerson, Essays, Self-Reliance

Greed   see also CONTENTMENT; COVETOUSNESS

The most grievous kind of destitution is to want money in the midst of wealth.
Seneca

Avarice is generally the last passion of those lives of which the first part has been squandered in pleasure, and the second devoted to ambition.
Samuel Johnson

Nothing is enough to the man for whom enough is too little.
Epicurus

A surfeit of the sweetest things,
The deepest loathing to the stomach brings.
William Shakespeare

The covetous man is ever in want.
Horace

Avarice and happiness never saw each other; how then should they be acquainted?
Benjamin Franklin

A greedy rector in gaining loaf loses a hundred.
Spanish proverb, referring to the loaf offered to the priest, who if he berates his parishioners for not bringing loaves may find they take offfence and stop bringing them altogether

Grief   see also BEREAVEMENT; SORROW; TEARS

Grief is the agony of an instant; the indulgence of grief, the blunder of a life.
Benjamin Disraeli

Grief is itself a medicine.
William Cowper, Charity

Growing up

When I was a boy of fourteen, my father was so ignorant I could hardly stand to have the old man around. But when I got to be twenty-one, I was astonished at how much he had learned in seven years.
Mark Twain

Growth, Personal   see also PROGRESS

The Word is all things to the infant: father, mother, teacher and nurse. 'Eat my flesh,' he says, 'and drink my blood.' The Lord gives us this proper nourishment; he offers his flesh and pours out his blood, and the children lack nothing they need for growth.
Clement of Alexandria, Paedagogus, 1.6

Growth is beauty. That's why children are beautiful. Learn from them. Grow mentally.
Author unknown

Everybody wants to *be* somebody: nobody wants to *grow*.
Goethe

I say that man was meant to grow, not stop.
Robert Browning

Growth is the only evidence of life.
J.H. Newman

Growth, Spiritual

It is no good a tree budding and blossoming if the blossom does not develop into fruit. Many people perish in blossom. . . . A man's existence is always in a state of non-being, becoming, and being. . . . He is always in sin, in justification, in righteousness. Always a sinner, always penitent, always justified.
Martin Luther, The Epistle to the Romans

There is nothing that is more dangerous to your own salvation, more unworthy of God and more harmful to your own happiness than that you should be content to remain as you are.
François Fénelon, Christian Perfection

Four stages in the growth of Christian maturity:
Love of self for self's sake;
Love of God for self's sake;
Love of God for God's sake;
Love of self for God's sake.
Bernard of Clairvaux

What you are must always displease you, if you would attain that which you are not.
Augustine of Hippo, Sermons

God's greatest gifts to me are three. First, cessation of carnal desires and pleasures. Secondly, divine light enlightens me in everything I do. Thirdly, daily I grow and am renewed in God's grace.
Meister Eckhart

O Jesus Christ, grow thou in me
And all things else recede. . . .
Let faith in thee and in thy might
My every motive move,
Be thou alone my soul's delight,
My passion and my love.
Johann Kaspar Lavater

Grumbling   see also CONTENTMENT

Do everything without complaining.
The Bible, The apostle Paul, Philippians 2:14

Not even Jupiter can please everybody.
Latin proverb

He labours in vain who tries to please everybody.
Latin proverb

To complain of the age we live in, to murmur at the present possessors of power, to lament the past, to conceive extravagant hopes of the future, are the common dispositions of the greatest part of mankind.

Edmund Burke, Thoughts on the Present Discontents, 1770

Guidance

I praise the Lord, because he guides me.

The Bible, Psalm 16:7

The Lord says, 'I will teach you the way you should go;
I will instruct you and advise you.
Don't be stupid like a horse or mule, which must be controlled with a bit and bridle
to make it submit.'

The Bible, Psalm 32:8–9

Remember the Lord in everything you do, and he will show you the right way.

The Bible, Proverbs 3:6

A nation will fall if it has no guidance. Many advisers mean security.

The Bible, Proverbs 11:14

You may make your plans, but God directs your actions.

The Bible, Proverbs 16:9

Men cast lots to learn God's will, but God himself determines the answer.

The Bible, Proverbs 16:33

Man proposes, God disposes.

Proverb

I hurl the spear, but Jove directs the blow.

Lord Derby, after Homer

Lead us on our journey,
Be thyself the way
Through terrestrial darkness
To celestial day.

G.R. Prynne

Never undertake anything unless you have the heart to ask Heaven's blessing on your undertaking!

Lichtenberg, Aphorisms

I am satisfied that when the Almighty wants me to do or not to do any particular things, he finds a way of letting me know it.

Abraham Lincoln

Guilt

The offender never forgives.

Russian proverb

H

Habits

Good habits are hard to acquire but easy to live with. Bad habits are easy to acquire but hard to live with.

Author unknown

What is most contrary to salvation is not sin, but habit.

Charles Péguy, Basic Verities

The strength of a man's virtue should not be measured by his special exertions, but by his habitual acts.

Blaise Pascal

Habit is a shirt made of iron.

Czech proverb

Habits begin like threads in a spider's web, but end up like ropes.

Spanish proverb

Habit with him was all the test of truth,
'It must be right: I've done it from my youth.'

George Crabbe

Habit both shows and makes the man, for it is at once historic and prophetic, the mirror of the man as he is to be.

A.T. Pierson, George Müller of Bristol

Don't let your sins turn into bad habits.

Teresa of Avila

First we build our habits; then our habits build us.

Author unknown

Sow and act, and you reap a habit. Sow a habit, and you reap a character. Sow a character, and you reap a destiny.

Charles Reade

Habits, Overcoming

The chains of habit are too weak to be felt until they are too strong to be broken.

Samuel Johnson

Nothing is stronger than habit.

Ovid

It is easier to prevent ill habits than to break them.

Thomas Fuller, Gnomologia

I never knew a man to overcome a bad habit gradually.

John R. Mott

Who is strong? He that can conquer his bad habits.

Benjamin Franklin, Poor Richard's Almanac, 1744

Habit is overcome by habit.
> *Thomas à Kempis, The Imitation*
> *of Christ*

Happiness

If you want to be happy, be.
> *Alexei Tolstoy, Kosma Prutkov*

Happiness is the practice of the virtues.
> *Clement of Alexandria*

There is no duty we so much underrate as the duty of being happy. By being happy we sow anonymous benefits upon the world.
> *Robert Louis Stevenson*

Complete happiness is knowing God.
> *John Calvin, The Institutes of*
> *Christian Religion, 1.5.1*

Happiness depends upon ourselves.
> *Aristotle, Nicomachean Ethics*

Happy is the man that findeth wisdom, and the man that getteth understanding.
> *The Bible, Proverbs 3:13 (AV)*

Ask yourself why you are happy, and you cease to be so.
> *John Stuart Mill, Autobiography*

Happiness is a mystery like religion, and should never be rationalised.
> *G.K. Chesterton, Heretics*

Happiness, Effects of

Happiness has many friends.
> *Latin proverb*

Cheerfulness and content are great beautifiers, and are famous preservers of good looks.
> *Charles Dickens*

A cheerful look makes a dish a feast.
> *George Herbert*

Happiness, Lack of

Imperial power is an ocean of miseries.
> *Marcus Aurelius*

In a word, I do not live: I am dead before my time. I have no interest in the world. Everything conspires to embitter my life. My life is a continual death.
> *Mme de Pompadour, Louis XV's*
> *mistress and favourite*

If we only wanted to be happy it would be easy; but we want to be happier than other people, which is almost always difficult, since we think them happier than they are.
> *Montesquieu*

Happiness, Sources of

Seek your happiness in the Lord,
  and he will give you your heart's desire.
> *The Bible, Psalm 37:4*

The supreme happiness of life is the conviction of being loved for yourself, or, more correctly, of being loved in spite of yourself.
> *Victor Hugo, Les Misérables*

Happiness; how little attains
  happiness.
Thus I spoke once and thought myself
  wise.
But it was blasphemy: I have learned
  that now.
Wise fools speak better.
Precisely the least thing, the gentlest,
  the rustling of a lizard, a breath, a
  moment, a twinkling of the eye –
  little makes up the quality of the
  best happiness. Soft!
The world is perfect.
> *Friedrich Nietzsche, Thus Spake*
> *Zarathustra*

Human felicity is produced not so much by great pieces of good fortune that seldom happen as by little advantages that occur every day.
> *Benjamin Franklin*

There is no happiness in having or in getting, but only in giving.
> *Henry Drummond*

There is nothing which has yet been contrived by man by which so much happiness is produced as by a good tavern.
> *Samuel Johnson*

It is the chiefest point of happiness that a man is willing to be what he is.
> *Erasmus*

Wine that maketh glad the heart of man.
> *The Bible, Psalm 104:15 (AV)*

Let him who would be happy for a day, go to the barber; for a week, marry a wife; for a month, buy him a new horse; for a year, build him a new house; for all his life time, be an honest man.
> *Thomas Fuller, History of the*
> *Worthies of England*

Hard times   see also ADVERSITY

Can anybody remember when the times were not hard and money not scarce?
> *Ralph Waldo Emerson, Society*
> *and Solitude*

Haste see RUSH

Hate

Whoever hates his brother is a murderer, and you know that a murderer
has not got eternal life in him.
The Bible, 1 John 3:15

If someone says he loves God, but
hates his brother, he is a liar.
The Bible, 1 John 4:20

Hate is blind as well as love.
Author unknown

Love, friendship, respect, do not unite
people as much as a common hatred
for something.
Anton Chekhov, Note Books

Love blinds us to faults, but hatred
blinds us to virtues.
Moses ibn Ezra

It is human nature to hate the man you
have hurt.
Tacitus

Hatred ceases not to be hatred at any
time. Hatred ceases by love.
Buddha

Love makes everything lovely; hatred
concentrates itself on the one thing
hated.
George Macdonald

It is a short road that leads from fear to
hate.
Italian proverb

Hated by fools, and fools to hate,
Be that my motto and my fate.
Jonathan Swift

Hatred is like fire; it makes even light
rubbish deadly.
George Eliot

Healing see also PAIN

God heals, and the doctor takes the
fee.
*George Herbert, Outlandish
Proverbs*

But unto you that fear my name shall
the Sun of righteousness arise with
healing in his wings.
The Bible, God, Malachi 4:2 (AV)

Health

The mere pursuit of health always
leads to something unhealthy. Physical nature must not be made the direct
object of obedience.
G.K. Chesterton

Hearts

To put the world in order, we must first
put the nation in order; to put the
nation in order, we must put the family
in order; to put the family in order, we
must cultivate our personal life; and to
cultivate our personal life, we must
first set our hearts right.
Confucius

God wants the heart.
The Talmud

Heaven

In my Father's house are many mansions. . . . I go to prepare a place for
you.
*The Bible, Jesus Christ,
John 14:2 (AV)*

Because of his great mercy he gave us
new life by raising Jesus Christ from
death. This fills us with a living hope,
and so we look forward to possessing
the rich blessings that God keeps for
his people. He keeps them for you in
heaven, where they cannot decay or
spoil or fade away.
The Bible, 1 Peter 1:3–4

I was told that the number of those
who were marked with God's seal on
their foreheads was 144,000.
The Bible, Revelation 7:4

A great multitude, which no man
could number, of all nations, and
kindred, and people, and tongues,
stood before the throne, and before
the Lamb.
The Bible, Revelation 7:9 (AV)

Those who live in the Lord never see
each other for the last time.
German proverb

Heaven goes by favour. If it went by
merit, you would stay out and your
dog would go in.
Mark Twain

Hold thou thy cross before my closing
eyes;
Shine through the gloom, and point
me to the skies;
Heaven's morning breaks, and earth's
vain shadows flee;
In life, in death, O Lord, abide with me.
Henry Francis Lyte

Finish then thy New Creation,
Pure and spotless let us be;
Let us see thy great salvation
Perfectly restored in thee,

Changed from glory into glory
  Till in heaven we take our place,
Till we cast our crowns before thee,
  Lost in wonder, love, and praise!
Charles Wesley

When I get to heaven, I shall see three
wonders there. The first wonder will
be to see many there whom I did not
expect to see; the second wonder will
be to miss many people who I did
expect to see; the third and greatest of
all will be to find myself there.
John Newton

The main object of religion is not to
get a man into heaven, but to get
heaven into him.
Thomas Hardy

How far away is heaven? It is not so far
as some imagine. . . . Men full of the
Spirit can look right into heaven.
Dwight L. Moody

Heaven, Nature of

Here lies a poor woman
  who always was tired,
For she liv'd in a place
  where help wasn't hired.
Her last words on earth
  were, Dear friends I am going
Where washing ain't done
  nor sweeping nor sewing,
And everything there
  is exact to my wishes,
For there they don't eat
  and there's no washing of dishes. . . .
Don't mourn for me now,
  don't mourn for me never,
For I'm going to do nothing
  for ever and ever.
*Epitaph quoted in a letter to the
Spectator, 2 September 1922*

We shall rest and we shall see, we shall
see and we shall love, we shall love and
we shall pray, in the end which is no end.
Augustine of Hippo

Bring us, O Lord God, at our last
awakening into the house and gate of
heaven, to enter that gate and dwell in
that house, where there shall be no
darkness nor dazzling, but one equal
light; no noise nor silence, but one
equal music; no fears nor hopes, but
one equal possession; no ends nor
beginnings, but one equal eternity; in
the habitations of thy glory and domin-
ion, world without end.
John Donne

He will wipe away all tears from their
eyes. There will be no more death, no
more grief or crying or pain. The old
things have disappeared.
The Bible, Revelation 21:4

I did not see a temple in the city,
because its temple is the Lord God
Almighty and the Lamb.
The Bible, Revelation 21:22

There is a land of pure delight,
  Where saints immortal reign;
Infinite day excludes the night,
  And pleasures banish pain.
*Isaac Watts, Hymns and Spiritual
Songs*

The only air of the soul, in which it can
breathe and live, is the present God
and the spirits of the just: that is our
heaven, our home, our all-right place.
George Macdonald

Heaven, Ways to

All the way to heaven is heaven.
Catherine of Siena

Here in this world he bids us come,
there in the next he shall bid us welcome.
John Donne

Many might go to heaven with half the
labour they go to hell.
Ben Jonson

Though with great difficulty I am got
hither, yet now I do not repent me of
all the trouble I have been at to arrive
where I am. My sword, I give to him
that shall succeed me in my pilgrimage, and my courage and skill to him
that can get it. My marks and scars I
carry with me, to be a witness for me,
that I have fought his battles, who will
now be my rewarder. . . . So he passed
over, and the trumpets sounded for
him on the other side.
*John Bunyan, The Pilgrim's
Progress, ii*

Hebrews 11

Hebrews 11 is the Westminster Abbey
of the Bible.
Author unknown

Hell

He will give relief to you who suffer
and to us as well. He will do this when
the Lord Jesus appears from heaven
with his mighty angels, with a flaming
fire, to punish those who reject God

and who do not obey the Good News about our Lord Jesus. They will suffer the punishment of eternal destruction, separated from the presence of the Lord and from his glorious might.

The Bible, The apostle Paul,
2 Thessalonians 1:7–9

Disbelieve hell, and you unscrew, unsettle, and unpin everything in scripture.

J.C. Ryle, Practical Religion

The lost enjoy for ever the horrible freedom they have demanded, and are therefore self-enslaved.

C.S. Lewis, The Problem of Pain

If I never spoke of hell, I should think I had kept back something that was profitable, and should look on myself as an accomplice of the devil.

J.C. Ryle, Practical Religion

Beware of new and strange doctrines about hell and the eternity of punishment.

J.C. Ryle, Practical Religion

There is no greater delusion than the common idea that it is possible to live wickedly, and yet rise again gloriously; to be without religion in this world, and yet to be a saint in the next.

J.C. Ryle, Practical Religion

Grace leads the right way – if you choose the wrong,
Take it, and perish, but restrain your tongue;
Charge not, with light sufficient and left free,
Your wilful suicide on God's decree.

William Cowper

The watchman who keeps silent when he sees a fire is guilty of gross neglect. The doctor who tells us we are getting well when we are dying is a false friend, and the minister who keeps back hell from his people in his sermons is neither a faithful nor a charitable man.

J.C. Ryle

Hell is paved with priests' skulls.

John Chrysostom, Letters

Men are not in hell because God is angry with them: they are in wrath and darkness because they have done to the light which infinitely flows forth from God as that man does to the light of the sun who puts out his own eyes.

William Law

The hottest places in hell are reserved for those who in time of great moral crises maintain their neutrality.

Dante

Hell, Nature of

Hell is nothing else but nature departed or excluded from the beams of divine light.

William Law

Annihilation is an everlasting punishment, though it is not unending torment.

William Temple

The one principle of hell is: 'I am my own.'

George Macdonald

Hell, Ways to

Then I saw that there was a way to Hell, even from the gates of heaven.

John Bunyan, The Pilgrim's
Progress

The safest road to Hell is the gradual one – the gentle slope, soft underfoot, without sudden turnings, without milestones, without signposts.

C.S. Lewis, The Screwtape letters

The road to hell is easy to travel.

Bion, quoted in Diogenes Laertius

The road to hell is paved with good intentions.

Proverb

Heresy see also DOCTRINE; PERSECUTION

Anyone who does not stay with the teaching of Christ, but goes beyond it, does not have God.

The Bible, 2 John 9

Avoid heretics like wild beasts; for they are mad dogs who bite in secret. You must be on your guard against them; their bite is not easily cured.

Ignatius of Antioch

Heresy is a spiritual thing, cut with no iron, burned with no fuse, drowned with no water. Even if we burned by force every Jew and heretic, there neither would be, nor will there be, one person conquered or converted thereby.

Martin Luther, Of Worldly Power

A heretic . . . is a fellow who disagrees with you regarding something neither of you knows anything about.

William Cowper Brann

You are not to suppose, brethren, that heresies could be produced through any little souls. None save great men have been the authors of heresies.

Augustine of Hippo

History

History is bunk.

Henry Ford

Those who cannot remember the past are doomed to repeat it.

George Santayana

The study of history is the beginning of political wisdom.

Jean Bodin

History is a set of lies agreed upon.

Napoleon

History: an account mostly false, of events mostly unimportant, which are brought about by rulers mostly knaves, and soldiers mostly fools.

Ambrose Bierce, The Devil's Dictionary

Dwell in the past and you'll lose an eye. Forget the past and you'll lose both eyes.

Russian proverb

Study the past if you would divine the future.

Confucius, Analects

He who learns nothing from the past will be punished by the future.

Author unknown

History is philosophy teaching by examples.

Dionysius of Halicarnassus, Ars rhetorica

History is the essence of innumerable biographies.

Thomas Carlyle, Essay on History

There is properly no history; only biography.

Ralph Waldo Emerson, Essays, History

History and Jesus Christ

All history is incomprehensible without Christ.

Ernest Renan

Christ is the central fact in the world's history. To him everything looks forward or backward. All the lines of history converge upon him. All the great purposes of God culminate in him. The greatest and most momentous fact which the history of the world records is the fact of his birth.

C.H. Spurgeon

History, which is, indeed, little more than the register of the crimes, follies, and misfortunes of mankind.

Edward Gibbon, Decline and Fall of the Roman Empire, ch. 3.

Holiness   see also GOD'S HOLINESS; PERFECTION; UNION WITH GOD

To reform the nation, particularly the church, and to spread scriptural holiness over the land.

John Wesley's objective

How little people know who think that holiness is dull. When one meets the real thing . . . it is irresistible.

C.S. Lewis, Letters to an American Lady

The Christian must be consumed by the conviction of the infinite beauty of holiness and the infinite damnability of sin.

Thomas Carlyle

Take time to be holy,
　let him be thy guide;
And run not before him,
　whatever betide;
In joy or in sorrow,
　still follow thy Lord,
And, looking to Jesus,
　still trust in his word.

W.D. Longstaff

There is no greater holiness than in procuring and rejoicing in another's good.

Herbert

The perfume of holiness travels even against the wind.

Indian proverb

It is not great talents God blesses so much as great likeness to Jesus. A holy minister is an aweful weapon in the hand of God.

Robert Murray M'Cheyne

Study universal holiness of life. Your whole usefulness depends on this.

Robert Murray M'Cheyne

The more we appropriate God into our lives the more progress we make on the road of Christian godliness and holiness.

Madame Guyon, A Short and Easy Method of Prayer

Nothing but the name of Jesus can restrain the impulse of anger, repress the swelling of pride, cure the world of envy, bridle the onslaught of luxury, extinguish the flame of carnal desire –

can temper avarice, and put to flight
impure and ignoble thoughts.
Bernard of Clairvaux

If you Christians would live like Jesus
Christ, India would be at your feet
tomorrow.
*Bara Dada, quoted by E. Stanley
Jones, The Christ of the Indian
Road*

Let him who would indeed be a Christian . . . learn from . . . the lives of
eminent Christians the best ways to
overcome temptation and to grow in
every aspect of holiness.
*William Wilberforce, A Practical
View*

A holy life will produce the deepest
impression. Lighthouses blow no
horns; they only shine.
Dwight L. Moody

The serene beauty of a holy life is the
most powerful influence in the world
next to the power of God.
Blaise Pascal

Things that are holy are revealed only
to men who are holy.
Hippocrates

Holy Spirit

Afterwards I will pour out my spirit on
   everyone:
   your sons and daughters will
     proclaim my message;
   your old men will have dreams,
and your young men will see visions.
At that time I will pour out my spirit
   even on servants, both men and
   women.
The Bible, God, Joel 2:28–29

I will ask the Father, and he will give
you another Helper, who will stay with
you for ever. He is the Spirit who
reveals the truth about God. The
world cannot receive him, because it
cannot see him or know him. But you
know him, because he remains with
you and is in you. When I go, you will
not be left all alone; I will come back to
you.
*The Bible, Jesus Christ,
John 14:16–18*

That anyone should be represented as
just and God-fearing who does not
have the Spirit would be the same as if
Belial were called Christ.
Martin Luther

We share in the divine nature through
our sharing of the Spirit.
Athanasius, Letter to Serapion

What gives life is God's Spirit.
The Bible, Jesus Christ, John 6:63

Just as someone who does right things
becomes more enlightened, so the
shining spirit comes closer to him.
*Clement of Alexandria,
Stromateis, 4.17*

When the Spirit came to Moses, the
plagues came upon Egypt, and he had
power to destroy men's lives; when the
Spirit came upon Elijah, fire came
down from heaven; when the Spirit
came upon Joshua, he moved around
the city of Jericho, and the whole city
fell into his hands. But when the Spirit
came upon the Son of Man, he gave his
life, he healed the broken-hearted.
Dwight L. Moody

All the minister's efforts will be vanity
or worse than vanity if he have not
unction. Unction must come from
heaven and spread a savour and feeling and relish over his ministry.
Richard Cecil

There is not a better evangelist in the
world than the Holy Spirit.
Dwight L. Moody

Those who have the gale of the Holy
Spirit go forward even in sleep.
Brother Lawrence

What God chooses, he cleanses.
What God cleanses, he moulds.
What God moulds, he fills.
What God fills, he uses.
J.S. Baxter

Holy Spirit, Fruit of the

The fruit of the Spirit is love, joy, peace,
longsuffering, gentleness, goodness,
faith, meekness, temperance.
*The Bible, The apostle Paul,
Galatians 5:22 (AV)*

The Spirit of God first imparts love; he
next inspires hope, and then gives liberty; and that is about the last thing we
have in many of our churches.
Dwight L. Moody

Holy Spirit, Gifts of the

Come, Holy Ghost, our souls inspire,
And lighten with celestial fire;
Thou the anointing Spirit art,
Who dost thy sevenfold gifts impart.
J. Cosin, based on a Latin hymn

Now there are diversities of gifts, but the same Spirit.

The Bible, The apostle Paul,
1 Corinthians 12:4 (AV)

Some people drive out devils . . . some can see into the future . . . others heal the sick through the laying on of hands . . . and even the dead have been raised before now and have remained with us for many years.

Irenaeus, Against Heresies, 2.32.4

Gifts . . . excite and stir up grace unto its proper exercise and operation. How often is faith, love, and delight in God, excited and drawn forth unto especial exercise in believers by the use of their own gifts!

John Owen, Of Spiritual Gifts

Prayer is a principal means for their attainment. This the apostle directs unto when he enjoins us earnestly to desire the best gifts; for this desire is to be acted by prayer, and no otherwise.

John Owen, Of Spiritual Gifts

Sir, the pretending to extraordinary revelations and gifts of the Holy Ghost is a horrid thing, a very horrid thing.

Joseph Butler, to John Wesley

Holy Spirit, Indwelling of the

The philosophers of old made reason the sole ruler of man and listened only to her, as the arbiter of conduct. But Christian philosophy makes her move aside and give complete submission to the Holy Spirit, so that the individual no longer lives, but Christ lives and reigns in him (Galatians 2:20).

John Calvin, The Institutes of
Christian Religion, 3.7.1

Ephesians 5.18 is not just an experience to be enjoyed but a command to be obeyed. If we do not open ourselves to a daily encounter with the Holy Spirit, then the inevitable conclusion is that we are disobedient Christians.

Dwight L. Moody

Holy Spirit and free will

God works immediately by his Spirit in and on the wills of his saints.

John Owen

Our nature is so vitiated, and has such a propensity to sin, that unless it is renewed by the Holy Spirit, no man can do or will what is good of himself.

Confession of Basil

Holy Spirit and the Bible   see also BIBLE, INSPIRATION OF

The Spirit breathes upon the Word,
And brings the truth to sight.

William Cowper

Holy Spirit and the Church

If you do not join in what the church is doing, you have no share in this Spirit. . . . For where the church is, there is the Spirit of God; and where the Spirit of God is, there is the church and every kind of grace.

Irenaeus, Against Heresies, 3.24.1

Holy Spirit and work

For the attainment of divine knowledge, we are directed to combine a dependence on God's Spirit with our own researches. Let us, then, not presume to separate what God has thus united.

Charles Simeon

We need the Spirit of Christ, without whom all our works are only worthy of condemnation.

Martin Luther

Home   see also HOSPITALITY

Except the Lord build the house, they labour in vain that build it.

The Bible, Psalm 126:1 (AV)

The strength of a nation is derived from the integrity of its home.

Confucius

Pity the home where everyone is the head.

Jewish proverb

Let a man behave in his own house as a guest.

Ralph Waldo Emerson

A charcoal-burner is master in his own house.

French proverb, alluding to the
story of the charcoal-burner who
set before his guest, who turned out
to be the king, a boar's head
poached from the royal forest

Like a bird in the forest
    whose home is its nest,
My home is my all
    and my centre of rest.

John Clare

A comfortable house is a great source of happiness. It ranks immediately after health and a good conscience.

Sydney Smith

Home is where the heart is.
Pliny the Elder

Honesty

Wealth that you get by dishonesty will do you no good, but honesty can save your life.
The Bible, Proverbs 10:2

The Lord wants weights and measures to be honest and every sale to be fair.
The Bible, Proverbs 16:11

An honest man's the noblest work of God.
Alexander Pope, Essay on Man

No legacy is so rich as honesty.
William Shakespeare, All's Well that Ends Well, III.v

Honesty is the first chapter of the book of wisdom.
Thomas Jefferson

Honour

A godly mind prizes honour above worldly good.
Rembrandt; written in a guest book

It is better to deserve honours and not have them than to have them and not deserve them.
Mark Twain

Dignity does not consist in possessing honours, but in deserving them.
Aristotle

Hope

If you do not hope, you will not find what is beyond your hopes.
Clement of Alexandria, Stromateis

The virtue of hope is an orientation of the soul towards a transformation after which it will be wholly and exclusively love.
Simone Weil

Hope is a waking dream.
Aristotle, quoted in Diogenes Laertius, Lives and Opinions of Eminent Philosophers

Every blade of grass, each leaf, each separate petal, is an inscription speaking of hope.
Richard Jefferies

Under the shadow of thy throne
    Thy saints have dwelt secure;
Sufficient is thine arm alone,
    And our defence is sure.
Isaac Watts

Totally without hope one cannot live. To live without hope is to cease to live.

Hell is hopelessness. It is no accident that above the entrance to Dante's hell is the inscription: 'Leave behind all hope, you who enter here.'
Fyodor Dostoevsky

Whatever enlarges hope will also exalt courage.
Samuel Johnson

Let your hook be always cast; in the pool where you least expect it, there will be a fish.
Ovid

Hope springs eternal in the human breast;
Man never is, but always to be blest.
Alexander Pope, Essay on Man, 1.95

Everything that is done in the world is done by hope.
Martin Luther

In God alone is there faithfulness and faith in the trust that we may hold to him, to his promise, and to his guidance. To hold to God is to rely on the fact that God is there for me, and to live in this certainty.
Karl Barth

Hope deferred makes the heart sick.
Proverb

Great hopes make great men.
Thomas Fuller

Hope is the pillar that holds up the world.
Hope is the dream of a waking man.
Pliny the Elder

It is not necessary to hope in order to undertake, nor to succeed in order to persevere.
Charles the Bold

A religious hope does not only bear up the mind under her sufferings, but makes her rejoice in them.
Joseph Addison

The word 'hope' I take for faith; and indeed hope is nothing else but the constancy of faith.
John Calvin

Hopelessness

In every department of our nation, industry, commerce and agriculture, there is no hope.
Benjamin Disraeli, 1852

I thank God I shall be spared the consummation of ruin that is gathering around us.
Duke of Wellington

Hospitality

Remember to welcome strangers in your homes. There were some who did that and welcomed angels without knowing it.

The Bible, Hebrews 13:2

If a man be gracious to strangers it shows that he is a citizen of the world and that his heart is no island, cut off from other islands, but a continent that joins them.

Francis Bacon

To welcome a fellow man is to welcome the Shekhinah [divine presence].

Jewish proverb

To succour the orphans and widows, and those who through sickness or any other cause are in want, and those who are in bonds, and the strangers sojourning amongst us.

Justin Martyr, A.D. 170, describing the duty of the president of the Christian congregation, having received offerings from the well-to-do members

Human nature   see BELONGING; MANKIND; RELATIONSHIPS

Human rights

We hold these truths to be self-evident, that all men are created equal, that they are endowed by their Creator with certain unalienable rights, that among these are life, liberty and the pursuit of happiness.

American Declaration of Independence, 1776

All human beings are born free and equal in dignity and rights.

Universal Declaration of Human Rights, 1948

Humility

The greatest in the Kingdom of heaven is the one who humbles himself and becomes like this child.

The Bible, Jesus Christ, Matthew 18:4

The church must learn humility, as well as teach it.

George Bernard Shaw

Christian humility is based on the sight of self, the vision of Christ, and the realisation of God.

William Barclay, The Letter to the Ephesians

Humility comes from the constant sense of our own creatureliness.

R.C. Trench

Christ is with the humble, not with those who set themselves up over his flock.

Clement of Rome, Epistle to the Corinthians

Christ is the humility of God embodied in human nature; the Eternal Love humbling itself, clothing itself in the garb of meekness and gentleness, to win and serve and save us.

Andrew Murray

Humility is simply the disposition which prepares the soul for living on trust.

Andrew Murray

The only wisdom we can hope to acquire is the wisdom of humility.

T.S. Eliot

My children, said my grandfather, you will never see anything worse than yourselves.

Ralph Waldo Emerson

Man knows mighty little, and may some day learn enough of his own ignorance to fall down and pray.

Henry Adams

Without humility there can be no humanity.

John Buchan

An able yet humble man is a jewel worth a kingdom.

William Penn

When the church is prostrated in the dust before God, and is in the depth of agony in prayer, the blessing does them good. While at the same time, if they had received the blessing without this deep prostration of soul, it would have puffed them up with pride. But as it is, it increases their holiness, their love, their humility.

Charles G. Finney

An ass laden with sacred relics.

La Fontaine's fable in which a donkey thinks the worship of his load is being accorded to himself

The first test of a really great man is his humility.

John Ruskin, Modern Painters

In peace there's nothing so becomes a man
As modest stillness and humility.

William Shakespeare, Henry V, III.i

Humility, Examples of

The first I knew the delight of being lowly; of saying to myself, 'I am what I am, nothing more.'

George Macdonald

God's most holy eyes have not found among sinners any smaller man, nor any more insufficient and sinful, therefore he has chosen me to accomplish the marvellous work which he has undertaken; he chose me because he could find none more worthless, and he wished to confound the nobility and grandeur, the strength, the beauty and the learning of this world.

Francis of Assisi

I do not know that I ever had what Christians call zeal.

Dr Buchanan, who exhausted body and mind in the effort to awaken Christians to the importance of missions

Lord, help me to begin to begin.

George Whitefield, whose indefatigable preaching was the means of conversion of thousands in England and America

None but God knows what an abyss of corruption is in my heart. It is perfectly wonderful that ever God could bless such a ministry.

Robert Murray M'Cheyne, who died at 29 after bringing untold blessing to the Church of Scotland through his preaching

Humility, Exhortations to

Humble yourself in all things.

Thomas à Kempis, The Imitation of Christ

Let every day be a day of humility; condescend to all the weaknesses and infirmities of your fellow-creatures, cover their frailties, love their excellencies, encourage their virtues, relieve their wants, rejoice in their prosperities, compassionate their distress, receive their friendship, overlook their unkindness, forgive their malice, be a servant of servants, and condescend to do the lowliest offices of the lowest of mankind.

William Law, A Serious Call to a Devout and Holy Life

Humility, False

Too humble is half proud.

Hanan J. Ayalti, Yiddish Proverbs

What we suffer from today is humility in the wrong place. Modesty has settled on the organ of conviction; where it was never meant to be. A man was meant to be doubtful about himself but undoubting about the truth. This has been exactly reversed.

G.K. Chesterton

False humility is to believe that one is unworthy of God's goodness and does not dare to seek it humbly. True humility lies in seeing one's own unworthiness, giving up oneself to God, not doubting for a moment that he can perform the greatest results for us and in us.

François Fénelon, Christian Perfection, letter of 22 July 1690

I am well aware that I am the 'umblest person going . . . 'umble we are, 'umble we have been, 'umble we ever shall be.

Charles Dickens, David Copperfield

Humility, Importance of in Christianity

We must view humility as one of the most essential things that characterise true Christianity.

Jonathan Edwards, Treatise Concerning the Religious Affections

Humility is not a mere ornament of a Christian, but an essential part of the new creature. It is a contradiction to be a true Christian and not humble. All that will be Christians must be Christ's disciples and come to him to learn, and their lesson is to be 'meek and lowly'.

Richard Baxter

We may as well try to see without eyes, or live without breath, as to live in the spirit of religion without humility.

William Law

There is no love of God without patience, and no patience without lowliness and sweetness of spirit. Humility and patience are the surest proofs of the increase of love.

John Wesley, A Plain Man's Guide to Holiness

The foundation of our philosophy is humility.

John Chrysostom

When certain rhetorician was asked what was the chief rule of eloquence he replied, 'Delivery.' What was the second rule? 'Delivery.' What was the third rule? 'Delivery.' So if you ask me about the precepts of the Christian religion, first, second, third and always I would answer, 'Humility.'

Augustine of Hippo

Humility, Learning

What you lack and not what you have is the quickest path to humility.

Author unknown, The Cloud of Unknowing

Life is a long lesson in humility.

J.M. Barrie

Humility is not a grace that can be acquired in a few months: it is the work of a lifetime.

François Fénelon, Christian Perfection, letter to a lady

Humility, Nature of

Humility is to make a right estimate of one's self.

C.H. Spurgeon, Gleanings Among the Sheaves

The reason why God is so great a lover of humility is because he is the great lover of truth. Now humility is nothing but truth, while pride is nothing but lying.

Vincent de Paul

True humility is a kind of self-annihilation, and this is the centre of all virtues.

John Wesley, A Plain Man's Guide to Holiness

The sufficiency of my merit is to know that my merit is not sufficient.

Augustine of Hippo

Humility, a sense of reverence before the sons of heaven –
of all the prizes that a mortal man might win,
these, I say, are wisest; these are best.

Euripides, The Bacchae

Love to be unknown and esteemed as nothing.

Thomas à Kempis, The Imitation of Christ

Humility, Rewards of

You save those who are humble, but you humble those who are proud.

The Bible, Psalm 18:27

It is better to be asked to take a higher position than to be told to give your place to someone more important.

The Bible, Proverbs 25:7

Blessed are the meek: for they shall inherit the earth.

The Bible, Jesus Christ, Matthew 5:5 (AV)

Humour   see also LAUGHTER

Humour is mankind's greatest blessing.

Mark Twain

True humour springs not more from the head than from the heart; it is not contempt, its essence is love.

Thomas Carlyle

Hunger

You cannot reason with a hungry belly, since it has no ears.

Greek proverb

Hurry   see RUSH

Husbands

Husbands, love your wives.

The Bible, The apostle Paul, Colossians 3:19

A husband's power over his wife is paternal and friendly, not magisterial and despotic.

Jeremy Taylor

It is necessary to be almost a genius to make a good husband.

Honoré de Balzac, Physiology of Marriage

Being a husband is a whole-time job. That is why so many husbands fail. They cannot give their entire attention to it.

Arnold Bennett, The Title, Act I

Hypocrisy

A hypocrite hides his hate behind flattering words.

The Bible, Proverbs 26:24

Do not live one way in private, and another in public.

Quintilian

One may smile, and smile, and be a villain.

William Shakespeare

A bad man is worse when he pretends to be a saint.

Francis Bacon

Hypocrisy can plunge the mind of a man into a dark abyss, when he believes his own self-flattery instead of God's verdict.

John Calvin, The Institutes of Christian Religion, 3.13.3

I

Ideals

An ideal is never yours until it comes out of your finger tips.
Florence Allshorn

Ideas

A man with a new idea is a crank, until the idea succeeds.
Mark Twain

Neither man nor nation can exist without a sublime idea.
Fyodor Dostoevsky

There is one thing that is stronger than armies – an idea whose time has come.
Victor Hugo

Daring ideas are like chessmen moved forward; they may be beaten, but they may start a winning game.
Goethe

Whoso shrinks from ideas ends by having nothing but sensations.
Goethe

One of the greatest pains to human nature is the pain of a new idea.
Walter Bagehot, Physics and Politics

Idleness   see also Action; Effort

Go to the ant, thou sluggard; consider her ways, and be wise.
The Bible, Proverbs 6:6 (AV)

Being lazy will make you poor, but hard work will make you rich.
The Bible, Proverbs 10:4

Hard work will give you power; being lazy will make you a slave.
The Bible, Proverbs 12:24

A lazy person is as bad as someone who is destructive.
The Bible, Proverbs 18:9

When a man is too lazy to repair his roof, it will leak, and the house will fall in.
The Bible, Ecclesiastes 10:18

'You bad and lazy servant!'
The Bible, the master in Jesus Christ's parable of the three servants, Matthew 25:26

Work hard and do not be lazy.
The Bible, The apostle Paul, Romans 12:11

We do not want you to become lazy.
The Bible, Hebrews 6:12

Never be entirely idle; but either be reading, or writing, or praying, or meditating, or endeavouring something for the public good.
Thomas à Kempis

To do nothing is in every man's power.
Samuel Johnson

Men were created to do something, that they might not be idle and unoccupied. God condemned in his person all idleness.
John Calvin, Commentary on Genesis 2:15

Let us use the gifts of God lest they be extinguished by our slothfulness.
John Calvin

Idleness is the key to Poverty's door.
German proverb

The true, living faith, which the Holy Spirit instils into the heart, simply cannot be idle.
Martin Luther

Idleness is the mother of want.
Greek proverb

Shun idleness even if you are wealthy.
Thales

Hunger is the constant companion of the idle man.
Hesiod

As worms breed in a pool of stagnant water, so evil thoughts breed in the mind of the idle.
Latin proverb

Satan finds work for idle hands to do.
Proverb

Activity may lead to evil; but inactivity cannot be led to good.
Hannah More, Tracts

Idleness, Sacred

Work is not always required of a man. There is such a thing as sacred idleness, the cultivation of which is now fearfully neglected.
George Macdonald

Idols

If you are going to turn to the Lord with all your hearts, you must get rid of all the foreign gods and the images of the goddess Astarte. Dedicate yourselves completely to the Lord and worship only him.
The Bible, Samuel, 1 Samuel 7:3

Idolatry is an attempt to use God for man's purposes, rather than to give oneself to God's service.
C.F.D. Moule

They did not stop worshipping demons, nor the idols of gold, silver, bronze, stone, and wood, which cannot see, hear, or walk.

The Bible, Revelation 9:20

Three things there be in Man's opinion dear:
Fame, many *Friends*, and *Fortune*'s dignities;
False visions all, which in our sense appear
To sanctify desire's Idolatries.

Fulke Greville

The dearest idol I have known,
    Whate'er that idol be,
Help me to tear it from thy throne,
    And worship only thee.

William Cowper

Idols defined

The calves of Jeroboam still remain in the world, and will remain to the last day . . . but whatever a man depends on or trusts, except for God, this is the calves of Jeroboam, that is, other and strange gods, honoured and worshipped instead of the only, true, living and eternal God, who only can and will help and comfort in time of need. Similarly, all those who rely and depend on their art, wisdom, strength, sanctity, riches, honour, power, or anything else which the world builds on, whatever it is called, they make and worship the calves of Jeroboam.

Martin Luther

That to which your heart clings is your god.

Martin Luther

My sin was this, that not in him but in his creatures – myself and others – I sought for pleasures, honours, and truths, and so fell headlong into sorrows, confusions, errors.

Augustine of Hippo

Ignorance

Herein is the evil of ignorance, that he who is neither good nor wise nevertheless satisfied with himself: he has no desire for that of which he feels no want.

Socrates

One part of knowledge consists in being ignorant of such things as are not worthy to be known.

Crates

Ignorance is not innocence, but sin.

Robert Browning, The Inn Album

There is nothing more frightful than ignorance in action.

Goethe

Ignorance of what is better is often the cause of sin.

Democritus

We are all ignorant, only on different subjects.

Will Rogers

It is worse still to be ignorant of your ignorance.

Jerome, Letters, 53

We need not be ashamed to be ignorant in an area where to realise our ignorance is to be learned.

John Calvin, The Institutes of Christian Religion, 3.21.2

I believe in the forgiveness of sins and the redemption of ignorance.

Adlai Stevenson

I have never met a man so ignorant that I couldn't learn something from him.

Galileo

Illness

Before all things and above all things, care must be taken of the sick, so that they may be served in very deed as Christ himself.

Benedict, Rule

All diseases of Christians are to be ascribed to demons.

Augustine of Hippo

Imagination

Imagination cannot make fools wise; but she can make them happy, to the envy of reason, who can only make her friends miserable.

Blaise Pascal

Imagination is more important than knowledge.

Albert Einstein

Imitation of God

First you must learn what is the nature of the gods, for as the gods are found to be, so must man try to resemble them, if he would please and obey them.

Epictetus

Immortality

Even Pliny, one of the most intelligent Latin writers, in his *Natural History*, says there were two things which were beyond the power of God – one was to give immortality to mortals, and the other was to give bodily life again to the dead.

J.C. Ryle, The Upper Room

Spring – an experience in immortality.

Henry David Thoreau

Surely God would not have created such a being as man . . . to exist only for a day! No, no, man was made for immortality.

Abraham Lincoln

Incarnation

Never can man and God meet.

Plato

God is away beyond everything.

Celsus, ridiculing the description of God as Father

The Word was made man in order that we might be made divine.

Athanasius, On the Incarnation, 54

Christ, by highest heaven adored,
Christ, the everlasting Lord,
Late in time behold him come,
Offspring of a virgin's womb.
Veiled in flesh the Godhead see;
Hail, the incarnate Deity,
Pleased as Man with man to dwell,
Jesus our Immanuel!

Charles Wesley

Indecision

There is no more miserable human being than one in whom nothing is habitual but indecision.

William James

They are decided only to be un-decided, resolved to be irresolute, adamant for drift, all-powerful for impotence.

Winston Churchill

Indifference

Nothing is so fatal to religion as indif-ference, which is, at least, half infidelity.

Edmund Burke, letter to William Smith, 1795

Silence is the worst form of persecu-tion.

Blaise Pascal

When Jesus came to Golgotha
they hanged him on a tree;
they drove great nails through hands and feet,
and made a Calvary;

they crowned him with a crown of thorns,
red were his wounds and deep,
for those were crude and cruel days,
and human flesh was cheap.
When Jesus came to Birmingham
they simply passed him by,
they never hurt a hair of him,
they only let him die;
for men had grown more tender,
and they would not give him pain,
they only just passed down the street
and left him in the rain.
Still Jesus cried, 'forgive them
for they know not what they do'.
And still it rained the wintry rain
that drenched him through and through;
the crowds went home and left the streets
without a soul to see,
and Jesus crouched against the wall
and cried for Calvary.

G.A. Studdert-Kennedy

Individuals

A whole bushel of wheat is made up of single grains.

Thomas Fuller

We forfeit three-fourths of ourselves in order to be like other people.

Arthur Schopenhauer

A man like Verdi must write like Verdi.

Giuseppina Verdi

It is not best that we should all think alike; it is difference of opinion which makes horse races.

Mark Twain

If [God] has no use for all these differ-ences, I do not see why he should have created more souls than one. . . . Your soul has a curious shape because it is a hollow made to fit a particular swelling in the infinite contours of the divine substance, or a key to unlock one of the doors in the house with many mansions.

C.S. Lewis, The Problem of Pain

Indulgences

Let none of you obtain tickets of indulgence. Leave that for the lazy half-asleep Christians. You get on without them. . . . I know nothing about souls dragged out of purgatory by an indulgence. I do not even believe it, in spite of all the new-fangled doctors who say so. ... They [indulgences] are not based on scripture. Therefore, have no doubt about them, whatever the scholastic doctors say.

Martin Luther, sermon on indulgences and grace

Infallibility

I'm sorry we're late, we misread the timetables. But there – nobody's infallible.

Geoffrey Fisher to John XXIII, on the occasion of the first meeting of an Archbishop of Canterbury with a Pope since before the Reformation

Infant baptism   see also BAPTISM

The divine sign given to the child in baptism confirms the promise given to godly parents, and proclaims that the Lord is not only their God, but their children's. All this is to God's glory and increases the believer's love towards him, as they realise that his love is not only for them, but for their offspring.

John Calvin, The Institutes of Christian Religion, 4.16.9

Ingratitude   see GRATITUDE

Inner life

We must have richness of soul.

Antiphanes, Greek Comic Fragments

If there is only a little water in the stream, the fault is with the channel, not the source.

Jerome, Letters

If better were within, better would come out.

Thomas Fuller, Gnomologia, 1732

Insight

A moment's insight is sometimes worth a life's experience.

Oliver Wendell Holmes, The Professor at the Breakfast Table

Inspiration

No man was ever great without some degree of divine inspiration.

Cicero

Institutions

An institution is the lengthened shadow of one man.

Ralph Waldo Emerson

Instruction

Give instruction to a wise man, and he will be yet wiser: teach a just man, and he will increase in learning.

The Bible, Proverbs 9:9 (AV)

Insults

Sensible people will ignore an insult.

The Bible, Proverbs 12:16

An injury is much sooner forgotten than an insult.

Lord Chesterfield, Letters, 9 October 1746

A smiling face, and forgiveness, are the best way to avenge an insult.

Spanish proverb

Integrity

Integrity is the noblest possession.

Latin proverb

Intolerance   see also TOLERATION

I have seen gross intolerance shown in support of tolerance.

Samuel Taylor Coleridge

Invitations

When the ass was invited to the wedding feast, he said, 'They need more wood and water.'

Bosnian proverb

J

Jealousy

Peace of mind makes the body healthy, but jealousy is like a cancer.

The Bible, Proverbs 14:30

Anger is cruel and destructive, but it is nothing compared to jealousy.

The Bible, Proverbs 27:4

The ear of jealousy heareth all things.

The Bible (Apocrypha), Wisdom of Solomon 1:5 (AV)

Jealousy sees with opera glasses, making little things big; dwarfs are changed into giants and suspicions into truths.

Cervantes

O! beware, my lord, of jealousy;
It is the green-eyed monster which doth mock
The meat it feeds on.

William Shakespeare, Othello, III.iii

Jesus see Christ

Job, Book of

One of the grandest things ever written with pen.
Thomas Carlyle

The greatest poem of ancient and modern times.
Alfred, Lord Tennyson

Magnificent and sublime as no other book in the Bible.
Martin Luther

John 3:16

The most famous sentence in the English language.
Author unknown

Joy

The joy that the Lord gives you will make you strong.
The Bible, Nehemiah 8:10

The whole point of the letter [to the Philippians] is: I do rejoice – do you rejoice.
Bengel

He who kisses the joy as it flies
Lives in eternity's sunrise.
William Blake

Into all our lives, in many simple, familiar, homely ways, God infuses this element of joy from the surprises of life . . . the strain of music . . . or sunset glory . . . the unsought word of encouragement . . . these are the overflowing riches of his grace, these are his free gifts.
S. Longfellow

If I have faltered more or less
In my great task of happiness;
If I have moved among my race
And shown no glorious morning face;
If beams from happy human eyes
Have moved me not; if morning skies,
Books, and my food, and summer rain
Knocked on my sullen heart in vain:
Lord, thy most pointed pleasure take
And stab my spirit broad awake;
Or, Lord, if too obdurate I,
Choose Thou, before that spirit die,
A piercing pain, a killing sin,
And to my dead heart run them in!
Robert Louis Stevenson, The Celestial Surgeon

Judaism

The amount of this debt [the debt the Christian faith has to Judaism] is so large that one might almost venture to claim the Christian mission as a continuation of the Jewish propaganda.
Adolf Harnack, The Mission and Expansion of Christianity

Judgement see also Criticism; God's Judgement

Experience teaches that excellent memories are too often joined to weak judgements.
Montaigne

A smattering of philosophy had liberated his [Nero's] intellect without maturing his judgement.
Tacitus

Judging others

Do not be angry that you cannot make others as you would wish them to be, since you cannot make yourself as you wish to be.
Thomas à Kempis, The Imitation of Christ

It is easy to be heavy; hard to be light.
G.K. Chesterton, Orthodoxy

It is the property of fools, to be always judging.
Thomas Fuller, Gnomologia

It is not failure of others to appreciate your abilities that should trouble you, but rather your failure to appreciate theirs.
Confucius, Analects

Judge not, that ye be not judged.
The Bible, Jesus Christ, Matthew 7:1 (AV)

You hypocrite! First take the log out of your own eye, and then you will see clearly to take the speck out of your brother's eye.
The Bible, Jesus Christ, Matthew 7:5

He that is without sin among you, let him first cast a stone at her.
The Bible, Jesus Christ, John 8:7 (AV)

How seldom we weigh our neighbour in the same balance with ourselves.
Thomas à Kempis

I hate to think the worst of others when I might think the best.
Samuel Chadwick

We keep other people's vices in our eyes, our own we keep on our back.
Seneca

Do not punish with a scourge a fault which merits only the strap.
Horace, referring to the scourge which was used on prisoners, and which could kill

The cobbler should stick to his last.
Latin proverb

I see no fault that I might not have committed myself.
Goethe

The three essential rules when speaking of others are: Is it true? Is it kind? Is it necessary?
Author unknown

If we had no faults ourselves, we should not take so much delight in noticing those of others.
La Rochefoucauld

Before I judge my neighbour, let me walk a mile in his moccasins.
Sioux proverb

We hand folks over to God's mercy, and show none ourselves.
George Eliot, Adam Bede, ch. 42

Justice

Let justice be done, though the world perish.
Ferdinand I

To no man will we sell, or deny, or delay, right or justice.
Magna Carta

Justice is my being allowed to do whatever I like. Injustice is whatever prevents my doing so.
Samuel Johnson

If we will have peace without a worm in it, lay we the foundations of justice and good will.
Oliver Cromwell

One hour of justice is worth a hundred of prayer.
Arab proverb

Faith is the sister of justice.
Latin proverb

Justice is the foundation of kingdoms.
Latin proverb

Act justly and you will have heaven as your ally.
Menander

He hurts the good who spares the bad.
Publius Syrus

I tremble for my country when I reflect that God is just.
Thomas Jefferson, Notes on the State of Virginia

Justice delayed is justice denied.
William Ewart Gladstone

Justice and power must be brought together, so that whatever is just may be powerful, and whatever is powerful may be just.
Blaise Pascal

Injustice anywhere is a threat to justice everywhere.
Martin Luther King

The eleventh commandment: Thou shalt not be found out.
Author unknown

Children are innocent and love justice, while most adults are wicked and prefer mercy.
G.K. Chesterton

Justification by faith

Justification by faith is the principal article of all Christian doctrine, which maketh true Christians indeed.
Martin Luther

K

Kindness   see also CHARITY

Righteous people know the kind thing to say, but the wicked are always saying things that hurt.
The Bible, Proverbs 10:32

You do yourself a favour when you are kind. If you are cruel, you only hurt yourself.
The Bible, Proverbs 11:17

If you want to be happy, be kind to the poor; it is a sin to despise anyone.
The Bible, Proverbs 14:21

Kind words bring life, but cruel words crush your spirit.
The Bible, Proverbs 15:4

Kind words are like honey – sweet to the taste and good for your health.
The Bible, Proverbs 16:24

Kindness is a language the blind can see and the deaf can hear.
Author unknown

Great people are able to do great kindnesses.
Cervantes, Don Quixote, 3.32

Kindness is the noblest weapon to conquer with.
Thomas Fuller, Gnomologia

No act of kindness, no matter how small, is ever wasted.

Æsop, The Lion and the Mouse

I expect to pass through life but once. If therefore, there be any kindness I can show, or any good thing I can do to any fellow being, let me do it now, and not defer or neglect it, as I shall not pass this way again.

William Penn

Be kind! Everyone you meet is fighting a hard battle. Be kind!

Alexander Maclaren

There are ten strong things. Iron is strong, but fire melts it. Fire is strong, but water quenches it. Water is strong, but the clouds evaporate it. Clouds are strong, but wind drives them away. Man is strong, but fears cast him down. Fear is strong, but sleep overcomes it. Sleep is strong, yet death is stronger. But loving kindness survives death.

The Talmud

He was so benevolent, so merciful a man that he would have held an umbrella over a duck in a shower of rain.

Douglas Jerrold

Kindness in words creates confidence. Kindness in thinking creates profoundness. Kindness in giving creates love.

Lao Tzu

Getting money is not all a man's business: to cultivate kindness is a valuable part of the business of life.

Samuel Johnson

Every act of kindness and compassion done by any man for his fellow Christian is done by Christ working within him.

Julian of Norwich, Revelations of Divine Love

If we're not kind to the unkind, our brand of kindness is shallow.

Author unknown

If someone hurts you, do something nice to someone. That will restore the balance.

Author unknown

Wise sayings often fall on barren ground; but a kind word is never thrown away.

Arthur Helps

Deeds of kindness weigh as much as all the commandments.

The Talmud

Kindness, Response to

The first thing a kindness deserves is acceptance, the second, transmission.

George Macdonald

Kindness has converted more souls than zeal, eloquence or learning.

F.W. Faber

Have you had a kindness shown?
    Pass it on!
'Twas not given for thee alone,
    Pass it on!
Let it travel down the years,
Let it wipe another's tears,
Till in heaven the deed appears –
    Pass it on!

Henry Burton

Kingdom of God

The kingdom of God is within you.

*The Bible, Jesus Christ,
Luke 17:21 (AV)*

To want all that God wants, always to want it, for all occasions and without reservations, this is the kingdom of God which is all within.

François Fénelon

There is no structural organisation of society which can bring about the coming of the Kingdom of God on earth, since all systems can be perverted by the selfishness of man.

*The Malvern Manifesto of the
York province of the Church of
England, 1941*

Kingdom of heaven

Blessed are the poor in spirit: for theirs is the kingdom of heaven.

*The Bible, Jesus Christ,
Matthew 5:3 (AV)*

Knowledge see also LEARNING; REASON; SELF-KNOWLEDGE

All wish to know, but none want to pay the price.

Juvenal

To know a thing is nothing in your eyes, unless some other person is aware of your knowledge.

Bernard of Clairvaux, The Song of Songs

We should not seek to learn anything just so that we can pander to our pride, indulge our curiosity, but only so that we can edify ourselves and our neighbours.

Bernard of Clairvaux, The Song of Songs

We are as stupid as St Augustine and St Paul, St Louis and St Francis, and Joan of Arc, and – why not say it – Pascal and Corneille. We others make *no progress*. It is the moderns who make progress. We are stupid once and for all.

Charles Péguy, Men and Saints, The Humanities

I am never afraid of what I know.

Anna Sewell, Black Beauty

A smattering of everything, and a knowledge of nothing.

Charles Dickens, Sketches by Boz, Tales, ch. 3

Knowledge is the small part of ignorance that we arrange and classify.

Ambrose Bierce

We both exist and know that we exist, and rejoice in this existence and this knowledge.

Augustine of Hippo

What man does not understand, he does not possess.

Goethe

To be conscious that you are ignorant is a great step to knowledge.

Benjamin Disraeli, Synil, Bk. 1, ch. 5

Knowledge is power.

Francis Bacon

Knowledge, Means to

The next best thing to knowing something is knowing where to find it.

Samuel Johnson

The preservation of the means of knowledge among the lowest ranks is of more importance to the public than all the property of all the rich men in the country.

John Adams

Knowledge, Warnings concerning

Men, not books, are the proper subject for study.

La Rochefoucauld

Knowledge is not the most important thing in the world. Love is essential.

François Fénelon

Knowledge puffeth up, but charity edifieth.

The Bible, The apostle Paul, 1 Corinthians 8:1 (AV)

Knowledge without integrity is dangerous and dreadful.

Samuel Johnson

Beware you be not swallowed up in books! An ounce of love is worth a pound of knowledge.

John Wesley

Cease from an excessive desire of knowing, for you will find much distraction and delusion in it.

Thomas à Kempis, The Imitation of Christ

Knowledge of God

To know God, so as thereby to be made like unto him, is the chief end of man.

John Owen, The Person of Christ

In proportion as we have the Spirit of Jesus we have the true knowledge of Jesus.

Albert Schweitzer

If your conception of God is radically false, then the more devout you are the worse it will be for you. You are opening your soul to be moulded by something base. You had much better be an atheist.

William Temple

Unknown makes unloved.

Dutch proverb

Ah, my dear God, though I am clean forgot,
Let me not love thee, if I love thee not.

George Herbert, The Temple

O world invisible, we view thee,
O world intangible, we touch thee,
O world unknowable, we know thee,
Inapprehensible, we clutch thee!

Francis Thompson

The knowledge of God is very far from the love of him.

Blaise Pascal

We must observe that the knowledge of God which we are invited to cultivate is not that which, resting satisfied with empty speculation, only flutters in the brain, but a knowledge which will prove substantial and fruitful whenever it is duly perceived and rooted in the heart.

John Calvin

Until people feel that they owe everything to God, that they are protected by his fatherly care and that he is the author of all their blessings, so that nothing should be sought apart from him, they will never submit to him voluntarily.

John Calvin, The Institutes of Christian Religion, 1.2.1

God is more truly imagined than expressed, and he exists more truly than he is imagined.

Augustine of Hippo

Knowledge of God, Limits of

We cannot know God in his greatness, for the Father cannot be measured.

Irenaeus, Against Heresies, 4.20.1

Through his love and infinite kindness God comes within the grasp of man's knowledge. But this knowledge is not of his greatness or true being, for no one has measured or comprehended that.

Irenaeus, Against Heresies, 3.24.1

Knowledge of God, Means of

By faith we know his existence; in glory we shall know his nature.

Blaise Pascal

God never meant that man should scale the heavens
By strides of human wisdom. In his works,
Though wondrous, he commands us in his word
To seek him rather where his mercy shines.

William Cowper

This is how men get to know God – by doing his will.

Henry Drummond

Knowledge of God, Possibility of

Don't imagine that God is like a human carpenter, who works or doesn't work as he chooses, who can do his work or leave it undone as the mood takes him. It is not like that with God. When he finds you ready, he is obliged to act, to flow into you, just as the sun must shine out and is unable to stop itself whenever the air is bright and clear.

Meister Eckhart

Blind unbelief is sure to err,
    And scan his work in vain;
God is his own interpreter,
    And he will make it plain.

William Cowper

According to Jesus, God is to be known not by theory, but by practice, not through mental investigation, but

through spiritual trust and fellowship. Only a son can know the Father. The consequence of this is that the knowledge of God is available to children and to all whom God chooses to reveal himself.

W.N. Clarke, The Christian Doctrine of God

The Lord has taught us that no one can know God unless he is taught by God; that is, God cannot be known without his help. But it is the Father's will that he should be known; for he is known by those to whom the Son reveals him.

Irenaeus, Against Heresies, 4.6.4

L

Language

In Paris they simply stared when I spoke to them in French; I never did succeed in making those idiots understand their own language.

Mark Twain

Last words

Truth sits upon the lips of dying men.

Matthew Arnold

Sir, you often told me of Christ and salvation: why did you not oftener remind me of hell and danger?

A dying member of John Newton's congregation

[The following examples of reputed 'last words' are arranged in alphabetical order of the speaker.]

See in what peace a Christian can die.

Joseph Addison

I have pain (there is no arguing against sense); but I have peace, I have peace.

Richard Baxter

The same lad, named Wilbert, said, again, 'Dear Master, there is still one sentence unfinished.' He replied, 'Write it down.' After a time the lad said, 'Now it is finished.' 'You have spoken truly,' he replied. 'It is well finished.' Now raise my head in your hands, for it would give me great joy to sit facing the holy place where I used to pray, so that I can sit and call upon my Father.' And thus on the floor of his cell he chanted, 'Glory be to the Father, and to the Son, and to the Holy Spirit,' to its ending and breathed his last.

Bede

We all make mistakes, but everyone makes different mistakes.

Ludwig van Beethoven

Dearest brethren, I do not wish to say much to you, but you should bear in mind that my condition now will be yours some day, just as you hold the same vocation. I found in my soul that I would not have renounced the service of Christ for a thousand worlds like this. For every sin I have committed, I accuse myself before my Saviour Jesus Christ and you. I beg you, dearest brethren, love one another.

Bernard, early Franciscan brother

While women weep, as they do now, I'll fight; while men go to prison, in and out, in and out, as they do now, I'll fight; while there is a drunkard left, while there is a poor lost girl upon the streets, where there remains one dark soul without the light of God – I'll fight! I'll fight to the very end!

William Booth, end of his last speech

I was a little better than speechless all day. O my God, I am speedily coming to thee! Hasten the day, O Lord, if it be thy blessed will. Oh, come, Lord Jesus, come quickly.

David Brainerd

This is a beautiful country.

John Brown

Beautiful!

Elizabeth Barrett Browning

I am going to a place where few kings and great men will come.

Buchanan, tutor to James I

Though I have endeavoured to avoid sin, and to please God to the utmost of my power, yet, from the consciousness of perpetual infirmities, I am still afraid to die. [His chaplain replied: 'My Lord, you have forgotten that Jesus Christ is a Saviour.'] True, but how shall I know that he is a saviour for me? ['My Lord,' answered the chaplain, 'it is written, "Him that cometh to me I will in no wise cast out."'] True, and I am surprised that, although I have read that Scripture a thousand times over, I have never felt its virtue till this moment; and now I die happy.

Joseph Butler

You bruise me, Lord, but I am abundantly satisfied, since it is from your hand.

John Calvin

I know now that patriotism is not enough; I must have no hatred and no bitterness toward anyone.

Edith Cavell

The issue is now clear. It is between light and darkness and everyone must choose his side.

G.K. Chesterton

This was the hand that wrote it, therefore it shall suffer the first punishment.

Archbishop Cranmer, burnt at the stake in 1555 for writing heresy

It is not my design to drink or to sleep, but my design is to make what haste I can to be gone.

Oliver Cromwell

The fog is rising.

Emily Dickinson

Weep not, I shall not die; and as I leave the land of the dying I trust to see the blessings of the Lord in the land of the living.

Edward the Confessor

I have sinned against my brother the ass. . . . Welcome, Sister Death!

Francis of Assisi

Humility.

Francis de Sales, when asked the virtue he most desired

More light!

Goethe

Here die I, Richard Grenville, with a joyful and quiet mind, that I have ended my life as a true soldier ought to do that hath fought for his country, Queen, religion and honour. Whereby my soul most joyfully departeth out of this body, and shall always leave behind it an everlasting fame of a valiant and true soldier that hath done his duty as he was bound to do.

Richard Grenville

God will forgive me. It's his job.

Heinrich Heine, quoting from Voltaire, Candide

How thankful I am for death! It is the passage to the Lord and giver of eternal life. O welcome, welcome death! Thou mayest well be reckoned among the treasures of the Christian! To live is Christ, but to die is gain! Lord, now lettest thou thy servant depart in peace, according to thy most holy and comfortable Word; for mine eyes have seen thy precious salvation.

James Hervey

You have been used to take notice of the sayings of dying men. This is mine: that a life spent in the service of God, and communion with him, is the most comfortable and pleasant life that anyone can live in this world.

Matthew Henry

I shall be glad then to find a hole to creep out of the world at.

Thomas Hobbes

Let nothing cause thy heart to fail;
Launch out thy boat, hoist up thy sail,
   Put from the shore;
And be sure thou shalt attain
Unto the port that shall remain
   For evermore.

John Hooper, written the night
before his execution
as a heretic in 1555

O holy simplicity!

John Huss, at the stake in 1415

Let us cross over the river and rest under the shade of the trees!

Thomas 'Stonewall' Jackson

God bless you!

Samuel Johnson

You have conquered, O Galilean.

The emperor Julian

Live in Christ, live in Christ, and the flesh need not fear death.

John Knox

Away with these filthy garments. I feel a sacred fire kindled in my soul, which will destroy everything contrary to itself, and burn as a flame of divine love to all eternity.

William Law

I give my dying testimony to the truth of Christianity. The promises of the gospel are my support and consolation. They, alone, yield me satisfaction in a dying hour. I am not afraid to die. The gospel of Christ has raised me above the fear of death; for I know that my redeemer liveth.

John Leland

Abe, I'm going to leave you now and I shall not return. I want you to be kind to your mother and live as I have taught you. Love your heavenly Father and keep his commandments.

Thomas Lincoln, father of
Abraham, then aged 9

'God so loved the world that he gave his only begotten Son, that whosoever believeth in him should not perish but have everlasting life.' [Repeated three times. Then, asked if he would stand by Christ and the doctrine Luther had preached, he answered:] Yes.

Martin Luther

God gave me a message to deliver and a horse to ride. Alas, I have killed the horse and now I cannot deliver the message.

Robert Murray M'Cheyne, as he
lay dying at the age of 29

You will tell the others I am going home a little sooner than I thought. Then tell them not to talk about the servant but to talk about the Saviour.

F.B. Meyer

Earth is receding; heaven is approaching. This is my crowning day!

Dwight L. Moody

She declared she felt nothing but 'an inexpressible tranquillity and peace with God through Jesus Christ.' Her mouth was full of the praises of God, and she emphatically expressed herself by saying, 'I am nothing but joy.'

Olympia Fulvia Morata, described
by David Simpson, A Plea for
Religion and the Sacred Writings

Too kind – too kind!

Florence Nightingale, when
presented on her deathbed with the
Order of Merit

See now, I commend my soul to God for whom I am an ambassador because he chose me for this task, despite my obscurity, to be one of the least among his servants. This is my confession before I die.

Patrick

Love God, and begin betimes. In him you shall find true, everlasting, and endless comfort. When you have travelled and wearied yourself with all sorts of worldly cogitations, you shall sit down by sorrow in the end. Teach your son also to serve and fear God whilst he is young, that the fear of God may grow up in him. Then will God be an husband to you, and a father to him, an husband and a father that can never be taken from you.

Walter Raleigh

Even such is time which takes in trust
Our youth, our joys, and all we have
And pays us but with age and dust:
Who in the dark and silent grave
When we have wandered all our ways

Shuts up the glory of our days.
And from the earth and grave and dust
The Lord shall raise me up, I trust.

*Walter Raleigh (written on the day
before he was beheaded)*

(To his wife, or mistress:) How happy
a thing it is to die, when one has no
reason for remorse, or self-reproach!
(To God:) Eternal Being! The soul
that I am going to give you back is as
pure, at this moment, as it was when it
proceeded from you: render it par-
taker of your felicity!

Jean-Jacques Rousseau

Neither my imprisonment nor fear of
death have been able to discompose
me in any degree. On the contrary I
have found the assurances of the love
and mercy of God, in and through my
blessed redeemer, in whom I only
trust. And I do not question but I am
going to partake of that fulness of joy
which is in his presence; the hopes of
which do so wonderfully delight me,
that I think this is the happiest time of
my life, though others may look upon
it as the saddest.

William, Lord Russell

If he should slay me ten thousand
times, ten thousand times I'll trust. I
feel, I feel, I believe in joy and rejoice;
I feed on manna. O for arms to
embrace him! O for a well-tuned harp!

Samuel Rutherford

Sir Walter Scott expressed the wish, as
he lay dying, that I should read to him,
and when I asked him from what book,
he said, 'Need you ask? There is but
one.' I chose the fourteenth chapter of St
John's Gospel. Then Sir Walter Scott
said, 'Well, this is a great comfort.'

*J.G. Lockhart, Life of Sir Walter
Scott*

Love my memory; cherish my friends;
but above all, govern your will and
affection by the will and word of your
creator; in me beholding the end of
this world, with all her vanities.

Philip Sidney

I wish to be alone, with my God, and to
lie before him as a poor, wretched, hell-
deserving sinner. . . . But I would also
look to him as my all-forgiving God –
and as my all-sufficient God – and as my
all-atoning God – and as my covenant-
keeping God. . . . I would lie here to

the last, at the foot of the cross, looking
unto Jesus; and go as such into the presence of my God. . . . Jesus Christ is all
in all for my soul, and now you must be
all for my body. I cannot tell you any
longer what I want. My principles were
not founded on fancies or enthusiasm;
there is a reality in them, and I find
them sufficient to support me in death.

Charles Simeon

We owe a cock to Æsculapius; by no
means forget to give it.

*Socrates, as he died of poisoning (a
cock used to be sacrificed as a
thanksgiving offering to the god of
healing, Æscupalius)*

Whether or no God will approve my
actions, I know not; but this I am sure
of, that I have at all times made it my
endeavour to please him, and I have a
good hope that this my endeavour will
be accepted by him.

Socrates (again!)

My son, may you be more fortunate
than your father; in all else be like him;
then you will be no base man.

Sophocles

I have taken a look into eternity. Oh, if
I could come back and preach again,
how differently would I preach from
what I have done before!

Summerfield

I am so weak that I can hardly write, I
cannot read my Bible, I cannot even
pray. I can only lie still in God's arms
like a little child, and trust.

Hudson Taylor

The sky is clear; there is no cloud;
come, Lord Jesus, come quickly.

Augustus Toplady

I am abandoned by God and man. . . .
Doctor, I will give you half of what I
am worth, if you will give me six
months' life. (The doctor answered,
Sir, you cannot live six weeks.) Then I
shall go to hell, and you will go with me!

Voltaire

I shall be satisfied with thy likeness –
satisfied, satisfied.

Charles Wesley

The best of all is, God is with us.
Farewell!

John Wesley

I am tired in the Lord's work, but not
tired of it.

George Whitefield

Laughter   see also HUMOUR

Laughter is a bodily exercise precious to health.

Aristotle

It better befits a man to laugh at life than to lament over it.

Seneca

If you're not allowed to laugh in heaven, I don't want to go there.

Martin Luther

A good laugh is sunshine in a house.

William Makepeace Thackeray

The man who cannot laugh is not only fit for treasons, stratagems, and spoils; but his whole life is already a treason and a stratagem.

Thomas Carlyle

It is the heart that is not yet sure of its God that is afraid to laugh in his presence.

George Macdonald

That day is the most utterly wasted in which one has not laughed.

Chamfort

Law

Agree, for the law is costly.

William Camden, Remains, 1623

Laws are like cobwebs, which may catch small flies, but let wasps and hornets break through.

Jonathan Swift

Draco wrote his law in blood, not in ink.

Demades (Draco, in 7th-century Athens, held that all crimes were equally deserving of the severest punishment)

Laws grind the poor, and rich men rule the law.

Oliver Goldsmith

Laws follow the roads that kings wish them to take.

Spanish proverb, after Alfonso VI threw Roman and Gothic Missals into the fire saying he would choose whichever came out unburned, and then threw back the Gothic one which was unburned and chose the Roman

Fifteen million laws have been passed to try to enforce the Golden Rule and the ten commandments.

Author unknown

Bad laws are the worst sort of tyranny.

Edmund Burke

Law of God

The law of the Lord is perfect;
   it gives new strength.
The commands of the Lord are
   trustworthy,
   giving wisdom to those who lack it.

The Bible, Psalm 19:7

Remember that as long as heaven and earth last, not the least nor the smallest detail of the Law will be done away with – not until the end of all things.

The Bible, Jesus Christ, Matthew 5:18

What is hateful to you, do not do to another. That is the whole law and all else is explanation.

Rabbi Hillel

The Lord humbles us and absolutely terrifies us with the Law and the prospect of our sins so that we . . . seem to be nothing but fools and evil men. And in truth that is exactly what we are.

Martin Luther at the Heidelberg Disputation

The Law and the will are against one another, and without the grace of God are irreconcilable.

Martin Luther, Thesis 71

The Law is a kind of mirror. When we look in the mirror we notice any dirty marks on our faces, so in the Law we are made aware first of our helplessness, then of our sin and finally the judgement.

John Calvin, The Institutes of Christian Religion, 2.7.7

If the Spirit of grace is absent, the law is present only to convict and kill.

Augustine of Hippo

In the maxims of the Law, God is seen as the rewarder of perfect righteousness and the avenger of sin. But in Christ, his face shines out, full of grace and gentleness to poor, unworthy sinners.

John Calvin, The Institutes of Christian Religion, 2.7.8

Laziness   see IDLENESS

Leadership

There are only three kinds of people in the world – those that are movable, those that are immovable, and those that move them.

Li Hung Chang, when General Charles Gordon asked about the nature of leadership

I made all my generals out of mud.
Napoleon

He who knows not, and knows not that
he knows not, is a fool – shun him.
He who knows not, and knows that he
knows not, is a child – teach him.
He who knows, and knows not that he
knows, is asleep – wake him.
He who knows, and knows that he
knows, is wise – follow him.
Persian proverb

A leader is best when he is neither seen
nor heard,
Not so good when he is adored and
glorified,
Worst when he is hated and despised.
'Fail to honour people, they will fail to
honour you.'
But of a good leader, when his work is
done, his aim fulfilled,
The people will say, 'We did this
ourselves.'
Lao Tzu

Spiritual power is the outpouring of
spiritual life, and like all life, from that
of the moss and lichen on the wall to
that of the archangel before the
throne, is from God. Therefore those
who aspire to leadership must pay the
price, and seek it from God.
*Samuel Brengle, The
Soul-Winner's Secret*

I'd rather get ten men to do the job
than to do the job of ten men.
Dwight L. Moody

If you command wisely, you'll be
obeyed cheerfully.
Thomas Fuller, Gnomologia

Learning   see also EDUCATION;
EXPERIENCE; WISDOM

What we have to learn to do, we learn
by doing.
Aristotle, Nicomachean Ethics

He not only overflowed with learning,
but stood in the slop.
Sydney Smith

The university brings out all abilities
including incapability.
Anton Chekhov

To spend too much time in studies is
sloth.
Francis Bacon, Essays, Of Studies

If I hear, I forget; if I see, I remember;
if I do, I make it my own.
Chinese saying

One picture is worth more than a
thousand words.
Chinese proverb

Learning after unpromising beginnings

A boy was expelled from his Latin
class for slow learning. He resolved to
excel in English where he was slow in
Latin. He was Winston Churchill.

A six-year-old boy was sent home
from school with a note saying he was
too stupid to learn. His name was
Thomas Edison.

Sir Walter Scott's teacher called him a
hopeless dunce.

Louis Pasteur was reckoned the
slowest learner in his chemistry class.

Learning from all sources

It is allowable to learn even from an
enemy.
Latin proverb

Improve yourself by others' experience: so shall you quickly acquire what
others labour long for.
Socrates

From the errors of others a wise man
corrects his own.
Publilius Syrus

I make it my rule to lay hold of light
and embrace it, though it be held forth
by a child or an enemy.
Jonathan Edwards

You will find many things help honest
living, and you should not refuse whatever an author (even though a gentile)
teaches well. . . . It is profitable to
taste all manner of learning of the gentiles, if it is done with caution and
judgement discreetly—and further-
more with speed and like someone
intending only to pass through the
country and not to stay or live there. In
conclusion (and this is the most important) everything must be applied and
referred to Christ.
*Erasmus, The Manual of the
Christian Knight*

Learning throughout life

Anyone who stops learning is old,
whether at twenty or eighty. Anyone
who keeps learning stays young. The
greatest thing in life is to keep your
mind young.
Henry Ford

Unless we accept lifelong learning as a habit, we're shortening our lives.
Author unknown

Leisure

Neither in your actions be sluggish, nor in your conversation without method, nor wandering in your thoughts, nor let there be inward contention in your soul, nor be so busy in life as to have no leisure.
Marcus Aurelius

If all the year were playing holidays, To sport would be as tedious as to work.
William Shakespeare

Leisure is the mother of philosophy.
Thomas Hobbes, Leviathan

Leprosy

No other disease reduces a human being for so many years to so hideous a wreck.
E.W.G. Masterman

[Lepers are treated] as if they were, in effect, dead men.
Josephus

Letter-writing

Everyone reveals his own soul in his letters. In every other form of composition it is possible to discern the writer's character, but in none so clearly as the epistolary.
Demetrius, On Style

Liberty   see FREEDOM

Lies   see also TRUTH

Have nothing to do with lies and misleading words.
The Bible, Proverbs 4:24

A lie has a short life, but truth lives on for ever.
The Bible, Proverbs 12:19

A little lie can travel half way round the world while Truth is still lacing up her boots.
Mark Twain

When in doubt, tell the truth.
Mark Twain, Following the Equator

A little lie is like a little pregnancy – it doesn't take long before everyone knows.
C.S. Lewis

Dare to be true: nothing can need a lie; A fault, which needs it most, grows two thereby.
George Herbert, The Temple

A lie which is all a lie May be met and fought outright. But a lie which is a part of truth Is a harder matter to fight.
Author unknown

Lying is the acme of evil. White lies are non-existent, for a lie is wholly a lie; falsehood is the personification of evil; Satan has two names: he is called Satan, and he is called the Father of Lies.
Victor Hugo

The essence of lying is in deception, not in words; a lie may be told in silence, by equivocation, by the accent on a syllable, by a glance of the eye attaching a peculiar significance to a sentence; and all these kinds of lies are worse and baser by many degrees than a lie plainly worded; so that no form of blinded conscience is so far sunk than that which comforts itself for having deceived because the deception was by gesture or silence, instead of utterance.
John Ruskin

Lying covers a multitude of sins – temporarily.
Dwight L. Moody

A lie is a snowball: the further you roll it, the bigger it becomes.
Martin Luther

The great masses of the people . . . will more easily fall victims to a great lie than to a small one.
Adolf Hitler, Mein Kampf

Life   see also AGES OF MAN

So teach us to number our days, that we may apply our hearts unto wisdom.
The Bible, Psalm 90:12 (AV)

Life is love.
Goethe

Life is real! Life is earnest! And the grave is not its goal; Dust thou art, to dust returnest, Was not spoken of the soul.
Henry Wadsworth Longfellow, A Psalm of Life

My life reminded me of a ruined temple. What strength, what proportion in some parts! What unsightly gaps, what prostrate ruins in others!
Robert Burns

We are born crying, live complaining, and die disappointed.
Thomas Fuller, Gnomologia

123 LITTLE THINGS

Everything passes, everything perishes, everything palls.
French proverb

Life is not a holiday, but an education. And the one eternal lesson for us all is how better we can love.
Henry Drummond

Life, Meaning of see MEANING OF LIFE; MEANINGLESSNESS

Life, Spiritual

Man must not depend on bread alone to sustain him, but on everything that the Lord says.
The Bible, Deuteronomy 8:3

Whoever has the Son has this life; whoever does not have the Son of God does not have life.
The Bible, 1 John 5:12

Life after death

We shall all be changed, in a moment, in the twinkling of an eye.
The Bible, The apostle Paul, 1 Corinthians 15:51–52 (AV)

This life is the cradle in which we are prepared for the other one.
Joubert

We know and feel that we are eternal.
Benedict Spinoza, Ethics

But though life's valley be a vale of tears,
A brighter scene beyond that vale appears.
William Cowper, Conversation

Even such is Time, that takes in trust
Our youth, our joys, our all we have,
And pays us but with age and dust;
Who in the dark and silent grave,
When we have wandered all our ways,
Shuts up the story of our days;
But from this earth, this grave, this dust,
My God shall raise me up, I trust.
Walter Raleigh, written the night before his death

He is not dead, this friend, not dead,
But, in the path we mortals tread,
Gone some few, trifling steps ahead
And nearer to the end;
So that you, too, once past the bend,
Shall meet again, as face to face,
This friend you fancy dead.
Robert Louis Stevenson

Life in Jesus

In Christ there is no East or West,
In him no South or North,

But one great fellowship of love
Throughout the whole wide earth.
John Oxenham

My life is like a faded leaf,
My harvest dwindled to a husk;
Truly my life is void and brief
And tedious in the barren dusk;
My life is like a frozen thing,
No bud or greenness can I see:
Yet rise it shall – the sap of Spring;
O Jesus, rise in me.
Christina Rossetti

Light

Lead me from the unreal to the real!
Lead me from darkness to light!
Lead me from death to immortality!
Brihadaranyaka Upanishad 1.3.28

Listening see also Speech

Listen before you answer. If you don't you are being stupid and insulting.
The Bible, Proverbs 18:13

Blessed are those who listen, for they shall learn.
Author unknown

It takes two to speak the truth – one to speak, and another to hear.
Henry David Thoreau

The only way to entertain some folks is to listen to them.
Kin Hubbard

His thoughts were slow,
His words were few and never formed to glisten.
But he was a joy to all his friends,
You should have heard him listen!
Author unknown

The most effective remedy for self-love and self-absorption is the habit of humble listening.
E. Herman

None so deaf as those who won't hear.
Proverb

God gave a man two ears and only one mouth. Why don't we listen twice as much as we talk?
Chinese proverb

The surest rule [for excelling in conversation] is to listen much, speak little, and say nothing that you may be sorry for.
La Rochefoucauld

Little things see also FAITHFULNESS

Do little things as if they were great, because of the majesty of the Lord Jesus Christ, who dwells in thee;

and do great things as if they were little and easy, because of his omnipotence.
Blaise Pascal

Exactness in little duties is a wonderful source of cheerfulness.
F.W. Faber

Be great in little things.
Augustine of Hippo

Attention to little things is a great thing.
John Chrysostom

I am only one. I can't do everything, but that won't stop me from doing the little I can do.
Everett Hale

Liturgy

It hath been the wisdom of the Church of England, ever since the first coming of her public liturgy, to keep the mean between the two extremes, of too much stiffness in refusing, and of too much easiness in admitting any variation from it.
Book of Common Prayer, 1662, Preface

Living   see also BEHAVIOUR; MOTTOES

All of us should eat and drink and enjoy what we have worked for. It is God's gift.
The Bible, Ecclesiastes 3:13

Take care of the means and the end will take care of itself.
Mahatma Gandhi

I could not at any age be content to take my place in a corner by the fireside and simply look on. Life was meant to be lived. One must never, for whatever reason, turn one's back on life.
Eleanor Roosevelt

Manifest plainness,
Embrace simplicity,
Reduce selfishness,
Have few desires.
Lao Tzu

Many words do not satisfy the soul; but a good life refreshes the mind.
Thomas à Kempis, The Imitation of Christ

We are always getting ready to live but never living.
Ralph Waldo Emerson

How many people eat, drink, and get married; buy, sell, and build; make contracts and attend to their fortune;

have friends and enemies, pleasures and pains, are born, grow up, live and die – but asleep!
Joubert

Things worth remembering:
The value of time.
The success of perseverance.
The pleasure of working.
The dignity of simplicity.
The worth of character.
The improvement of talent.
The influence of example.
The obligation of duty.
The wisdom of economy.
The virtue of patience.
The joy of originating.
The power of darkness.
Author unknown

Not everything that is more difficult is more meritorious.
Thomas Aquinas

RESOLVED: To live with all might while I do live.
Jonathan Edwards

Life is given not as a lasting possession, but merely for use.
Lucretius

Life is long, if we know how to use it.
Seneca

He preaches best that lives well.
Proverb

Take time to think:
   it is the course of power.
Take time to play:
   it is the secret of perpetual youth.
Take time to read:
   it is the fountain of wisdom.
Take time to pray:
   it is the greatest power on earth.
Take time to laugh:
   it is the music of the soul.
Take time to give:
   it is too short a day to be selfish.
Author unknown

May you live all the days of your life.
Jonathan Swift

Be careful for nothing, prayerful for everything, thankful for anything.
Dwight L. Moody

Life is something to do when you can't get to sleep.
Fran Lebowitz

It is better to wear out than to rust out.
Richard Cumberland

The most important thing in the Olympic Games is not winning but taking part. . . . The essential thing in life is not conquering but fighting well.

Pierre de Coubertin, speech to officials of the Olympic Games, 24 July 1908, London

Living, Day by day

Look to this day. . . . In it lie all the realities and verities of existence, the bliss of growth, the splendour of action, the glory of power. For yesterday is but a dream and tomorrow is only a vision. But today, well lived, makes every yesterday a dream of happiness and every tomorrow a vision of hope.

Sanskrit proverb

If on our daily course our mind
Be set to hallow all we find
New treasures still of countless price
God will provide for sacrifice.

John Keble

Living, God's help for

I asked God for strength that I might achieve;
I was made weak that I might learn humbly to obey.
I asked for help that I might do greater things;
I was given infirmity that I might do better things.
I asked for riches that I might be happy;
I was given poverty that I might be wise.
I asked for all things that I might enjoy life;
I was given life that I might enjoy all things.
I was given nothing that I asked for;
But everything that I had hoped for.
Despite myself, my prayers were answered;
I am among all men most richly blessed.

Author unknown

To live righteously, man needs a twofold help from God. First a habitual gift, by which corrupted nature may be healed, and, after being healed, is lifted up so as to work deeds meriting everlasting life which exceed

the capacity of nature. Second, he needs the help of grace in order to be moved by God to act.

Thomas Aquinas

Living, Purpose of   see also GOALS

He who has a *why* to live for can bear with almost any *how*.

Friedrich Nietzsche

Living and dying

He that will not live a saint cannot die a martyr.

Thomas Fuller, Gnomologia

Die when I may, I want it said of me by those who knew me best, that I always plucked a thistle and planted a flower, where I thought a flower would grow.

Abraham Lincoln

Lives of great men all remind us
We can make our lives sublime,
And, departing, leave behind us
Footprints on the sands of time.

Henry Wadsworth Longfellow, A Psalm of Life

It matters not how a man dies, but how he lives.

Samuel Johnson

Live in such a way as, when you come to die, you will wish you had lived.

Gellert

Teach me to live, that I may dread
The grave as little as my bed;
Teach me to die, that so I may
Rise glorious at the awful day.

Thomas Ken

Live in such a manner that death may not find you unprepared.

Thomas à Kempis, The Imitation of Christ

Let us endeavour so to live that when we come to die even the undertaker will be sorry.

Mark Twain

Living and human relationships

Lord, make me a channel of your peace:
where there is hatred, may I bring love;
where there is wrong, may I bring the spirit of forgiveness;
where there is discord, may I bring harmony;
where there is error, may I bring truth;
where there is doubt, may I bring hope;

where there are shadows, may I bring light;
where there is sadness, may I bring joy.
Lord, grant that I may seek
  rather to comfort than to be comforted;
rather to understand than to be understood;
rather to love than to be loved,
for it is by forgetting myself that I find;
it is by forgiving that I am forgiven.

Francis of Assisi

May I be no man's enemy, and may I be the friend of that which is eternal and abides.
May I never quarrel with those nearest to me; and if I do, may I be reconciled quickly.
May I love, seek, and attain only what is good.
May I wish for all men's happiness and envy no one.
May I never rejoice in the ill fortune of someone who has wronged me.
May I win no victory that harms either me or my opponent.

Eusebius

Live among men as if the eye of God was upon you; pray to God as if men were listening to you.

Seneca

Of one thing I am convinced. Religion is the reverse of any one, cubby-holed experience. If I am not religious in the way I eat and drink, and in the way I deal with my wife, or my crew, or my students, or my customers, as the case may be, the fact that I accept all the theology ever taught me does not make me so.

Wilfred Grenfell

Living for God

I have held many things in my hands, and I have lost them all; but whatever I have placed in God's hands, that I still possess.

Martin Luther

Live in the world as if God and your soul only were in it; that your heart may be captive to no earthly thing.

John of the Cross, Maxims

Forth in thy name, O Lord, I go,
My daily labour to pursue;
Thee, only thee, resolved to know,
In all I think, or speak, or do.

The task thy wisdom hath assigned
O let me cheerfully fulfil:
In all thy works thy presence find,
And prove thine acceptable will.

Charles Wesley

The Son of God has redeemed us solely to this end: that we should, by a right life and devotion, live to the glory of God. This is the one and only rule and standard for living.

William Law

Enrich, Lord, heart, mouth, hands in me,
With faith, with hope, with charity:
That I may run, rise, rest with thee.

George Herbert

If I had a thousand lives, China should have them. No! Not *China*, but *Christ*. Can we do too much for him?

Hudson Taylor

Loneliness

Loneliness is the first thing which God's eye named not good.

John Milton

At home you can never know what it is to be absolutely alone, amidst thousands, everyone looking on you with curiosity, with contempt, with suspicion or with dislike. Thus to learn what it is to be despised and rejected of men . . . and then to have the love of Jesus applied to your heart by the Holy Spirit . . . *this is precious, this is worth coming for*.

Hudson Taylor

I hope no missionary will ever be as lonely as I have been.

Lottie Moon

Longevity   see also OLD AGE

Like anybody else, I would like to live a long life. Longevity has its place. But I'm not concerned about that now. I just want to do God's will.

Martin Luther King,
the night before he was assassinated

Longing for God

You called, you cried, you shattered my deafness, you sparkled, you

blazed, you drove away my blindness,
you shed your fragrance, and I drew in
my breath, and I pant for you.

Augustine of Hippo

As a deer longs for a stream of cool
    water,
  so I long for you, O God.

The Bible, Psalm 42:1

Blest are the pure in heart,
  For they shall see our God;
The secret of the Lord is theirs,
  Their soul is Christ's abode.

John Keble

Lord's Prayer

This, then, is how you should pray:
  Our Father in heaven:
    May your holy name be
      honoured;
    may your kingdom come;
    may your will be done on earth
      as it is in heaven.
    Give us today the food we need.
    Forgive us the wrongs we have
      done,
      as we forgive the wrongs that
        others have done to us.
    Do not bring us to hard testing,
      but keep us safe from the Evil
      One.

The Bible, Jesus Christ,
Matthew 6:9–13

The Lord's Prayer contains the sum
total of religion and morals.

Duke of Wellington

I cannot say 'our' if I live only for
myself.
I cannot say 'Father' if I do not
endeavour each day to act like his
child.
I cannot say 'who art in heaven' if I am
laying up no treasure there.
I cannot say 'hallowed be thy name' if I
am not striving for holiness.
I cannot say 'thy kingdom come' if I
am not doing all in my power to hasten
that wonderful event.
I cannot say 'thy will be done' if I am
disobedient to his word.
I cannot say 'on earth as it is in heaven'
if I'll not serve him here and now.
I cannot say 'give us this day our daily
bread' if I am dishonest or am seeking
things by subterfuge.

I cannot say 'forgive us our debts' if I
harbour a grudge against anyone.
I cannot say 'lead us not into temptation' if I deliberately place myself in its
path.
I cannot say 'deliver us from evil' if I
do not put on the whole armour of
God.
I cannot say 'thine is the kingdom' if I
do not give the King the loyalty due
him from a faithful subject.
I cannot attribute to him 'the power' if
I fear what men may do.
I cannot ascribe to him 'the glory' if
I'm seeking honour only for myself,
and I cannot say 'for ever' if the hori-
zon of my life is bounded completely
by time.

Author unknown

Lord's Supper   see also MASS

Jesus took a piece of bread, gave a
prayer of thanks, broke it, and gave it
to his disciples. 'Take and eat it,' he
said; 'this is my body.'

The Bible, Matthew 26:26

The cup we use in the Lord's Supper
and for which we give thanks to God:
when we drink from it, we are sharing
in the blood of Christ. And the bread
we break: when we eat it, we are sharing in the body of Christ.

The Bible, The apostle Paul,
1 Corinthians 10:16

Take great care to keep one eucharist,
for there is one flesh of our Lord Jesus
Christ and one cup to unite us by his
blood.

Ignatius of Antioch, To the
Philadelphians (being the first
occasion on which the word
eucharist was applied to the
sacrament of the Lord's Supper)

The flesh feeds on the body and blood
of Christ so that the soul may be fat-
tened on God.

Tertullian, The Resurrection of the
Body

The sacrament is the eaten word of
God.

Martin Luther

The chief object of the [Lord's Supper]
is to seal and confirm his promise by
which he testifies that his flesh is our
food and his blood our drink, feeding
us to eternal life. He is the bread of life
and whoever eats it shall live for ever.
Thus the sacrament sends us to the

cross of Christ, where that promise was carried out perfectly. We cannot eat Christ aright unless we see the efficacy of his death.

John Calvin, The Institutes of Christian Religion, 4.17.4

I believe what the Church has always believed, that the sacred mystery of the Lord's Supper consists of two things – the physical signs and the spiritual truth. There is the thing meant, the matter which depends on it, and the effectiveness of both. The thing meant consists in the promises which are included in the sign. By the matter I mean Christ, with his death and resurrection. By the effect, I mean redemption, justification, sanctification, eternal life and all the other benefits Christ bestows on us. When I say that Christ is received by faith, I do not mean only by intellect and imagination. He is offered by the promises, not for us to stop short at mere sight or knowledge of him, but so that we may enjoy true communion with him.

John Calvin, The Institutes of Christian Religion, 4.17.11

If anyone asks me about the process, I do not mind admitting that it is too high a mystery for my mind to grasp or my words to express. I feel rather than understand it. I can rest safely in the truth of God and embrace it without question. He declares that his flesh is the food, his blood the drink for my soul. I give my soul to him to be fed with such food.

John Calvin, The Institutes of Christian Religion, 4.17.32

Lord's Supper, Physical elements in

There is only one body of Christ, which both mouth and heart eat, each in its own way. The heart cannot physically eat it and the mouth cannot eat it spiritually. So God arranges for the mouth to eat physically for the heart, and the heart to eat spiritually for the mouth. This way, both are satisfied and saved by the same food.

Martin Luther

The body and blood of Christ feed our souls, just as bread and wine support our bodily life. There would be no point in the signs, if our souls did not find their nourishment in Christ. This can only be because Christ is made one with us and refreshes us by the eating of his flesh and the drinking of his blood. Although it seems an incredible thing that the flesh of Christ, so far removed physically, should be food to us, we have to remember the immense inward power of the Holy Spirit and how stupid it is to try to measure its immensity by our feeble efforts. What our minds cannot grasp, faith must engender – that the Spirit really does unite things separated by space. Christ transfuses his life into us by that sacred communion of flesh and blood, just as if it entered our very bones and marrow.

John Calvin, The Institutes of Christian Religion, 4.17.10

'Twas God the word that spake it,
He took the bread and brake it;
And what the word did make it,
That I believe, and take it.

Elizabeth I, asked what she believed about the presence of Christ in the sacrament; Samuel Clarke, Marrow of Ecclesiastical History, 1675

Love is that liquor sweet and most divine
Which my God sees as blood; but I as wine.

George Herbert

Lord's Supper ineffective by itself

We do not become good just by eating. What causes our deprivation is wickedness and sin; what causes our abundance is righteousness and doing good deeds.

Origen, Commentary on Matthew

The teaching of those who press all their congregation to come to the Lord's table, as if the coming *must* necessarily do every one good, is entirely without warrant of scripture.

J.C. Ryle, Practical Religion

Lord's Supper to be received worthily

If you have received worthily, you are what you have received.

Augustine of Hippo

On the Lord's Day come together and break bread and give thanks, first publicly confessing your faults, so that your sacrifice may be pure.

Didache

If anyone eats the Lord's bread or drinks from his cup in a way that dishonours him, he is guilty of sin against the Lord's body and blood.

The Bible, The apostle Paul, 1 Corinthians 11:27

We call this food the thanksgiving [*eucharist*], and the only people allowed to receive it are those who believe our teaching and have received the washing for the remission of sins and for regeneration; and who live according to the commands of Christ.

Justin Martyr, Apologia

Lordship of Christ

Jesus Christ will be Lord of all or he will not be Lord at all.

Augustine of Hippo

Lost souls

There is no one so far lost that Jesus cannot find him and cannot save him.

Andrew Murray

Love   see also CARING; GOD'S LOVE

Charity begins at home.

Terence, Andria

His banner over me was love.

The Bible, Song of Solomon 2:4 (AV)

My beloved is mine, and I am his: he feedeth among the lilies.
Until the day break, and the shadows flee away. . . .

The Bible, Song of Solomon 2:16 (AV)

Love of God is the root, love of our neighbour the fruit of the Tree of Life. Neither can exist without the other, but the one is cause and the other effect.

William Temple, Readings in St John's Gospel

Love is something more stern and splendid than mere kindness.

C.S. Lewis

Belief in the existence of other human beings as such is love.

Simone Weil

Love knows nothing of order.

Jerome, Letters

True love's the gift which God has given
To man alone beneath the heaven.

Walter Scott, The Lay of the Last Minstrel

Better is a dinner of herbs where love is, than a stalled ox and hatred therewith.

The Bible, Proverbs 15:17 (AV)

So let us love, dear Love, like as we ought;
Love is the lesson which the Lord us taught.

Edmund Spenser, Amoretti

Take away love and our earth is a tomb.

Robert Browning

He who loves, trusts.

Italian proverb

Love teaches even asses to dance.

French proverb

Love is bold, respect is timid.

A. Perez

She sat and wept, and with her untressed hair
Still wiped the feet she was blest to touch;
And He wiped off the soiling of despair
From her sweet soul – because she loved so much.

Dante Gabriel Rossetti

We cannot help conforming ourselves to what we love.

Francis de Sales

Love is responsibility of an *I* for a *Thou*

Martin Buber

Man while he loves is never quite depraved.

Charles Lamb

They love indeed who quake to say they love.

Philip Sidney

Love, Christian

You will find all that is lacking in your heart in the heart of Jesus, dying on the cross. Then you will be enabled to love those whom you would naturally, in your pride, hate and crush.

François Fénelon, Christian Perfection, letter of 17 November 1690

I may be able to speak the languages of men and even of angels, but if I have no love, my speech is no more than a noisy gong or a clanging bell. I may have the gift of inspired preaching; I may have all knowledge and under-stand all secrets; I may have all the faith needed to move mountains – but if I have no love, I am nothing. I may give away everything I have, and even give up my body to be burnt – but if I

have no love, this does me no good.
Love is patient and kind; it is not jealous or conceited or proud; love is not ill-mannered or selfish or irritable; love does not keep a record of wrongs; love is not happy with evil, but is nappy with the truth. Love never gives up; and its faith, hope, and patience never fail.
Love is eternal. . . . Meanwhile these three remain: faith, hope, and love; and the greatest of these is love.
The Bible, The apostle Paul,
1 Corinthians 13:1–8, 13

Love is the abridgement of all theology.
Francis de Sales

Love, Consistency of

Love will teach us all things: but we must learn how to win love; it is got with difficulty: it is a possession dearly bought with much labour and in long time; for one must love not sometimes only, for a passing moment, but always. There is no man who does not sometimes love: even the wicked can do that.
Fyodor Dostoevsky, The Brothers
Karamazov

Love, Lack of

All this famine of love, how it saddens my soul. There is not a drop of love anywhere.
Toyohiko Kagawa

Love, Learning

They who will learn love, will always be its scholars.
Byron, Don Juan

Love is a great teacher.
Augustine of Hippo

I loved not yet . . . I sought what I might love, in love with loving.
Augustine of Hippo

Love, Platonic

Platonic love is a delusion; it does not exist in nature.
Ninon de Lenclos

Love, Purity of

An instant of pure love is more precious to God and the soul, and more profitable to the church, than all other good works together, though it may seem as if nothing were done.
John of the Cross

Love one another in truth and purity, as children, impulsively, uncalculatingly.
Edward Wilson, diary

Love, Response to

Alexander, Caesar, Charlemagne and I founded empires; but upon what did we rest the creations of our genius? Upon force. Jesus Christ alone founded his empire upon love; and at this hour millions of men would die for him.
Napoleon

If you be loved, love and be lovable.
Benjamin Franklin, Poor
Richard's Almanac, 1755

Love begets love.
Latin proverb

We are too ready to retaliate rather than to forgive or to gain by love and information. Let us, then, try what love will do: for if men do once see we love them, we should find they would not harm us.
William Penn

Love, Sexual   see also COURTSHIP

There are four things that are too mysterious for me to understand:
an eagle flying in the sky,
a snake moving on a rock,
a ship finding its way over the sea,
and a man and a woman falling in love.
The Bible, Proverbs 30:18–19

Heaven has no rage like love to hatred turned,
Nor hell a fury like a woman scorned.
William Congreve, The Mourning
Bride, Act 3

Love is the selfishness of two.
De la Salle

There is no stronger tie upon a woman than the knowledge that she is loved.
Mme de Motteville

She who has never loved has never lived.
John Gay, The Captives, II.ii

All mankind love a lover.
Ralph Waldo Emerson, Essays,
Love

Love and actions

God regards with how much love a person performs a work, rather than how much he does.
Thomas à Kempis

Our Lord does not care so much for the importance of our works as for the love with which they are done.

Teresa of Avila

True affection is ingeniously inventive.

François Fénelon, Christian Perfection, letter to the Marquis de Seignelai, 2 July 1690

Love and anger

The anger of lovers is soon appeased.

Menander

Love and error

Love is infallible; it has no errors, for all errors are the want of love.

William Law

Love and fear

There is no fear in love; but perfect love casteth out fear.

The Bible, 1 John 4:18 (AV)

True love can fear no one.

Seneca

Love and giving

It is possible to give without loving, but it is impossible to love without giving.

Richard Braunstein

Love and God's nature

Human love is a reflection of something in the divine nature itself.

A.E. Brooke, commentary on the letters of John in the International Critical Commentary series

He who is filled with love is filled with God himself.

Augustine of Hippo

Love and humility

Love does not dominate; it cultivates.

Goethe

Love seeks not to possess, but to be possessed.

R.H. Benson

Love and prayer

It is not a matter of thinking a great deal but of loving a great deal, so do whatever arouses you most to love.

Teresa of Avila

Love and self

Love seeketh not itself to please
Nor for itself hath any care,
But for another gives its ease
And builds a heaven in hell's despair.

William Blake

Love is swift, sincere, pious, pleasant, faithful, prudent, long-suffering, manly and never seeking her own; for wherever you seek your own, you fall from love.

Thomas à Kempis, The Imitation of Christ

Love and suffering

Greater love hath no man than this, that a man lay down his life for his friends.

The Bible, Jesus Christ, John 15:13 (AV)

The one who will be found in trial capable of great acts of love, is ever the one who is doing considerate small ones.

F.W. Robertson

Love suffering on Calvary is far greater than love alive with excitement on Mount Tabor.

François Fénelon, Christian Perfection

Love and the faults of the beloved

When you love someone, you love him as he is.

Charles Péguy

Whatever a person may be like, we must still love him, because we love God.

John Calvin, The Institutes of Christian Religion, 2.8.55

Hate stirs up trouble, but love overlooks all offences.

The Bible, Proverbs 10:12

Love for Christians

If we love one another, God lives in union with us, and his love is made perfect in us.

The Bible, 1 John 4:12

Everyone who has been born of God must love those who have been similarly ennobled.

A.E. Brooke, commentary on the letters of John in the International Critical Commentary series

Love for enemies

If your enemy is hungry, feed him; if he is thirsty, give him a drink. You will make him burn with shame, and the Lord will reward you.

The Bible, Proverbs 25:21–22

You have heard that it was said, 'Love your friends, hate your enemies.' But now I tell you: love your enemies and pray for those who persecute you.

The Bible, Jesus Christ,
Matthew 5:43–44

Love for God

Love the Lord your God with all your heart, with all your soul, and with all your mind.

The Bible, Jesus Christ,
Matthew 22:37

The person who loves God is known by him.

The Bible, The apostle Paul,
1 Corinthians 8:3

We know that in all things God works for good with those who love him, those whom he has called according to his purpose.

The Bible, The apostle Paul,
Romans 8:28

Not by travelling, Lord,
men come to you,
but by the way of love.

Amy Carmichael

Origen kindled in our hearts the love of the divine Word, the supreme object of love who, by his unutterable loveliness, draws everyone irresistibly to himself.

Gregory Thaumaturgus

Man is the perfection of the universe; the spirit is the perfection of man; love is the perfection of the spirit; and charity the perfection of love. Hence, the love of God is the goal, the perfection and the crown of the whole universe.

Francis de Sales

You don't love him, or you would paint him better.

Doré's verdict on the painting of
Jesus which a young artist had
brought to show him

Too late I loved you, O beauty so ancient yet ever new! Too late I loved you! And, behold, you were within me, and I out of myself, and there I searched for you.

Augustine of Hippo

God does not need us to say many words to him, nor to think many thoughts. He sees our hearts, and that is enough for him. He sees very well our suffering and our submission. We have only to repeat continuously to a person we love, 'I love you with all my heart.' It even happens, often, that we go a long time without thinking that we love him, and we love him no less during this period than in those in which we make him the most tender protestations. True love rests in the depths of the heart.

François Fénelon

If you knew the whole Bible by heart, and the sayings of all the philosophers, what good would it do you without the love of God, without grace?

Thomas à Kempis

To love God is the greatest of virtues; to be loved by God is the greatest of blessings.

Portuguese proverb

The reason for loving God is God himself and how he should be loved is to love without limit.

Bernard of Clairvaux, On Loving
God

The will to love God is the whole of religion.

François Fénelon

Let us make God the beginning and end of our love, for he is the fountain from which all good things flow and into him alone they flow back. Let him therefore be the beginning of our love.

Richard Rolle

To love God is to hate oneself and to know nothing apart from God.

Martin Luther, Thesis 95

Where there is love, there is a trinity: a lover, a beloved and a spring of love.

Augustine of Hippo

To love God entirely, the soul must be pure and strong, staying faithful to God in times of trouble, alert against dishonesty and fraud. In this way man will not just find the supreme good, he will himself become like the supreme good – because he will be transformed into the image of God.

Augustine of Hippo, The Catholic
Church

The reason why God's servants love creatures so much is that they see how much Christ loves them, and it is one of the properties of love to love what is loved by the person we love.

Catherine of Siena

Love for neighbours see NEIGHBOUR

Loyalty

Ruth answered: 'Don't ask me to leave you! Let me go with you. Wherever you go, I will go; wherever you live, I will live. Your people will be my people, and your God will be my God. Wherever you die, I will be buried. May the Lord's worst punishment come upon me if I do let anything but death separate me from you!'

The Bible, Ruth 1:16–17

Never let go of loyalty and faithfulness.

The Bible, Proverbs 3:3

Lukewarmness

I know thy works, that thou art neither cold nor hot: I would thou wert cold or hot. So then because thou art lukewarm, and neither cold nor hot, I will spew thee out of my mouth.

The Bible, Jesus Christ to the church in Laodicea, Revelation 3:15

Lukewarmness I account as great a sin in love as in religion.

Abraham Cowley

Luxury

Luxury causes great care and produces great carelessness as to virtue.

Cato

Lying   see LIES

M

Mankind   see also HUMAN RIGHTS

The Lord God took some soil from the ground and formed a man out of it; he breathed life-giving breath into his nostrils and the man began to live.

The Bible, Genesis 3:9

Put no more confidence in mortal men.

The Bible, Isaiah 2:22

Man is only a reed, the weakest in nature; but he is a thinking reed.

Blaise Pascal, Pensées

At the bottom of the modern man there is always a great thirst for self-forgetfulness, self-distraction . . . and therefore he turns away from all those problems and abysses which might recall to him his own nothingness.

Henri Frédéric Amiel

People wish to be settled: only as far as they are unsettled is there any hope for them.

Ralph Waldo Emerson

I sometimes think that God in creating man somewhat overestimated His ability.

Oscar Wilde

There are only two kinds of men: the righteous who believe themselves sinners, and the rest, sinners who believe themselves righteous.

Blaise Pascal

Man – a being in search of meaning.

Plato

Human nature is like a drunk peasant. Lift him into the saddle on one side, over he topples on the other side.

Martin Luther

All that is human must retrograde if it does not advance.

Edward Gibbon

Man and woman are one body and soul.

The Talmud

Man is the measure of all things.

Protagoras

I've lost all hope, so what if God kills me?
    I am going to state my case to him.

The Bible, Job, Job 13:15

Man is only man at the surface. Remove his skin, dissect, and immediately you come to machinery.

Paul Valéry

Our Saviour knew mankind better than Socrates.

Boerhaave, on Jesus' warning to check thought as well as action (Matthew 5:28)

The tree which moves some to tears of joy is, in the eye of others, only a green thing which stands in the way. As a man is, so he sees.

William Blake

No great man lives in vain. The history of the world is but the biography of great men.

Thomas Carlyle, Heroes and Hero-Worship

Mankind, Christ's redemption of   see also SALVATION

He who denies the necessary perishing of all that live and die in the state of corrupted nature, denies all the use of the incarnation and mediation of the

Son of God: for if we may be saved without the renovation of our natures, there was no need nor use of the new creation of all things by Jesus Christ, which principally consists therein; and if men may be saved under all the evils that came upon us by the fall, then did Christ die in vain.

John Owen, The Nature, Causes, and Means of Regeneration

Jesus Christ taught men the simple truth about themselves: that they were selfish; enslaved to their appetites; blind, sick, unhappy, sinners; that it was laid upon himself to deliver, enlighten, bless, and heal them; and that this would be brought about by hatred of self, and by following him through poverty to the death of the cross.

Blaise Pascal

Mankind, compared with animals

The question is this: Is man an ape or an angel? I, my lord, am on the side of the angels.

Benjamin Disraeli, speech on 25 November 1864

Man with all his noble qualities . . . still bears in his bodily frame the indelible stamp of his lowly origin.

Charles Darwin, The Descent of Man

Brutes find out where their talents lie;
A bear will not attempt to fly,
A foundered horse will oft debate
Before he tries a five barred gate.
A dog by instinct turns aside
Who sees the ditch too deep and wide,
But man we find the only creature
Who, led by folly, combats nature;
With obstinacy fixes there;
And where the genius least inclines,
Absurdly bends his whole designs.

Jonathan Swift

This is the quality peculiar to man, wherein he differs from other animals, that he alone is endowed with perception to distinguish right from wrong, justice from injustice.

Aristotle

It is dangerous to make man see how like he is to animals without keeping his greatness in view. It is dangerous also to show him his greatness and not his baseness; and still more to leave

him ignorant of both. But it is most profitable to show him both.

Blaise Pascal

Man is the only animal that laughs and weeps; for he is the only animal that is struck by the difference between what things are and what they might have been.

William Hazlitt

All creatures kill – there seems to be no exception. But of the whole list man is the only one that kills for fun; he is the only one that kills in malice, the only one that kills for revenge.

Mark Twain

Wild animals never kill for sport. Man is the only one to whom the torture and death of his fellow creatures is amusing in itself.

J.A. Froude

Man is a tool-making animal.

Benjamin Franklin, quoted in James Boswell, Life of Johnson

Brutes never meet in bloody fray,
Nor cut each other's throats for pay.

Jonathan Swift

Man is the only animal that blushes. Or needs to.

Mark Twain

Mankind, Depravity of   see also ORIGINAL SIN

Men loved darkness rather than light, because their deeds were evil.

The Bible, John 3:19 (AV)

Man is very far gone from original righteousness.

Book of Common Prayer, Article 9

It is easier to denature plutonium than to denature the evil spirit of man.

Albert Einstein

Out of the crooked timber of humanity no straight thing can ever be made.

Immanuel Kant, Idee zu einer allgemeinen Geschichte in weltbürgerlicher Absicht

Our nature is not only completely empty of goodness, but so full of every kind of wrong that it is always active. Those who call it lust use an apt word, provided it is also stated (though not everyone will agree) that everything which is in man, from the intellect to the will, from the soul to the body, is defiled and imbued with this lust. To put it briefly, the whole man is in himself nothing but lust.

> *John Calvin, The Institutes of*
> *Christian Religion, 2.1.8*

Eichmann is in us, each of us.

> *Dinur*

The true problem lies in the hearts and thoughts of men. It is not a physical but an ethical one. . . . What terrifies us is not the explosive force of the atomic bomb but the power of the wickedness of the human heart.

> *Albert Einstein, lecture, 1948*

No clever arrangement of bad eggs will make a good omelette.

> *C.S. Lewis*

The natural man cannot want God to be God. Rather he wants himself to be God, and God not to be God.

> *Martin Luther, Thesis 17*

There is no man so good who, if all his actions and thoughts were put to the test of the laws, would not deserve hanging ten times in his life.

> *Montaigne*

Use every man after his desert, and who should 'scape whipping?

> *William Shakespeare, Hamlet, II.ii*

Mankind, Exalted estimates of

The world is full of wonders, but nothing is more wonderful than man.

> *Sophocles*

Man is naturally inclined to beneficence.

> *Marcus Aurelius*

Glory to Man in the Highest! for Man is the master of things.

> *Alfred, Lord Tennyson, Hymn of*
> *Man*

Mankind, Inhumanity to man

[Herod] gave orders to kill all the boys in Bethlehem and its neighbourhood who were two years old and younger.

> *The Bible, Matthew 2:16*

It is men, not God, who have produced racks, whips, prisons, slavery, guns, bayonets, and bombs; it is by human avarice or human stupidity, not by the churlishness of nature, that we have poverty and overwork.

> *C.S. Lewis, The Problem of Pain*

Mankind, Insignificance of

When a man is wrapped up in himself he makes a pretty small package.

> *John Ruskin*

Man is a little soul carrying around a corpse.

> *Epictetus*

Man is but a breath and shadow.

> *Euripides*

The state of man is inconstancy, boredom, anxiety.

> *Blaise Pascal, Pensées*

The life of man, solitary, poor, nasty, brutish, and short.

> *Thomas Hobbes*

Cursed is everyone who places his hope in man.

> *Augustine of Hippo*

Men are all like a puff of breath;
  great and small are worthless.
Put them on the scales, and they weigh
  nothing;
  they are lighter than a mere breath.

> *The Bible, Psalm 62:9*

Man that is born of a woman hath but a short time to live, and is full of misery.

> *Book of Common Prayer, Burial*
> *of the Dead*

Our helplessness in necessary things.

> *Seneca*

Man – a creature made at the end of the week's work when God was tired.

> *Mark Twain*

He [God] remembers what we are
  made of;
  he remembers that we are dust.

> *The Bible, Psalm 103:14*

Mankind, Middle state of

Man is neither angel nor beast; and the misfortune is that he who would act the angel acts the beast.

> *Blaise Pascal*

Know then thyself, presume not God
  to scan;
The proper study of mankind is man.
Plac'd on this isthmus of a middle
  state,
A being darkly wise, and rudely great:
With too much knowledge for the
  sceptic side,
With too much weakness for the stoic's
  pride,
He hangs between; in doubt to act, or
  rest,
In doubt to deem himself a God, or
  beast;
In doubt his mind or body to prefer;
Born but to die, and reas'ning but to
  err;

Alike in ignorance, his reason such,
Whether he thinks too little, or too
    much:
Chaos of thought and passion, all
    confus'd;
Still by himself abus'd, or disabus'd;
Created half to rise, and half to fall;
Great lord of all things, yet a prey to
    all;
Sole judge of truth, in endless error
    hurl'd:
The glory, jest, and riddle of the
    world!
                    Alexander Pope, Essay on Man

Mankind, Nature of

The inclination to goodness is
imprinted deeply in the nature of man:
insomuch, that if it issue not towards
men, it will take unto other living creatures.
                    Francis Bacon, Essays, Goodness,
                    and Goodness of Nature

I'm a man and a man's a mixture
    Right down from his very birth;
For part of him comes from heaven,
    And part of him comes from earth.
                    G.A. Studdert-Kennedy

Man is a gaming animal. He must
always be trying to get the better in
something or other.
                    Charles Lamb, Essays of Elia

Our nature is very bad in itself, but
very good to them that use it well.
                    Jeremy Taylor

It is the nature of man to believe and to
love: if he has not the right objects for
his belief and love, he will attach himself to wrong ones.
                    Blaise Pascal

Man . . . is a being born to believe.
                    Benjamin Disraeli, speech at
                    Oxford diocesan conference, 1864

It will be very generally found that
those who will sneer habitually at
human nature, and affect to despise it,
are among its worst and least pleasant
samples.
                    Charles Dickens

Human action can be modified to
some extent, but human nature cannot
be changed.
                    Abraham Lincoln

Man is by his constitution a religious
animal.
                    Edmund Burke, Reflections on the
                    Revolution in France

Mankind, potential with God

And ah for a man to arise in me, that
the man I am may cease to be.
                    Alfred, Lord Tennyson

All great knowledge is this, for a man
to know that he himself by himself is
nothing; and that, whatever he is, he is
from God and on account of God.
                    Augustine of Hippo, on Psalm 70

Whatever else may be said of man, this
one thing is clear: He is not what he is
capable of being.
                    G.K. Chesterton

God created man in order to have
someone on whom to shower his love.
                    Irenaeus of Lyons

No man need stay the way he is.
                    Harry Emerson Fosdick

Our humanity were a poor thing were
it not for the divinity which stirs within
us.
                    Francis Bacon

Mankind, Social aspects of

Man is a political animal.
                    Aristotle

Man is a social animal.
                    Seneca

Hand rubs hand, and hand washes
hand.
                    Latin proverb

To be honest;
to be kind;
to earn a little
and to spend a little less;
to make, upon the whole,
a family happier for his presence;
to renounce, when that shall be
    necessary,
and not be embittered;
to keep a few friends,
but these without capitulation;
above all, in the same condition,
to keep friends with himself;
here is a task for all that a man has of
    fortitude and delicacy.
                    Robert Louis Stevenson

Manners   see also BEHAVIOUR; POLITENESS

Good manners is the art of making
those people easy with whom we converse. Whoever makes the fewest
people uneasy is the best bred in the
company.
                    Jonathan Swift

The test of good manners is being able to put up pleasantly with bad ones.
Author unknown

Good breeding consists in concealing how much we think of ourselves and how little we think of the other person.
Mark Twain, Notebooks

Marriage   see also DIVORCE; FAMILIES; HUSBANDS; WIVES

It is not good that man should be alone; I will make him an help meet for him.
The Bible, God, Genesis 2:18 (AV)

Therefore shall a man leave his father and his mother, and shall cleave unto his wife; and they shall be one flesh.
The Bible, Genesis 2:24 (AV)

Each one has a special gift from God, one person this gift, another one that gift.
The Bible, The apostle Paul, 1 Corinthians 7:7

Wedlock is a padlock.
John Ray, A Collection of English Proverbs, 1678

An archaeologist is the best husband any woman can have; the older she gets, the more interested he is in her.
Agatha Christie

Marriage was ordained for a remedy and to increase the world and for the man to help the woman and the woman the man, with all love and kindness.
William Tyndale, The Obedience of a Christen Man

Mutual society, help and comfort, that the one ought to have of the other, both in prosperity and adversity.
Thomas Cranmer, Book of Common Prayer

The marital love is a thing pure as light, sacred as a temple, lasting as the world.
Jeremy Taylor

All that can be called happy in the life of man, is summed up in the state of marriage; that is the centre to which all the lesser delights of life tend, as a point in the circle.
Daniel Defoe, Use and Abuse of the Marriage Bed

Marriage: A community consisting of a master, a mistress, and two slaves, making in all, two.
Ambrose Bierce, The Devil's Dictionary

Women – one half the human race at least – care fifty times more for a marriage than a ministry.
Walter Bagehot, The English Constitution, The Monarchy

Marriage, Christian

You husbands must live with your wives with the proper understanding that they are the weaker sex. Treat them with respect, because they also will receive, together with you, God's gift of life.
The Bible, The apostle Peter, 1 Peter 3:7

Nowhere in the New Testament is a wife exhorted to obey her husband.
Mary Evans, Woman in the Bible

The virginity of Mary and her child-bearing was hidden from the prince of this world; so likewise was the death of the Lord – three mysteries that are to be proclaimed with a shout, which were effected in the quiet of God.
Ignatius of Antioch, To the Ephesians

Marriage and celibacy

It is better to marry than to burn with passion.
The Bible, The apostle Paul, 1 Corinthians 7:9

Wholly abstain or wed.
George Herbert

Bishops, priests and deacons are not commanded by God's law either to vow the estate of single life, or to abstain from marriage.
Book of Common Prayer, Article 32

Marriage and faithfulness

Marriage is to be honoured by all, and husbands and wives must be faithful to each other. God will judge those who are immoral and those who commit adultery.
The Bible, Hebrews 13:4

Marriage and heaven

When the dead rise to life, they will be like the angels in heaven and will not marry.
The Bible, Jesus Christ, Matthew 22:30

Marriage and love

A WIFE TO A HUSBAND

How do I love thee? Let me count the ways.

I love thee to the depth and breadth
and height
My soul can reach, when feeling out of
sight
For the end of Being and ideal Grace.
I love thee to the level of everyday's
Most quiet need, by sun and
candlelight.
I love thee freely, as men strive for
Right;
I love thee purely, as they turn from
Praise.
I love thee with the passion put to use
In my old griefs, and with my
childhood's faith.
I love thee with a love I seemed to lose
With my lost saints, – I love thee with
the breath,
Smiles, tears, of all my life! – and, if
God choose,
I shall but love thee better after death.
Elizabeth Barrett Browning,
Sonnets from the Portuguese

Martyrdom

I was some time in being burned.
At last a hand came through
The flames and drew
My soul to Christ whom now I see;
Sergius a brother writes for me
This testimony on the wall.
For me – I have forgot it all.
Robert Browning, of a martyr's
memorial tablet

The tyrant dies and his rule ends, the
martyr dies and his rule begins.
Søren Kierkegaard

When I was delighting in the doctrines
of Plato, and heard the Christians slandered, and saw them fearless of death
. . . I perceived that it was impossible
that they could be living in wickedness
and pleasure.
Justin Martyr

You can kill us, but not hurt us.
Justin Martyr, to the emperor

No man ever laid down his life for the
honour of Jupiter, Neptune, or
Apollo; but how many thousands have
sealed their Christian testimony with
their blood.
Beattie

Love makes the whole difference
between an execution and a martyrdom.
Evelyn Underhill

It is not the pain but the purpose that
makes the martyr.
Augustine of Hippo

It is the cause, not the death, that
makes the martyr.
Napoleon, Maxims

Martyrdom, Effects of

The church owes Paul to the prayer of
Stephen.
Augustine of Hippo

The more they mow us down, the
more we grow; the seed is the blood of
Christians.
Tertullian

Martyrdom welcomed

Eighty-six years have I served Jesus
and he has done me no wrong. How can
I blaspheme my king who saved me?
Polycarp, when asked to deny his
faith and so avoid martyrdom

I have committed my cause to the
great judge of all mankind, so I am not
moved by threats, nor are your swords
more ready to strike than is my soul for
martyrdom.
Thomas Beckett, when facing the
knights ready to murder him

Now do I begin to be a disciple of my
master, Christ.
Ignatius of Antioch, travelling
cheerfully to the place where he
was to be thrown to the lions

[Upon being urged to recant, or be
burned – since 'Life is sweet and death
is bitter':] True, quite true! But eternal
life is more sweet, and eternal death is
more bitter.
John Hooper

I die for Christ of my own choice,
unless you hinder me. I beseech you
not to show 'inopportune kindness' to
me. Let me be given to the wild beasts,
for by their means I can attain to God.
I am God's wheat, and I am being
ground by the teeth of the beasts so
that I may be like pure bread. Rather
coax the beasts, that they may become
my tomb, and leave no part of my body
behind, so that I may not be a nuisance
to anyone when I have fallen asleep.
Ignatius of Antioch, To the Romans

Marxism

Property is theft.
Proudhon; used as a basis of
Marxism

Mary   see also ANNUNCIATION; VIRGIN
BIRTH

My heart praises the Lord;
   my soul is glad because of God my
      Saviour,
   for he has remembered me, his
      lowly servant!
From now on all people will call me
   happy,
   because of the great things the
      Mighty God has done for me.
His name is holy.
                        The Bible, Mary, Luke 1:46–49

Not as the mother of grace, but as the
daughter of grace.
                                        Bengel

Mass   see also LORD'S SUPPER

The sacrifices of masses, in the which it
was commonly said, that the priest did
offer Christ for the quick and the dead,
to have remission of pain or guilt, were
blasphemous fables, and dangerous
deceits.
                        Book of Common Prayer,
                                      Article 31

No part of Christian religion was ever
so vilely contaminated and abused by
profane wretches, as this pure, holy,
plain action and institution of our
Saviour: witness the Popish horrid
monster of transubstantiation, and
their idolatrous mass.
                John Owen, The Principles of the
                              Doctrine of Christ

Maturity   see also GROWTH

Love slays what we have been that we
may be what we were not.
                              Augustine of Hippo

He is only advancing in life, whose
heart is getting softer, his blood
warmer, his brain quicker, and his
spirit entering into living peace.
                                    John Ruskin

Meaning of life

The only reason why man as man has
individual significance is that Christ
died for him.
                              George MacLeod

Only religion is able to answer the
question of the purpose of life. One
can hardly go wrong in concluding that
the idea of a purpose in life stands and
falls with the religious system.
                Sigmund Freud, Civilisation and
                                 its Discontents

Meaninglessness

If there are no gods all our toil is without meaning.
                        Euripides, Iphigenia in Aulis

The universe is indifferent. Who
created it? Why are we here on this
puny mud-heap spinning in infinite
space? I have not the slightest idea,
and I am quite convinced that no one
has the least idea.
                                    André Maurois

Every existing thing is born without
reason, prolongs itself out of weakness
and dies by chance.
                                  Jean-Paul Sartre

It is useless, useless, said the
Philosopher. Life is useless, all useless. You spend your life working,
labouring, and what do you have to
show for it?
                        The Bible, Ecclesiastes 1:2–3

All is vanity and vexation of spirit.
                        The Bible, Ecclesiastes 1:14 (AV)

No mortal is happy of all on whom the
sun looks down.
                                        Theognis

Life is one long struggle in the dark.
                        Lucretius, The Nature of the
                                         Universe

The mass of men lead lives of quiet
desperation.
                        Henry David Thoreau, Walden

Drank every cup of joy, drank early,
deeply drank, drank draughts which
common millions might have drunk,
then died of thirst because there was
no more to drink.
                                         Byron

Life is a bad joke.
                                        Voltaire

Tomorrow, and tomorrow, and
   tomorrow,
Creeps in this petty pace from day to day
To the last syllable of recorded time,
And all our yesterdays have lighted
   fools
The way to dusty death. Out, out,
   brief candle!
Life's but a walking shadow, a poor
   player,
That struts and frets his hour upon the
   stage,
And then is heard no more; it is a tale
Told by an idiot, full of sound and fury,
Signifying nothing.
                William Shakespeare, Macbeth V.v

Life is as tedious as a twice-told tale,
Vexing the dull ear of a drowsy man.
*William Shakespeare, King John,
III.iv*

All the world's a stage,
And all the men and women merely
players;
They have their exits and their
entrances;
. . . Last scene of all,
That ends this strange eventful
history,
Is second childishness and mere
oblivion;
Sans teeth, sans eyes, sans taste, sans
everything.
*William Shakespeare, As You
Like It, II.vii*

As flies to wanton boys, are we to the
gods;
They kill us for their sport.
*William Shakespeare, Gloucester
in King Lear*

Life is one long process of getting
tired.
Samuel Butler, Notebooks

Meditation   see also CONTEMPLATION

My spirit has become dry because it
forgets to feed on you.
John of the Cross

When you meditate, imagine that
Jesus Christ in person is about to talk
to you about the most important thing
in the world. Give him your complete
attention.
*François Fénelon, Christian
Perfection, letter to the Duchesse
de Beauvilliers*

It is preferable to be very humble and
ashamed of the faults one has committed than to be satisfied with one's
meditation and puffed up with the idea
that one is very advanced in spiritual
matters.
*François Fénelon, Christian
Perfection, letter to a lady*

Those who draw water from the
wellspring of meditation know that
God dwells close to their hearts.
Toyohiko Kagawa

Spend an hour every day, some time
before the midday meal, in meditation; and the earlier the better,
because your mind will then be less
distracted, and fresh after a night's
sleep.
Francis de Sales

Wilt thou love God, as he thee! then
digest,
My soul, this wholesome meditation,
How God the Spirit by angels waited
on
In heaven, doth make his Temple in
thy heart.
John Donne, Holy Sonnets

Work of sight is done.
Now do heart work
On the pictures within you.
Rainer Maria Rilke

All the troubles of life come upon us
because we refuse to sit quietly for a
while each day in our rooms.
Blaise Pascal

In the rush and noise of life, as you
have intervals, step home within yourselves and be still. Wait upon God,
and feel his good presence; this will
carry you evenly through your day's
business.
William Penn

Whatsoever things are true, whatsoever things are honest, whatsoever
things are just, whatsoever things are
pure, whatsoever things are lovely,
whatsoever things are of good report;
if there be any virtue, and if there be
any praise, think on these things.
*The Bible, The apostle Paul,
Philippians 4:8 (AV)*

Melancholy   see also DEPRESSION

Give no place to despondency. This is
a dangerous temptation of the adver-
sary. Melancholy contracts and withers
the heart.
Mme Guyon

Mercy   see also GOD'S MERCY

Mercy is compassion plus action.
Author unknown

The quality of mercy is not strained,
It droppeth as the gentle rain from
heaven
Upon the place beneath; it is twice
blest;
It blesseth him that gives, and him that
takes:
'Tis mightiest in the mightiest: it
becomes
The thronèd monarch better than his
crown;
His sceptre shows the force of
temporal power,
The attribute to awe and majesty,

Wherein doth sit the dread and fear of
kings;
But mercy is above this sceptred sway;
It is enthronèd in the hearts of kings,
It is an attribute of God himself;
And earthly power doth then show
likest God's
When mercy seasons justice.
Therefore, Jew,
Though justice be thy pleas, consider
this –
That in the course of justice none of us
Should see salvation; we do pray for
mercy,
And that same prayer doth teach us all
to render
The deeds of mercy.
William Shakespeare, Merchant of
Venice, IV.i

To Mercy, Pity, Peace, and Love
All pray in their distress;
And to these virtues of delight
Return their thankfulness.
William Blake, Songs of Innocence

Methodism

A Methodist is one who loves the Lord
his God with all his heart, with all his
soul, with all his mind, and with all his
strength. God is the joy of his heart,
and the desire of his soul.
John Wesley, The Character of a
Methodist

Our societies were formed from those
who were wandering upon the dark
mountains, that belonged to no Christian church; but were awakened by the
preaching of the Methodists, who had
pursued them through the wilderness
of this world to the highways and the
hedges – to the markets and the fairs –
to the hills and the dales – who set up
the standard of the Cross in the streets
and lanes of the cities, in the villages,
in the barns, and farmers' kitchens, etc.
– and all this done in such a way, and to
such an extent, as never had been done
before since the apostolic age.
John Wesley

Millionaires

Millionaires seldom smile.
Andrew Carnegie

Mind   see also THINKING

It is riches of the mind only that make a
man rich and happy.
Thomas Fuller, Gnomologia

The human mind is so constructed that
it resists vigour and yields to gentleness.
Francis de Sales

Choose to have a vigorous mind rather
than a vigorous body.
Pythagoras

The mind is its own place, and in itself
Can make a heaven of hell, a hell of
heaven.
John Milton

It is not enough to have a good mind.
The main thing is to use it well.
René Descartes, Discourse on
Method

Ministers of religion   see also WOMEN'S
MINISTRY

Some ministers would make good
martyrs. They are so dry, they would
burn well.
C.H. Spurgeon

[The Mayflower pilgrims] held (in
opposition to the church) that the
priesthood is not a distinct order, but
an office temporarily conferred by the
vote of the congregation.
John Masefield, introduction to
Chronicles of the Pilgrim Fathers,
Everyman's Library edition

What village parson would not like to
be a pope?
Voltaire, Letters on the English

It will, I believe, be everywhere found,
that as the clergy are, or are not what
they ought to be, so are the rest of the
nation.
Jane Austen, Mansfield Park, ch. 9

As the French say, there are three
sexes, men, women and clergymen.
Sydney Smith

Prayer and temptation, the Bible and
meditation make a true minister of the
gospel.
Martin Luther

Ministers of religion, Authority of

Be eager to act always in godly agreement; with the bishop presiding as the
counterpart of God, the presbyters as
the counterpart of the council of the
apostles, and the deacons (most dear
to me) who have been entrusted with a
service [*diaconate*] under Jesus Christ,
who was with the Father before all
ages and appeared at the end of time.
Ignatius of Antioch, To the
Magnesians

One ought to think as follows about ministers. The office does not belong to Judas but to Christ alone. When Christ said to Judas, 'Go, baptise,' Christ himself was the baptiser and not Judas because the command comes from above even if it passes down through a stinking pipe. Nothing is taken from the office on account of the unworthiness of a minister.

Martin Luther

Ministers of religion, Choice of

Appoint bishops and deacons worthy of the Lord – mild men, who are not out to get money, men who are genuine and approved; for they are your prophets and teachers.

Didache

When appointing priests we should choose only those of spotless and upright character as our leaders.

Cyprian of Carthage, Epistle 67

In order to prove a man's call [to the ministry], he must see a measure of conversion-work going on under his efforts.

C.H. Spurgeon

Miracles

The Spirit gives one person the power to work miracles.

The Bible, The apostle Paul, 1 Corinthians 12:10

As to me, I know of nothing else but miracles.

Walt Whitman

Miracles do not happen.

Matthew Arnold, Literature and Dogma, Preface to 1883 edition

If a man is a fool for believing in a Creator, then he is a fool for believing in a miracle; but not otherwise.

G.K. Chesterton

It is not necessary for me to go far afield in search of miracles. I am a miracle myself. My physical birth and my soul's existence are miracles. First and foremost, the fact that I was even born is a miracle.

Toyohiko Kagawa

I never have any difficulty believing in miracles, since I experienced the miracle of a change in my own heart.

Augustine of Hippo

Miracles are the swaddling clothes of infant churches.

Thomas Fuller

Miracles are not contrary to nature, but only contrary to what we know about nature.

Augustine of Hippo

God never wrought miracles to convince atheism, because his ordinary works convince it.

Francis Bacon, Essays, Atheism

Miracles of Jesus

The miracles of Jesus were the ordinary works of his Father, wrought small and swift that we might take them in.

George Macdonald

Misery

It is a miserable state of mind to have few things to desire and many things to fear.

Francis Bacon, Essays, Of Empire

Misery loves company.

John Ray, English Proverbs

Mission   see also EVANGELISM

We cannot hesitate to believe that the great mission of Christianity was in reality accomplished by means of informal missionaries.

Adolf Harnack, The Mission and Expansion of Christianity

The church exists by mission, as fire exists by burning.

Emil Brunner

I will go down, if you will hold the ropes.

William Carey's prayer, likening his missionary work to exploring a mine

Perpetual tutelage and everlasting leading strings would enfeeble angels.

David Livingstone, warning against over-emphasising consolidation in missionary strategy, as against continued expansion

The crowning wonder of [God's] scheme is that he entrusted it to *men*. It is the supreme glory of humanity that the machinery for its redemption should have been placed within itself.

Henry Drummond

When God wills to convert the heathen world, young man, he'll do it without consulting you or me.

The advice which William Carey was given, and which led him in 1792 to start a fund for the Baptist Missionary Society

Those who deblaterate against missions have only one thing to do: to come and see them on the spot.
Robert Louis Stevenson

Missionaries

There are three indispensable requirements for a missionary: 1. Patience. 2. Patience. 3. Patience.
Hudson Taylor

God had an only Son, and he was a missionary and a physician.
David Livingstone

Missionary call

Then I heard the Lord say, 'Whom shall I send? Who will be our messenger?'
I answered, 'I will go! Send me!'
The Bible, Isaiah 6:8

Go not to those who want you, but to those who want you most.
John Wesley

My son, if God has called you to be a missionary, your Father would be grieved to see you shrivel down into a king.
C.H. Spurgeon

Millions have never heard the name of Jesus. Hundreds of millions have seen a missionary only once in their lives, and know nothing of our King. Shall we let them perish? Can we go to our beds and sleep while China, India, Japan, and other nations are being damned? Are we clear of their blood? Have they no claim upon us? We ought to put it on this footing – not 'Can I prove that I *ought* to go?' but 'Can I prove that I *ought not* to go?'
C.H. Spurgeon, Lectures to my Students, Second Series

Cannibals Need Missionaries.
Poster outside a Liverpool hall, advertising a meeting at which C.T. Studd heard of the need of Africa for missionaries

We were enabled to renounce a life of usefulness in another and more distant land.
Thomas Barnardo's description of his call to work in London's East End

Mistakes see also CONFESSION; FAULTS; PERFECTION

There is no one on earth who does what is right and never makes a mistake.
The Bible, Ecclesiastes 7:20

A life spent making mistakes is not only more honourable but more useful than a life spent doing nothing.
George Bernard Shaw, The Doctor's Dilemma

I beseech you, in the bowels of Christ, think it possible you may be mistaken.
Oliver Cromwell, Letter to the General Assembly of the Church of Scotland, 3 August 1650

There is nothing progressive about being pig-headed and refusing to admit a mistake.
C.S. Lewis, Mere Christianity

The burned fool's bandaged finger goes wobbling back to the fire.
Rudyard Kipling, on the human tendency to repeat mistakes

Great blunders are often made, like large ropes, of a multitude of fibres.
Victor Hugo

Never let mistakes or wrong directions, of which every man . . . falls into many, discourage you. There is precious instruction to be got by finding where we were wrong.
Thomas Carlyle

A man should never be ashamed to own he has been in the wrong, which is but saying, in other words, that he is wiser today than he was yesterday.
Jonathan Swift

We often discover what *will* do, by finding out what will not do; and probably he who never made a mistake never made a discovery.
Samuel Smiles, Self-Help

The man who makes no mistakes does not usually make anything.
Edward John Phelps, speech at the Mansion House in London on 24 January 1899

Mobs

The mob has many heads but no brains.
Proverb

Mockery

If Jesus Christ were to come today, people would not even crucify him. They would ask him to dinner, and hear what he had to say, and make fun of it.
Thomas Carlyle

Moderation see also EXCESS

Moderation is the silken string running through the pearl chain of all virtues.
Joseph Hall, Christian Moderation

Modesty

Modesty is a becoming ornament in a young man.

Plautus

Beauty is truly beauty when its comrade is a modest mind.

Greek proverb

Modesty is the citadel of beauty and virtue.

Demades

Modesty once gone never returns.

Seneca

He who speaks without modesty will find it difficult to make his words good.

Confucius, Analects

Great modesty often hides great merit.

Benjamin Franklin, Poor Richard's Almanac, 1758

Money   see also WEALTH

The surface above gold mines is generally very barren.

Author unknown

Money is like muck, not good except it be spread.

Francis Bacon, Essays, Of Seditions and Troubles

Money often costs too much.

Ralph Waldo Emerson

Get all you can, save all you can and give all you can.

John Wesley

If the devil were made of gold, he would turn into money.

Angot

Asses' dung.

How the Franciscans are said to have regarded money

Money is life to wretched mortals.

Hesiod

Money is round, so it must circulate.

French proverb

Money, you are the cause of the anxieties of life, and through you we go down to the grave before our time.

Plautus

Dally not with money or women.

George Herbert, Outlandish Proverbs

Money, Dissatisfaction with

If you love money, you will never be satisfied; if you long to be rich, you will never get all you want. It is useless.

The Bible, Ecclesiastes 5:10

Money, Limits to the usefulness of

Nothing that is God's can be obtained with money.

Tertullian

Money will buy a pretty good dog but it won't buy the wag of his tail.

Josh Billings

Money really adds no more to the wise than clothes can to the beautiful.

Jewish proverb

Money, Love of

The love of money is the root of all evil.

The Bible, The apostle Paul, 1 Timothy 6:10 (AV)

It has been said that the love of money is the root of all evil. The want of money is so quite as truly.

Samuel Butler, Erewhon, ch. 20

The love of money is the parent of all wickedness.

Philoctetes

There are three causes for inordinate love of money – desire for pleasure, vain glory and lack of trust. And the last is stronger than the other two.

Maximus the Confessor

To be clever enough to get a great deal of money, one must be stupid enough to want it.

G.K. Chesterton

Your heart will always be where your riches are.

The Bible, Jesus Christ, Matthew 6:21

Money, Spending

Ask thy purse what thou shouldst buy.

Thomas Fuller, Gnomologia

Who has ears, let him hear; who has money, let him spend it.

Goethe

Money and the service of God

No one can be a slave of two masters; he will hate one and love the other; he will be loyal to one and despise the other. You cannot serve both God and money.

The Bible, Jesus Christ, Matthew 6:24

How hard it is for rich people to enter the Kingdom of God!

The Bible, Jesus Christ, Luke 18:24

Nothing I am sure has such a tendency to quench the fire of religion as the possession of money.
J.C. Ryle, Practical Religion

You can see what God thinks of money when you see the people he gives it to.
Abraham Lincoln

Money is always either our master or our slave.
Latin proverb

Monks

Monks are really Pelagians. They trust in themselves and their own works and consequently undermine both the church and the faith.
Martin Luther, The Epistle to the Romans

Monuments

Those only deserve a monument who do not need one.
William Hazlitt

Morality

We must not be guilty of sexual immorality.
The Bible, The apostle Paul, 1 Corinthians 10:8

Give up money, give up fame, give up science, give up the earth itself and all it contains, rather than do an immoral act.
Thomas Jefferson

If morality was Christianity, Socrates was the Saviour.
William Blake, Annotations to Dr Thornton's 'New Translation of the Lord's Prayer'

A piano has not got two kinds of notes on it, the 'right' notes and the 'wrong' ones. Every single note is right at one time and wrong at another.
C.S. Lewis, Mere Christianity

It is not, what a lawyer tells me I *may* do; but what humanity, reason, and justice tell me I ought to do.
Edmund Burke

Two blacks make no white
Two wrongs do not make a right.
H.G. Bohn, Proverbs

Nothing is settled until it is settled right.
Abraham Lincoln

Better, though difficult, the right way to go

Than wrong, tho' easy, where the end is woe.
John Bunyan, The Pilgrim's Progress

Lord, give us faith that right makes might.
Abraham Lincoln, Speeches and Letters

If your morals make your dreary, depend upon it, they are wrong. I do not say give them up, for they may be all you have, but conceal them like a vice lest they should spoil the lives of better and simpler people.
Robert Louis Stevenson

Motherhood   see also CHRISTIAN UPBRINGING

God could not be everywhere and therefore he made mothers.
Jewish proverb

You have omitted to mention the greatest of my teachers – my mother.
Winston Churchill, on being asked to check a list of those who had taught him

It is impossible that the son of these tears should perish.
Augustine of Hippo, Confessions

What the mother sings to the cradle goes all the way down to the coffin.
Henry Ward Beecher, Proverbs from a Plymouth Pulpit

If I were hanged on the highest hill,
Mother o' mine, O mother o' mine!
I know whose love would follow me still,
Mother o' mine, O mother o' mine!

If I were drowned in the deepest sea,
Mother o' mine, O mother o' mine!
I know whose love would come down to me,
Mother o' mine, O mother o' mine!

If I were damned of body and soul,
Mother o' mine, O mother o' mine!
I know whose prayers would make me whole,
Mother o' mine, O mother o' mine!
Rudyard Kipling

Pride is one of the seven deadly sins; but it cannot be the pride of a mother in her children, for that is a compound of two cardinal virtues – faith and hope.
Charles Dickens

Most of the stones for the buildings of the City of God, and all the best of them, are made by mothers.
Henry Drummond

That great academy, a mother's knee.
Thomas Carlyle

Jesus Christ, who returns good for evil, is our true Mother. We have our being from him, the ground and source of all motherhood, and with it we have all love's sweet protection for ever more. . . . We know that our own mother bore us for pain and for death. But what is it that Jesus, our true Mother, does? He who is all-love bears us for joy and eternal life! Praise him!
Julian of Norwich, Revelations of Divine Love

Mothers-in-law

Go not empty unto thy mother in law.
The Bible, Ruth 3:17 (AV)

Motivation   see also GOALS

When a man has not a good reason for doing a thing, he has one good reason for letting it alone.
Walter Scott

Motives

You may think that everything you do is right, but remember that the Lord judges your motives.
The Bible, Proverbs 21:2

No man does anything from a single motive.
S.T. Coleridge

Mottoes

Liberty! Equality! Fraternity!
Motto of the French Revolution

All for one, and one for all.
Alexandre Dumas, The Three Musketeers

The doctor's job: to cure occasionally; to help frequently; to comfort always.
Motto from an American country doctor's surgery

Mottoes, corporate

Have you got any rivers they say are uncrossable?
Have you got any mountains you can't tunnel through?
We specialise in the wholly impossible,
Doing the job that no man can do.
Motto of the American engineers

No absolutely destitute child ever refused admission.
Motto of Dr Barnardo's Homes

Through struggle to the stars.
Motto (in the Latin form 'Per ardua ad astra') of the Royal Air Force, and previously of the Mulvany family

To the greater glory of God.
Motto of the Society of Jesus

Unless the Lord is with us, our efforts are in vain.
Motto (in the Latin form 'Nisi Dominus, frustra') of the city of Edinburgh

Let Glasgow flourish by the preaching of the Word.
Motto of the city of Glasgow

Evil to him who evil thinks.
Motto (in the French form 'Honi soit qui mal y pense') of the Order of the Garter

Be prepared.
Motto of the Scouts

Either learn or depart, there is no third choice here.
Motto (in its Latin form) of Winchester College

Mottoes, personal and family

Union makes strength.
Motto (in its French form) of the King of the Belgians

Speaking the truth in love.
Motto (from the Bible, The apostle Paul, Ephesians 4:15 (AV)) used on letters to friends by Professor Blackie

Go for souls, and go for the worst.
Motto of William Booth

My heart I give you, Lord, eagerly and entirely.
Motto of John Calvin

What God wills, I will.
Motto (in its Italian form) of Lord Dormer

Find a way or make one.
Motto of Henry Ford

In God is my hope.
Motto (in its French form) of the Gerard family

Virtue is the only nobility.
Motto (in its French form) of the Earl of Guildford

To a valiant heart nothing is impossible.
Motto of Henri IV of France

Never speak of others' faults nor your own virtues.
Motto of Bob Hope

O God, make me like Jesus Christ.
Motto of Toyohiko Kagawa

I will go anywhere provided it is forward.
> *Motto of David Livingstone*

He that has prayed well has studied well.
> *Motto of Martin Luther*

Night is coming.
> *Motto of Samuel Johnson, Walter*
> *Scott and Robert Murray*
> *M'Cheyne*

Let me burn out for God.
> *Motto of Henry Martyn*

Send me where workers are most needed and difficulties are greatest.
> *Motto of Robert Morrison*

At the all-powerful disposal of God.
> *Motto (in its French form) of the*
> *Earl of Mount Edgecumbe*

Heart speaks to heart.
> *Motto (in its Latin form) of J.H.*
> *Newman*

God only do I seek.
> *Motto (in its French form 'Je ne*
> *cherche qu'ung' – strictly, 'I seek*
> *only one') of the Marquis of*
> *Northampton*

Hope in God.
> *Motto (in its French form) of the*
> *Duke of Northumberland and*
> *others*

Fidelity is of God.
> *Motto (in its French form) of*
> *Viscount Powerscourt*

The first principle God's honour, the second man's happiness, the means prayer and unremitting diligence.
> *Motto of Lord Shaftesbury*

I serve.
> *Motto (in its German form 'Ich*
> *dien') since 1346 of the Prince of*
> *Wales, having been the motto of*
> *King John of Bohemia, who was*
> *killed at the Battle of Crecy in that*
> *year by the then Prince of Wales*

Love loyalty.
> *Motto of the Marquis of*
> *Winchester*

I have one passion, and it is He, only He.
> *Motto of Count von Zinzendorf*

Mourning   see also BEREAVEMENT

Blessed are they that mourn: for they shall be comforted.
> *The Bible, Jesus Christ,*
> *Matthew 5:4 (AV)*

Silent sorrow is only the more fatal.
> *Racine*

Man's inhumanity to man
Makes countless thousands mourn!
> *Robert Burns, Man was Made to*
> *Mourn*

When I am dead, my dearest,
Sing no sad songs for me.
> *Christina Rossetti*

Murder

The poor man raises his sons, but the daughters, if one is poor, we expose.
> *Stobaeus, Eclogues*

Murphy's law

1. Nothing is as easy as it looks.
2. Everything takes longer than you think.
3. If anything can go wrong, it will.
> *Author unknown*

Music   see also SINGING

Music, the greatest good that mortals know,
And all of heaven we have below.
> *Joseph Addison, A Song for St*
> *Cecilia's Day*

The most poetic musician who ever lived.
> *Franz Liszt, referring to Schubert*

God has preached the gospel through music, too, as may be seen in Josquin, all of whose compositions flow freely, gently, and cheerfully, are not forced or cramped by rules, and are like the song of the finch.
> *Martin Luther*

Music is the poetry of the air.
> *Jean Paul Richter*

The purest and most sympathetic interpreter of poetry, love, and grief, is music.
> *E. Legouvé*

The man that hath no music in himself,
Nor is not mov'd with concord of sweet sounds,
Is fit for treasons, stratagems, and spoils;
The motions of his spirit are dull as night,
And his affections dark as Erebus.
Let no such man be trusted. Mark the music.
> *William Shakespeare*

Without music life would be a mistake.
> *Friedrich Nietzsche*

Music is the thing of the world that I love most.
> *Samuel Pepys, Diary, 1666*

Music, Effects of

Like the fingers of a threatening fist which straighten in friendship.
> *Goethe, on the effect music had on*
> *his comparatively unmusical spirit*

Music strikes in me a profound contemplation of the First Composer.
Thomas Browne

Music is for the soul what wind is for the ship, blowing her onwards in the direction in which she is steered.
William Booth

I adore art. . . . When I am alone with my notes, my heart pounds and the tears stream from my eyes, and my emotion and my joys are too much to bear.
Giuseppe Verdi

Music and the devil

Music is hateful and intolerable to the devil. I truly believe, and I do not mind saying, that there is no art like music, next to theology. It is the only art, next to theology, that can calm the agitations of the soul, which plainly shows that the devil, the source of anxiety and sadness, flees from the sound of music as he does from religious worship. That is why the scriptures are full of psalms and hymns, in which praise is given to God. That is why, when we gather round God's throne in heaven, we shall sing his glory. Music is the perfect way to express our love and devotion to God. It is one of the most magnificent and delightful presents God has given us.
Martin Luther

[Rowland Hill] did not see any reason why the devil should have all the good tunes.
E.W. Broome, Rev. Rowland Hill

Music in church services

First we must take heed that in music be not put the whole sum and effect of godliness and of the worshipping of God. . . . Further, we must take heed that in it be not put merit or remission of sins. Thirdly, that singing be not so much used and occupied in the church that there be no time, in a manner, left to preach the Word of God and holy doctrine. . . . Fourthly, that rich and large stipends be not so appointed for musicians that either very little or, in a manner, nothing is provided for the ministers which labour in the word of God. Fifthly, neither may that broken and quavering music be used wherewith the standers-by are so letted

[hindered] that they cannot understand the words, not though they would never so fain. Lastly, we must take heed that in the church nothing be sung without choice, but only those things which are contained in the holy scriptures, or which are by just reason gathered out of them, and do exactly agree with the word of God.
John Northbrooke, A Treatise wherein Dicing, Dauncing, etc. are Reproved, 1577

Mystery

A religion without mystery must be a religion without God.
Jeremy Taylor

Mysticism

Mysticism keeps men sane.
G.K. Chesterton

N

Name of Jesus

The name of Jesus is not only light but food. It is oil without which food for the soul is dry and salt without which it is insipid. It is honey in the mouth, melody in the ear and joy in the heart. It has healing power. Every discussion where his name is not heard is pointless.
Bernard of Clairvaux

How sweet the Name of Jesus sounds
  In a believer's ear!
It soothes his sorrows, heals his
  wounds,
  And drives away his fear!
John Newton

Nations

A nation without God's guidance is a nation without order.
The Bible, Proverbs 29:18

By three things will a nation endure: truth, justice, and peace.
Rabbinical saying

Nature see also EVENING; GOD, AS CREATOR

You will find something more in woods than in books. Trees and stones will teach you what you cannot learn from masters.
Bernard of Clairvaux, letter to an Archbishop of York

And this our life, exempt from public
haunt,
Finds tongues in trees, books in the
running brooks,
Sermons in stones, and good in everything.

William Shakespeare

Nothing comes of nothing.
*Lucretius, who believed the world
began in the chance collision of
atoms*

The more I study nature, the more I
am amazed at the creator.

Louis Pasteur

In all things of nature there is something of the marvellous.
Aristotle, Historia Animalium

[Speaking of his studies and discoveries:] O God, I am thinking your
thoughts after you.
*Johann Kepler, founder of
physical astronomy*

Nature, as far as in her lies,
Imitates God and turns her face
To every land beneath the skies,
Counts nothing that she meets with base
But lives and loves in every place.
Alfred, Lord Tennyson

Nature, to be commanded, must be
obeyed.

Francis Bacon, Novum Organum

Nature, Redeemed

Wolves and sheep will live together in
peace,
and leopards will lie down with
young goats.
Calves and lion cubs will feed together,
and little children will take care of
them.
Cows and bears will eat together,
and their calves and cubs will lie
down in peace.
Lions will eat straw as cattle do.
Even a baby will not be harmed
if it plays near a poisonous snake.
On Zion, God's sacred hill,
there will be nothing harmful or
evil.
The land will be as full of knowledge of
the Lord
as the seas are full of water.
The Bible, Isaiah 11:6–9

Nature and the praise of God

Praised be you, my Lord, through our
Sister Mother Earth, who sustains us,
governs us, and who produces varied
fruits with coloured flowers and herbs.
Praised be you, my Lord, through
Brother Wind and through the air,
cloudy and serene, and every kind of
weather.
Praised be you, my Lord, through Sister Moon and the stars in heaven: you
formed them clear and precious and
beautiful.
Praised be you, my Lord, through
Brother Fire, through whom you light
the night and he is beautiful and play-
ful and robust and strong.
Praised be you, my Lord, with all your
creatures, especially Sir Brother Sun,
who is the day and through whom you
give us light. And he is beautiful and
radiant with great splendours and
bears likeness of you, most high one.
Francis of Assisi

Let all the world in ev'ry corner sing
My God and King.
The heav'ns are not too high,
His praise may thither fly;
The earth is not too low,
His praises there may grow.
Let all the world in ev'ry corner sing
My God and King.
The Church with psalms must shout,
No door can keep them out:
But above all, the heart
Must bear the longest part.
George Herbert, The Temple

O God, we thank you for this earth,
our home;
for the wide sky and the blessed sun,
for the salt sea and the running water,
for the everlasting hills and the never-
resting winds,
for trees and the common grass underfoot.

Walter Rauschenbusch

God made the country, and man made
the town.

William Cowper, after Varro

Nature as revealing God

The heavens declare the glory of God;
and the firmament showeth his
handiwork.
The Bible, Psalm 19:1 (AV)

It is a remarkable fact that no canoni-
cal writer has ever used Nature to
prove God.

Blaise Pascal, Pensées

Jesus taught men to see the operation of God in the regular and the normal – in the rising of the sun and the falling of the rain and the growth of the plant.

William Temple

I love to think of nature as an unlimited broadcasting station through which God speaks to us every hour, if we will only tune in.

George Washington Carver

For the beauty of the earth,
For the beauty of the skies,
For the love which from our birth
Over and around us lies:
  Father, unto thee we raise
  This our sacrifice of praise.

F.S. Pierpoint

The angels keep their ancient places –
Turn but a stone, and start a wing!
'Tis we, 'tis our estrangèd faces,
That miss the many-splendoured thing.

Francis Thompson

What inexpressible joy for me, to look up through the apple-blossom and the fluttering leaves, and to see God's love there; to know that if I could unwrap fold after fold of God's universe, I should only unfold more and more blessing and see deeper and deeper into the love which is at the heart of it all.

Elizabeth Charles

Need of God

O God, never suffer us to think that we can stand by ourselves, and not need thee.

John Donne

Neighbour, Love for

Love your neighbour as you love yourself.

The Bible, Leviticus 19:18

Do not waste time bothering about whether you love your neighbour; act as if you did. . . . When you are behaving as if you love someone, you will presently come to love him.

C.S. Lewis

Love your neighbour.

Thales

He passed by on the other side.

The Bible, Jesus Christ, Luke 10:31 (AV)

No one should be looking to his own interests, but to the interests of others.

The Bible, The apostle Paul, 1 Corinthians 10:24

Anyone taking up his neighbour's load, willing to use his higher position for the benefit of one who is not as well off, giving what he has been given by God to those who need it, becomes a god to his neighbour, and imitates God.

Epistle to Diognetus

It is easier to love humanity as a whole than to love one's neighbour.

Eric Hoffer

The Bible tells us to love our neighbours, and also to love our enemies; probably because they are generally the same people.

G.K. Chesterton

The love of our neighbour is the only door out of the dungeon of self.

George Macdonald

As we think of [the Lord], we can achieve the difficult and unnatural: we can love those that hate us, give good for evil, and blessing for cursing (Matthew 5:44), remembering that we are not to dwell on the evil in men, but look to the image of God in them. This image covers and obliterates their faults, and by its beauty and dignity draws us to love and to embrace them.

John Calvin, The Institutes of Christian Religion, 3.7.6

Charity begins at home, and justice begins next door.

Charles Dickens

There is no principle of the heart that is more acceptable to God than a universal, ardent love for all mankind, which seeks and prays for their happiness.

William Law

I am to become a Christ to my neighbour and be for him what Christ is for me.

Martin Luther

Neighbour, Love for, and love for God

Though we do not have our Lord with us in bodily presence, we have our neighbour, who, for the ends of love and loving service, is as good as our Lord himself.

Teresa of Avila

You can never love your neighbour without loving God.

Bossuet

In order to love our neighbour properly we must seek God's help. It is not possible to love our neighbour with a pure heart without loving God first. We cannot pass on God's love if we do not possess God's love ourselves.

Bernard of Clairvaux, On Loving God

The love of God is the first and greatest commandment. But love of our neighbour is the means by which we obey it. Since we cannot see God directly, God allows us to catch sight of him through our neighbour. By loving our neighbour we purge our eyes to see God. So love your neighbour and you will discover that in doing so you come to know God.

Augustine of Hippo, Treatise on St John's Gospel

We cannot know whether we love God, although there may be strong reasons for thinking so, but there can be no doubt about whether we love our neighbour or no.

Teresa of Avila

He alone loves the creator perfectly who manifests a pure love for his neighbour.

Bede

Neighbour, Love for, and the 'Golden Rule'

What is hateful to thyself do not unto thy neighbour.

The Talmud

What you hate to suffer, do not do to anyone else.

Isocrates

Is not *reciprocity* such a word [that can act as a rule for all life]? What you do not want done to yourself, do not do to others.

Confucius

Neighbours

Never tell your neighbour to wait until tomorrow if you can help him now.

The Bible, Proverbs 3:28

Don't visit your neighbour too often; he may get tired of you and come to hate you.

The Bible, Proverbs 25:17

A neighbour near by can help you more than a brother who is far away.

The Bible, Proverbs 27:10

New birth   see REGENERATION

New creation   see also NATURE, REDEEMED

The Lord says, 'I am making a new earth and new heavens. The events of the past will be completely forgotten.'

The Bible, Isaiah 65:17

New Testament   see also EPHESIANS; HEBREWS 11; JOHN 3:16; ROMANS

The New Testament is the very best book that ever was or ever will be known in the world.

Charles Dickens

One does well to put on gloves when reading the New Testament; the proximity of so much impurity almost compels to this. . . . I have searched in it vainly for even a single congenial trait . . . everything in it is cowardice and self-deception.

Friedrich Nietzsche

New Year

I said to the man who stood at the gate of the year: 'Give me a light, that I may tread safely into the unknown.'
And he replied: 'Go out into the darkness and put your hand into the hand of God. That shall be to you better than light and safer than a known way.'

M. Louise Haskins

Nicknames

A nickname is the hardest stone that the devil can throw at a man.

William Hazlitt

Non-violence

Preach and pray, but do not fight.

Martin Luther, advising those reformers who might have become revolutionaries

In my opinion non-violence is not passivity in any shape or form. Non-violence as I understand it is the most active force in the world.

Mahatma Gandhi

The Spirit of Christ, which leads us into all Truth, will never move us to fight and war against any man with outward weapons, neither for the kingdom of Christ, nor for the kingdoms of this world.

Quaker Declaration, 1660

This house will in no circumstances fight for its King and country.

Motion passed at the Oxford Union, 9 February 1933

Novelty

It is in the nature of man to long for novelty.

Pliny the Elder

O

Obedience   see also SERVICE

Which does the Lord prefer: obedience or offerings and sacrifices? It is better to obey him than to sacrifice the best sheep to him.

The Bible, Samuel, 1 Samuel 15:22

Give me the desire to obey your laws rather than to get rich.

The Bible, Psalm 119:36

The test of progress is obedience.

A.E. Brooke, commentary on the letters of John in the International Critical Commentary series

I find the doing of the will of God leaves me no time for disputing about his plans.

George Macdonald, The Marquis of Lossie

It is much safer to obey than to rule.

Thomas à Kempis, The Imitation of Christ

The lips are slow to obey the brain when the heart is mutinous.

Voltaire

Obedience is the key of knowledge.

Christina Rossetti

The golden rule for understanding in spiritual matters is not intellect, but obedience.

Oswald Chambers

We are [God's] glory, when we follow his ways.

Florence Nightingale

It is so hard to believe because it is so hard to obey.

Søren Kierkegaard

No man is a successful commander who has not first learned to obey.

Classical proverb

Put aside your own will so as to go to war under Christ the Lord, the real King, picking up the keen and glittering weapons of obedience.

Benedict, Rule

That thou art happy, owe to God;
That thou continuest such, owe to
    thyself,
That is, to thy obedience.

John Milton, Paradise Lost

Offence, Giving

The truth is like the light to sore eyes. . . . He who never offended anyone never did anyone any good.

Diogenes

Old age

Getting old is not so bad when you think of the opposite!

Owen Hendrix

To grow old is to pass from passion to compassion.

Albert Camus

I prefer old age to the alternative.

Maurice Chevalier

Accept it, adjust to it, adorn it.

Guy King

Next to the very young, I suppose the very old are the most selfish.

William Makepeace Thackeray

When your friends begin to flatter you on how young you look, it's a sure sign you're getting old.

Mark Twain

I no longer live; I am merely a spectator of life.

Lamartine, when he was poor and neglected after being a famous writer

Grow old along with me,
The best is yet to be.

Robert Browning

Never regret growing old. Not everyone has that privilege.

Author unknown

Grey hairs are a proof of age, but not of wisdom.

Menander

The greatest need of the handicapped, the backward, and the aged is the need to be needed.

Author unknown

Lord, save me from being a wicked old man.

George Müller

Old age, Respect for

Learn all you can from old people. They've been down the road you must travel.

Author unknown

The older the fiddle the sweeter the tune.

Proverb

Respect grey hairs.

Greek proverb

Old age and action

Keeping useful keeps us youthful.
Author unknown

When I feel old age creeping upon me, and know that I must soon die – I hope it is not wrong to say it – I cannot bear to leave this world with all the misery in it.
Lord Shaftesbury, who prayed daily for Christ's second coming

Old age and maturing

We never grow old. We get old when we stop growing.
Author unknown

Age is not all decay; it is the ripening, the swelling, of the fresh life within, that withers and bursts the husk.
George Macdonald

It is always the season for the old to learn.
Æschylus, Fragments

To know how to grow old is the master work of wisdom, and one of the most difficult chapters in the great art of living.
Henri Frédéric Amiel

The righteous will flourish like
   palm-trees;
   they will grow like the cedars of
   Lebanon.
They are like trees planted in the
   house of the Lord,
   that flourish in the Temple of our
   God,
   that still bear fruit in old age
and are always green and strong.
The Bible, Psalm 92:12–14

Old Testament see also JOB, BOOK OF

I beg every devout Christian not to despise the simplicity of language and the stories found in the Old Testament. He should remember that, however simple the Old Testament may seem, it contains the words, works, judgements and actions of God himself. Indeed the simplicity makes fools of the wise and clever, and allows the poor and simple to see the ways of God. Therefore submit your thoughts and feelings to the stories you read, and let yourself be carried like a child to God.
Martin Luther

In the Old Testament the New is concealed, in the New Testament the Old is revealed.
Augustine of Hippo

Opinions, Other people's

It is dangerous to be concerned with what others think of you, but if you trust the Lord, you are safe.
The Bible, Proverbs 29:25

The real black, diabolical Pride, comes when you look down on others so much that you do not care what they think of you.
C.S. Lewis, Mere Christianity

Remember, no one can make you feel inferior without your consent.
Eleanor Roosevelt

A good name is better than riches.
Latin proverb

The thirst for fame is greater than for virtue.
Latin proverb

I am not sure which of the two occupies the lower sphere, he who hungers for money or he who thirsts for applause.
J.H. Jowett

Opportunity

No great man ever complains of want of opportunity.
Ralph Waldo Emerson

I do not like crises; but I like the opportunities which they supply.
Lord Reith

A man must make his opportunity as oft as find it.
Francis Bacon, Advancement of Learning

A wise man will make more opportunities than he finds.
Francis Bacon, Essays, Of Ceremonies and Respects

Every man is guilty of all the good he didn't do.
Voltaire

Three things come not back – the spoken word, the spent arrow, and the lost opportunity.
Proverb

Opposition

Receive [opposition] from men with humility, meekness, submissiveness, gentleness, sweetness. Why should not even your outward appearance and manner be soft? Remember the character of Lady Cutts: 'It was said of the Roman Emperor Titus, never anyone came displeased from him. But it might be said of her, Never anyone went displeased to her: so secure were all of the kind and favourable reception which they would meet with from her.'

John Wesley, A Plain Man's Guide to Holiness

Muscle is made by resistances.
Author unknown

The Christian life is a fight, not a picnic; a battlefield, not a parade ground.
F.P. Wood

Optimism

As you travel on through life,
Whatever be your goal,
Keep your eye upon the doughnut
And not upon the hole.
Author unknown

Only optimists make history. No monument was ever built to a pessimist.
Author unknown

Pessimism is an investment in nothing; optimism is an investment in hope.
Author unknown

Order

Order is Heaven's first law.
Alexander Pope, Essay on Man

Good order is the foundation of all good things.
Edmund Burke

Original sin   see also MANKIND, DEPRAVITY OF

Original sin may be defined as the hereditary corruption and depravity of our nature. This reaches every part of the soul, makes us abhorrent to God's wrath and produces in us what Scripture calls works of the flesh.
John Calvin, The Institutes of Christian Religion, 1.1.8

We repudiated all versions of the doctrine of original sin, of there being instances and irrational springs of wickedness in most men.
John Maynard Keynes, recalling his undergraduate days

Certain new theologians dispute original sin, which is the only part of Christian theology which can really be proved.
G.K. Chesterton

The glad news brought by the gospel was the good news of original sin.
Francis of Assisi

Everything is good when it leaves the hands of the Creator; everything degenerates in the hands of man.
Jean-Jacques Rousseau

Originality

The more intelligent a man is, the more originality he discovers in men. Ordinary people see no difference between men.
Blaise Pascal

Everything has been thought of before, but the problem is to think of it again.
Goethe

P

Pacifism   see NON-VIOLENCE

Pain   see also HEALING

No pain, no palm; no thorn, no throne.
William Penn, No Cross, No Crown

When pain is to be borne, a little courage helps more than much knowledge, a little human sympathy more than much courage, and the least tincture of the love of God more than all.
C.S. Lewis, The Problem of Pain

All the great religions were first preached, and long practised, in a world without chloroform.
C.S. Lewis, The Problem of Pain

There was a faith-healer of Deal,
Who said, 'Although pain isn't real,
   If I sit on a pin
   And it punctures my skin,
I dislike what I fancy I feel.'
Author unknown

Let me not beg for the stilling of my pain, but for the heart to conquer it.
Rabindranath Tagore

Pain insists upon being attended to. God whispers to us in our pleasures, speaks in our conscience, and shouts in our pain. It is his megaphone to rouse a deaf world.
C.S. Lewis, The Problem of Pain

Parables in nature   see NATURE

Parenthood   see also CHRISTIAN
UPBRINGING; FAMILIES; FATHERHOOD;
MOTHERHOOD

Teach a child how he should live, and
he will remember it all his life.
The Bible, Proverbs 22:6

Train your child in the way in which
you know you should have gone yourself.
C.H. Spurgeon

Spare the rod and spoil the child. It is
true. But beside the rod keep an apple
to give him when he does well.
*Martin Luther, whose own father
was so stern that Martin found it
hard to pray to God as Father*

The thing that impresses me most
about America is the way parents obey
their children.
Duke of Windsor

Parents, Respect for

A wise son makes his father happy.
Only a fool despises his mother.
The Bible, Proverbs 15:20

Listen to your father; without him you
would not exist. When your mother is
old, show her your appreciation.
The Bible, Proverbs 23:22

Anyone who makes fun of his father or
despises his mother in her old age
ought to be eaten by vultures or have
his eyes picked out by wild ravens.
The Bible, Proverbs 30:17

Children, it is your Christian duty to
obey your parents, for this is the right
thing to do.
*The Bible, The apostle Paul,
Ephesians 6:1*

Parley

Neither a fortress nor a maidenhead
will hold out long after they begin to
parley.
*Benjamin Franklin, Poor
Richard's Almanac, 1734*

Passion

Rule your passions, or they will rule
you.
Horace

It is more grievous to be a slave to
one's passions than to be ruled by a
despot.
Pythagoras

A wise man will be master of his passions, a fool their slave.
Publius Syrus

Do not give in to bodily passions, which
are always at war against the soul.
The Bible, 1 Peter 2:11

Patience   see also RUSH

It is better to be patient than powerful.
The Bible, Proverbs 16:32

Stupid people express their anger
openly, but sensible people are patient
and hold it back.
The Bible, Proverbs 29:11

Patience is a bitter plant but it bears
sweet fruit.
German proverb

Beware the fury of a patient man.
John Dryden

Patience and diligence, like faith,
remove mountains.
*William Penn, Some Fruits of
Solitude*

I can well wait a century for a reader,
since God has waited six thousand
years for a discoverer.
Johannes Kepler

All things come to those who wait.
Proverb

Faith takes up the cross, love binds it
to the soul, patience bears it to the
end.
Horatius Bonar

What cannot be amended is made
easier by patience.
Horace

Our patience will achieve more than
our force.
*Edmund Burke, Reflections on the
Revolution in France*

We must wait for God, long, meekly,
in the wind and wet, in the thunder and
lightning, in the cold and the dark.
Wait, and he will come. He never
comes to those who do not wait.
F.W. Faber

O God, grant me the courage to
change what I can, the patience to
endure what I cannot, and the wisdom
to know the difference.
Author unknown

The weak man is impetuous, the
strong is patient.
Proverb

Patience is power; with time and patience the mulberry leaf becomes silk.
Chinese proverb

Patience is the queen of virtues.
John Chrysostom

My greatest temptation is to lose my temper over the slackness and inefficiency so disappointing to those on whom I depended. It is no use to lose my temper – only kindness. But oh, it is such a trial.

Hudson Taylor

Paul, The apostle

A man small in size, bald-headed, bandy-legged, well built, with eyebrows meeting, rather long-nosed, full of grace – for sometimes he seemed like a man, and sometimes he had the countenance of an angel.

(Apocryphal) Acts of Paul and Thecla

No sooner had Jesus knocked over the dragon of superstition than Paul boldly set it on its legs again in the name of Jesus.

George Bernard Shaw

Paul stakes all his life upon the truth of what he says about the death and resurrection of Jesus.

J. Gresham Machen

Peace

A day is coming when human pride will be ended and human arrogance destroyed. Then the Lord alone will be exalted.

The Bible, Isaiah 2:11

Turn away from evil and do good;
strive for peace with all your heart.
The Bible, Psalm 34:14

While the emperor may give peace from war on land and sea, he is unable to give peace from passion, grief and envy. He cannot even give peace of heart, for which man yearns more than even for outward peace.

Epictetus

Even peace may be purchased at too high a price.

Benjamin Franklin

Reason's whole pleasure, all the joys of sense,
Be in three words: health, peace, and competence.
Alexander Pope

When the voices of children are heard on the green
And laughter is heard on the hill,
My heart is at rest within my breast
And everything else is still.
William Blake

All that matters is to be one with the living God
to be a creature in the house of the God of life.
Like a cat asleep on a chair
at peace.
D.H. Lawrence

Great peace is found in little busyness.
Geoffrey Chaucer

If you would preserve peace, then prepare for peace.
Barthélemy Enfantin

The shortest path to world peace is world trade. The shortest path to domestic peace and marital peace is communication.
Author unknown

Peace, False

They have healed also the hurt of the daughter of my people slightly, saying, Peace, peace; when there is no peace.
The Bible, Jeremiah 6:14 (AV)

Peace and its source in the self

A man who cannot find tranquillity within himself will search for it in vain elsewhere.
La Rochefoucauld

First keep the peace within yourself, then you can bring peace to others too.
Thomas à Kempis, The Imitation of Christ

Nothing can bring you peace but yourself.
Ralph Waldo Emerson, Essays, Self-Reliance

Peace and truth

I love peace, but I love truth even more.
Latin proverb

Love and faithfulness will meet;
righteousness and peace will embrace.
The Bible, Psalm 85:10

Peace of God

And I smiled to think God's greatness flowed around our incompleteness –
Round our restlessness, his rest.
Elizabeth Barrett Browning

Anoint and cheer our soiled face
With the abundance of thy grace:
Keep far our foes, give peace at home;
Where thou art guide no ill can come.
J. Cosin, based on Veni creator Spiritus

Peace I leave with you, my peace I give unto you: not as the world giveth, give I unto you.

The Bible, Jesus Christ,
John 14:27 (AV)

The peace of God, which passeth all understanding, shall keep your hearts and minds through Christ Jesus.

The Bible, The apostle Paul,
Philippians 4:7 (AV)

Peace reigns where our Lord reigns.

Julian of Norwich, Revelations of
Divine Love

Drop thy still dews of quietness,
  Till all our strivings cease;
Take from our souls the strain and
    stress,
And let our ordered lives confess
  The beauty of thy peace.

John Greenleaf Whittier

All glory be to God on high,
  And to the earth be peace;
Goodwill henceforth from heaven to
    men
Begin and never cease!

Nahum Tate

Where there is charity and wisdom, there is neither fear nor ignorance. Where there is patience and humility, there is neither anger nor vexation. Where there is poverty and joy, there is neither greed nor avarice. Where there is peace and meditation, there is neither anxiety nor doubt.

Francis of Assisi

My soul, there is a country
  Far beyond the stars,
Where stands a wingèd sentry
  All skilful in the wars,
There above noise, and danger,
  Sweet peace sits crown'd with smiles.

George Herbert

Keep your heart in peace; let nothing in this world disturb it: everything has an end.

John of the Cross

Son, now will I teach you the way of peace and true freedom. (Lord, do as you say; for this is delightful for me to hear.) Study, son, to do the will of another rather than your own. Choose always to have less rather than more. Seek always the lowest place; and to be inferior to everyone. Wish always and pray; that the will of God may be

wholly fulfilled in you. Behold, such a man enters the land of peace and rest.

Thomas à Kempis

Peace of God and the death of Jesus

God made peace through his Son's sacrificial death on the cross and so brought back to himself all things, both on earth and in heaven.

The Bible, The apostle Paul,
Colossians 1:20

Peace, perfect peace, in this dark world of sin?
The blood of Jesus whispers peace within.

E.H. Bickersteth, Songs in the
House of Pilgrimage

When Christ came into the world, peace was sung; and when he went out of the world, peace was bequested.

Francis Bacon

A great many people are trying to make peace, but that has already been done. God has not left it for us to do; all we have to do is to enter into it.

Dwight L. Moody

Peace of God desired

Late have I loved you, O Beauty so ancient and so new; late have I loved you! For behold you were within me, and I outside; and I sought you outside and in my unloveliness fell upon those things that you have made. You were with me and I was not with you. I was kept from you by those things, yet had they not been in you, they would not have been at all. You called and cried to me and broke open my deafness; you sent your shafts of light to shine on me and chase away my blindness; you breathed your fragrant breath on me, and I took a breath and now pant for you; I tasted you, and now I hunger and thirst for you; you touched me and I have burned for your peace.

Augustine of Hippo

Peace of God foretold

They shall beat their swords into ploughshares, and their spears into pruning-hooks: nation shall not lift up sword against nation, neither shall they learn war any more.

The Bible, Isaiah 2:4 (AV)

I offer peace to all, both near and far! I will heal my people.

The Bible, God, Isaiah 57:19

Everyone will live in peace
among his own vineyards and
fig-trees,
and no one will make him afraid.
The Bible, Micah 4:4

Peace of mind   see also CONTENTMENT;
STILLNESS

With peace of mind a poor man is rich;
without it, a rich man is poor.
Author unknown

Each one has to find his peace from
within, and peace to be real must be
unaffected by outside circumstances.
Mahatma Gandhi

What is the quiet mind? A quiet mind
is one which nothing weighs on, nothing worries, which, free from ties and
all self-seeking, is wholly merged into
the will of God and dead to its own.
Meister Eckhart

He has great tranquillity of heart who
sets nothing by praisings or blamings.
He whose conscience is clean will soon
be content and pleased.
You are no holier for being praised,
nor viler for being blamed or dis-
praised.
What you are, that you are; that God
knows you to be and you cannot be
said to be greater.
If you take heed what you are within,
you will not care what men say about
you: man looks on the face and God on
the heart; man considers the deeds and
God praises the thoughts.
Thomas à Kempis

True peace of heart is found by resisting our passions, not by serving them.
*Thomas à Kempis, The Imitation
of Christ*

Peacemaking

Have you ever thought seriously of the
meaning of that blessing given to the
peacemakers? People are always
expecting to get peace in heaven; but
you know whatever peace they get
there will be ready-made. Whatever
making of peace they can be blessed
for, must be on the earth here: not the
taking of arms against, but the building of nests amidst, its 'sea of troubles'
(like the halcyons). Difficult enough,
you think? Perhaps so, but I do not see
that any of us try. We complain of the
want of so many things – we want

votes, we want liberty, we want
amusement, we want money. Which
of us feels or knows that he wants
peace?
John Ruskin

I would sooner reconcile all Europe
than two women.
Louis XIV

First keep yourself in peace, and then
you will be able to pacify others. A
peaceable man does more good than a
learned one.
Thomas à Kempis

Penitent thief   see THIEF ON THE CROSS

Pentecost

And suddenly there came a sound
from heaven as of a rushing mighty
wind, and it filled all the house where
they were sitting. And there appeared
unto them cloven tongues like as of
fire.
The Bible, Luke, Acts 2:2–3

People

The voice of the people is the voice of
God.
*Alcuin, Epistles, Letter to
Charlemagne*

The Lord prefers common-looking
people. That is the reason he makes so
many of them.
Abraham Lincoln

Perfection   see also HOLINESS;
MISTAKES

You must be perfect – just as your
Father in heaven is perfect!
*The Bible, Jesus Christ,
Matthew 5:48*

I do not claim that I have already succeeded or have already become perfect. I keep striving to win the prize for
which Christ Jesus has already won me
to himself.
*The Bible, The apostle Paul,
Philippians 3:12*

If you say, 'It is enough. I have
reached perfection,' all is lost, since it
is the function of perfection to make
one know one's imperfections.
Augustine of Hippo

No mortal is wise at all times.
Pliny

I want you to remember what a difference there is between perfection and
perfectionism. The former is a Bible

truth: the latter may or may not be a human perversion of that truth. I fear much that many, in their horror of perfectionism, reject perfection too.

Andrew Murray

Christian perfection is loving God with all our heart, mind, soul, and strength. This implies that no wrong frame of mind, nothing contrary to love, remains in the soul; and that all the thoughts, words and actions, are governed by pure love.

John Wesley, A Plain Man's Guide to Holiness

[Perfection] is the devoting, not a part but all our soul, body and substance to God.

John Wesley, A Plain Man's Guide to Holiness

We even take issue with perfection.

Blaise Pascal, Pensées

Perfection in the church

If the Lord himself teaches that the Church will struggle with the burden of countless sinners until the day of judgement, it is obviously futile to look for a Church totally free from faults.

John Calvin, The Institutes of Christian Religion, 4.1.13

Persecution   see also HERESY; MARTYRDOM

Everyone who wants to live a godly life in union with Christ Jesus will be persecuted.

The Bible, The apostle Paul, 2 Timothy 3:12

Christians who are daily being punished flourish all the more. This is the high calling to which God has appointed them, and we must not look to be let off.

Epistle to Diognetus

In the midst of the flame and the rack I have seen men not only not groan, that is little; not only not complain, that is little; not only not answer back, that too is little; but I have seen them smile, and smile with a good heart.

Seneca

Persecution for righteousness' sake is what every child of God must expect.

Charles Simeon, Sermon 2336

The parting with my wife and poor children hath often been to me in this place, as the pulling the flesh from my bones; and that not only because I am somewhat too fond of these great mercies, but also because I should have often brought to my mind the many hardships, miseries, and wants that my poor family was like to meet with, should I be taken from them, *especially my poor blind child*, who lay nearer my heart than all I had besides. O the thought of the hardship I thought my blind one might go under, would break up my heart to pieces. . . . But yet, recalling myself, thought I, I must venture all with God, though it goeth to the quick to leave you; O I saw in this condition, I was a man who was pulling down his house upon the head of his wife and children; yet thought I, I must do it, I must do it.

John Bunyan, contemplating his imprisonment

Against the persecution of a tyrant the godly have no remedy but prayer.

John Calvin

Christians have burned each other, quite persuaded
That all the apostles would have done as they did.

Lord Byron, Don Juan

There is only one thing left, my weak and broken body. If they take that away, they will rob me of an hour or two of life. But they cannot take my soul. I know perfectly well that from the beginning of the world the word of Christ has been such that whoever wants to carry it into the world must, like the apostles, renounce everything and expect death at any and every hour. If it were not so, it would not be the word of Christ. By death it was bought, by deaths spread, by deaths safeguarded. It must also take many deaths to keep it, or bring it back again. Christ is a bloody partnership for us.

Martin Luther at the Heidelberg Disputation

If it were an art to overcome heresy with fire, the executioners would be the most learned doctors on earth.

Martin Luther, To the Christian Nobility of the German States

The true Christian is like sandalwood, which imparts its fragrance to the axe which cuts it, without doing any harm in return.

Sundar Singh

Persecution in the early church

If the Tiber has left its bed, if the Nile has not poured its waters over the fields, if there is an earthquake, if famine or pestilence threatens, the cry immediately arises, 'The Christians to the lions!'

Tertullian

Those who persisted in declaring themselves Christians, I ordered to be led away to punishment, for I did not doubt, whatever it was that they confessed, that contumacy and inflexible obstinacy ought to be punished.

Pliny the Younger

[Nero] laid the guilt, and inflicted the most cruel punishments, upon a set of people who were held in abhorrence for their crimes, and popularly called Christians. . . . Their sufferings at their execution were aggravated by insult and mockery, for some were disguised in the skins of wild beasts and worried to death by dogs, some were crucified, and others were wrapped in pitched shirts and set on fire when the day closed, that they might serve as lights to illuminate the night. Nero lent his own gardens for these executions. . . . This made the sufferers pitied, and though they were criminals and deserving the severest punishments, they were considered as sacrificed not so much out of a regard to the public good as to gratify the cruelty of one man.

Tacitus

Through zeal and envy, the most faithful and righteous pillars of the church have been persecuted even to the most grievous deaths. . . . To [the] holy apostles were joined a very great number of others who . . . have left a glorious example to us. For this, not only men, but women, have been persecuted and, having suffered very grievous and cruel punishments, have finished the course of their faith with firmness.

Clement of Rome

The church of Christ has been founded by shedding its own blood,

not that of others; by enduring outrage, not by inflicting it. Persecutions have made it grow; martyrdoms have crowned it.

Jerome, Letters

All these have not run in vain, but in faith and righteousness, and are gone to the place that was due to them from the Lord, with whom also they suffered. For they loved not this present world, but him who died and was raised again by God for us.

Polycarp

For this cause (i.e., having felt and handled Christ's body after his resurrection, and being convinced, as Ignatius expresses it, both by his flesh and spirit), they [i.e. Peter, and those who were present with Peter at Christ's appearance] despised death, and were found to be above it.

Ignatius of Antioch, quoted by William Paley, Evidences of Christianity

They are put to death, and they gain new life. They are poor, and make many rich; they lack everything, and in everything they abound. They are dishonoured, and their dishonour becomes their glory; they are reviled and they are justified. They are abused and they bless; they are insulted, and they repay insult with honour. They do good, and they rejoice as gaining new life therein.

Eusebius

The sufferings of all the other martyrs were blessed and generous, which they underwent according to the will of God. For so it becomes us who are more religious than others to ascribe the power and ordering of all things to him. And indeed who can choose but admire the greatness of their minds, and that admirable patience and love of their Master, which then appeared in them?

A letter from the early church in Smyrna, quoted by William Paley, Evidences of Christianity

Religious persecution may shield itself under the guise of a mistaken and over-zealous piety.

Edmund Burke, speech on 17 February 1788

Perseverance see also ENDURANCE; GENIUS

Let us not become tired of doing good; for if we do not give up, the time will come when we will reap the harvest.

The Bible, The apostle Paul, Galatians 6:9

Think of what he [Jesus] went through; how he put up with so much hatred from sinners! So do not let yourselves become discouraged and give up.

The Bible, Hebrews 12:3

Perseverance is the sister of patience, the daughter of constancy, the friend of peace, the cementer of friendships, the bond of harmony and the bulwark of holiness.

Bernard of Clairvaux, The Song of Songs

Let therefore none presume on past mercies, as if they were out of danger.

John Wesley

The drop of rain maketh a hole in the stone, not by violence, but by oft falling.

Hugh Latimer

Nothing can take the place of persistence. Talent will not. Thousands with talents are drifters. Genius will not. Unrewarded genius is almost a proverb. Education will not. The world is full of educated derelicts. Persistence alone solves all the world's big problems.

Author unknown

The saints are the sinners who keep on going.

Robert Louis Stevenson

Give us grace and strength to forbear and to persevere. Give us courage and gaiety and the quiet mind, spare to us our friends, soften to us our enemies.

Robert Louis Stevenson

By gnawing through a dike, even a rat may drown a nation.

Edmund Burke

There are only two creatures that can surmount the pyramids, the eagle and the snail.

Eastern proverb

I can plod. I can persevere in any definite pursuit. To this I owe everything.

William Carey

Multiply our graces,
   Chiefly love and fear,

But, dear Lord, the chiefest,
   Grace to persevere.

F.W. Faber

Who perseveres succeeds at last.

Proverb

By perseverance the snail reached the Ark.

C.H. Spurgeon

Slow and steady wins the race.

Æsop, The Hare and the Tortoise

'Tis a lesson you should heed,
Try, try again.
If at first you don't succeed,
Try, try again.

William Edward Hickson, Try and Try Again

All things are possible to him who believes, yet more to him who hopes, more still to him who loves, and most of all to him who practises and perseveres in these three virtues.

Brother Lawrence

You're looking at a man who spent two years trying to learn to wiggle his big toe.

Franklin D. Roosevelt, when asked how he could do so much without being tired; referring to his recovery after polio

Perseverance in politics

Abraham Lincoln failed in business in 1831.
Was defeated for Legislature in 1832.
Second business failure in 1833.
Suffered nervous breakdown in 1836.
Was defeated as candidate for Speaker in 1838.
Was defeated as candidate for Elector in 1840.
Was defeated as candidate for Congress in 1843.
Was defeated as candidate for Congress in 1848.
Was defeated as candidate for Senate in 1855.
Was defeated as candidate for Vice-Presidency in 1856.
Was defeated as candidate for Senate in 1858.
Was elected President in 1860.

Our motto must continue to be *perseverance*. And ultimately I trust the Almighty will crown our efforts with success.

William Wilberforce, message to the Anti-Slavery Society

My hands are too full, Jews, chimney-sweeps, factory children, church extension, etc., etc., I shall succeed I fear, partially in all, and completely in none. Yet we must persevere; there is hope.

Lord Shaftesbury

Perseverance to the end

There must be a beginning of any great matter, but the continuing unto the end until it be thoroughly finished yields the true glory.

Francis Drake to Francis Walsingham, 17 May 1587

With malice toward none; with charity for all; with firmness in the right, as God gives us to see the right – let us strive on to finish the work we are in.

Abraham Lincoln

Of evil works we ought to repent, and forsake them before we die: lest the day find us in them. But we ought to persevere till the end in good works, that in them our soul may be taken out of life.

Anselm

The doctrine of the final perseverance of the saints has as its corollary the salutary teaching that the saints are the people who persevere to the end.

F.F. Bruce

I have seen too many men fall out in the last lap.

Author unknown – a well-known man who thus explained why he would not have his biography written during his lifetime

Persistence   see PERSEVERANCE

Personality

We boil at different degrees.

Ralph Waldo Emerson, Society and Solitude, Eloquence

Persuasion

You have not converted a man because you have silenced him.

John Morley

Pessimism   see OPTIMISM

Philosophy

Philosophers have only interpreted the world differently; the point is, however, to change it.

Karl Marx

Unintelligible answers to insoluble problems.

Henry Adams

The first step towards philosophy is incredulity.

Diderot

When he who hears doesn't know what he who speaks means, and when he who speaks doesn't know what he himself means – that's philosophy.

Voltaire

Philosophy has shown itself over and over again to be full of arguments but lacking in conclusions.

Hugh Silvester, Arguing with God

Philosophy, Pagan

What has Athens to do with Jerusalem? What has the Academy to do with the church?

Tertullian

Pilgrimage

Here we have no continuing city, but we seek one to come.

The Bible, Hebrews 13:14 (AV)

They live in their own countries, but as travellers. They share everything as citizens, they suffer everything as foreigners. Every foreign land is their own country, their own country a foreign land. . . . They pass their life here on earth, but are citizens of heaven. They obey the laws of the land, but they out-do the laws in their own lives.

Epistle to Diognetus

Paradise is our native country, and we in this world be as exiles and strangers.

Richard Greenham

As I walk'd through the wilderness of this world. . .

John Bunyan, The Pilgrim's Progress

Who would true valour see,
   Let him come hither;
One here will constant be,
   Come wind, come weather.
There's no discouragement
Shall make him once relent
His first avowed intent
   To be a pilgrim.

John Bunyan, The Pilgrim's Progress

Fullness to such, a burden is,
   That go on pilgrimage:
Here little, and hereafter bliss,
   Is best from age to age.

John Bunyan, The Pilgrim's Progress

Give me my scallop-shell of quiet,
My staff of faith to walk upon,
My scrip of joy, immortal diet,
My bottle of salvation,
My gown of glory, hope's true gage,
And thus I'll take my pilgrimage.
Walter Raleigh, Diaphantus, The
Passionate Man's Pilgrimage
(Written when he was imprisoned
in the Tower of London. The
scallop shell was the badge of the
medieval pilgrim.)

Blest be the day that I began
A pilgrim for to be;
And blessèd also be that man
That thereto movèd me.
John Bunyan, The Pilgrim's
Progress

Pioneers

Never be a pioneer. It's the Early
Christian that gets the fattest lion.
Saki, Reginald

Plagiarism

Whatever is well said by another, is
mine.
Seneca

Pleasing God   see also SERVICE

Doing little things with strong desire to
please God makes them really great.
Francis de Sales

Pleasure

There is nothing – absolutely nothing –
half so much worth doing as simply
messing about in boats.
Kenneth Grahame, The Wind in
the Willows, ch. 1

Where pleasure prevails, all the greatest virtues will lose their power.
Cicero

Take all the pleasures of all the
spheres,
And multiply each through endless
years –
One minute of heaven is worth
them all.
Thomas Moore, Lalah Rookh

I do not think there is anyone who takes
such a fierce pleasure in things being
themselves as I do. The startling wet-
ness of water excites and intoxicates
me: the fieriness of fire, the steeliness
of steel, the unutterable muddiness of
mud.
G.K. Chesterton, quoted by
Maisie Ward, Gilbert Keith
Chesterton

He remains a fool his whole life long
Who loves not women, wine and song.
Martin Luther

Pleasure, in itself harmless, may
become mischievous, by endearing to
us a state which we know to be trans-
ient and probatory, and withdrawing
our thoughts from that of which every
hour brings us nearer to the beginning
and of which no length of time will
bring us to the end.
Samuel Johnson, Rasselas, ch. 47

What is more frequent, than to see
religion make men cynical, and sour in
their tempers, morose and surly in
their conversation.
Daniel Defoe, The Religious
Courtship, 1722

Poetry

If I had my life again, I would have
made a rule to read some poetry and
listen to some music at least once every
week; for perhaps the parts of my
brain now atrophied would thus have
been kept active through use.
Charles Darwin

Politeness   see also BEHAVIOUR; MANNERS

Politeness is to human nature what
warmth is to wax.
Arthur Schopenhauer

Politeness is the blossom of our
humanity.
Joubert

Politeness is worth much and costs
little.
Spanish proverb

There is a politeness of the heart, and
it is allied to love. It produces the most
agreeable politeness of outward
behaviour.
Goethe

Politics   see also ELECTIONS, GOVERNMENT

Man is by nature a political animal.
Aristotle

You cannot create a new world except
by creating a new heart and a new purpose in common men.
Bishop Percival

Politics is the only profession for which
no preparation is thought necessary.
Robert Louis Stevenson

What is morally wrong can never be politically right.

Lord Shaftesbury

That action is best, which procures the greatest happiness of the greatest numbers.

Francis Hutcheson, Concerning Moral Good and Evil

A man who acts from the principles I profess reflects that he is to give an account of his political conduct at the judgement seat of Christ.

William Wilberforce, in a letter to a constituent in 1789

Polygamy

A Mormon challenged Mark Twain to cite any passage of scripture forbidding polygamy. 'Nothing easier,' replied Twain. 'No man can serve two masters.'

Edmund Fuller, Thesaurus of Anecdotes

Pope, The

Primacy is given to Peter. . . . If someone deserts the throne of Peter, on whom the church is founded, is he sure that he is in the church?

Cyprian of Carthage, On the Unity of the Catholic Church

Both the pope and the higher clergy who are so liberal in granting indulgences for the temporal support of the churches are more credulous than credulity itself if they are not, for God's sake, as solicitous or more so for grace and the cure of souls. They have freely received all they have, and they ought freely to give it. 'But they are corrupt and have become abominable in their ways' (Psalm 14:1). They themselves have been misled and are now leading the people of Christ away from the true worship of God.

Martin Luther, The Epistle to the Romans

Positive thinking

I can do all things through Christ which strengtheneth me.

The Bible, St Paul, Philippians 4:13 (AV)

Faith, belief, positive thinking make better people and a better world since the outer world shapes itself to our inner thinking. Quit thinking and talking about war, poverty, hard times. Think and talk peace, health, plenty,

success to help bring them about. Guard your thoughts against negatives as you would your house against thieves.

Author unknown

Instead of deploring that roses have thorns, I am glad the thorny stem is capped with roses and that the tree bears bloom.

Joubert

Possessions

It is easier to renounce worldly possessions than it is to renounce the love of them.

Walter Hilton

These are things that make it difficult to die.

Samuel Johnson, being shown round a castle and its grounds

The riches and goods of Christians are not common, as touching the right, title, and possession of the same, as certain Anabaptists do falsely boast.

Book of Common Prayer, Article 38

Nobody can fight properly and boldly for the faith if he clings to a fear of being stripped of earthly possessions.

Peter Damian

Potential

Treat people as if they were what they ought to be and you help them become what they are capable of being.

Goethe

Poverty

Poverty . . . has no sharper pang than this, that it makes men ridiculous.

Juvenal

A hungry man is not a free man.

Adlai Stevenson

Wherever there is great property, there is great inequality. . . . For one very rich man, there must be at least five hundred poor.

Adam Smith

Give me neither poverty nor riches, but give me only my daily bread.

The Bible, Proverbs 30:8

What is the use of being kind to a poor man?

Cicero

He who mocks the poor shows contempt for their maker.

The Bible, Proverbs 17:5

The only way a rich man can be healthy is by exercise and abstinence – living like a poor man.
Author unknown

Every stable government in history has depended on the resignation of the poor to being poor.
Lammenais

Necessity hath no law.
Latin proverb

Poverty is no sin.
George Herbert

Debt is the worst form of poverty.
Author unknown

Better to go to heaven in rags than to hell in embroidery.
Thomas Fuller, Gnomologia

Poverty is not a shame, but the being ashamed of it.
Author unknown

Poverty breeds strife.
Author unknown

There is no scandal like rags, nor any crime so shameful as poverty.
George Farquhar, Archer in The Beaux' Stratagem, I.i

No society can surely be flourishing and happy, of which the far greater part of the members are poor and miserable.
Adam Smith, The Wealth of Nations, 1.8

With fingers weary and worn,
  With eyelids heavy and red,
A woman sat, in unwomanly rags,
  Plying her needle and thread –
    Stitch! stitch! stitch!
In poverty, hunger, and dirt.
Thomas Hood, The Song of the Shirt

Poverty, Relief of

A decent provision for the poor is the true test of civilisation.
Samuel Johnson, quoted by Boswell, Life of Johnson

If anyone has material possessions and sees his brother in need but has no pity on him, how can the love of God be in him?
The Bible, 1 John 3:17

Go and sell that thou hast, and give to the poor, and thou shalt have treasure in heaven.
The Bible, Jesus Christ, Matthew 19:21

Every cab-horse in London is given food, shelter and work. People ought to be looked after just as well as cab-horses are cared for.
William Booth

The real disgrace of poverty is not in admitting the fact but in declining to struggle against it.
Thucydides

Defend the rights of the poor and the orphans;
  be fair to the needy and the helpless.
The Bible, Psalm 82:3

Poverty, Spiritual

He who is poor in spirit no longer depends upon his material possessions. He can no longer say, 'I am rich and increasing in goods, and need nothing.' The poor in spirit knows that he is wretched, poor, miserable, blind, and naked. He is convinced that he is spiritually poor indeed. He knows that he has no spiritual good abiding in him. He says, 'In me dwells no good thing, but only that which is evil and abominable.'
John Wesley, The Nature of the Kingdom

He [Francis of Assisi] had become a lover of her [Poverty's] beauty. . . . He rejoiced to exchange a perishable treasure for the hundredfold.
An early biographer of Francis

When I see the curse of God upon many Christians that are now grown full of their parts, gifts, peace, comforts, abilities, duties, I stand adoring the riches of the Lord's mercies, through a little handful of poor believers, not only in making them empty, but in keeping them so all their days.
Thomas Shepherd, Sound Believer

Poverty, Understanding

Few, save the poor, feel for the poor.
Letitia Elizabeth Landon, The Poor

Unless he has genius, a rich man cannot imagine what poverty is like.
Charles Péguy, Basic Verities

Power

Power tends to corrupt, and absolute power corrupts absolutely. Great men are almost always bad men. . . . There is no worse heresy than that the office sanctifies the holder of it.

Lord Acton, Historical Essays and Studies, Letter to Bishop Creighton

Political power comes out of the barrel of a gun. . . . The gun must never slip from the grasp of the communist party.

Mao Tse-tung

Germany will be either a world power or will not be at all.

Adolf Hitler, Mein Kampf

'My name is Ozymandias, king of kings,
Look on my works, ye Mighty, and despair!'
Nothing beside remains. Round the decay
Of that colossal wreck, boundless and bare,
The lone and level sands stretch far away.

Percy Bysshe Shelley, Ozymandias, whose name and shattered statue are all that are left of his power

Guns will make us powerful; butter will only make us fat.

Hermann Goering, broadcast in 1936

Might before right.

Bismarck's policies as summed up by his opponent, Von Schwerin

The love of liberty is the love of others; the love of power is the love of ourselves.

William Hazlitt

Power gradually extirpates from the mind every humane and gentle virtue.

Edmund Burke

The measure of man is what he does with power.

Pittacus

Power, Spiritual

God has every bit of me.

William Booth's account of why his life displayed such power

There are in the world two powers – the sword and the spirit. And the spirit has always vanquished the sword.

Napoleon

Practice

The only way to become master of any skill is first to become its slave. And that takes practice, practice, practice.

Paderewski, on being asked by a youngster how he too could master the piano

Praise

As long as one can admire and love, then one is young for ever.

Pablo Casals

No sound is sweeter than the sound of praise.

Xenophon

The applause of a single human being is of great importance.

Samuel Johnson

Modesty is the only sure bait when you angle for praise.

G.K. Chesterton

Praise – of God   see also WORSHIP

What else can I, a lame old man, do but sing hymns to God? If, indeed, I were a nightingale, I would be singing as a nightingale; if a swan, as a swan. But, as it is, I am a rational being, therefore I must be singing hymns of praise to God. This is my task; I do it, and will not desert this post, as long as it may be given to me to fill it; and I exhort you to join with me in this same song.

The lame pagan slave Epictetus, Discourses 1.16.21

A man should utter a hundred daily benedictions.

Rabbi Meir

Let us with a gladsome mind
Praise the Lord, for he is kind:
   For his mercies ay endure,
   Ever faithful, ever sure.

John Milton

Praise to the holiest in the height,
   And in the depth be praise,
In all his words most wonderful,
   Most sure in all his ways.

J.H. Newman, The Dream of Gerontius

Man's chief work is the praise of God.

Augustine of Hippo, Discourses on the Psalms

He who does not praise God while here on earth shall in eternity be dumb.

John of Ruysbroeck

If anyone would tell you the shortest way to all happiness and all perfection, he must tell you to make it a rule to yourself to thank and praise God for everything that happens to you. For it is certain that whatever calamity happens to you, if you thank and praise God for it, you turn it into a blessing.

Could you, therefore, work miracles, you could not do more for yourself than by this thankful spirit; for it heals with a word speaking, and turns all that it touches into happiness.

William Law

Praise my soul, the King of heaven;
  To his feet thy tribute bring;
Ransomed, healed, restored, forgiven,
  Who like thee his praise should sing?
    Praise him, praise him, . . .
  Praise the everlasting King.

Henry Francis Lyte

Prayer is my chief work, by it I carry on all else.

William Law

Praise – of others   see also RIDICULE

As we must account for every idle remark, so we must account for every idle silence.

Benjamin Franklin

Usually we praise only to be praised.

La Rochefoucauld

A slowness to applaud betrays a cold temper or an envious spirit.

Hannah More

Glory paid to ashes comes too late.

Martial

Praise often turns losers into winners.

Author unknown

To be niggard in one's praise of others is a sure proof of mediocrity in oneself.

Vauvenargues

Praise – of self   see also BOASTING

Speaking ill of others is a cheap, dishonest way to praise ourselves.

Author unknown

Prayer

I will do whatever you ask for in my name, so that the Father's glory will be shown through the Son. If you ask me for anything in my name, I will do it.

The Bible, Jesus Christ,
John 14:13–14

When I stop praying, the coincidences stop happening.

William Temple

The end of prayer is the perfection of the whole Christian body.

B.F. Westcott

He did not pray to men, but to God. He seemed to realise that he was speaking to heaven's king.

A minister describing 'Stonewall'
Jackson

He who has learned to pray, has learned the greatest secret of a happy and holy life.

William Law

If you are to pray in the profitable way you desire it is best for you, from the start, to think of yourself as a poor, naked, miserable wretch, dying of hunger, who knows about one person who can help you and relieve you of your suffering.

François Fénelon, Christian
Perfection, letter to the Duchesse
de Beauvilliers

If an army advances on its stomach, a church advances on its knees.

Author unknown

Truly we have learned a great lesson when we have learned that 'saying prayers' is not praying!

J.C. Ryle

The brief hours are not lost in which ye learn
More of your Master and his rest in heaven.

E.H. Bickersteth

In my first prayer for deliverance from worldly thoughts, depending on the power and promises of God, for fixing my soul while I prayed, I was helped to enjoy much abstinence from the world for nearly an hour.

Henry Martyn, journal entry
describing a day of prayer and
fasting; John Sargent, Memoir

One single grateful thought raised to heaven is the most perfect prayer.

G.E. Lessing, Minna von
Barnhelm

The great masters and teachers in Christian doctrine have always found in prayer their highest source of illumination.

H.P. Liddon

If I had one gift, and only one gift, to make to the Christian church, I would offer the gift of prayer.

E. Stanley Jones

A little place of mystic grace
Of sin and self swept bare
Where I may look into thy face
And talk with thee in prayer.

Oxenham

You know the value of prayer: it is precious beyond all price. Never, never neglect it.

Thomas Buxton

The act of praying is the very highest energy of which the human mind is capable; praying, that is, with the total concentration of the faculties. The great mass of worldly men and of learned men are absolutely incapable of prayer.
Samuel Taylor Coleridge

I urge upon you communion with Christ, a growing communion.
Samuel Rutherford

He prayeth best, who loveth best
All things both great and small;
For the dear God who loveth us,
He made and loveth all.
Samuel Taylor Coleridge, The Ancient Mariner

Prayer is the first thing, the second thing, the third thing necessary to a minister. Pray, then, my dear brother, pray, pray, pray.
Edward Payson

The soul which gives itself to prayer – whether a lot or only a little – must absolutely not have limits set on it.
Teresa of Avila

From depth of sin and from a deep despair,
From depth of death, from depth of heart's sorrow,
From this deep cave of darkness' deep repair,
Thee have I called, O Lord, to be my borrow.
Thomas Wyatt

Our Lord is the ground from whom our prayer grows and in his love and grace he himself gives us our prayer.
Julian of Norwich, Revelations of Divine Love

There is but one road which reaches God and that is prayer; if anyone shows you another, you are being deceived.
Teresa of Avila

The very act of prayer honours God and gives glory to God, for it confesses that God is what he is.
Charles Kingsley

There are few men who dare publish to the world the prayers they make to Almighty God.
Montaigne, Essays, Of Prayer

Certain thoughts are prayers. There are moments when whatever be the attitude of the body, the soul is on its knees.
Victor Hugo, Les Misérables

Prayer and faith

Prayer digs up the treasures which the Gospel reveals to the eye of faith.
John Calvin, The Institutes of Christian Religion, 3.20.2

Faith is to prayer what the feather is to the arrow; without prayer it will not hit the mark.
J.C. Ryle

Prayer and the devil

Satan dreads nothing but prayer.
Samuel Chadwick

And Satan trembles when he sees
The weakest saint upon his knees.
William Cowper

Satan rocks the cradle when we sleep at our devotions.
Joseph Hall

The one concern of the devil is to keep the saints from praying. He fears nothing from prayerless studies/work/ Christian activity. He laughs at our toil, mocks our wisdom, but trembles when we pray.
Samuel Chadwick

Prayer and the heart's desire

The best prayers have more often groans than words.
John Bunyan

Prayer is not merely expressing our present desires. Its purpose is to exercise and train our desires, so that we want what he is getting ready to give us. His gift is very great, and we are small vessels for receiving it. So prayer involves widening our hearts to God.
Augustine of Hippo, Letter to Proba

In prayer it is better to have a heart without words than words without a heart.
John Bunyan

In prayer the lips ne'er act the winning part,
Without the sweet concurrence of the heart.
Robert Herrick

Why, why is Heaven silent still
When I have prayed so long?

Ah! answerless the silence speaks,
And tells me that the heart that seeks,
The heart, the heart is wrong.

*P. Wilkes, Missionary Joys in
Japan*

Your desire is your prayer; and your
desire is without ceasing; your prayer
will also be without ceasing.

*Augustine of Hippo, Discourses
on the Psalms*

Prayer and the will of God

You cannot *alter* the will of God, but
the man of prayer can discover God's
will.

*Sundar Singh, At the Feet of the
Master*

When we speak with God, our power
of addressing him, of holding communion with him, and listening to his
still small voice, depends upon our will
being one and the same with his.

Florence Nightingale

Prayer is not overcoming God's reluctance; it is laying hold of his highest
willingness.

Richard Chevenix Trench

Prayer, Definitions of

What you love you worship; true
prayer, real prayer, is nothing but loving: what you love, that you pray to.

Augustine of Hippo

Prayer is love in need appealing to love
in power.

Robert Moffatt

Prayer is the burden of a sigh,
  The falling of a tear,
The upward glancing of an eye
  When none but God is near.

James Montgomery

Prayer is fellowship with God, and it is
from such that the servant of God
draws his strength and inspiration, and
the enablement to serve him accepta-
bly. There can be no doubt that we
avail ourselves all too little of this great
privilege.

William Dobbie

Prayer is an effort to lay hold of God
himself, the author of life.

*Sundar Singh, At the Feet of the
Master*

Prayer is a cry of hope.

Alfred de Musset

Prayer is the application of the heart to
God, and the internal exercise of love.

*Madame Guyon, A Short and
Easy Method of Prayer*

Prayer. The chief exercise of faith, by
which we daily receive God's benefits.

*John Calvin, The Institutes of
Christian Religion, 3.20*

Prayer is the overflowing of the heart
in the presence of God.

*Madame Guyon, A Short and
Easy Method of Prayer*

There are always burning winds to
pass over the soul of man and dry it up.
Prayer is the dew which refreshes it.

Lamennais

As soon as we are with God in faith
and in love, we are in prayer.

François Fénelon

Prayer, the church's banquet, angel's
  age
God's breath in man returning to his
  birth,
The soul in paraphrase, heart in
  pilgrimage,
The Christian plummet sounding
  heaven and earth.

George Herbert

To work is to pray.

Latin proverb

Prayer, Effects of on person praying

No spring of water pours out sweet
water and bitter water from the same
opening.

*The Bible, The apostle James
writing about the tongue,
James 3:11*

The child of many prayers shall never
perish.

*An old Christian, to Monnica,
mother of Augustine of Hippo*

One bright benison which private
prayer brings down upon the ministry
is an indescribable and inimitable
something – an unction from the Holy
One.

C.H. Spurgeon

Prayer – secret, fervent, believing
prayer – lies at the root of all personal
godliness.

Carey's Brotherhood, Serampore

The sure relief of prayer.

William Wordsworth

Prayer is a breathing in of the Holy
Spirit. God so pours his Holy Spirit

into the life of the prayerful that they become 'living souls' (Genesis 2; John 20:22). They will never die. The Holy Spirit pours himself into their spiritual lungs through prayer, filling them with health, power and eternal life.
Sundar Singh

When God wants to perform in us and through us and with us some act of great charity, he first proposes it to us by his inspiration, then we favour it, and finally we consent to it.
Francis de Sales

There is nothing that makes us love a man so much as praying for him.
William Law

Prayer unites the soul to God.
Julian of Norwich, Revelations of Divine Love

Prayer makes things possible for men which they find otherwise impossible.
Sundar Singh, At the Feet of the Master

Prayer has the salutary effect of purifying, refining, and ennobling our heart. It banishes evil thoughts, and thus saves us much pain and sorrow.
M. Friedländer

Prayer is the guide to perfection, and delivers us from every vice, and gives us every virtue; for the one way to become perfect is to walk in the presence of God.
Madame Guyon, A Short and Easy Method of Prayer

Prayer does not change God, but it changes him who prays.
Søren Kierkegaard

Prayer, Extempore

We pray without a prompter because from the heart.
Tertullian, Defence of Christianity

Prayer, Humility in

There is a sense in which every man when he begins to pray to God should put his hand upon his mouth.
Martyn Lloyd-Jones, Studies in the Sermon on the Mount

Prayer, Intercessory

When God has something very great to accomplish for his church it is his will that there should precede it, the extraordinary prayers of his people

. . . And it is revealed that when God is about to accomplish great things for his church, he will begin by remarkably pouring out the spirit of grace and supplication.
Author unknown

Prayer must carry on our work as much as preaching: he preacheth not heartily to his people, that will not pray for them.
Richard Baxter

Our prayer must not be self-centred. It must arise not only because we feel our own need as a burden which we must lay upon God, but also because we are so bound up in love for our fellow-men that we feel their need as acutely as our own. To make intercession for men is the most powerful and practical way in which we can express our love for them.
John Calvin

Take time and realise, when you are alone with God: Here am I now, face to face with God, to intercede for his servants. Do not think that you have no influence, or that your prayer will not be missed. Your prayer and faith will make a difference.
Andrew Murray

True intercession is a sacrifice, a bleeding sacrifice.
J.H. Jowett

Prayer, Lack of

What a dreadful delusion has overshadowed most of mankind, as they suppose that they are not called to a state of prayer! The truth of the matter is that everyone who is called and who is capable of salvation is also called to and is capable of prayer.
Madame Guyon, A Short and Easy Method of Prayer

To be prayerless is to be without God – without Christ – without grace – without hope – and without heaven. It is to be in the road to hell.
J.C. Ryle, Practical Religion

If I wished to humble anyone, I should question him about his prayers. I know nothing to compare with this topic for its sorrowful self-confessions.
C.J. Vaughan

I wish I had prayed more, even if I had worked less; and from the bottom of my heart I wish I had prayed better.
Samuel Chadwick

Little of the Word with little prayer is death to the spiritual life. . . . A full measure of the Word and prayer each day gives a healthy and powerful life.
Andrew Murray, The Prayer Life

He judged he had dedicated too much time to public ministrations, and too little to private communion with God.
John Sargent, Memoir of Henry Martyn

Your greatest lack is that you do not know how to pray.
Toyohiko Kagawa, speaking to a meeting of American ministers

I suspect I have been allotting habitually too little time to religious exercises, as private devotion and religious meditation, scripture-reading, etc. Hence I am lean and cold and hard. I had better allot two hours or an hour and a half daily. I have been keeping too late hours, and hence have had but a hurried half-hour in a morning to myself. Surely the experience of all good men confirms the proposition that without a due measure of private devotions the soul will grow lean.
William Wilberforce

If I should neglect prayer but a single day, I should lose a great deal of the fire of faith.
Martin Luther

The leading defect in Christian ministers is want of a devotional habit.
Richard Cecil

The principal cause of my leanness and unfruitfulness is owing to an unaccountable backwardness to pray.
Richard Newton

He that flees from prayer flees from all that is good.
John of the Cross

Who goes to bed and does not pray
Maketh two nights to every day.
George Herbert, The Temple

Whoever has it in his power to pray on behalf of his neighbour, and fails to do so, is called a sinner.
Rabbinical saying

The worst sin is prayerlessness.
P.T. Forsyth, The Soul in Prayer

O what peace we often forfeit,
O what needless pain we bear,
All because we do not carry
Everything to God in prayer.
J.M. Scriven

Prayer, Length of

If I fail to spend two hours in prayer each morning, the devil gets the victory through the day. I have so much business I cannot get on without spending three hours daily in prayer.
Martin Luther

He prayed me into a good frame of mind, and if he had stopped there, it would have been very well; but he prayed me out of it again by keeping on.
George Whitefield

Lord's Day, April 25th. This morning spent about two hours in sacred duties, and was enabled, more than ordinarily, to agonise for immortal souls; though it was early in the morning, and the sun scarcely shone at all, yet my body was quite wet with sweat.
David Brainerd, diary

I have so much to do that I must spend several hours in prayer before I am able to do it.
John Wesley

Prayer, Method of

You must literally prostrate yourself before him in the quietness of your own room, and through this outward physical action express the humiliation of your soul as you view the terrible sight of your own faults.
François Fénelon, Christian Perfection, letter to the Duchesse de Beauvilliers

In our Lord's teaching about petitionary prayer there are three main principles. The first is confidence, the second is perseverance, and the third, for lack of a better word, I will call correspondence with Christ.
William Temple

We must understand that the only ones who prepare themselves for prayer adequately are those who are so impressed with God's majesty that they can be free from all earthly worries and affections.

John Calvin, The Institutes of Christian Religion, 3.20.5

There is no need to talk a lot in prayer, but stretch out your hands often and say, 'Lord, as you want and as you know, have mercy on me.' But if there is war in your soul, add, 'Help me.' And because he knows what we need, he shows us his mercy.

Macarius

To ask timidly is to invite refusal. Ask as though you expect to receive.

Author unknown

Do not turn to prayer hoping to enjoy spiritual delights; rather come to prayer totally content to receive nothing or to receive great blessing from God's hand, whichever should be your heavenly Father's will for you at that time.

Madame Guyon, A Short and Easy Method of Prayer

Receive each day as a resurrection from death, as a new enjoyment of life; meet every rising sun with such thoughts of God's goodness, as if they were visible and newly created for you.

William Law

For though the spirit of devotion is the gift of God and cannot be attained by any mere powers of our own, yet it is mostly given to, and never withheld from, those who by a wise and steady use of the right methods prepare themselves for the reception of it.

William Law

The one who comes into God's presence to pray must get rid of all boasting and self-opinionated ideas. Self-confidence must be thrown aside and God be given all the glory. Pride always means turning away from God. The holier the servant of God, the lower he will bow down in the presence of the Lord.

John Calvin, The Institutes of Christian Religion, 3.20.8

The first rule of true prayer is to have heart and mind in the right mood for talking with God.

John Calvin, The Institutes of Christian Religion, 3.20.4

No one should give the answer that it is impossible for a man occupied with worldly cares to pray always. You can set up an altar to God in your mind by means of prayer. And so it is fitting to pray at your trade, on a journey, standing at a counter or sitting at your handicraft.

John Chrysostom

Some men will spin out a long prayer telling God who and what he is, or they pray out a whole system of divinity. Some people preach, others exhort people, till everybody wishes they would stop and God wishes so, too, most undoubtedly.

C.H. Spurgeon

You can't pray a lie.

Mark Twain, The Adventures of Huckleberry Finn

Tell God that you have, alas! no inclination to pray, and that you have dragged yourself to your knees. Still you will be welcome!

W.E. Sangster

You need not cry very loud: he is nearer to us than we think.

Brother Lawrence

Do not pray for easy lives. Pray to be stronger men. Do not pray for tasks equal to your powers. Pray for powers equal to your tasks.

Phillips Brooks

Enter into the inner chamber of your mind. Shut out all things save God and whatever may aid you in seeking God; and having barred the door of your chamber, seek him.

Anselm of Canterbury

Early to bed and early to rise
Makes a man healthy, wealthy, and wise.

Author unknown

Take time to be holy;
Speak oft with thy Lord.

W.D. Longstaff

Prayer, Occasions and times of

You can only pray all the time everywhere if you bother to pray some of the time somewhere.

J. Dalrymple, The Christian Affirmation

Prayer should be the key of the day and the lock of the night.

Thomas Fuller, Gnomologia

If I have accomplished anything in the world, I attribute it to the fact that the first hour of every day of my life for years has been given to communion with God in secret prayer and the study of his word. . . . Do you suppose I come to a Cabinet meeting without first having talked it over with God?

Earl Cairns

The man who says his prayers in the evening is a captain posting his sentries. After that, he can sleep.

Charles Baudelaire

Make conscience of beginning the day with God, and the best way to begin the day well is to begin it the night before.

John Bunyan

I ought to spend the best hours in communion with God. It is my noblest and most fruitful employment, and is not to be thrust into a corner. The morning hours, from six to eight, are the most uninterrupted and should be thus employed.

Robert Murray M'Cheyne

From four or five in the morning, private prayer; from five to six in the evening, private prayer.

Methodists

When the clock strikes, or however else you shall measure the day, it is good to say a short ejaculation every hour, that the parts and returns of devotion may be the measure of your time: and do so also in the breaches of thy sleep; that those spaces, which have in them no direct business of the world, may be filled with religion.

Jeremy Taylor

Endeavour seven times a day to withdraw from business and company and lift up thy soul to God in private retirement.

Adoniram Judson

Vows made in storms are forgotten in calm.

Proverb

Affliction teacheth a wicked person sometime to pray: prosperity never.

Ben Jonson, Timber

I ought to pray before seeing anyone.

Robert Murray M'Cheyne

The spirit of prayer is for all times and all occasions, it is a lamp that is to be always burning, a light to be ever shining; everything calls for it, everything is to be done in it and governed by it, because it is and means and wills nothing else but the whole totality of the soul, not doing this or that, but wholly, incessantly given up to God to be where and what and how he pleases.

William Law, Letters

Prayer, People of

I have read the lives of many eminent Christians who have been on earth since the Bible days. Some of them, I see, were rich, and some poor. Some were learned, some unlearned. Some of them were Episcopalians, and some Christians of other denominations. Some were Calvinists, and some were Arminians. Some have loved to use a liturgy, and some choose to use none. But one thing, I see, they all had in common. They all have been men of prayer.

J.C. Ryle

At the time of his health he did rise constantly at or before four of the clock, and would be much troubled if he heard smiths or other craftsmen at their trades before he was at communion with God; saying to me often, 'How this noise shames me. Does not my Master deserve more than theirs?' From four till eight he spent in prayer, holy contemplation, and singing of psalms, in which he much delighted and did daily practise alone, as well as in the family.

Of Joseph Alleine, by his wife

Give me a man of God – one man,
    One mighty prophet of the Lord,
And I will give you peace on earth,
    Bought with a prayer and not a sword.

George Liddell

I would be undone if I did not have access to his chamber when I can show him all my business.

Samuel Rutherford

Consider the lives of the most outstanding and shining servants of God, whether they be in the Bible or out of the Bible. In all of them you will find that they were men of prayer. Depend on prayer; prayer is powerful.

J.C. Ryle

Above all [George Fox] excelled in prayer. . . . He knew and lived nearer to the Lord than other men, for they that know God most will see most reason to approach him with reverence and fear.

William Penn

I overheard him in prayer, but, good God, with what life and spirit did he pray! It was with so much reverence, as if he were speaking to God, yet with so much confidence as if he were speaking to his friend.

Theodorus, writing of Martin Luther

The great leaders of the Bible were not leaders because of brilliancy of thought, because they were exhaustless in resources, because of their magnificent culture or native endowment, but because, by the power of prayer, they could command the power of God.

E.M. Bounds, Prayer and Praying Men

Prayer, Persistence in

Pray without ceasing.

The Bible, The apostle Paul, 1 Thessalonians 5:17 (AV)

Put the word of God and the world of God side by side; the one he himself gave, the other he gave himself for.

S.D. Gordon, The Quiet Time

If we do pray, let it be a settled rule with us, never to leave off the habit of praying, and never to shorten our prayers. A man's state before God may always be measured by his prayers. Whenever we begin to feel careless about our private prayers, we may depend upon it, there is something very wrong in the condition of our souls. There are breakers ahead. We are in imminent danger of shipwreck.

J.C. Ryle

Pray inwardly, even if you do not enjoy it. It does good, though you feel nothing, see nothing, yes, even though you think you are doing nothing. For when you are dry, empty, sick or weak, at such a time is your prayer most pleasing, though you find little enough to enjoy in it. This is true of all believing prayer.

Julian of Norwich, Revelations of Divine Love

God's acquaintance is not made hurriedly. He does not bestow his gifts on the casual or hasty comer and goer. To be much alone with God is the secret of knowing him and of influence with him.

E.M. Bounds

I am convinced that every man who, amidst his serious projects, is apprised of his dependence on God, as completely as that dependence is a fact, will be impelled to pray, almost every hour.

Foster

When it is hardest to pray, we ought to pray the hardest.

Dwight L. Moody

Be not afraid to pray – to pray is right.
Pray, if thou canst, with hope; but ever
    pray,
Though hope be weak, or sick with
    long delay;
Pray in the darkness, if there be no
    light.
Far is the time, remote from human
    sight,
When war and discord on the earth
    shall cease;
Yet every prayer for universal peace
Avails the blessed time to expedite.
Whate'er is good to wish, ask that of
    Heaven,
Though it be what thou canst not hope
    to see;
Pray to be perfect, though material
    leaven
Forbid the spirit so on earth to be:
    But if for any wish thou darest not
        pray,
    Then pray to God to cast that wish
        away.

Hartley Coleridge

Do not forget prayer. Every time you pray, if your prayer is sincere, there will be new feeling and new meaning in it, which will give you fresh courage.

Fyodor Dostoevsky

Hold yourself in prayer before God, like a dumb or paralytic beggar at a rich man's gate: let it be your business to keep your mind in the presence of God.

Brother Lawrence, The Practice of the Presence of God

A man, sir, should keep his friendship in constant repair.

Samuel Johnson

Prayer, Power of

Prayer moves the hand that moves the world.

Author unknown

I fear John Knox's prayers more than an army of ten thousand men.

Mary Queen of Scots

God does nothing redemptively in the world – except through prayer.

John Wesley

A generous prayer is never presented in vain.

Robert Louis Stevenson

It is possible to move men, through God, by prayer alone.

Hudson Taylor

Give me one hundred preachers who fear nothing but sin, and desire nothing but God, and I care not a straw whether they be clergymen or laymen; such alone will shake the gates of hell and set up the kingdom of heaven on earth. God does nothing but in answer to prayer!

John Wesley

To little men the gods send little things.

Callimachus

Thou art coming to a king,
Large petitions with thee bring;
For his grace and power are such,
None can ever ask too much.

John Newton

Even the gods are moved by the voice of entreaty.

Ovid, The Art of Love

Prayer is a powerful thing, for God has bound and tied himself thereto. None can believe how powerful prayer is, and what it is able to effect, but those who have learned it by experience.

Martin Luther

Prayer is a strong wall and fortress of the church; it is a good Christian weapon.

Martin Luther

The privilege of prayer, to me, is one of the most cherished possessions, because faith and experience alike convince me that God himself sees and answers, and his answers I never venture to criticise. It is only my part to ask.

Wilfred Grenfell

More things are wrought by prayer than this world dreams of:

For what are men better than sheep or goats
If, knowing God, they lift not hands of prayer
Both for themselves and those who call them friend.

Alfred, Lord Tennyson

Where two or three are gathered together in thy name, thou wilt grant their requests.

Book of Common Prayer, prayer of St John Chrysostom

Prayer, Prevailing

Five grand conditions of prevailing prayer were ever before his mind:

1. Entire dependence upon the merits and mediation of the Lord Jesus Christ, as the only ground of any claim for blessing. . . .
2. Separation from all known sin. . . .
3. Faith in God's word of promise. . . .
4. Asking in accordance with his will. . . .
5. Importunity in supplication. There must be *waiting* on God and waiting for God.

A.T. Pierson, George Müller of Bristol

Preaching

An irritable man cannot teach.

Rabbi Hillel

Logic on fire = preaching.

Martyn Lloyd-Jones

When you preach the gospel, beware of preaching it as the religion which explains everything.

Albert Schweitzer

Latimer! Latimer! Latimer! Be careful what you say. Henry the king is here. [Pause.] Latimer! Latimer! Latimer! Be careful what you say. The King of kings is here.

Hugh Latimer, preaching before Henry VIII

Preaching is not the performance of an hour. It is the outflow of a life. It takes twenty years to make a sermon, because it takes twenty years to make a man.

E.M. Bounds, Power through Prayer

Once in seven years I burn all my sermons; for it is a shame if I cannot write better sermons now than I did seven years ago.

John Wesley

If I profess with the loudest voice and clearest exposition every portion of God's word except precisely that little point which the world and the devil are attacking, I am not confessing Christ, however boldly I may be professing Christ. Where the battle rages, there the loyalty of the soldier is tested. To be steady in all the battlefields besides is mere flight and disgrace, if the soldier flinches at that one point.

Martin Luther

I simply taught, preached, wrote God's word: I did nothing . . . the Word did it all.

Martin Luther

Whoever does not find in holy scriptures, and the works of the fathers, wherewithal to affect his hearers, is not worthy of mounting the pulpit.

Pope Clement XIV (Ganganelli)

Preaching, Manner of

Whatever you do, let the people see that you are in good earnest. . . . You cannot break men's hearts by jesting with them, or telling them a smooth tale, or patching up a gaudy oration. Men will not cast away their dearest pleasures upon a drowsy request of one that seemeth not to mean as he speaks, or to care much whether his request be granted.

Richard Baxter

I preach as though Christ was crucified yesterday; rose again from the dead today; and is coming back to earth tomorrow.

Martin Luther

A good preacher should have these qualities and virtues: first, he should teach systematically; second, he should have a ready wit; third, he should be eloquent; fourth, he should have a good voice; fifth, a good memory; sixth, he should know when to stop; seventh, he should be sure of his doctrine; eighth, he should go out and grapple with body and blood, wealth and honour, in the word; ninth, he should let himself be mocked and jeered at by everybody.

Martin Luther, Table Talk

I preached as never sure to preach again,
And as a dying man to dying men.

Richard Baxter

The most reverent preacher that speaks as if he saw the face of God doth more affect my heart though with common words, than an irreverent man with the most exquisite preparations.

Richard Baxter

The pastor who wants to keep his church full of people should first of all preach the gospel. Then he should preach the gospel keeping the following three adverbs in his mind: earnestly, interestingly, and fully.

C.H. Spurgeon

The want of a familiar tone and expression is a great fault in most of our deliveries, and that which we should be very careful to amend.

Richard Baxter

Preaching, Open-air

Being excommunicated, and forbidden to preach in any church or churchyard, he [William Swinderby] made a pulpit of two mill-stones in the High Street of Leicester, and there preached 'in contempt of the bishop'. 'There,' says Knighton, 'you might see throngs of people from every part, as well from the town as the country, double the number there used to be when they might hear him lawfully.'

Quoted by C.H. Spurgeon,
Lectures to my Students, Second
Series

It is said that the first field-preaching in the Netherlands took place on the 14th of June, 1566, and was held in the neighbourhood of Ghent. The preacher was Herman Modet, who had formerly been a monk, but was now the reformed pastor at Oudenard. 'This man,' says a Popish chronicler, 'was the first who ventured to preach in public, and there were 7,000 persons at his first sermon.'

Wylie, History of Protestantism

Saturday, 31 [March 1731]. In the evening I reached Bristol, and met Mr Whitefield there. I could scarce reconcile myself at first to this strange way of preaching in the fields, of which he set me an example on Sunday; having been all my life (till very recently) so tenacious of every point relating to decency and order, that I should have

thought the saving of souls almost a sin, if it had not been done in a church.
John Wesley, Journal

I love a commodious room, a soft cushion and a handsome pulpit, but field preaching saves souls.
John Wesley

As soon as I began to preach, a man came straight forward, and presented a gun at my face; swearing that he would blow my brains out, if I spake another word. However, I continued speaking, and he continued swearing, sometimes putting the muzzle of the gun to my mouth, sometimes against my ear. While we were singing the last hymn, he got behind me, fired the gun, and burned off part of my hair.
John Furz

But when I was in the middle of my discourse, one at the outside of the congregation threw a stone, which cut me on the head: however, that made the people give greater attention, especially when they saw the blood running down my face; so that all was quiet till I had done, and was singing a hymn.
John Nelson

Preaching, Purpose of

To humble the sinner, to exalt the Saviour, and to promote holiness.
Charles Simeon

To comfort the disturbed and to disturb the comfortable.
Chad Walsh

Doctrine should be such as should make men in love with the lesson, and not with the teacher.
Francis Bacon, The Advancement of Learning

Every sermon should be an agony of soul, a passion to beget Christ in the souls of men.
John Chrysostom

The chief end of preaching is comfort.
Ian Maclaren

People want to be comforted. . . . They need consolation – really need it, and do not merely long for it.
R.W. Dale

Some are dead; you must rouse them. Some are troubled; you must comfort them. Others are burdened; you must point them to the burden-bearer. Still more are puzzled; you must enlighten

them. Still others are careless and indifferent; you must warn and woo them.
C.H. Spurgeon

The test of a preacher is that his congregation goes away saying, not 'What a lovely sermon!' but, 'I will do something!'
Francis de Sales

Preach not because you have to say something, but because you have something to say.
Richard Whateley

It is a marvel to me how men continue at ease in preaching year after year without conversions.
C.H. Spurgeon

Preaching is thirty minutes in which to raise the dead.
John Ruskin

Preaching, Simplicity in

No man can at one and the same time prove that he is clever and that Christ is wonderful.
James Denney

Be sparing in allegorising or spiritualising.
John Wesley

You will never attain simplicity in preaching without plenty of trouble. Pains and trouble, I say emphatically, pains and trouble. When Turner, the great painter, was asked by someone how it was he mixed his colours so well, and what it was that made them so different from those of other artists, he replied: 'Mix them? Mix them? Mix them? Why, with brains, sir.' I am persuaded that, in preaching, little can be done except by trouble and by pains.
J.C. Ryle, The Upper Room

No one can be a good preacher to the people, who is not willing to preach in a manner that seems childish and vulgar to some.
Martin Luther

The Lord said, 'Feed my sheep,' not 'Feed my giraffes'!
C.H. Spurgeon, Lectures to my Students, Second Series

A preacher should have the skill to teach the unlearned simply, roundly and plainly; for teaching is of more importance than exhorting. When I preach I regard neither doctors nor magistrates, of whom I have over forty in the congregation. I have all my eyes on the servant maids and the children. And if the learned men are not well pleased with what they hear, well, the door is open.

Martin Luther

A fellow of Billingsgate cannot understand a fellow of Brazenose. Now as the costermonger cannot learn the language of the college, let the college learn the language of the costermonger.

C.H. Spurgeon, Lectures to my Students, Second Series

We use the language of the market.

George Whitefield

Preaching, Skill in

Skill [is] necessary, to make plain the truth, to convince the hearers, to let in the irresistible light into their consciences, and to keep it there and drive all home; to screw the truth into their minds and work Christ into their affections. . . . This should surely be done with a great deal of holy skill.

Richard Baxter, The Reformed Pastor, 6.vi

If elephants can be trained to dance, lions to play, and leopards to hunt, surely preachers can be taught to preach.

Erasmus

He is the best speaker who can turn the ear into an eye.

Arabian proverb

Preaching and love

Whoever preaches with love preaches effectively.

Francis de Sales

To love to preach is one thing, to love those to whom we preach is quite another. The trouble with some of us is that we love preaching, but we are not always careful to make sure we love the people to whom we are actually preaching. If you lack this element of compassion for the people you will also lack the pathos which is a very vital element in all true preaching. Our Lord looked out upon the multitude and 'saw them as sheep without a shepherd', and was 'filled with compassion'. And if you know nothing of

this you should not be in a pulpit for this is certain to come out in your preaching.

Richard Cecil

Preaching and practice

Practise yourself what you preach.

Plautus, Asinaria, III.iii

It is no use walking anywhere to preach unless we preach as we walk.

Francis of Assisi

Preachers say, Do as I say, not as I do.

John Selden, Table Talk

With their doctrine they build, and with their lives they destroy.

Augustine of Hippo

No man preaches his own sermon well to others if he doth not first preach it to his own heart.

John Owen

Every preacher should sound out more by his deeds than by his words. He should, by his good life, make footprints for men to follow rather than, by speaking, merely show them the way to walk in.

Gregory the Great

He preaches well that lives well.

Proverb

Truth through *personality*.

Phillips Brooks' definition of great preaching

We must study as hard how to live well as how to preach well.

Richard Baxter

He that means as he speaks will surely do as he speaks.

Richard Baxter

Preaching and the gospel message

How beautiful upon the mountains are the feet of him that bringeth good tidings, that publisheth peace; that bringeth good tidings of good, that publisheth salvation; that saith unto Zion, Thy God reigneth!

The Bible, Isaiah 52:7 (AV)

There are two things in sermons – the one informing, and the other inflaming.

George Herbert, The Country Parson, 21

Brethren, first and above all things, keep to plain evangelical doctrines; whatever else you do or do not preach, be sure incessantly to bring forth the soul-saving truth of Christ and him crucified.

C.H. Spurgeon, Lectures to my Students

The celebrated lawyer, Blackstone, had the curiosity early in the reign of George III, to go from church to church and hear every clergyman of note in London. He says that he did not hear a single discourse which had more Christianity in it than the writings of Cicero, and that it would have been impossible for him to discover, from what he had heard, whether the preacher were a follower of Confucius, of Muhammad or of Christ!

J.C. Ryle, Five Christian Leaders

Preach nothing down but the devil, and nothing up but Jesus Christ.

Berridge

One lesson I learned that night . . . is that I [must] preach to press Christ upon the people then and there, and try to bring them to a decision on the spot. Ever since that night I have determined to make more of Christ than in the past.

Dwight L. Moody, describing the fire which, by burning down the hall where he had just asked people to think about Christ, prevented them ever coming back with their decision

Depend upon it, if we brought the intellect of a Locke or a Newton, and the eloquence of a Cicero, to bear upon the simple doctrine of 'believe and live,' we should find no surplus strength.

C.H. Spurgeon, Lectures to my Students

I would like to see no questions asked . . . as to what denomination a chaplain belongs, but let the question be, 'Does he preach the gospel?'

'Stonewall' Jackson, on the recruitment of army chaplains

Preaching and the Holy Spirit

On the one hand it deserves attention, that the most eminent and successful preachers of the gospel in different communities, a Brainerd, a Baxter, and a Schwartz, have been the most conspicuous for simple dependence on spiritual aid; and on the other that no success whatever has been attended the ministrations of those by whom the power of the Holy Spirit has been either neglected or denied.

Robert Hall

The preaching of the Word and the observance of the sacraments cannot happen anywhere without producing fruit and prospering because of God's blessing.

John Calvin, The Institutes of Christian Religion, 4.1.10

The gospel is preached in the ears of all; it only comes with power to some. The power that is in the gospel does not lie in the eloquence of the preacher; otherwise men would be converters of souls. Nor does it lie in the preacher's learning; otherwise it would consist in the wisdom of men. We might preach till our tongues rotted, but unless there were mysterious power going with it – the Holy Ghost changing the will of man. O, sirs! We might as well preach to stone walls as to preach to humanity unless the Holy Ghost be with the Word, to give it power to convert the soul.

C.H. Spurgeon

My endeavour is *to bring out of scripture what is there, and not to thrust in what I think might be there. I have a great jealousy on this head;* never to speak more or less than I believe the mind of the Spirit, in the passage I am expounding.

Charles Simeon to his publisher, 1832

Preaching by God's command

Everyone who can preach the truth and does not preach it, incurs the judgement of God.

Justin Martyr

I have no right to boast just because I preach the gospel. After all, I am under orders to do so. And how terrible it would be for me if I did not preach the gospel!

The Bible, The apostle Paul, 1 Corinthians 9:16

Predestination   see also CALVINISM V. ARMINIANISM; DESTINY; ELECTION, DIVINE

Those who had been chosen for eternal life became believers.

The Bible, Luke, Acts 13:48

Those whom God had already chosen he also set apart to become like his Son, so that the Son would be the first among many brothers. And so those whom God set apart, he called; and those he called, he put right with himself, and he shared his glory with them.

The Bible, The apostle Paul,
Romans 8:29–30

Even before the world was made, God had already chosen us to be his through our union with Christ, so that we would be holy and without fault before him.

The Bible, The apostle Paul,
Ephesians 1:4

To those who are elect and have the Spirit, predestination is the very sweetest of all doctrines, but to the worldly-wise it is the bitterest and hardest of all. . . . The reason God saves in this way is to show that he saves not by our merits but by election pure and simple, and by his unchanging will. . . . We are saved by his unchanging love. . . . Where then is our righteousness? Where our good works? Where is our free will?

Martin Luther, The Epistle to the
Romans

Predestination we call the eternal decree of God by which he determined in himself what he would have to become of every individual of mankind. For they are not all created with a similar destiny, but eternal life is foreordained for some and eternal death for others.

John Calvin, Institutes of Christian
Religion, 3.21.5

Scripture clearly proves that God, by his eternal and unchanging will, determined once and for all those whom he would one day admit to salvation and those whom he would consign to destruction. His decision about the elect is based on his free mercy with no reference to human deserving. Equally, those whom he dooms to destruction are shut off from eternal life by his perfect, but incomprehensible, judgment.

John Calvin, The Institutes of
Christian Religion, 3.21.7

God invites all indiscriminately by outward preaching.

John Calvin, Tracts

God draws, but he draws the willing one.

John Chrysostom

The promise of the gospel ought to be promiscuously and without distinction declared and published to all men and people.

Synod of Dort, 1619

The perfectly infallible preparation for grace, the only one, is eternal election and the predestination of God.

Martin Luther, Thesis 29

Although it is true that no one can be saved unless he is predestined, and has faith and grace, we must be very careful how we speak and treat these subjects.

Ignatius Loyola, Spiritual
Exercises

He who cannot believe is cursed, for he reveals by his unbelief that God has not chosen to give him grace.

Blaise Pascal

Predestination to life is the everlasting purpose of God, whereby (before the foundations of the world were laid) he hath constantly decreed by his counsel secret to us, to deliver from curse and damnation those whom he hath chosen in Christ out of mankind, and to bring them by Christ to everlasting salvation, as vessels made to honour.

Book of Common Prayer,
Article 17

The elect are whosoever will, and the non-elect, whosoever won't.

Henry Ward Beecher

Prejudice

Prejudice is wrong. But some judges will do wrong to get even the smallest bribe.

The Bible, Proverbs 28:21

A good many people think they are thinking when they are merely rearranging their prejudices.

William James

Prejudice is the child of ignorance.

William Hazlitt

It is never too late to give up your prejudices.

Henry David Thoreau

All looks yellow to a jaundiced eye.

Alexander Pope

Prejudice not being founded on reason cannot be removed by argument.

Samuel Johnson

Preoccupation

Those who are much occupied with the care of the body usually give little care to the soul.

Proverb

Preparation

Have thy tools ready. God will find thee work.

Charles Kingsley

Presence of God   see GOD'S PRESENCE

Pride

I know thy pride, and the naughtiness of thine heart.

The Bible, Eliab to David,
1 Samuel 17:28 (AV)

Pride always means enmity – it *is* enmity.

C.S. Lewis, Mere Christianity

A cold, self-righteous prig who goes regularly to church may be far nearer to hell than a prostitute. But, of course, it's better to be neither.

C.S. Lewis, Mere Christianity

Pride is the only disease known to man that makes everyone sick except the one who has it.

Author unknown

I pray God to keep me from being proud.

Samuel Pepys, Diary, 22 March
1660

Of all the marvellous works of the Deity, perhaps there is nothing that angels behold with such supreme astonishment as a proud man.

C.C. Colton, Lacon

The greatest fault is to be conscious of none.

Thomas Carlyle

He was like a cock who thought the sun had risen to hear him crow.

George Eliot, Adam Bede, ch. 33

Though various foes against the Truth combine,
Pride above all opposes her design;
Pride, of a growth superior to the rest,
The subtlest serpent with the loftiest crest,
Swells at the thought and, kindling into rage,
Would hiss the cherub Mercy from the stage.

William Cowper

Pride, or the loss of humility, is the root of every sin and evil.

Andrew Murray

Pride is the defect of the English, vanity of the French.

Jean-Jacques Rousseau

Other sins find their vent in the accomplishment of evil deeds, whereas pride lies in wait for good deeds to destroy them.

Augustine of Hippo

Haughtiness towards men is rebellion to God.

Moses Maimonides

Pride is the disorder of the fallen world. It can exist only where ignorance and sensuality, lies and falsehood, lust and impurity reign.

William Law

He that is down need fear no fall;
He that is low, no pride.

John Bunyan, Pilgrim's Progress,
Shepherd Boy's Song

God sends no one away empty except those who are full of themselves.

Dwight L. Moody

So narrow is the entry to heaven, that our knots, our bunches and lumps of pride, and self-love, and idol-love, and world-love, must be hammered off us, that we may throng in, stooping low, and creeping through that narrow and thorny entry.

Samuel Rutherford

Be not proud of race, face, place or grace.

C.H. Spurgeon

Pride and its correction

Pride is like a beard. It just keeps growing. The solution? Shave it every day.

Author unknown

When you become like a child, your pride will melt away and you will be like Christ himself in the stable at Bethlehem.

Martin Luther

Our pride must have winter weather to rot it.

Samuel Rutherford

Pride and its source

Pride comes from a deeply buried root – it comes from the devil himself. Where pride is fostered a person will be insincere, harsh, bitter, cutting, disdainful.

François Fénelon, Christian
Perfection, letter to an officer,
4 April 1701

Pride and what it leads to

Without a doubt it is pride that is the greatest of sins. Pride causes us to use our gifts as though they came from ourselves, not benefits received from God, and to usurp our benefactor's glory.

Bernard of Clairvaux, On Loving God

Pride is at the bottom of all great mistakes.

John Ruskin

The more proud anyone is himself, the more impatient he becomes at the slightest instance of it in other people. And the less humility anyone has, the more he demands and is delighted with it in other people.

William Law

You can have no greater sign of a confirmed pride than when you think you are humble enough.

William Law

The source of sin is pride. Pride makes the soul desert God, to whom it should cling as the source of life, and to imagine itself instead as the source of its own life.

Augustine of Hippo, The City of God

Excessive scruple is only hidden pride.

Goethe

If you harden your heart with pride, you soften your brain with it too.

Jewish proverb

What is the sign of a proud man? He never praises anyone.

The Zohar

Pride leads to destruction, and arrogance to downfall.

The Bible, Proverbs 16:18

People who do not get along with others are interested only in themselves; they will disagree with what everyone else knows is right.

The Bible, Proverbs 18:1

Principles

In matters of principle, stand like a rock; in matters of taste, swim with the current.

Thomas Jefferson

Prison

Though my body is enslaved, still my thoughts are free.

Sophocles

Stone walls do not a prison make,
Nor iron bars a cage.

Richard Lovelace, To Althea from Prison

Procrastination

Give me chastity and continence, but not yet.

Augustine of Hippo

Procrastination is the thief of time.

Edward Young, Night Thoughts, The Complaint

Never do today what you can put off till tomorrow.

Punch, 1849

Never put off till tomorrow what you can do the day after tomorrow.

Mark Twain

Procrastination is the assassination of motivation.

Author unknown

Business tomorrow.

Archias, the Spartan commander, refusing to give attention to a report of a plot against him: he continued to eat and drink, but the plot brought about his death

The man who procrastinates is always struggling with misfortunes.

Hesiod

A ripe crop must not wait for tomorrow.

Latin proverb

Tomorrow's life is too late, so live today.

Martial

The devil's favourite tool is tricking people to put things off. Outsmart him. Do it now.

Author unknown

Lose this day loitering, 'twill be the same story, tomorrow, and the next more dilatory,
For indecision brings its own delays, and days are lost lamenting o'er lost days.

Goethe

It is better to cleanse ourselves of our sins now, and to give up our vices, than to reserve them for cleansing at some future time.

Thomas à Kempis

Progress   see also GROWTH

Pigmies placed on the shoulders of giants see more than the giants themselves.

Lucan, Civil War, 2.10

Progress means getting nearer to the place where you want to be. And if you have taken a wrong turning, then to go forward does not get you any nearer.
C.S. Lewis, Mere Christianity

If I have seen further it is by standing on the shoulders of giants.
Isaac Newton

The dwarf sees further than the giant, when he has the giant's shoulder to mount on.
Samuel Taylor Coleridge, The Friend, 1828

The Roman pontiff can and ought to reconcile himself, and come to terms with progress, liberalism, and modern civilisation.
Pope Pius IX

'Peace upon Earth!' was said. We sing it,
And pay a million priests to bring it.
After two thousand years of mass
We've got as far as poison gas.
Thomas Hardy

You can't say that civilisation don't advance, for in every war they kill you a new way.
Will Rogers

You're not very smart if you're not a little kinder and wiser than yesterday.
Abraham Lincoln

Don't be yourself. Be superior to the fellow you were yesterday.
Author unknown

Promises

Those who are quick to promise are generally slow to perform.
C.H. Spurgeon

Promises of God

The promises of the Lord can be trusted;
   they are as genuine as silver
refined seven times in the furnace.
The Bible, Psalm 12:6

God keeps every promise he makes.
The Bible, Proverbs 30:5

I beseech you do not treat God's promises as if they were curiosities for a museum; but use them as everyday sources of comfort.
C.H. Spurgeon

Every promise of scripture is a writing of God which may be placed before him in reasonable request, 'Do as thou hast said.' The creator will not cheat the creature who depends upon his truth; and far more the heavenly Father will not break his own word to his own child.
C.H. Spurgeon

There is a living God; he has spoken in the Bible. He means what he says and will do all he has promised.
Hudson Taylor

God's lips know not how to lie, but he will accomplish all his promises.
Æschylus

What greater rebellion, impiety, or insult to God can there be, than not to believe his promises?
Martin Luther

The main hinge on which faith turns is this: we must not imagine that the Lord's promises are true objectively but not in our experience. We must make them ours by embracing them in our hearts.
John Calvin, The Institutes of Christian Religion, 3.2.16

Prophecy

Well, then, the Lord himself will give you a sign: a young woman who is pregnant will have a son and will name him 'Immanuel'.
The Bible, Isaiah 7:14

Prophets

Allow the prophets to give thanks as much as they want.
Didache

Not everyone who speaks in a spirit is a prophet; he is only a prophet if he walks in the ways of the Lord.
Didache

It was concerning this salvation that the prophets made careful investigation, and they prophesied about this gift which God would give you. They tried to find out when the time would be and how it would come. This was the time to which Christ's Spirit in them was pointing, in predicting the sufferings that Christ would have to endure and the glory that would follow. God revealed to these prophets that their work was not for their own benefit, but for yours, as they spoke about those things which you have now heard.
The Bible, 1 Peter 1:10–12

Propitiation

We propitiate only a person: we expiate only a fact or act or thing.
Horace Bushnell

Prosperity   see also WEALTH

Adversity makes a man, and prosperity makes monsters.
French proverb

Prosperity tries the souls even of the wise.
Sallust, Catiline War

It is prosperity that we cannot endure.
Martin Luther

For a hundred that can bear adversity there is hardly one that can bear prosperity.
Thomas Carlyle

Proverbs

Here are proverbs that will help you to recognise wisdom and good advice, and understand sayings with deep meaning.
The Bible, Proverbs 1:2

Every man like myself, who never went to college, can largely make up for that lack by reading the wise sayings of the great men of the past, who gladly left their wisdom and experience in proverbs for us who follow them.
Winston Churchill

Learning from the wise sayings of great men is like riding to success on the shoulders of giants.
Elbert Hubbard

Proverbs give us quality, not quantity. An hour of reading proverbs is usually worth weeks, even months or years, of ordinary reading. Here is wisdom, not knowledge.
Montaigne

A proverb is a short sentence with long experience.
Author unknown

In the proverbs, a drop of ink makes thousands think.
Bennet Cerf

Now back to my real people – to my 2000 page book of wise sayings, proverbs, and epigrams.
Eleanor Roosevelt, leaving a political rally

Proverbs introduce us to ourselves – to that bigger, grander man we never knew, beating beneath that dwarf of a man we always knew. That bigger man often haunts us until we express him.
Ralph Waldo Emerson

Wise sayings are lamps that light our way, from darkness to the light of day.
Henry Ward Beecher, Proverbs from a Plymouth Pulpit

One of the greatest treasures is a collection of wise sayings and proverbs for sharpening the mind.
Toynbee

These wise sayings seem to have some strange power to discover our rich, hidden talents – those hidden seeds of greatness that God plants inside every one of us.
Thomas Carlyle

Fire your ambition and courage by studying the priceless advice in the proverbs and wise sayings. They're the shortest road to wisdom you'll ever find.
Alexander Graham Bell

Time has weeded out of the great books all the unnecessary details and left us the gist, the essentials – the proverbs. They are the wisdom of the ages in the fewest words.
Goethe

In this hectic age, when most of us are unsure, confused and troubled, the surest anchors, guides and advisers are the wise sayings of great men of the past.
Clifton Fadiman

Any reading is better than none, but I prefer the book of the century rather than the book of the week or any cheap novel. Better still the book of four centuries – the book of proverbs. Time and the mind are too precious to waste – spend on anything but the best.
Theodore Roosevelt

Mankind would lose half its wisdom built up over the centuries if it lost its great sayings. They contain the best parts of the best books.
Thomas Jefferson

I use all the brains I have and borrow all I can from the classics and wise sayings.
Thomas Woodrow Wilson

Providence of God   see also GOD'S
PROVISION

Everything that happens in this world happens at the time God chooses.

He sets the time for birth and the time
   for death,
   the time for planting and the time
   for pulling up,
   the time for killing and the time for
   healing;
   the time for tearing down and the
   time for building.
He sets the time for sorrow and the
   time for joy,
   the time for mourning and the time
   for dancing,
   the time for making love and the
   time for not making love,
   the time for kissing and the time for
   not kissing.
He sets the time for finding and the
   time for losing,
   the time for saving and the time for
   throwing away,
   the time for tearing and the time for
   mending,
   the time for silence and the time for
   talk.
He sets the time for love and the time
   for hate,
   the time for war and the time for
   peace.

The Bible, Ecclesiastes 3:1–8

Man proposes but God disposes.

Thomas à Kempis

God moves in a mysterious way
   His wonders to perform;
He plants his footsteps in the sea,
   And rides upon the storm.

William Cowper

Prudence

We must not trust every word of others
or feeling within ourselves, but cautiously and patiently try the matter, to
see whether it is of God.

Thomas à Kempis

Psychoanalysis

Psychoanalysis is confession without
absolution.

G.K. Chesterton

Public opinion

Its name is Public Opinion. It is held in
reverence. It settles everything. Some
think it is the voice of God.

Mark Twain

In matters of conscience, the law of the
majority has no place.

Mahatma Gandhi

The voice of the people is the voice of
God.

Latin proverb

Follow the wise few rather than the
vulgar many.

Proverb

The man tenacious of purpose fears
neither the despot's tyranny nor that
of the mob.

Author unknown

The first qualification of a ruler is the
ability to endure unpopularity.

Seneca

We are all of us, more or less, the
slaves of opinion.

William Hazlitt

I do not believe in the collective wisdom of individual ignorance.

Thomas Carlyle

The world is governed by opinion.

Thomas Hobbes

It is a besetting vice of democracies to
substitute public opinion for law. This
is the usual form in which masses of
men exhibit their tyranny.

James Fenimore Cooper

Public opinion in this country is everything.

Abraham Lincoln

Punctuality

No man ever waited five minutes for
me in my life, unless for reasons quite
beyond my power.

Charles Simeon

Punishment

All who are strangers to the true God,
however excellent they may be,
deserve punishment if only because
they contaminate the pure gifts of
God.

Augustine of Hippo

Distrust all in which the impulse to
punish is powerful.

Friedrich Nietzsche

Men are not hanged for stealing horses,
but that horses may not be stolen.

Halifax

Man punishes the action, but God the
intention.

Thomas Fuller, Gnomologia

Purgatory

The Romish doctrine concerning purgatory, pardons, worshipping, and
adoration, as well of images as of

relics, and also invocation of saints, is a fond thing vainly invented, and grounded upon no warranty of scripture, but rather repugnant to the word of God.

Book of Common Prayer,
Article 22

The Bible teaches plainly, that as we die, whether converted or unconverted, whether believers or unbelievers, whether godly or ungodly, so shall we rise again when the last trumpet sounds. There is no repentance in the grave: there is no conversion after the last breath is drawn.

J.C. Ryle, Practical Religion

The scripture never represents the state of future misery as a state of purgation and purification, or anything like analogous to a state of trial, where men may fit and qualify themselves for some better state of existence: but always as a state of retribution, punishment, and righteous vengeance, in which God's justice . . . vindicates the power of his majesty, his government, and his love, by punishing those who have despised them.

Horbery

This life is the time of our preparation for our future state. Our souls will continue for ever what we make them in this world.

John Tillotson, Sermon on
Philippians 3:20

Purity   see also HOLINESS

There cannot be perfect transformation without perfect pureness.

John of the Cross, The Ascent of
Mount Carmel

How to be pure? By steadfast longing for the one good, that is, God.

Meister Eckhart

Still to the lowly soul
He doth himself impart,
And for his dwelling and his throne
Chooseth the pure in heart.

Lord, we thy presence seek;
May ours this blessing be;
Give us a pure and lowly heart,
A temple meet for thee.

John Keble

Make and keep me pure within.

Charles Wesley

My strength is as the strength of ten,
Because my heart is pure.

Alfred, Lord Tennyson

Purpose   see AMBITION; GOALS

Q

Quakers

Justice Bennett of Derby was the first that called us Quakers, because I bid them tremble at the word of the Lord. That was in the year 1650.

George Fox, Journal

He [Oliver Cromwell] said: 'I see there is a people risen, that I cannot win either with gifts, honours, offices or places; but all other sects and people I can.'

George Fox, Journal

Questions

The first key to wisdom is assiduous and frequent questioning. For by doubting we come to inquiry, and by inquiry we arrive at truth.

Peter Abelard

The important thing is not to stop questioning.

Albert Einstein

A prudent question is one-half of wisdom.

Francis Bacon

Judge a man by his questions rather than by his answers.

Voltaire

I keep six honest serving men
(They taught me all I knew);
Their names are What and Why and
   When
And How and Where and Who.

Rudyard Kipling

Quietness   see also SILENCE; STILLNESS

If we have not quiet in our minds, outward comfort will do no more for us than a golden slipper on a gouty foot.

John Bunyan

Sometimes quiet is disquieting.

Seneca, Epistles, 56

The holy time is quiet as a nun.

William Wordsworth

Quotation

Next to the originator of good sentence is the first quoter of it.

Ralph Waldo Emerson, Letters and Social Arms, Quotation and Originality

Everything has been said before, but since nobody listens we have to keep going back and beginning all over again.

André Gide, Le Traité du Narcisse

It is a good thing for an uneducated man to read books of quotations.

Winston Churchill, My Early Life

To make good use of a thought found in a book requires almost as much cleverness as to originate it. Cardinal du Perron said that the apt quotation of a line of Virgil was worthy of the highest talent.

Stendhal

Quotations are useful, ingenious, and excellent, when not overdone, and aptly applied.

Edouard Fournier

The wisdom of the wise and the experience of the ages are perpetuated by quotations.

Benjamin Disraeli

I quote others only the better to express myself.

Montaigne

R

Race

God knew what he was doing when he made me black. On a piano you cannot play a good tune using only the white notes: you must use the black and white notes together. God wants to play tunes with both his white notes and his black ones.

Dr Aggrey

All who are not of good race in this world are chaff.

Adolf Hitler

A heavy guilt rests upon us for what the whites of all nations have done to the coloured peoples. When we do good to them, it is not benevolence – it is atonement.

Albert Schweitzer

I have a dream that my four little children will one day live in a nation where they will not be judged by the colour of their skin but by the content of their character.

Martin Luther King

I want to be the white man's brother, not his brother-in-law.

Martin Luther King

Labour in a white skin cannot be free as long as labour in a black skin is branded.

Karl Marx

The Americans ought to be ashamed of themselves for letting their medals be won by negroes.

Adolf Hitler

Rainbows

My heart leaps up when I behold
A rainbow in the sky.

William Wordsworth

Reading   see also READING THE BIBLE

Show me an army of leaders and I'll show you an army of readers.

Napoleon

Some people judge the value of books by their thickness, as though they were written to exercise the arms rather than the brains.

Gracian

To read without reflecting is like eating without digesting.

Edmund Burke

Master those books you have. Read them thoroughly. Bathe in them until they saturate you. Read and reread them, masticate them and digest them. Let them go into your very self.

C.H. Spurgeon

In your reading, let not your end be to seek and find out curiosities and subtleties, but to find and meet with Christ.

Thomas Taylor, Exposition of Titus

In reading let your motto be 'much, not many'.

C.H. Spurgeon

A classic is something that everybody wants to have read and nobody wants to read.

Mark Twain

Much reading is an oppression of the mind, and extinguishes the natural

candle, which is the reason of so many senseless scholars in the world.
William Penn

We read books to prevent their being read by others.
Latin saying, originally used of censors and reviewers

Read, mark, learn, and inwardly digest.
Book of Common Prayer, Collect for the second Sunday in Advent

Some books are to be tasted, others to be swallowed, and some few to be chewed and digested.
Francis Bacon, Essays, Of Studies

Read not to contradict and confute, nor to believe and take for granted, nor to find talk and discourse, but to weigh and consider.
Francis Bacon, Essays, Of Studies

Reading is to the mind what exercise is to the body.
Richard Steele, The Tatler, no 147

Guard against the habit of mere reading. Promote yourself to more doing.
Author unknown

Reading, Devotional

If you would benefit, read with humility, simplicity and faith, and never seek the fame of being learned.
Thomas à Kempis, The Imitation of Christ

Read to refill the wells of inspiration.
Harold J. Ockenga

Christian devotional reading helps us find intimate union with God, its motivation being to love God with all our heart, mind, and will.
Jonathan Edwards, Treatise Concerning the Religious Affections

Seek by reading, and you will find meditating; cry in prayer, and the door will be opened in contemplation.
John of the Cross, Maxims

Reality

Beware that you do not lose the substance by grasping at the shadow.
Æsop, Fables, The Dog and the Shadow

Reality is usually something you could not have guessed.
C.S. Lewis, Mere Christianity

Reason

Reason is God's crowning gift to man.
Sophocles, Antigone

Without the capacity of rational argument, all our proof of God ceases.
Jonathan Edwards

He that will not reason is a bigot; he that cannot reason is a fool; and he that dares not reason is a slave.
William Drummond

There is a difficulty about disagreeing with God. He is the source from which all your reasoning power comes.
C.S. Lewis, Mere Christianity

Reason, Limitations of

Human reason cannot begin to answer the great questions as to what God is in himself, and what he is in relation to us.
John Calvin, The Institutes of Christian Religion, 2.2.18

If the greatest philosopher in the world find himself on a plank wider than actually necessary, but hanging over a precipice, his imagination will prevail, though his reason convince him of his safety.
Blaise Pascal

Reason acts slowly and with so many views, on so many principles, which it must always keep before it, that it constantly slumbers and goes astray from not having its principles to hand. The heart does not act thus; it acts in a moment, and is always ready to act. We must then place faith in the heart or it will always be vacillating.
Blaise Pascal

We know truth not only by reason but also by the heart, and it is from this last that we know first principles.
Blaise Pascal, Pensées

The ultimate purpose of reason is to bring us to the place where we see that there is a limit to reason.
Blaise Pascal

Reason is the greatest enemy faith has: it never comes to the aid of spiritual things, but – more frequently than not – struggles against the divine Word, treating with contempt all that emanates from God.
Martin Luther, Table Talk

To accept everything is an exercise, to understand everything is a strain. . . .

The poet only asks to get his head into the heavens. It is the logician who seeks to get the heavens into his head. And it is his head that splits.

G.K. Chesterton, Orthodoxy

Rebellion   see REVOLUTION

Rebuke   see also CRITICISM

Open rebuke is better than secret love.
The Bible, Proverbs 25:5 (AV)

Redemption   see also SALVATION

A person cannot redeem himself;
  he cannot pay God the price for his life,
  because the payment for a human life is too great.
The Bible, Psalm 49:7–8

Reform

A nation without the means of reform is without means of survival.
Edmund Burke

Reformation, Church

The church needs a reformation. This reformation is not, however, the concern just of the pope, nor of the cardinals; this was plainly shown by the recent council [the Fifth Lateran Council of 1512–17]. It is the concern of all Christendom, or better still, of God alone. Only he knows the hour of this reformation.
Martin Luther, explanation of Thesis 89

The Bishop of Rome hath no jurisdiction in this Realm of England.
Book of Common Prayer, Article 37

[Calvin] dreams of reforming the whole world. One Lord, one faith, one baptism.
William Whittingham

Reformation, Personal

Repentance may begin instantly, but reformation often requires a sphere of years.
Henry Ward Beecher

Reformers

The best reformers the world has ever seen are those who commence on themselves.
George Bernard Shaw

Refreshment, Spiritual

The dead dry days were gone. I was all the time tugging and carrying water, but now I have a river carrying me.
Dwight L. Moody

Regeneration   see also CONVERSION

A light from above entered and permeated my heart, now cleansed from its defilement. The Spirit came from heaven, and changed me into a new man by the second birth. Almost at once in a marvellous way doubt gave way to assurance, and what I had thought impossible could be done.
Cyprian, To the Donatists

The manner of regeneration cannot be fully comprehended by believers in this life. Notwithstanding which, they rest satisfied with knowing and experiencing that by this grace of God they are enabled to believe with the heart, and to love their Saviour.
Canons of the Synod of Dort, Article 13

To be the people of God without regeneration, is as impossible as to be the children of men without generation.
Richard Baxter

The very first and indispensable sign is self-loathing and abhorrence.
Charles Simeon, asked about the principal mark of regeneration

If life had a second edition, how I would correct the proofs!
John Clare

Rejection

A prophet is respected everywhere except in his home town and by his own family.
The Bible, Jesus Christ, Matthew 13:57

Rejoicing

Rejoice in the Lord alway: and again I say, Rejoice.
The Bible, The apostle Paul, Philippians 4:4 (AV)

Relationships   see also ANGER; BEHAVIOUR; KINDNESS; PRAISE

A man's feelings of good will *toward* others is the strongest magnet for drawing good will *from* others.
Chesterfield

You can never establish a personal relationship without opening up your own heart.
Paul Tournier

Use your head to handle yourself, your heart to handle others.
Author unknown

Charm may in seven words be found: Forget yourself and think of those around.
Author unknown

We are interested in others if they are interested in us.
Horace

If you want people to be glad to meet you, you must be glad to meet them – and show it.
Goethe

Religion see also ATHEISM; CHRISTIANITY; FAITH

What God the Father considers to be pure and genuine religion is this: to take care of orphans and widows in their suffering and to keep oneself from being corrupted by the world.
The Bible, James 1:27

Men will wrangle for religion; write for it; fight for it; anything but – live for it.
C.C. Colton, Lacon

The true meaning of religion is thus not simply morality, but morality touched by emotion.
Matthew Arnold, Literature and Dogma

One religion is as true as another.
Robert Burton, The Anatomy of Melancholy, 4.2.1

Religion, credit and the eyes are not to be touched.
George Herbert, Jacula Prudentum

We have just enough religion to make us hate, but not enough to make us love one another.
Jonathan Swift, Thoughts on Various Subjects

Man is by his constitution a religious animal.
Edmund Burke, letter to William Smith, 1795

Every religion is false which, as to its faith, does not worship one only God as the origin of all things, and, as to its morality, does not worship one only God as the goal of all things.
Blaise Pascal, Pensées

Religion without piety hath done more mischief in the world than all other things put together.
Thomas Fuller, Gnomologia

Men never do evil so completely and cheerfully as when they do it from religious conviction.
Blaise Pascal, Pensées

No one can deny how great is the
    secret of our religion:
He appeared in human form,
    was shown to be right by the
    Spirit,
    and was seen by angels.
He was preached among the
    nations,
    was believed in throughout the
    world,
    and was taken up to heaven.
The Bible, The apostle Paul, 1 Timothy 3:16

Religion, Hostile views of

Religion is an illusion and it derives its strength from the fact that it falls in with our instinctual desires.
Sigmund Freud, New Introductory Lectures on Psychoanalysis, A Philosophy of Life

Religion . . . is the opium of the people.
Karl Marx, Criticism of the Hegelian Philosophy of Right, Introduction

The first requisite for the happiness of the people is the abolition of religion.
Karl Marx, A Criticism of the Hegelian Philosophy of Religion

Religions, Non-Christian

May they know that you alone are the
    Lord,
    supreme ruler over all the earth.
The Bible, Psalm 83:18

God has no partner.
Muhammad

One person in seven is a Muslim.

Jesus Christ *arrived in* the world – all other religions *arose from* the world.
Richard Bewes

It is simple religions that are the made-up ones. . . . We cannot compete, in simplicity, with people who are inventing religions. . . . Anyone can be simple if he has no facts to bother about.
C.S. Lewis, Mere Christianity

Religious fanaticism

Defoe says that there were a hundred thousand country fellows in his time ready to fight to the death against popery, without knowing whether popery was a man or a horse.

William Hazlitt

Religious practice

There's a kind of religious practice without any inward experience which is of no account in the sight of God. It is good for nothing.

Jonathan Edwards, Treatise Concerning the Religious Affections

Remembering

People need to be reminded more often than they need to be instructed.

Samuel Johnson

Remuneration

The Lord has ordered that those who preach the gospel should get their living from it.

The Bible, The apostle Paul, 1 Corinthians 9:14

Renunciation

The Protestant Church has perhaps taught too exclusively the duty of consecrating to God the life we are born into, and left too little room for the truth that in the present evil world there must be great renunciations as well if there are to be great Christian careers.

John Sung

Renewal

They that wait upon the Lord shall renew their strength: they shall mount up with wings as eagles; they shall run, and not be weary; and they shall walk, and not faint.

The Bible, Isaiah 40:31 (AV)

Repentance

When the wicked man turneth away from his wickedness that he hath committed, and doeth that which is lawful and right, he shall save his soul alive.

The Bible, Ezekiel 18:27 (AV)

I have sinned against you [God] – only against you.

The Bible, Psalm 51:4

God have pity on me, a sinner!

The Bible, The tax collector in Jesus' parable, Luke 18:13

To do so no more is the truest repentance.

Martin Luther

Repentance . . . is not something God demands of you before he will take you back . . . it is simply a description of what going back to him is like.

C.S. Lewis, Mere Christianity

One of the most fundamental marks of true repentance is a disposition to see our sins as God sees them.

Charles Simeon, Sermon 587

O God, though our sins be seven, though our sins be seventy times seven, though our sins be more than the hairs of our head, yet give us grace in loving penitence to cast ourselves down into the depths of thy compassion.

Christina Rossetti

He shows himself worthy, in that he confesses himself unworthy.

Augustine of Hippo

Here on this lowly ground,
Teach me how to repent; for that's as good
As if thou hadst seal'd my pardon, with thy blood.

John Donne

You cannot repent too soon, because you do not know how soon it may be too late.

Thomas Fuller

Years of repentance are necessary in order to blot out a sin in the eyes of men, but one tear of repentance suffices with God.

French proverb

Before God can deliver us we must undeceive ourselves.

Augustine of Hippo

Who after his transgression doth repent,
Is half, or altogether, innocent.

Robert Herrick

Whatever is foolish, ridiculous, vain or earthly, or sensual, in the life of a Christian is something that ought not to be there. It is a spot and a defilement that must be washed away with tears of repentance.

William Law, A Serious Call to a Devout and Holy Life

A noble mind disdains not to repent.

Alexander Pope

When preaching has failed to reform a man, try a little ridicule.

Santeuil

Reputation   see also OPINIONS, OTHER PEOPLE'S

I know that you have the reputation of being alive, even though you are dead!

The Bible, Revelation 3:1

Respect

He that respects not is not respected.

George Herbert, Outlandish Proverbs

Distance increases respect.

Latin proverb

Without feelings of respect, what is there to distinguish men from beasts?

Confucius, Analects

Without respect, love cannot go far or rise high: it is an angel with but one wing.

Alexandre Dumas fils

In his private heart no man much respects himself.

Mark Twain

Respect of persons

You must never treat people in different ways according to their outward appearance.

The Bible, James 2:1

Responsibility

Some grow under responsibility, others swell.

Author unknown

Liberty means responsibility. That is why most men dread it.

George Bernard Shaw

Rest

Come unto me, all ye that labour and are heavy laden, and I will give you rest. Take my yoke upon you, and learn of me; for I am meek and lowly in heart: and ye shall find rest unto your souls. For my yoke is easy, and my burden is light.

The Bible, Jesus Christ, Matthew 11:28–30 (AV)

You have created us for yourself, and our heart cannot be stilled until it finds rest in you.

Augustine of Hippo

Restoration

I will restore to you the years that the locust hath eaten.

The Bible, God, Joel 2:25 (AV)

Results

Leave results to God.

Elizabeth Barrett Browning

Resurrection   see also LIFE AFTER DEATH

I am the resurrection and the life. Whoever believes in me will live, even though he dies.

The Bible, Jesus Christ, John 11:35

No Resurrection. No Christianity.

Michael Ramsey

I am he that liveth, and was dead; and, behold, I am alive for evermore, Amen; and have the keys of hell and of death.

The Bible, Jesus Christ, Revelation 1:18 (AV)

I know that my redeemer liveth, and that he shall stand at the latter day upon the earth: And though after my skin worms destroy this body, yet in my flesh shall I see God.

The Bible, Job, Job 19:25–26 (AV)

If our hope in Christ is good for this life only and no more, then we deserve more pity than anyone else in all the world.

The Bible, The apostle Paul, 1 Corinthians 15:19

But if the dead are not raised to life, then, as the saying goes, 'Let us eat and drink, for tomorrow we will die.'

The Bible, The apostle Paul, 1 Corinthians 15:32

My knowledge of that life is small,
The eye of faith is dim;
But 'tis enough that Christ knows all,
And I shall be with him.

Richard Baxter

Let us look at the resurrection which happens regularly. Day and night show us a resurrection; night goes to sleep, day rises: day departs, night arrives.

Clement of Rome, Epistle to the Corinthians

Christ has turned all our sunsets into dawns.

Clement of Alexandria

On Easter day tomorrow has become today.

Author unknown

Although we have complete salvation through his death, because we are reconciled to God by it, it is by his resurrection, not his death, that we are said to be born again to a living hope (1 Peter 1:3).

John Calvin, The Institutes of
Christian Religion, 2.16.13

Resurrection appearances

He [Christ] appeared to Peter and then to all twelve apostles. Then he appeared to more than five hundred of his followers at once, most of whom are still alive, although some have died. Then he appeared to James, and afterwards to all the apostles. Last of all he appeared also to me.

The Bible, The apostle Paul,
1 Corinthians 15:5–8

Resurrection of Jesus

Christ died for sins once and for all, a good man on behalf of sinners, in order to lead you to God. He was put to death physically, but made alive spiritually.

The Bible, 1 Peter 3:18

The truth is that Christ has been raised from death, as the guarantee that those who sleep in death will also be raised. For just as death came by means of a man, in the same way the rising from death comes by means of a man.

The Bible, The apostle Paul,
1 Corinthians 15:20–21

If these acts of our Lord [his death and resurrection] were just appearances, then so are my chains. Why then have I exposed myself to death, fire, sword and wild beasts? Ah, but 'He who is near the sword is near God,' so if I am in the presence of wild beasts I am in the presence of God. Only let it be in the name of Jesus Christ so that I share his passion. I endure all things, since he who is perfect man gives me the power.

Ignatius of Antioch, To the
Smyrnaeans

Why seek ye the living among the dead?

The Bible, Luke 24:5 (AV)

Resurrection of Jesus, Evidence for

I know pretty well what evidence is, and I tell you, such evidence as that for

the resurrection has never broken down yet.

John Singleton Copley, English
lawyer and Chancellor

Resurrection of the body

This is how it will be when the dead are raised to life. When the body is buried, it is mortal; when raised, it will be immortal.

The Bible, The apostle Paul,
1 Corinthians 15:42

The seed dies into a new life, and so does man.

George Macdonald

We therefore commit his body to the ground; earth to earth, ashes to ashes, dust to dust; in sure and certain hope of the Resurrection to eternal life.

Book of Common Prayer, Burial
of the Dead

Retirement

If I followed my own inclination I would sit in my armchair and take it easy for the rest of my life. But I dare not do it. I must work as long as life lasts.

Lord Shaftesbury

Retreat

One must draw back in order to leap better.

French proverb

Revelations

There are some things that the Lord our God has kept secret; but he has revealed his Law, and we and our descendants are to obey it for ever.

The Bible, Deuteronomy 29:29

All the principles of godliness are undermined by fanatics who substitute revelations for Scripture. . . . The work of the Spirit promised to us is not to create new and unfamiliar revelations, or to coin some novel type of teaching by which we may be led away from the received doctrine of the Gospel, but to seal on our minds the very doctrine which the Gospel recommends.

John Calvin, The Institutes of
Christian Religion, 1.9.1

All visions, revelations, heavenly feelings and whatever is greater than these, are not worth the least act of humility, being the fruits of that charity which neither values nor seeks itself, which thinketh well, not of self, but of others. Many souls, to whom visions have never come, are incomparably more advanced in the way of perfection than others to whom many have been given.

John of the Cross

Revenge

Don't take it on yourself to repay a wrong. Trust the Lord and he will make it right.

The Bible, Proverbs 20:22

Don't give evidence against someone else without good reason, or say misleading things about him. Don't say, 'I'll do to him just what he did to me! I'll get even with him!'

The Bible, Proverbs 24:28–29

You have heard that it was said, 'An eye for an eye and a tooth for a tooth.' But now I tell you: do not take revenge on someone who wrongs you. If anyone slaps you on the right cheek, let him slap your left cheek too.

The Bible, Jesus Christ, Matthew 5:38–39

It costs more to revenge injuries than to bear them.

Thomas Wilson, Maxims

A man that studieth revenge keeps his own wounds green.

Francis Bacon

The smallest revenge will poison the soul.

Jewish proverb

Blood that has been shed does not rest.

Jewish proverb

Revenge is often like biting a dog because the dog bit you.

Austin O'Malley

Revenge is an inhuman word.

Seneca

Revenge never healed a wound.

Guarini

Revenge is the abject pleasure of an abject mind.

Juvenal

Reverence for God

To have knowledge, you must first have reverence for the Lord.

The Bible, Proverbs 1:7

Reverence for the Lord is a fountain of life.

The Bible, Proverbs 14:27

Reverence for the Lord is an education in itself.

The Bible, Proverbs 15:33

Only let reverence for God be the guardian of innocence, so that the Lord, who in his kindness has poured into our minds his heavenly mercy, may through good deeds be kept as a guest of the soul that delights in him, or else the security we have will produce heedlessness and the old enemy will creep in unawares once again.

Cyprian of Carthage, To Donatus

A few formal, ready-made, prayers serve me as a corrective of – well, let's call it 'cheek'.

C.S. Lewis, Letters to Malcolm Chiefly on Prayer

Our courteous Lord wants us to be as homely with him as heart may think or soul may desire. But let us be careful not to take this homeliness recklessly and leave courtesy.

Julian of Norwich, Revelations of Divine Love

Revival

A revival may be expected whenever Christians are found willing to make the sacrifices necessary to carry it on. They must be willing to sacrifice their feelings, their business, their time, to help forward the work.

Charles G. Finney

At first glance the work of change in a saint appears confused chaos. The saints do not know what to make of it, because the manner of the Spirit's proceeding in them is very often extremely mysterious and unsearchable.

Thomas Shepard

From the day of Pentecost downwards revivals of religion, as a matter of history, have had far more influence on the theology of the church than historians of dogma have recognised.

P. Carnegie Simpson

Every revival from the twelfth century onwards speaks to us plainly, and church history is as clear. God has always blessed and moved a nation through the people. In Japan the agricultural classes are [1911] practically untouched. Strange it is, that with all history and experience behind us we can still blunder.

P. Wilkes, Missionary Joys in Japan

From the Day of Pentecost until now, there has not been any one great spiritual awakening in any land which has not begun in a union of prayer though only among two or three, and no such outward or upward movement has continued after such prayer meetings have declined.

A.T. Pierson

Kneel down and with a piece of chalk draw a complete circle all around you – and pray to God to send revival on everything inside the circle. Stay there until he answers, and you will have revival.

Gipsy Smith, when asked how to have revival

Lord, revive your church and begin with me.

Chinese Christian

It presupposes that the church is sunk down in a backslidden state, and a revival consists in the return of the church from her backslidings, and in the conversion of sinners. . . . A revival is nothing else than a new beginning of obedience to God.

Charles G. Finney, Lectures on Revivals of Religion

Where there is a want of brotherly love and Christian confidence among professors of religion, then a revival is needed. Then there is a loud call for God to revive his work.

Charles G. Finney, Lectures on Revivals of Religion

If such things are enthusiasm or the fruit of a distempered brain, let my brain be evermore possessed of that happy distemper! If this be distraction, I pray God that the world of mankind may be seized with this benign, meek, beneficent, glorious distraction.

Jonathan Edwards

Revolutions

Inferiors revolt in order that they may be equal, and equals that they may be superior. Such is the state of mind which creates revolutions.

Aristotle

Rebellion to tyrants is obedience to God.

John Bradshaw

If our revolution does not have the goal of changing men, it doesn't interest me.

Che Guevara

Those who make peaceful revolution impossible will make violent revolution inevitable.

John F. Kennedy

Reward

Every athlete in training submits to strict discipline, in order to be crowned with a wreath that will not last; but we do it for one that will last for ever.

The Bible, The apostle Paul, 1 Corinthians 9:25

When God crowns our merits, it is nothing other than his own gifts that he crowns.

Augustine of Hippo

Ridicule

It is easier to ridicule than to commend.

Thomas Fuller, Gnomologia

Ridiculousness

From the sublime to the ridiculous is but a step.

Napoleon, on the retreat from Moscow

Righteousness

Righteousness is the road to life; wickedness is the road to death.

The Bible, Proverbs 12:28

Righteousness makes a nation great.

The Bible, Proverbs 14:34

Except your righteousness shall exceed the righteousness of the scribes and Pharisees, ye shall in no case enter into the kingdom of heaven.

The Bible, Jesus Christ, Matthew 5:20 (AV)

The most important ingredient of righteousness is to render to God the service and homage due to him. He is shamefully cheated whenever we do not submit to his authority.

John Calvin, The Institutes of Christian Religion, 3.3.7

Righteousness from God

I now have the righteousness that is given through faith in Christ, the righteousness that comes from God and is based on faith.

The Bible, The apostle Paul, Philippians 3:9

God does not want to save us by our own personal and private righteousness and wisdom. He wants to save us by a righteousness and wisdom completely separate from this – a righteousness which does not come from ourselves and is not brought to birth by ourselves. It is a righteousness which comes into us from somewhere else. It is not a righteousness which originates on this earth of ours. It is a righteousness which comes from heaven.

Martin Luther, The Epistle to the Romans

No condemnation now I dread.
   Jesus, and all in him, is mine;
Alive in him, my living Head,
   And clothed in Righteousness divine,
Bold I approach the eternal throne,
And claim the crown, through Christ, my own.

Charles Wesley

The righteousness of God is not acquired by acts frequently repeated, as Aristotle taught, but is imparted by faith.

Martin Luther at the Heidelberg Disputation

'The righteousness of God': I suddenly began to understand that this righteousness of God is a gift of God, through faith. Paul teaches us that the righteousness of God revealed in the gospel is passive, given to us in Christ. As this truth dawned, I felt I was born again, and was entering in at the gates of paradise itself. There and then the whole face of scripture changed. Just as much as I had hated the phrase 'the righteousness of God', I now loved it – it seemed the sweetest and most joyous phrase ever written.

Martin Luther

My hope is built on nothing less
Than Jesus' blood and righteousness.

Edward Mote

Rights of man   see HUMAN RIGHTS

Roman Catholic Church

Here is everything which can lay hold of the eye, ear and imagination – everything which can charm and bewitch the simple and ignorant. I wonder how Luther ever broke the spell.

John Adams

Rome has spoken; the case is concluded.

Augustine of Hippo, Sermons

Romans, Paul's letter to the

This Epistle is the chief part of the New Testament and the very purest gospel, which indeed deserves that a Christian should not only know it word for word by heart, but deal with it daily as with the daily bread of the soul, for it can never be read or considered too much or too well, and the more it is handled the more delightful it becomes and the better it tastes.

Martin Luther

It is the profoundest piece of writing in existence.

Samuel Taylor Coleridge

Rush

God never imposes a duty without giving time to do it.

John Ruskin, Lectures on Architecture and Planning

Hurry is not of the devil. Hurry is the devil.

Carl Gustav Jung

Though I am always in haste, I am never in a hurry.

John Wesley

How paltry must be the devotions of those who are always in a hurry.

William Law

Go placidly amid the noise and the haste, and remember what peace there may be in silence.

Max Ehrmann

Good and quickly seldom meet.

George Herbert, Outlandish Proverbs

Haste in every business brings failures.

Herodotus, Histories, Bk 7 ch. 10

Great haste makes great waste. Adopt the pace of nature. Her pace is patience.

Author unknown

This perpetual hurry of business and company ruins me in soul if not in body.

William Wilberforce

S

Sabbath

The conscionable keeping of the Sabbath, is the Mother of all Religion.
Lewis Bayly, Practise of Pietie, 1613

Sacraments see also BAPTISM; LORD'S SUPPER

Grace sometimes precedes the sacrament, sometimes follows it, and sometimes does not even follow it.
Theodoret

A sacrament is God's witness to us of his favour towards us, by means of an outward sign.
John Calvin, The Institutes of Christian Religion, 4.14.1

A sacrament is a visible sign of a sacred thing, or a visible form of an invisible grace.
Augustine of Hippo

The sacraments can only fulfil their function when accompanied by the Spirit within, whose power alone can penetrate the heart and stir the emotions.
John Calvin, The Institutes of Christian Religion, 4.14.9

The sacraments have the same function as God's Word: they offer Christ to us, and in him, the treasures of grace. They are useless if not received in faith just as wine and oil, when poured out, will go to waste unless they are poured into an open vessel. If the vessel is not open, it will remain empty even if the liquid is poured on to it.
John Calvin, The Institutes of Christian Religion, 4.14.17

Sacrifice

Not what we stand for but what we fall for is the true test of strength.
Author unknown

No sacrifice is worth the name unless it is a joy. Sacrifice and a long face go ill together.
Mahatma Gandhi

To save your world you asked this man to die:
Would this man, could he see you now, ask why?
W.H. Auden, Epitaph for an Unknown Soldier

It is a far, far better thing that I do, than I have ever done; it is a far, far better rest that I go to, than I have ever known.
Charles Dickens, A Tale of Two Cities

Greater love hath no man than this, that a man lay down his life for his friends.
The Bible, Jesus Christ, John 15:13 (AV)

No sacrifice can be too great to make for him who gave his life for me.
C.T. Studd

I never made a sacrifice. We ought not to talk of 'sacrifice' when we remember the great sacrifice which he made who left his Father's throne on high to give himself for us.
David Livingstone

We can offer up much in the large, but to make sacrifices in little things is what we are seldom equal to.
Goethe

Saints

Saint: A dead sinner revised and edited.
Ambrose Bierce, The Devil's Dictionary

During their lifetime saints are a nuisance.
George Bernard Shaw

Salvation

If you confess that Jesus is Lord and believe that God raised him from death, you will be saved.
The Bible, The apostle Paul, Romans 10:9

Work out your own salvation with fear and trembling.
The Bible, The apostle Paul, Philippians 2:12 (AV)

I am sure that God, who began this good work in you, will carry it on until it is finished on the Day of Christ Jesus.
The Bible, The apostle Paul, Philippians 1:6

Salvation comes from our God, who sits on the throne, and from the Lamb!
The Bible, Revelation 7:10

He who created you without you will not justify you without you.
Augustine of Hippo, Sermons

Eve, by disobeying, brought death on herself and all humankind; Mary, by obeying, brought salvation.
Irenaeus, Against Heresies, 3.22.4

Lord my God, you have formed and reformed me.

Anselm

Salvation is God's way of making us real people.

Augustine of Hippo

If ever a man could be saved by monkery, that man was I.

Martin Luther

Salvation comes through a cross and a crucified Christ. Salvation is the fellowship with the crucified Christ in the Spirit of his cross. Salvation is union with and delight in . . . the humility of Jesus.

Andrew Murray

Salvation consists wholly in being saved from ourselves, or that which we are by nature.

Andrew Murray

To follow the Saviour is to participate in salvation, to follow the light is to perceive the light.

Irenaeus

Three things are necessary for the salvation of man: to know what he ought to believe; to know what he ought to desire; and to know what he ought to do.

Thomas Aquinas, Two Precepts of Charity

To know Christ is not to speculate about the mode of his incarnation, but to know his saving benefits.

Philip Melanchthon

Scripture alone [for authority]; grace alone [for salvation].

Reformation theologians

[The fundamental principles of Christianity are] these two – the doctrine of justification, and that of the new birth; the former relating to that great work God does *for us*, in forgiving our sins; the latter to the great work of God *in us*, in renewing our fallen nature.

John Wesley

Salvation, as experienced by Bilney

When I read that Christ Jesus came into the world to save sinners, it was as if day suddenly broke on a dark night.

Thomas Bilney

Salvation, as experienced by Wesley

I felt my heart strangely warmed. I felt I did trust in Christ, Christ alone, for

salvation; an assurance was given me that he had taken away my sins, even mine, and saved me from the law of sin and death.

John Wesley, Journal

Salvation, as God's gift

God so loved the world, that he gave his only begotten Son, that whosoever believeth in him should not perish, but have everlasting life.

The Bible, John 3:16 (AV)

How did you come to God? By believing. Watch out that you don't fall from the right way, by claiming merit for finding it yourself. I came, you say, by free choice, by my own will. Why do you boast? Don't you know that even this was a gift? Listen to Christ exclaiming 'No one can come to me, unless the Father who sent me draws him' (John 6:44).

Augustine of Hippo, The Predestination of the Saints, quoted in John Calvin, The Institutes of Christian Religion

Salvation, Mankind's need of

No man can resolve himself into heaven.

Dwight L. Moody

Nothing in my hand I bring;
Simply to Thy Cross I cling;
Naked, come to Thee for dress;
Helpless, look to Thee for grace;
Foul, I to the Fountain fly;
Wash me, Saviour, or I die!

Augustus Montague Toplady

Sanctification

Justification is at once an accomplished fact, but sanctification is gradual.

Abraham Kuyper, The Work of the Holy Spirit

Sanctification is glory begun. Glory is sanctification completed.

F.F. Bruce

Sanctification is a gracious work of God, whereby in a supernatural way he gradually divests from sin the inclinations and dispositions of the regenerate and clothes them with holiness.

Abraham Kuyper, The Work of the Holy Spirit

He is not a Christian that thinks he is a finished Christian and is insensible how far short he falls. . . . That man without doubt, has never so much as begun to be renewed, nor did he ever taste what it is to be a Christian.

Bernard of Clairvaux

Satan   see DEVIL

Saving   see also THRIFT

If you add a little to a little and do it often enough you can become skilled, learned, or rich. A little practice every day makes the champion athlete; a little learning every day makes the scientist; a little saving every day makes the millionaire.

Author unknown

Saviour   see also CHRIST

Only these two things I know . . . I am a great sinner and Christ is a great saviour.

John Newton

Jesus, the saviour of mankind.

Meaning of the common Latin letters 'I.H.S.' (Iesus hominum salvator)

Scandal

Nothing travels more swiftly than scandal.

Virgil

Science   see also DISCOVERIES

Science does not know its debt to imagination.

Ralph Waldo Emerson

Science without religion is lame, religion without science is blind.

Albert Einstein

Science and Christianity

There is but one God the Father of whom are all things and we in him and one Lord Jesus Christ by whom are all things and we by him.

Isaac Newton

Science commits suicide when it adopts a creed.

T.H. Huxley

Since the Holy Ghost did not intend to teach us whether heaven moves or stands still . . . nor whether the earth is located at its centre or off to one side, then so much the less was it intended to settle for us any other conclusion of the same kind. . . . Now if the Holy Spirit has purposely neglected to teach us propositions of this sort as irrelevant to the highest goal

(that is, to our salvation), how can anyone affirm that it is obligatory to take sides on them? . . . I would say here something that was heard from an ecclesiastic of the most eminent degree: 'The intention of the Holy Ghost is to teach us how one goes to heaven, not how heaven goes.'

Galileo

The works of the Lord are great, sought out of all them that have pleasure therein.

The Bible, Psalm 111:2, inscribed over the entrance to the Cavendish laboratory in Cambridge

Searching for God   see also LONGING FOR GOD

Seek ye the Lord while he may be found, call ye upon him while he is near.

The Bible, Isaiah 55:6 (AV)

Those who seek God in isolation from their fellow-men . . . are apt to find, not God, but a devil whose countenance bears an embarrassing resemblance to their own.

R.H. Tawney

Seeking with faith, hope and love pleases our Lord and finding him pleases the soul, filling it full of joy. And so I learnt that as long as God allows us to struggle on this earth, seeking is as good as seeing.

Julian of Norwich, Revelations of Divine Love

The whole round world is not enough to fill the heart's three corners, but it craveth still; only after the Trinity that made it, can suffice the vast triangled heart of man.

Francis Quarles

The kingdom of heaven is not for the well-meaning but for the desperate.

James Denney

If you seek anything for yourself, you will never find God, for you are not simply seeking God, you are seeking for something with God. You are, as it were, making a candle out of God with which to find something.

Meister Eckhart

When I looked for Christ it seemed to me I saw the devil.

Martin Luther

In all things throughout the world, the men who look for the crooked will see the crooked, and the men who look for the straight will see the straight.

John Ruskin

Nobody has found God by walking his own way.

Ram Das

There are but three classes of men: those who have found God, and serve him; those that have not yet found him, but seek him earnestly; those who spend their lives neither seeking nor finding. The first know where the true values lie, and they are happy; the last are stupid and unhappy; the class in the middle are unhappy, but they are rational.

Blaise Pascal

If the pleasures of love can attract a man to a woman, if hunger and loneliness can make a man travel miles in search of food and shelter, how much more will the desire for truth and holiness make a man seek God.

Augustine of Hippo, Treatise on St John's Gospel

Searching for God in one's emptiness

For a heart to be perfectly ready [to receive God] it has to be perfectly empty.

Meister Eckhart

I never ask God to give himself to me, I beg him to purify, to empty, me. If I am empty, God of his very nature is obliged to give himself to me to fill me.

Meister Eckhart

Searching for God in one's interior

Descend into yourself. Go beneath your clothing, beneath your flesh. Go right into the secret chamber of your soul. If you cannot come close to your own soul, you can never come close to God. It is not your body, but your soul which has been created in the image of God. Seek God within your soul, for in understanding your own soul you will recognise its creator.

Augustine of Hippo, Treatise on St John's Gospel

Second coming of Christ

Then the sign of the Son of Man will appear in the sky; and all the peoples of earth will weep as they see the Son of Man coming on the clouds of heaven with power and great glory.

The Bible, Jesus Christ, Matthew 24:30

After I go and prepare a place for you, I will come back and take you to myself, so that you will be where I am.

The Bible, Jesus Christ, John 14:3

There will be the shout of command, the archangel's voice, the sound of God's trumpet, and the Lord himself will come down from heaven. Those who have died believing in Christ will rise to life first.

The Bible, The apostle Paul, 1 Thessalonians 4:16

If Christ were coming again tomorrow, I would plant a tree today.

Martin Luther

He who loves the coming of the Lord is not he who affirms it is far off, nor is it he who says it is near. It is he who, whether it be far or near, awaits it with sincere faith, steadfast hope, and fervent love.

Augustine of Hippo

Martin Luther said he had only two days on his calendar: today and 'that day'.

I wish that he would come during my lifetime so that I could take my crown and lay it at his feet.

Queen Victoria, after hearing a clergyman preach on the Second coming

Secrets

If someone is angry with you, a gift given secretly will calm him down.

The Bible, Proverbs 21:14

If you wish someone else to keep your secret, first keep it yourself.

Seneca

Security

I give them eternal life, and they shall never die. No one can snatch them away from me. What my Father has given me is greater than everything, and no one can snatch them away from the Father's care.

The Bible, Jesus Christ, John 10:28–29

Seeking God   see SEARCHING FOR GOD

Self

To conquer self is the best and noblest victory; to be vanquished by one's own nature is the worst and most ignoble defeat.

Plato

God, harden me against myself,
The coward with pathetic voice
Who craves for ease and rest and joy.
Myself, arch-traitor to myself,
My hollowest friend,
My deadliest foe,
My clog, whatever road I go.
Amy Carmichael

'I' is hateful.
Blaise Pascal, Pensées

Some conjurors say that three is the magic number, and some say number seven. It's neither, my friend, neither. It's number one.
Charles Dickens, Fagin in Oliver Twist

If a man conquer in battle a thousand times a thousand, and another conquer himself, he who conquers himself is the greater conqueror.
Buddha

It is a poor centre of a man's action, himself.
Francis Bacon, Essays, Of Wisdom for a Man's Self

Who sits in solitude and is quiet has escaped from three wars: hearing, speaking, seeing; yet against one thing shall he continually battle: that is, his own heart.
Antony

Talk to a man about himself and he will listen for hours.
Benjamin Disraeli

Men may rise on stepping-stones
Of their dead selves to higher things.
Alfred, Lord Tennyson

That favourite subject, Myself.
James Boswell

If I long to improve my brother, the first step toward doing so is to improve myself.
Christina Rossetti

There is endless room for rebellion against ourselves.
George Macdonald

To fight against sin is to fight against the devil, the world and oneself. The fight against oneself is the worst fight of all.
Martin Luther, The Epistle to the Hebrews

I am more afraid of my own heart than of the pope and all his cardinals. I have within me the great pope, Self.
Martin Luther

Self is the root, the branches, the tree, of all the evil of our fallen state.
Andrew Murray

Self, Death of

There was a day when I died, utterly died, died to George Müller, his opinions, preferences, tastes and will, died to the world, its approval or censure, died to the approval or blame even of my brethren and friends, and since then I have studied to show myself approved unto God.
George Müller

The one true way of dying to self is the way of patience, meekness, humility, and resignation to God.
Andrew Murray

You will be dead so long as you refuse to die.
George Macdonald

The only way to achieve mortification is through inner recollection. The soul must meditate on Jesus Christ and so cease to concentrate on anything external and be consumed with the inner spiritual life and drawing close to God.
Madame Guyon, A Short and Easy Method of Prayer

Sever me from myself that I may be grateful to you;
may I perish to myself that I may be safe in you;
may I die to myself that I may live in you;
may I wither to myself that I may blossom in you;
may I be emptied of myself that I may abound in you;
may I be nothing to myself that I may be all to you.
Erasmus

Self, Value of

If a man is cruel to himself, how can we expect him to be compassionate to others?
Jewish proverb

In the world to come I shall not be asked, 'Why were you not Moses?' but God will ask me, 'Why were you not Zusya?'
Rabbi Zusya

Self love, my liege, is not so vile a sin as self neglecting.
William Shakespeare

Self-confidence

The men who really believe in themselves are in lunatic asylums. A man will certainly fail because he believes in himself. Complete self-confidence is not merely a sin; complete self-confidence is a weakness.

G.K. Chesterton, Orthodoxy

Self-control   see also TEMPERANCE

It is better to win control over yourself than over whole cities.

The Bible, Proverbs 16:32

If you are to be self-controlled in your speech you must be self-controlled in your thinking.

François Fénelon, Christian Perfection, letter to the Duc de Chevreuse

There never has been, and cannot be, a good life, without self-control.

Leo Tolstoy

Anything which increases the authority of the body over the mind is an evil thing.

Susannah Wesley, writing to her student son John

To enjoy freedom we have to control ourselves.

Virginia Woolf

Self-deception

Nothing is easier than self-deceit. For what each man wishes, that he also believes to be true.

Demosthenes, Third Olynthiac, 19

The greatest magnifying glasses in the world are a man's own eyes when they look upon his own person.

Alexander Pope

Self-denial

There is no greater valour nor sterner fight than that for self-effacement, self-oblivion.

Meister Eckhart

Self-denial is not a virtue; it is only the effect of prudence on rascality.

George Bernard Shaw

One's own desires are never satisfied when they have all they wish; but they are satisfied as soon as the wish is renounced.

Blaise Pascal

There are plenty to follow our Lord half-way, but not the other half. They will give up possessions, friends and honours, but it touches them too closely to disown themselves.

Meister Eckhart

Those who determine not to put self to death will never see the will of God fulfilled in their lives. Those who ought to become the light of the world must necessarily burn and become less and less. By denying self we are able to win others.

Sundar Singh

All the graces of a Christian spring from the death of self.

Madame Guyon

It is incredibly difficult to carry out our duty to seek our neighbour's good. Unless we stop thinking about ourselves, and in a way stop being ourselves, we will never achieve it.

John Calvin, The Institutes of Christian Religion, 3.7.5

The great Christian duty is self-denial, which consists in two things: first, in denying worldly inclinations and its enjoyments, and second, in denying self-exultation and renouncing one's self-significance by being empty of self.

Jonathan Edwards, Treatise Concerning the Religious Affections

Self-discipline

No wise man wants a soft life.

King Alfred

By his restrictions the master proclaims himself.

Goethe

Self-examination

Everyone should examine himself first, and then eat the bread and drink from the cup.

The Bible, The apostle Paul, 1 Corinthians 11:28

You will never be an inwardly religious and devout man unless you pass over in silence the shortcomings of your fellow men, and diligently examine your own weaknesses.

Thomas à Kempis

Consider well what your strength is equal to, and what exceeds your ability.

Horace

The unexamined life is not worth living.

Socrates

Self-knowledge   see also KNOWLEDGE

Know thyself.
*Inscription over the entrance to the
temple of Apollo at Delphi*

The longest journey is the journey within.
Dag Hammarskjold

'Know thyself'? If I knew myself, I'd run away.
Goethe

It has ever been allowed that to know one's self is the most valuable part of knowledge.
*Eliza Haywood, The Tea-Table,
1725*

A man has many skins in himself, covering the depths of his heart. Man knows so many things; he does not know himself. Why, thirty or forty skins or hides, just like an ox's or a bear's, so thick and hard, cover the soul. Go into your own ground and learn to know yourself there.
Meister Eckhart

One's own self is well hidden from one's own self: of all mines of treasure, one's own is the last to be dug up.
Friedrich Nietzsche

For the gift to see ourselves as others see us . . .
Prayer of Robbie Burns

Self-righteousness

If there be ground for you to trust in your own righteousness, then all that Christ did to purchase salvation, and all that God did to prepare the way for it, is in vain.
Jonathan Edwards

Self-sacrifice

The only gift is a portion of thyself.
Ralph Waldo Emerson

It is only through the mystery of self-sacrifice that a man may find himself anew.
Carl Gustav Jung

Self-preservation is the first law of human nature.
Jean-Jacques Rousseau

Selfishness

The things that will destroy America are peace at any price, prosperity at any cost, safety first instead of duty first, the love of soft living, and the get-rich-quick theory of life.
Theodore Roosevelt

No indulgence of passion destroys the spiritual nature so much as respectable selfishness.
George Macdonald

He who lives only to benefit himself confers a benefit on the world when he dies.
Tertullian

He that falls in love with himself, will have no rivals.
*Benjamin Franklin, Poor
Richard's Almanac, 1739*

Sensuality

No one is free who is a slave to his body.
Seneca

Service   see also CARING; OBEDIENCE

The service we render to others is really the rent we pay for our room on this earth.
Author unknown

He is no fool who gives what he cannot keep to gain what he cannot lose.
Jim Elliott

The object of love is to serve, not to win.
Woodrow Wilson

Life is an exciting business, and it is most exciting when it is lived for others.
Helen Keller

In other kingdoms they rule, whose privilege it is to be ministered unto. In the divine commonwealth, they rule who account it a privilege to minister.
*A.B. Bruce, The Training of the
Twelve*

Wash what is dirty, water what is dry, heal what is wounded. Bend what is stiff, warm what is cold, guide what goes off the road.
Stephen Langton

If Christ were here, he would help them, and so must I.
*Toyohiko Kagawa, on his mission
to help the slum-dwellers of Kobe*

The vocation of every man and woman is to serve other people.
Leo Tolstoy

In the New Testament it is the work and not the workers that is glorified.
*Alfred Plummer, Exegetical
Commentary on the Gospel
According to Saint Matthew*

Man must use in God's service all the abilities and powers with which God has provided him, otherwise he will not receive God's help. As soon as man does his part, God will complete it.

Sundar Singh, At the Feet of the Master

You should help everyone as much as you can: often you need someone smaller than yourself.

La Fontaine

Our lives will harmonise best with God's will and the demands of his Law when they serve other people best.

John Calvin, The Institutes of Christian Religion, 2.8.54

No one is useless in this world who lightens the burdens of another.

Charles Dickens

Christ has no body now on earth but yours;
yours are the only hands with which he can do his work,
yours are the only feet with which he can go about the world,
yours are the only eyes through which his compassion
can shine forth upon a troubled world.
Christ has no body now on earth but yours.

Teresa of Avila

When I consider how my life is spent
  Ere half my days in this dark world and wide,
  And that one talent is death to hide
  Lodged with me useless, though my soul more bent
To serve therewith my Maker, and present
  My true account, lest He returning chide,
  'Doth God exact day-labour, light denied?'
  I fondly ask. But Patience, to prevent
That murmur, soon replies, 'God doth not need
  Either man's work or his own gifts. Who best
  Bear his mild yoke, they serve him best. His state
Is kingly: thousands at his bidding speed,
  And post o'er land and ocean without rest;
  They also serve who only stand and wait.'

John Milton, On his Blindness

To give and give, and give again,
What God hath given thee;
To spend thyself nor count the cost,
To serve right gloriously
The God that gave all worlds that are,
And all that are to be.

G.A. Studdert-Kennedy

If I can stop one heart from breaking,
I shall not live in vain;
If I can ease one life the aching,
Or cool one pain,
Or help one fainting robin
Unto his nest again,
I shall not live in vain.

Emily Dickinson

Service, Prayers dedicating the self to

O Lord, who though thou wast rich, yet for our sakes didst become poor, and hast promised in thy gospel that whatsoever is done unto the least of thy brethren, thou wilt receive as done unto thee: give us grace, we humbly beseech thee, to be ever willing and ready to minister to the needs of our fellow creatures, to thy praise and glory who art God over all. Amen.

Augustine of Hippo

Teach us, good Lord, to serve thee as thou deservest;
To give, and not to count the cost,
To fight, and not to heed the wounds,
To toil, and not to seek for rest,
To labour, and not to ask for any reward
Save that of knowing that we do thy will.

Ignatius Loyola

Oh God, you put into my heart this great desire to devote myself to the sick and sorrowful; I offer it to you. Do with it what is for your service.

Florence Nightingale

Let the name of Whitefield perish, but Christ be glorified! And let me be but the servant of all!

George Whitefield

Teach me, my God and King,
In all things thee to see,
And what I do in any thing,
To do it as for thee.

George Herbert

I shall only last a year; use me as you can.

Joan of Arc's prayer when she knew she would not last out long against her enemies

Service and God's plans

I used to ask God to help me. Then I asked if I might help him. I ended up by asking him to do his work through me.

Hudson Taylor

I cannot invent
New things
Like the airship
Which sails
On silver wings;
But today
A wonderful thought
In the dawn was given,
And the stripes on my robe,
Shining from wear,
Were suddenly fair,
Bright with light
Falling from heaven –
Gold and silver and bronze
Light from the windows of heaven.
And the thought
Was this:
That a sacred plan
Is hid in my hand;
That my hand is big,
Big,
Because of this plan;
That God,
Who dwells in my hand,
Knows this sacred plan
Of the things he will do
For the world,
Using my hand.

Toyohiko Kagawa

We may make the best plans we can, and then carry them out to the best of our ability. Or, having carefully laid our plans, and determined to carry them through, we may ask God to help us. There is yet another mode of working: to begin with God, to ask his plans, and to offer ourselves to carry out his purposes.

Hudson Taylor

Service and humility

When God wants to do his great works he trains somebody to be quiet enough and little enough, then he uses that person.

Hudson Taylor

We may easily be too big for God to use, but never too small.

Dwight L. Moody

The measure of a man is not how many servants he has but how many men he serves.

Dwight L. Moody

. . . they who fain would serve thee best
Are conscious most of wrong within.

Henry Twells

Service and love for God

It is possible to be so active in the service of Christ as to forget to love him.

P.T. Forsyth

If you want to be of use, get rightly related to Jesus Christ, and he will make you of use unconsciously every moment you live.

Oswald Chambers

Service means the activity of the spiritual life. It is man's spontaneous love offering to God.

Sundar Singh, At the Feet of the Master

Service in small things

Small service is true service while it
  lasts:
Of humblest friends, bright creature,
  scorn not one:
The daisy, by the shadow that it casts,
Protects the lingering dew-drop from
  the sun.

William Wordsworth, verse written for a small child

To take up the cross of Christ is no great action done once for all; it consists in the continual practice of small duties which are distasteful to us.

J.H. Newman

Remember that there must be someone to cook the meals, and count yourselves happy in being able to serve like Martha.

Teresa of Avila

Be ashamed of nothing but sin: not of fetching wood, or drawing water, if time permit; not of cleaning your own shoes or your neighbour's.

John Wesley

All service ranks the same with God.

Robert Browning

Sex see also ADULTERY; LOVE, SEXUAL

Don't spend all your energy on sex and all your money on women; they have destroyed kings.

The Bible, Proverbs 31:3

An experiment of the serpent . . . the impediment which separates from the Lord.

The Acts of John

The degrading necessity of sex.

Augustine of Hippo

Be happy with your wife. . . . Let her charms keep you happy; let her surround you with her love.

The Bible, Proverbs 5:18–19

Enjoy life with the woman you love, as long as you live the useless life that God has given you in this world.

The Bible, Ecclesiastes 9:9

Sexual intercourse

Do not deny yourselves to each other, unless you first agree to do so for a while in order to spend your time in prayer; but then resume normal marital relations.

*The Bible, The apostle Paul,
1 Corinthians 7:5*

A desire of children, or to avoid fornication, or to lighten and ease the cares and sadnesses of household affairs, or to endear each other.

*Jeremy Taylor, Holy Living,
giving reasons for marital
intercourse*

Shame see also BLUSHING

I think that man is lost indeed who has lost the sense of shame.

Plautus

I never wonder to see men wicked, but I often wonder to see them not ashamed.

Jonathan Swift

Where there is yet shame, there may in time be virtue.

Samuel Johnson

The emotion of shame has been valued not as an emotion but because of the insight to which it leads.

C.S. Lewis

Little shame, little conscience, and much industry will make a man rich.

Thomas Fuller, Gnomologia

Sharing see also GIVING

You could read Kant by yourself if you wanted to; but you must share a joke with someone else.

Robert Louis Stevenson

Grief can take care of itself, but to get the full value of a joy you must have somebody to share it with.

Mark Twain

Sickness see also HEALING

For the love of God discipline your body and soul alike, keeping fit and healthy. If you should get ill, through circumstances beyond your control, bear it patiently and wait patiently upon God's mercy. That is all you need to do. It is true to say that patience in sickness and other forms of trouble pleases God much more than any splendid devotion that you might show in health.

*Author unknown, The Cloud of
Unknowing*

Sight see also VISION

Lord, purge our eyes to see
Within the seed a tree,
Within the glowing egg a bird,
Within the shroud a butterfly,
Till, taught by such, we see
Beyond all creatures, thee.

Christina Rossetti

As I am, so I see.

Ralph Waldo Emerson

Sight, Spiritual

So it is through tears of penitence, through striving after righteousness, and through constant compassionate living, that spiritual eyesight is made clear.

*Bernard of Clairvaux, The Twelve
Steps of Humility and Pride*

Silence

Quietude, which some men cannot abide, because it reveals their inward poverty, is as a palace of cedar to the wise, for along its hallowed courts the King in his beauty deigns to walk.

*C.H. Spurgeon, Lectures to my
Students*

Sacred silence! thou that art
Floodgate of the deeper heart,
Offspring of a heavenly kind;
Frost o' the mouth, and thaw o' the
  mind.

Richard Flecknoe

Priceless as the gift of utterance may be, the practice of silence in some aspects far excels it. Do you think me a Quaker? Well, be it so.

*C.H. Spurgeon, Lectures to my
Students*

Silence is deep as Eternity, speech is shallow as Time.

Thomas Carlyle

Outward silence is indispensable for the cultivation and improvement of inner silence.

Madame Guyon, A Short and Easy Method of Prayer

Silence is the element in which great things fashion themselves together.

Thomas Carlyle

Silence more musical than any song.

Christina Rossetti, Rest

The Father uttered one Word; that Word is his Son, and he utters him for ever in everlasting silence; and in silence the soul has to hear it.

John of the Cross

Silence, Reprehensible

To sin by silence when they should protest makes cowards out of men.

Abraham Lincoln

The cruellest lies are often told in silence.

Robert Louis Stevenson

Silence in society

Better to remain silent and be thought a fool than to speak and remove all doubt.

Abraham Lincoln

When you have nothing to say, say nothing.

C.C. Colton, Lacon

Silence is the unbearable repartee.

G.K. Chesterton

Simplicity see also CHILDLIKENESS

Our life is frittered away by detail. . . . Simply, simplify.

Henry David Thoreau

Blissful are the simple, for they shall have much peace.

Thomas à Kempis

It is very hard to be simple enough to be good.

Ralph Waldo Emerson

Sin see also CONFESSION; FORGIVENESS; ORIGINAL SIN

The reward for doing good is life, but sin leads only to more sin.

The Bible, Proverbs 10:16

It is because of your sins that he doesn't hear you. It is your sins that separate you from God when you try to worship him.

The Bible, Isaiah 59:2

All our righteousnesses are as filthy rags.

The Bible, Isaiah 64:6 (AV)

Can the Ethiopian change his skin, or the leopard his spots?

The Bible, Jeremiah 13:23 (AV)

Be sure your sin will find you out.

The Bible, Numbers 32:23 (AV)

I can contribute nothing to my own salvation, except the sin from which I need to be redeemed.

William Temple

For the religious man to do wrong is to defy his King; for the Christian it is to wound his Friend.

William Temple

Love the sinner but hate the sin.

Augustine of Hippo

Custom of sinning takes away the sense of it; the course of the world takes away the shame of it; and love to it makes men greedy in the pursuit of it.

John Owen, The Manner of Conversion Explained in the Instance of Augustine

Sometimes it does us good to make a slip: it keeps us humble. We cannot be conquered so long as we do not lose courage.

Francis de Sales

There is only one calamity – sin.

John Chrysostom

Natural man is bent inwards upon himself.

Martin Luther

There is a sleeping pig at the bottom of every human heart.

Sarcey

Near our vineyard was a pear tree laden with fruit, though the fruit was not all that attractive either to look at or to eat. I and some other wretched youth had the idea of shaking the pears off and taking them. We set out late that night – having played in the streets till that time, as we usually did in our depraved way – and stole all the fruit we could carry. We may have tasted a few, but it was not for food we stole them – we threw most of them to the pigs. I did not want to enjoy what I had got by stealing: my delight was in the act of theft and in sin. Our real pleasure was doing something forbidden.

Augustine of Hippo, Confessions

Sin, Awareness of

My conscience hath a thousand several
   tongues,
And every tongue brings a several
   tale,
And every tale condemns me for a villain.
William Shakespeare, Richard III

Dear Sir,
What's wrong with the world?
I am.
*G.K. Chesterton's letter to The
Times, after someone had asked
what was wrong with the world*

In youth, in middle age, and now after
many battles, I find nothing in me but
corruption.
John Knox

I have had a vastly greater sense of my
own wickedness and the badness of my
heart than ever I had before my
conversion. . . . It is affecting to think
how ignorant I was, when a young
Christian, of the bottomless, infinite
depths of wickedness, pride, hypocrisy, and deceit left in my heart.
Jonathan Edwards

It is an accustomed action with her, to
seem thus washing her hands: I have
known her continue in this a quarter of
an hour. . . . 'Out, out, damned spot!
out, I say! . . . Here's the smell of the
blood still: all the perfumes of Arabia
will not sweeten this little hand. Oh,
oh, oh!' . . . What a sigh is there! The
heart is sorely charged. . . . This disease is beyond my practice.
*William Shakespeare, Lady
Macbeth being observed by the
doctor*

If we say that we have no sin, we
deceive ourselves, and the truth is not
in us.
The Bible, 1 John 1:8 (AV)

Sin, Dealing with

Sin is not a monster to be mused on,
but an impotence to be got rid of.
Martin Luther

When you attack the roots of sin, fix
your thought more on the God you
desire than on the sin you abhor.
Walter Hilton

I will keep your law in my heart,
   so that I will not sin against you.
The Bible, Psalm 119:11

Sin, Defeat of

Sin must not be your master; for you
do not live under law but under God's
grace.
*The Bible, The apostle Paul,
Romans 6:14*

Behold the Lamb of God, which
taketh away the sin of the world.
*The Bible, John the Baptist,
John 1:29 (AV)*

Sin, Definition of

Sin is essentially a departure from God.
Martin Luther

Sin is believing the lie that you are self-
created, self-dependent, and self-
sustained.
Augustine of Hippo

Sin is to live according to one's own
will and cast aside the will of God.
*Sundar Singh, At the Feet of the
Master*

I see and approve of the better things;
I follow the worse.
Ovid

Sin, Effects of

The wages of sin is death.
*The Bible, The apostle Paul,
Romans 6:23 (AV)*

Commit a sin twice and it will not seem
a crime.
Rabbinical saying

As long as we meddle with any kind of
sin we shall never clearly see the
blessed face of our Lord.
*Julian of Norwich, Revelations of
Divine Love*

The gods will punish the man whose
heart is full of sin.
Euripides

Sin, Seriousness of

To understand the seriousness of sin,
we must fathom three oceans, the
ocean of human suffering, the ocean of
the sufferings of the Lord Jesus Christ,
the ocean of future suffering which
awaits impenitent sinners.
H. Guinness

No sin is small. No grain of sand is
small in the mechanism of a watch.
Jeremy Taylor

One leak will sink a ship, and one sin
will destroy a sinner.
*John Bunyan, The Pilgrim's
Progress, ii*

We have a strange illusion that mere time cancels sin.
C.S. Lewis, The Problem of Pain

The heart is deceitful above all things, and desperately wicked.
The Bible, Jeremiah 17:9 (AV)

The very animals whose smell is most offensive to us have no idea that they are offensive, and are not offensive to one another. And man, fallen man, just no idea what a vile thing sin is in the sight of God.
J.C. Ryle, Holiness

The weight of sin is not in substance of matter, but in the majesty of God that is offended, and be the thing never so little, yet the breach of his commandment deserveth death.
Edward Dering, A Part of a Register

Sin is the most expensive thing in the universe, pardoned or unforgiven – pardoned, its cost falls on the atoning sacrifice, unforgiven, it must forever lie upon the impenitent soul.
Charles Grandison Finney

Sin, Unforgivable

Whoever says evil things against the Holy Spirit will not be forgiven.
The Bible, Jesus Christ, Matthew 12:31

Sin and sins

The corruption [of original sin] is constantly called sin by Paul (Galatians 5:19) while the things which spring from it such as adultery, fornication, theft, hatred, murder and revellings, he calls sins. Sins are the fruits of sin. The two things must be looked at separately.
John Calvin, The Institutes of Christian Religion, 2.1.8

Sin forsaken

Sin forsaken is one of the best evidences of sin forgiven.
J.C. Ryle

Singing

God respects me when I work, but he loves me when I sing.
Rabindranath Tagore

The shepherds sing, and shall I be silent?
My God, no hymn for thee?

My soul's a shepherd too; a flock it feeds
Of thoughts and words and deeds:
The pasture of thy word; the streams of grace,
Enriching all the place.
Shepherds and flock shall sing, and all my powers
Out-sing the daylight hours.
George Herbert

When your heart is full of Christ, you want to sing.
C.H. Spurgeon

Singleness of mind   see also GOALS

Blessed are the single-hearted; for they shall enjoy much peace.
Thomas à Kempis

Who keeps one end in view makes all things serve.
Robert Browning

The Chicago Fire was the turning point of my life. I had become so mixed up with building Farwell Hall and was on committees for every kind of work, and in my ambition to make my enterprises succeed . . . I had taken my eyes off the Lord.
Dwight L. Moody

Sisters

For there is no friend like a sister
In calm or stormy weather;
To cheer one on the tedious way,
To fetch one if one goes astray,
To lift one if one totters down,
To strengthen whilst one stands.
Christina Rossetti, Goblin Market

Slander

The slanderous tongue kills three: the slandered, the slanderer, and the person listening to the slander.
The Talmud

The tongue of him who utters slander, and the ear of him to listens to it, are brothers.
Portuguese proverb

Slavery

Slaves are the excrement of mankind.
Cicero

That execrable villainy, which is the scandal of religion, of England, and of human nature.
John Wesley, Thoughts on Slavery

We cannot be free men if this is, by our national choice, to be a land of slavery. Those who deny freedom to others, deserve it not for themselves.
Abraham Lincoln, speech on 19 May 1856

Slaves are not slaves to us. We deem them brothers after the Spirit, in religion fellow-servants.
Lactantius

If in this hour of the world's need I should refuse to lend my aid, however small it may be, I should have no right to think myself a Christian.
Lucy Stone, when urged not to get involved in the abolitionist movement

Sloth see IDLENESS

Smiling

When people are happy, they smile, but when they are sad, they look depressed.
The Bible, Proverbs 15:13

1992 saw the first 'Laughter Clinic' open. It is run by the National Health Service in west Birmingham. Patients who suffer from stress go there and are taught to use laughter to relax.

Of all the things we wear, a smile and good humour are most important. Without them, we are not properly dressed.
Author unknown

We smile because we are happy. But we also become happy because we smile. Act the part and you'll become the part.
Author unknown

The smile that you send out returns to you.
Indian proverb

Most smiles are started by other smiles. Smile first.
Author unknown

Smoking

A custom loathsome to the eye, hateful to the nose, harmful to the brain, dangerous to the lungs, and in the black, stinking fume thereof, nearest resembling the horrible Stygian smoke of the pit that is bottomless.
James I, A Counterblast to Tobacco

Cigarette smoking won't send you to hell, but it may send you to heaven quicker than you expected!
Author unknown

Social action

I was hungry and you fed me, thirsty and you gave me a drink; I was a stranger and you received me in your homes, naked and you clothed me; I was sick and you took care of me, in prison and you visited me.
The Bible, Jesus Christ, Matthew 25:35–36

Whenever you did this for one of the least important of these brothers of mine, you did it for me!
The Bible, Jesus Christ, Matthew 25:40

None are true saints except those who have the true character of compassion and concern to relieve the poor, indigent, and afflicted.
Jonathan Edwards, Treatise Concerning the Religious Affections

It is impossible to comfort men's hearts with the love of God when their feet are perishing with cold.
William Booth

Social reform

It is vain to assert the dignity of human beings, if we do not try to transform them; strive to deal so that men can live worthily and gain their bread in honour.
Jacques Maritain

Social sin

The doctrines and miracles of our Saviour have required nearly two thousand years to convert but a small part of the human race, and even among Christian nations what gross errors still exist!
Robert E. Lee

Society

A population sodden with drink, steeped in vice, eaten up by every social and physical malady, these are the denizens of Darkest England amidst whom my life has been spent.
William Booth, In Darkest England and the Way Out

Merely to build schools and churches for the poor is to offer them stones for bread. There must be living, loving Christian workers, who, like Elisha of old, will take the dead into their arms, and prayerfully clasp them close until they come to life again.
Andrew Murray

Society and the Christian   see also
CHRISTIANS AND THE STATE; GOD AND
THE STATE; WORLD, CONCERN FOR

I might have chosen . . . the housing of
the poor . . . the material benefit of
the working classes . . . the interests of
the criminal world . . . the improvement of the community through politics. . . . The object I chose . . . contained in its heart the remedy for every
form of misery and sin to be found
upon the earth.
William Booth, in his last speech

We are neither Brahmins nor Indian
fakirs, nor do we live remote in the
woods. We despise none of God's
gifts, but we use them with discretion
and understanding. Moreover in living
in this world, we make use of your
forum, your meat market, your baths,
shops and workshops, your inns and
weekly markets, and whatever else
belongs to your economic life. We go
with you by sea, we are soldiers or
farmers, we exchange goods with you,
and whatever we make as a work of art
or for use serves your purposes.
Tertullian, Apologeticum

It is not a matter of getting individuals
into heaven, but of transforming the
life on earth into the harmony of
heaven.
Walter Rauschenbusch,
Christianity and the Social Crisis

The essential purpose of Christianity
[is] to transform human society into
the Kingdom of God by regenerating
all human relationships.
Walter Rauschenbusch,
Christianity and the Social Crisis

Solitude

Solitude is to the mind what diet is to
the body.
Vauvenargues

I never found the companion that was
so companionable as solitude.
Henry David Thoreau

By all means use sometimes to be alone.
George Herbert

Sorrow

We are tossed on a tide that puts us to
the proof, and if we could not sob our
troubles in your ear, what hope should
we have left to us?
Augustine of Hippo

Sorrow conceal'd, like an oven
stopped,
Doth burn the heart to cinders where it
is.
William Shakespeare, Titus
Andronicus

What man, ne'er pull your hat upon
your brows.
Give sorrow words; the grief that does
not speak
Whispers the o'er-fraught heart, and
bids it break.
William Shakespeare, Macbeth

Everyone can master a grief but he
that has it.
William Shakespeare

I was stunned. I felt as if the whole
world were coming to a standstill.
Opposite me on the wall was a picture of
Christ on the cross. I thought I could
understand it as never before. She talked
like a heroine, like an angel to me. I
could only kneel with her and try to pray.
William Booth, describing the day
his wife told him she had cancer

Rain, do not hurt my flowers, but
quickly spread
Your honey drops: press not to smell
them here:
When they are ripe, their odour will
ascend
And at your lodging with their thanks
appear.
George Herbert

As gold is purified in the furnace, so
the faithful heart is purified by sorrow.
Guarini

Sorrow makes us all children again,
destroys all differences of intellect.
Ralph Waldo Emerson

As long as skies are blue, and fields are
green,
Evening must usher night, night urge
the morrow,
Month follow month with woe, and
year wake year to sorrow.
Percy Bysshe Shelley, Adonais
(lament for Keats)

Sorrow, Remedies for

Time is a physician that heals every
grief.
Diphilus

The best remedy for grief is the counsel of a kind and honest friend.
Euripides

Earth has no sorrow that heaven cannot heal.

Thomas Moore, Come Ye
Disconsolate

Soul

One can hardly think too little of oneself. One can hardly think too much of
one's soul.

G.K. Chesterton

The body is the socket of the soul.

Author unknown

Plato located the soul of man in the
head; Christ located it in the heart.

Jerome

Sowing

A person will reap exactly what he sows.

The Bible, The apostle Paul,
Galatians 6:7

Specialists

A specialist is someone who knows
everything about something and nothing about anything else.

Ambrose Bierce

Speech see also CONVERSATION;
GARRULITY

We cannot always oblige, but we can
always speak obligingly.

Voltaire

A bore is a man who, when you ask
him how he is, tells you.

Bert Leston Taylor

One often contradicts an opinion
when what is uncongenial is really the
tone in which it was conveyed.

Friedrich Nietzsche

The language of the true is always
simple.

Euripides

Abderite by birth, Abderite by
speech.

Greek proverb (the people of
Abdera being thought boorish)

The spoken word cannot be recalled.

Proverb

Either be silent, or speak words that
are better than silence.

Pythagoras

Speech is silver, silence is golden.

Persian proverb

Speech, Godly

My distress compels me to speak out,
and my position demands that I do.
Teaching is most properly understood

when its relevance to present-day conditions is clearest. I must perform my
duty as a teacher holding office by apostolic authority. My duty is to speak out
on whatever I see happening that is not
right, even in the highest places.

Martin Luther, The Epistle to the
Romans

Speak for eternity.

Robert Murray M'Cheyne

A word spoken by you when your conscience is clear and your heart full of
God's Spirit is worth ten thousand
words spoken in unbelief and sin.

Robert Murray M'Cheyne

Speech, Thoughtless

One of the disadvantages of wine is
that it makes a man mistake words for
thoughts.

Samuel Johnson

If you want to stay out of trouble, be
careful what you say.

The Bible, Proverbs 21:23

Thoughtless words can wound as
deeply as any sword, but wisely
spoken words can heal.

The Bible, Proverbs 12:18

Be careful what you say and protect
your life. A careless talker destroys
himself.

The Bible, Proverbs 13:3

To talk without thinking is to shoot
without aiming.

Thomas Fuller, Gnomologia

Speech, Unkind

A sharp tongue is worse than a sharp
sword.

Proverb

There is no venom to that of the tongue.

Proverb

A man has no more right to say an
uncivil word to another man than he
has to knock him down.

Samuel Johnson

A sharp tongue is the only edged tool
that grows keener with constant use.

Washington Irving, The
Sketch-Book, Rip Van Winkle

Speech and action

Talkers are no good doers.

William Shakespeare, Richard III,
I.iii

He who speaks without modesty will
find it difficult to make his words good.

Confucius, Analects

Speech and listening

Here was an old owl liv'd in an oak,
The more he heard the less he spoke:
The less he spoke, the more he heard,
O, if men were all like that wise bird.
Punch, 1875

No one would talk so much in society if
he knew how often he misunderstands
others.
Goethe

Bore: A person who talks when you
wish him to listen.
Ambrose Bierce

Hear twice before you speak once.
Proverb

Speech and observation

Men are born with *two* eyes, but with
one tongue, in order that they would
see twice as much as they say; but,
from their conduct, one would suppose that they were born with two tongues, and one eye, for those talk the
most who have observed the least, and
obtrude their remarks upon everything, who have seen into nothing.
C.C. Colton, Lacon

Speech and self-control

Men govern nothing with more difficulty than their tongues, and can mod-
erate their desires more than their
words.
Benedict Spinoza

Do not talk much, neither long at a
time. Few can converse profitably
above an hour. Keep at the utmost distance from pious chit-chat, or religious
gossiping.
*John Wesley, A Plain Man's
Guide to Holiness*

Readiness of speech is often inability
to hold the tongue.
J.B. Rousseau

Blessed is the man who, having nothing to say, abstains from giving wordy
evidence of the fact.
*George Eliot, Impressions of
Theophrastus Such*

Set a watch, O Lord, before my
mouth; keep the door of my lips.
The Bible, Psalm 143:1 (AV)

Even a fool may be thought wise and
intelligent if he stays quiet and keeps
his mouth shut.
The Bible, Proverbs 17:27

The tongue can no man tame; it is an
unruly evil.
*The Bible, The apostle James,
James 3:8 (AV)*

Spiritual coolness

When I was threatening to become
cold in my ministry, and when I felt
Sabbath morning coming, and my
heart not filled with amazement at the
grace of God, or when I was making
ready to dispense the Lord's Supper,
do you know what I used to do? I used
to take a turn up and down among the
sins of my past life, and I always came
down with a broken and a contrite
heart, ready to preach, as it was
preached in the beginning, the forgiveness of sins.
*Thomas Goodwin, in a
letter to his son*

Spiritual gifts see HOLY SPIRIT, GIFTS
OF THE

Spiritual guides

There is no faithfulness like that which
ought to be between a guide of souls
and the person directed by him.
*John Wesley, A Plain Man's
Guide to Holiness*

Spirituality

Spirituality is the basis and foundation
of human life. . . . It must underlie
everything. To put it briefly, man is a
spiritual being, and the proper work of
his mind is to interpret the world
according to his higher nature, and to
conquer the material aspects of the
world so as to bring them into subjec-
tion to the spirit.
Robert Bridges, The Spirit of Man

Why do you hasten to remove anything which hurts your eye, while if
something affects your soul you post-
pone the cure until next year?
Horace

It would be wholly monstrous for a
man to be highest in office and lowest
in soul; first in station and last in life.
Bernard of Clairvaux

I doubt if there is any problem – political or economic – that will not melt
before the fire of a spiritual awakening.
Franklin D. Roosevelt

Statistics

There are three kinds of lies: lies, damned lies, and statistics.

Mark Twain, Autobiography

To understand God's thoughts we must study statistics, for these are the measure of his purpose.

Florence Nightingale

Stewardship

[When asked why he did not operate his evangelistic work totally on faith:] I do. Show me someone with the Lord's money and I have faith enough to ask him for it.

Dwight L. Moody

The living church ought to be dependent on its living members.

Thomas Barnardo

Stillness

Be still and cool in thy own mind and spirit.

George Fox

The very best and highest attainment in this life is to remain still and let God act and speak in you.

Meister Eckhart

To the quiet mind all things are possible. What is the quiet mind? A quiet mind is one which nothing weighs on, nothing worries, which, free from ties and from all self-seeking, is wholly merged into the will of God and dead to its own.

Meister Eckhart

Stoicism

Begin with a cup or a household utensil; if it breaks, say, 'I don't care.' Go on to a horse or pet dog; if anything happens to it, say, 'I don't care.' Go on to yourself, and if you are hurt or injured in any way, say, 'I don't care.' If you go on long enough, and if you try hard enough, you will come to a stage when you can watch your nearest and dearest suffer and die, and say, 'I don't care.'

Epictetus

The Stoics made of the heart a desert, and called it a peace.

T.R. Glover

Strangers

I have been a stranger in a strange land.

The Bible, Exodus 2:22 (AV)

Stubbornness

Stubbornness should have been my middle name.

Martin Luther

Study   see also KNOWLEDGE; LEARNING

For the attainment of divine knowledge we are directed to combine a dependence on God's Spirit with our own researches. Let us, then, not presume to separate what God has thus united.

Charles Simeon

A warmer cap, a candle, a piece of cloth to patch my leggings. . . . But above all, I beseech and entreat your clemency to be urgent with the Procureur that he may kindly permit me to have my Hebrew Bible, Hebrew Grammar and Hebrew Dictionary, that I may spend time with that in study.

William Tyndale's request to have some of his goods brought to him in prison

Stumbling-blocks

If anyone should cause one of these little ones to lose his faith in me, it would be better for that person to have a large millstone tied round his neck and be drowned in the deep sea.

The Bible, Jesus Christ, Matthew 18:6

Stupidity   see also FOOLISHNESS

Dead flies can make a whole bottle of perfume stink, and a little stupidity can cancel out the greatest wisdom.

The Bible, Ecclesiastes 10:1

Success

Success is full of promise till men get it; and then it is a last-year's nest from which the birds have flown.

Henry Ward Beecher

If successful, don't crow; if defeated, don't croak.

Samuel Chadwick

Success cloaks and obscures the evil deeds of good men.

Demosthenes

Success is the one unpardonable sin against one's fellows.

Ambrose Bierce

Dionysius' pupils asked him why Timothy outstripped them in perfection. Dionysius said, 'Timothy is a

God-receptive man. The one expert in this outstrips all men.'
Meister Eckhart

Success has ruined many a man.
Benjamin Franklin, Poor Richard's Almanac, 1752

Suffering   see also ADVERSITY; PAIN

The Lord gave, and now he has taken away. May his name be praised!
The Bible, Job, Job 1:21

Everyone wants to rejoice with Jesus; few are willing to bear anything for him.
Thomas à Kempis, The Imitation of Christ

The Lord gets his best soldiers out of the highlands of affliction.
C.H. Spurgeon

Suffering

The Son of God suffered unto the death, not that men might not suffer, but that their sufferings might be like his.
George Macdonald, Unspoken Sermons, First Series

Try to exclude the possibility of suffering which the order of nature and the existence of free-wills involve, and you find that you have excluded life itself.
C.S. Lewis, The Problem of Pain

It requires more courage to suffer than to die.
Napoleon

I have always loved to think of devoted suffering as the highest, purest, perhaps the only quite pure form of action.
Friedrich von Hügel

It is impossible to love God without loving the cross; and a heart that delights in the cross, finds the most bitter things sweet.
Madame Guyon, A Short and Easy Method of Prayer

Suffering, Causes of

Without doubt all your sufferings are because you have not turned to God and to God alone.
Meister Eckhart

Since God is good, we must regard him as the author of all our blessings; our misfortunes we must assign to other causes, but never to God.
Plato

Suffering, Learning from

Suffering is a stern teacher but a good one.
Proverb

Suffer in order to know, and toil in order to have.
Spanish proverb

If God had told me some time ago that he was about to make me happy as I could be in this world, and then had told me that he should begin by crippling me in arm or limb, and removing me from all my usual sources of enjoyment, I should have thought it a very strange mode of accomplishing his purpose. And yet, how is his wisdom manifested even in this! For if you should see a man shut up in a closed room, idolising a set of lamps and rejoicing in their light, and you wished to make him truly happy, you would begin by blowing out all his lamps, and then throwing open the shutter to let in the light of heaven.
Samuel Rutherford, Letters

Sufferings are lessons.
Æsop

Wisdom comes through suffering.
Æschylus, Agamemnon

Knowledge by suffering entereth,
And life is perfected by death.
Elizabeth Barrett Browning, A Vision of Poets

Sometimes it takes a painful experience to make us change our ways.
The Bible, Proverbs 20:30

Suffering, Patience in

Be patient in all the sufferings which God is pleased to send you. If your love of God is wholehearted you will seek him as much at Calvary as at Mount Tabor and you will definitely find that God's love towards you is even greater.
Madame Guyon, A Short and Easy Method of Prayer

If you can just hold your peace and suffer, you will without doubt see help from the Lord.
Thomas à Kempis, The Imitation of Christ

Suffering, Peace in

Either he will shield you from suffering or he will give you unfailing strength to bear it. Be at peace, then, and put aside all anxious thoughts and imaginings.

Francis de Sales

Suffering and prayer

I beg you to cultivate your inner spirit, as this gradually results in everything becoming prayer in you. You will not be free of suffering, but a peaceful suffering is twice as easy to bear as suffering in turmoil.

François Fénelon, Christian Perfection

Sunday

The people should come together to hear God's word, receive the sacraments, and give God thanks. That done, they may return unto their houses, and do their business as well as any other day. He that thinketh that a man sinneth which worketh on the holy day, if he be weak or ignorant, ought to be better instructed and so to leave his hold.

John Frith, 16th century, writing of Sundays and other religious festivals

Sunday clears away the rust of the whole week.

Joseph Addison, The Spectator, 1711

Superstition

Superstition is the religion of feeble minds.

Edmund Burke

Superstition is godless religion.

Joseph Hall

Surrender see also GOD'S WILL

The greatness of a man's power is the measure of his surrender.

William Booth

Swearing

Do not use any vow when you make a promise. Do not swear by heaven, for it is God's throne.

The Bible, Jesus Christ, Matthew 5:34

Symbolism

Think for a moment, and ask yourself if the business of the world could be carried on without the symbol of the cross. The sea cannot be crossed unless this sign of victory – the mast – remains unharmed. Without it there is no ploughing: neither labourers nor

engineers can do their work without tools of this shape. The human form differs from that of animals solely by its upright posture and the ability to stretch the arms out; and also by the nose, through which the creature gets its breath, and which is at right angles to the forehead and shows the shape of the cross.

Justin Martyr, Apologia

Sympathy

Sympathy is your pain in my heart.

Author unknown

Next to love, sympathy is the divinest passion of the human heart.

Edmund Burke

Systematic theology

Be Bible Christians, and not system Christians.

Charles Simeon

We are far too anxious to be definite and to have finished, well-polished, sharp-edged *systems* – fogetting that the more perfect the theory about the infinite, the surer it is to be wrong, the more impossible is it to be right.

George Macdonald

I am neither Arminian nor Calvinist. To no system would I subscribe.

George Macdonald

T

Tact

Tact is the intelligence of the heart. Mention not a halter in the house of him that was hanged.

George Herbert

Talents

All our talents increase in the using, and every faculty, both good and bad, strengthens by exercise.

Anne Brontë, The Tenant of Wildfell Hall

Talking see SPEECH

Taxes

Pay the Emperor what belongs to the Emperor, and pay God what belongs to God.

The Bible, Jesus Christ, Matthew 22:21

Teachers   see also EDUCATION

[Jesus] wasn't like the teachers of the Law; instead, he taught with authority.
The Bible, Matthew 7:29

He who can, does. He who cannot, teaches.
George Bernard Shaw, Man and Superman

To teach is to learn.
Japanese proverb

Between the alternatives of no teacher or a bad one, the sensible man does not hesitate: he replies at once, 'No teacher'.
Jules Simon

A teacher affects eternity.
Henry Adams

It is useful to have spiritual teachers; and if they be wise, it is wise to learn reverently from them; but their lessons have not been successful until the learner has gained an eye for seeing the truth, and believes no longer because of his teacher's word, but because he has an anointing from the Holy One, and knoweth all things.
F.W. Newman

Origen taught us in words which inspired as much by their humility as by their confidence that nature gives our minds a longing to know the truth of God and the causes of things, just as our eyes have a longing for light or our bodies for food.
Gregory Thaumaturgus

Teamwork

Locusts: they have no king, but they move in formation.
The Bible, Proverbs 30:27

The great cannot exist without the less, nor the less without the great.
Clement of Rome, Epistle to the Corinthians

It needs more skill than I can tell
To play the second fiddle well.
C.H. Spurgeon

The great fault, I think, in our missions is that no one likes to be second.
Robert Morrison

Tears

Sometimes tears have the weight of words.
Ovid

'It [weeping] opens the lungs, washes the countenance, exercises the eyes,

and softens down the temper,' said Mr Bumble. 'So cry away.'
Charles Dickens

To weep is to make less the depth of grief.
William Shakespeare

There is a kind of pleasure in weeping, for grief is assuaged and removed by tears.
Ovid

The good are always prone to tears.
Greek proverb

The tears which I had been holding back streamed down, and I let them flow as freely as they would, making of them a pillow for my heart. On them it rested, for my weeping sounded in your ears alone.
Augustine of Hippo

What soap is to the body, tears are for the soul.
Jewish proverb

I wept not, so to stone I grew within.
Dante

Technology

Technological progress has merely provided us with more efficient means for going backwards.
Aldous Huxley

Temperance

Temperate temperance is best; intemperate temperance injures the cause of temperance.
Martin Luther

Intemperate intemperance injures the cause of temperance, while temperate temperance helps it in its fight against intemperate intemperance.
Mark Twain, Notebooks

To go beyond the bounds of moderation is to outrage humanity.
Blaise Pascal

Temperance and work are the two best physicians of men.
Jean-Jacques Rousseau

Temptation

Temptation commonly comes through that for which we are naturally fitted.
B.F. Westcott

Let no man think himself to be holy because he is not tempted, for the holiest and highest in life have the most temptations. How much higher the hill is, so much is the wind there greater; so, how much higher the life is, so much the stronger is the temptation of the enemy.

John Wycliffe

When a good man is afflicted, tempted, or troubled with evil thoughts; then he understands better the great need he has of God, without whom he perceives he can do nothing that is good. . . . Yet we must be watchful, especially in the beginning of the temptation; for the enemy is then more easily overcome, if he is not allowed to enter the door of our hearts, but is resisted at his first knock at the gate. . . . For first there comes to the mind a mere thought of evil, then a strong imagination of it, afterwards delight, and an evil inclination, and then consent.

Thomas à Kempis

Sympathy with the sinner in his trial does not depend on the experience of sin, but on the experience of the temptation to sin, which only the sinless can know in its full intensity. He who falls yields before the last strain.

B.F. Westcott, on Hebrews 2:18

Temptation, Purpose of

Temptation reveals to us what we are.
Thomas à Kempis

The devil tempts that he may ruin; God tests that he may crown.

Ambrose

Blessed is the man that endureth temptation: for when he is tried, he shall receive the crown of life.

The Bible, James 1:12 (AV)

Temptation, Resisting

'Tis one thing to be tempted,
Another thing to fall.

William Shakespeare

I cannot keep birds from flying over my head, but I can keep them from building under my hat.

Martin Luther

God is better served in resisting a temptation to evil than in many formal prayers. This is but twice or thrice a day; but that every hour and moment of the day. So much more is our continual watch than our evening and morning devotion.

William Penn

I can resist everything except temptation.

Mark Twain

I couldn't help it. I can resist everything except temptation.

Oscar Wilde, Lady Windermere's Fan, Act I

When sinners tempt you, my son, don't give in.

The Bible, Proverbs 1:10

Resist the Devil, and he will run away from you.

The Bible, James 4:7

Temptation, Ways to escape

The only way to get rid of temptation is to yield to it.

Oscar Wilde, The Picture of Dorian Gray

In the greatest temptations, a single look to Christ, and the bare pronouncing of his name, suffices to overcome the wicked one, so it be done with confidence and calmness of spirit.

John Wesley, A Plain Man's Guide to Holiness

There hath no temptation taken you but such as is common to man: but God is faithful, who will not suffer you to be tempted above that ye are able; but will with the temptation also make a way to escape, that ye may be able to bear it.

The Bible, The apostle Paul, 1 Corinthians 10:13 (AV)

Ten Commandments

The Law of the Ten Commandments is the strength of sin because it creates self-knowledge.

Martin Luther, The Epistle to the Hebrews

No man can break any of the Ten Commandments. He can only break himself against them.

G.K. Chesterton

Testimonies to Christ

To me the most valuable of all the discoveries I ever made was when I discovered my saviour in Jesus Christ.

Lord Kelvin, when a student asked him which of his discoveries was the most valuable

Religion has done a big change in me. . . . I was brought up in a family where there was never any talk of God. But when I had become a grown-up person,

I found it impossible to exist without God in one's heart.

Svetlana Allilueva, speaking on a U.S. television programme

The greatest discovery I ever made was that I was a lost, guilty sinner, and that Jesus Christ, the saviour of sinners, is my saviour.

James Simpson, discoverer of chloroform, on being asked what his greatest discovery was

I do not know in what mood of pessimism I might have stood before you today had it not been that, ere the dew of youth had dried from off me, I made friends with the sinless Son of Man who is the well-head of the stream that vitalises all advancing civilisation and who claims to be the first and the last, and the living one who was dead and is alive for evermore.

James Simpson

Thanksgiving   see also GRATITUDE

Thanksgiving is the end of all human conduct, whether observed in words or works.

J.B. Lightfoot

Theology   see also SYSTEMATIC THEOLOGY

Jesus loves me, this I know,
for the Bible tells me so.

Karl Barth's summary of his theology

A theologian is a man who spends his time answering questions that nobody is asking.

William Temple

Everything a theologian does in the church contributes to the spread of the knowledge of God and the salvation of men.

Martin Luther

As wheels in a complicated machine may move in opposite directions and yet subserve a common end, so may truths apparently opposite be perfectly reconcilable with each other, and equally subserve the purposes of God in the accomplishment of man's salvation.

Charles Simeon

Theology is but an appendix to love, and an unreliable appendix!

Toyohiko Kagawa

It is the heart that makes the theologian.

Quintilian

Theology is but our ideas of truth classified and arranged.

Henry Ward Beecher

Brethren, if in your pastorates you are not theologians, you are just *nothing at all*.

C.H. Spurgeon, to his theological students

Thief on the cross

One thief on the cross was saved, that none should despair, and only one, that none should presume.

J.C. Ryle, The Upper Room

Thinking   see also MIND; REASON; WISHFUL THINKING

Let every Christian, as much as in him lies, engage himself openly and publicly, before all the World, in some mental pursuit for the building up of Jerusalem.

William Blake, Jerusalem

The spirit of the age is filled with disdain for thinking.

Albert Schweitzer

Most people think no more than twice or three times a year. I have become rich and famous by thinking twice or three times a week.

George Bernard Shaw

The soul is dyed the colour of its leisure thoughts.

W.R. Inge

It isn't that they can't see the solution. It is that they can't see the problem.

G.K. Chesterton

Question with boldness even the existence of God; because, if there be one, he must more approve of the homage of reason than that of blindfolded fear.

Thomas Jefferson

I do not feel obliged to believe that the same God who has endowed us with sense, reason, and intellect has intended us to forgo their use.

Galileo

The diseases of the mind are more destructive than those of the body.

Cicero

I think, therefore I am.

René Descartes, Discours de la Méthode

Our thoughts can help us more than doctors and harm us more than brickbats.

Author unknown

The heart has its reasons which reason does not know.

Blaise Pascal, Pensées

Life does not consist mainly – or even largely – of facts and happenings. It consists mainly of the storm of thoughts that are forever blowing through one's mind.

Mark Twain

Our greatest need is to teach people how to think – not what, but how.

Thomas Edison

Great minds discuss ideas;
average minds, events and happenings;
small minds, people and things.

Author unknown

Thinking, Avoiding

They don't think enough.

Albert Schweitzer, replying to the question, 'What's wrong with the world?'

There is no expedient to which man will not resort to avoid the real labour of thinking.

Joshua Reynolds

Iron rusts from disuse, stagnant water loses its purity, and in cold weather becomes frozen: even so does inaction sap the vigour of the mind.

Leonardo da Vinci, Notebooks

Learning without thought is labour lost; thought without learning is perilous.

Confucius, Analects

Thinking, Buddhist view of

The no-mind not-thinks no-thoughts about no-things.

Buddha

Thinking, Humility in

Listen less to your own thoughts and more to God's thoughts.

François Fénelon, Christian Perfection, letter to the Duc de Chevreuse

Thinking, Maturity in

We are to be children in heart, not in understanding.

Thomas Aquinas

A little learning is a dangerous thing;
Drink deep, or taste not the Pierian Spring;
There shallow draughts intoxicate the brain,
And drinking largely sobers us again.

Alexander Pope

Do not be like children in your thinking, my brothers; be children so far as evil is concerned, but be grown-up in your thinking.

The Bible, The apostle Paul, 1 Corinthians 14:20

Thinking, Resting from

The mind ought sometimes to be amused, that it may the better return to thought, and to itself.

Phaedrus

Thinking and action

You can't keep people from doing wrong until you keep them from thinking wrong.

Author unknown

Dynamic thought or belief helps create the actual fact.

William James

All thought tends to convert itself into action.

Thomas Edison

Whether you think you'll succeed, or think you'll fail, you are right.

Henry Ford

The decisive events of the world take place in the intellect.

Henri Frédéric Amiel

To think evil is very much the same as doing it.

Aristophanes

Nothing is more terrible than activity without insight.

Thomas Carlyle

Action and faith enslave thought, both of them in order not to be troubled or inconvenienced by reflection, criticism and doubt.

Henri Frédéric Amiel

Thinking and character

Be transformed by the renewing of your mind.

The Bible, The apostle Paul, Romans 12:2

Set your minds on things above, not on earthly things.

The Bible, The apostle Paul, Colossians 3:2

All that we are is the result of our past thoughts.

Buddha

We can't choose our relatives, but we can choose our thoughts, which influence us much more.

Author unknown

Whatever your habitual thoughts are like, so also will be the character of your mind; for the soul is dyed by the thoughts.
Marcus Aurelius

Be careful how you think; your life is shaped by your thoughts.
The Bible, Proverbs 4:23

Thought makes the whole dignity of man; therefore endeavour to think well, that is the only morality.
Blaise Pascal

Thinking and happiness

Most people are about as happy as they've made up their minds to be.
Abraham Lincoln

It's impure thoughts that produce the secretions that create passion.
Author unknown

Thinking and speech   see also SPEECH AND THOUGHT

They never taste who always drink;
They always talk, who never think.
Matthew Prior

Good people think before they answer. Evil people have a quick reply, but it causes trouble.
The Bible, Proverbs 15:28

As he thinketh in his heart, so is he.
The Bible, Proverbs 23:7 (AV)

There is more hope for a stupid fool than for someone who speaks without thinking.
The Bible, Proverbs 29:20

Thinking deeply

Second thoughts are best.
Euripides

Look to the essence of a thing, whether it be a point of doctrine, of practice, or of interpretation.
Marcus Aurelius, Meditations

I do not understand; I pause; I examine.
Montaigne, inscription for his library

To get the best out of life great matters have to be given a second thought.
Blaise Pascal

Thrift   see also SAVING

Good management goes further than good income. With thrift, little is enough. Without thrift, much is not.
Author unknown

Time

A thousand years to you are like one day;
   they are like yesterday, already gone.
The Bible, Psalm 90:4

One grain of time's inestimable sand is worth a golden mountain: let us not lose it.
Roger Williams

Gather ye rosebuds while ye may,
Old Time is still a-flying.
Robert Herrick

I recommend you to take care of the minutes: for hours will take care of themselves.
Chesterfield, letter to his son, 6 November 1747

The value of life is computed not by its duration, but by its donation.
William James

Tiredness

Life is one long process of getting tired.
Samuel Butler, Notebooks, Life, 7

Toleration

There is a limit at which forbearance ceases to be a virtue.
Edmund Burke

I may disapprove of what you say but I will defend to the death your right to say it.
Voltaire

Toleration means reverence for all the possibilities of truth, it means acknowledgement that she dwells in diverse mansions, and wears vesture of many colours, and speaks in strange tongues. It means frank respect for freedom of indwelling conscience against mechanic forms, official conventions, social force. It means the charity that is greater than faith or hope.
John Morley

The equal toleration of all religions . . . is the same thing as atheism.
Pope Leo XIII

Tolerance is the virtue of the man without convictions.
G.K. Chesterton

We ought to be much more tolerant about faulty behaviour. We can all fall into one of Satan's traps here: it is so easy to give a false impression of super holiness, as if we were already angels, and ignore the company of all who seem human in their shortcomings!

John Calvin, The Institutes of Christian Religion, 4.1.13

Tongues

I thank God that I speak in strange tongues much more than any of you. But in church worship I would rather speak five words that can be understood, in order to teach others, than speak thousands of words in strange tongues.

The Bible, The apostle Paul, 1 Corinthians 14:18–19

Tradition see also CHANGE; CUSTOM; HABIT

Loyalty to petrified opinion never yet broke a chain or freed a human soul.

Mark Twain

Tradition may be defined as an extension of the franchise. Tradition means giving votes to the most obscure of all classes, our ancestors. It is the democracy of the dead.

G.K. Chesterton

Tradition is an important help to history, but its statements should be carefully scrutinised before we rely on them.

Joseph Addison

Training

Training is everything. The peach was once a bitter almond; cauliflower is nothing but cabbage with a college education.

Mark Twain, Pudd'nhead Wilson's Calendar, ch. 5

Transformation

I am releasing the angel that is imprisoned in this marble.

Michelangelo's description of what he was doing as he began a sculpture

Travel

There are three states of misery – sickness, fasting and travel.

Eastern proverb

He that travels far knows much.

Clark, 1639

All travelling becomes dull in exact proportion to its rapidity.

John Ruskin

Tribulations see also ADVERSITY; DIFFICULTIES

Christians must be exhorted to follow Christ their head with complete utter devotion through punishment, through death, through hell.
In this way let them have confidence that they will enter heaven through many tribulations, rather than through a false assurance of peace.

Martin Luther, Theses 94 and 95

Man's extremity is God's opportunity.

John Flavel

Even the holiest of men would feel too secure in their own strength, if they were not made to know themselves more thoroughly by the trial of the cross.

John Calvin, The Institutes of Christian Religion, 3.8.2

Whatever sort of tribulation we suffer, we should always remember that its purpose is to make us spurn the present and reach out to the future. God knows very well that we are naturally drawn to love this world. So, to keep us from clinging to it too closely, he finds good reason to call us away and wake us up.

John Calvin, The Institutes of Christian Religion, 3.9.1

Trinity

Without the Spirit it is not possible to hold the Word of God nor without the Son can any draw near to the Father, for the knowledge of the Father is the Son and the knowledge of the Son of God is through the Holy Spirit.

Irenaeus

The Lord redeems us . . . and pours out the Spirit of the Father to unite God and mankind.

Irenaeus, Against Heresies, 5.1.2

The Father of all is one; the Word of all is one; the Holy Spirit is one and the same everywhere.

Clement of Alexandria, Paedagogus, 1.6

Think of the Father as a spring of life begetting the Son like a river and the Holy Spirit is like a sea, for the spring and the river and the sea are all one nature. Think of the Father as a root, of the Son as a branch, and of the Spirit as a fruit, for the substance in these three is one. The Father is a sun with the Son as rays and the Holy Spirit as heat.

John of Damascus

Since there is but one divine Being, why do you speak of three, Father, Son and Holy Ghost? Because God has revealed himself in his word that these three distinct persons are the one, true and eternal God.

Heidelberg Catechism

The names we use to distinguish between the different persons of Trinity refer to the relationships of the persons to each other, not to their common substance or nature – which is one.

Augustine of Hippo

We are enclosed in the Father, and we are enclosed in the Son, and we are enclosed in the Holy Ghost. And the Father is enclosed in us, and the Son is enclosed in us, and the Holy Ghost is enclosed in us: Almightiness, All Wisdom, All Goodness: one God, one Lord.

Julian of Norwich

Trouble   see also ADVERSITY;
DIFFICULTIES; DISASTER; TRIBULATIONS

Leave your troubles with the Lord, and he will defend you.

The Bible, Psalm 55:22

When things are going well for you, be glad, and when trouble comes, just remember: God sends both happiness and trouble; you never know what is going to happen next.

The Bible, Ecclesiastes 7:14

Trust

He who does not trust enough will not be trusted.

Lao Tzu, Tao Te Ching

Trust in God

Trust in the Lord with all your heart. Never rely on what you think you know.

The Bible, Proverbs 3:5

Please thank them for that, sir. . . . And I can only say that I am nothing but a poor sinner, trusting in Christ alone for salvation, and need all of the prayers they can offer for me.

Robert E. Lee, when told of the prayers people were offering for him

The Sovereign Lord, the holy God of Israel, says to the people, 'Come back and quietly trust in me. Then you will be strong and secure.'

The Bible, Isaiah 30:15

O give me light to see, a heart to close with and power to do thy will, O God.

Thomas Wilson

Trusting in him who can go with me, and remain with you, and be everywhere for good, let us confidently hope that all will yet be well.

Abraham Lincoln

Boundless is thy love for me,
Boundless then my trust shall be.

Robert Bridges

Trust in yourself and you are doomed to disappointment.
Trust in your friends and they will die and leave you.
Trust in money and you may have it taken away from you.
Trust in reputation and some slanderous tongues will blast it.
But trust in God and you are never to be confounded in time or in eternity.

Dwight L. Moody

He rides at ease whom the grace of God carries.

Thomas à Kempis

The heart that trusts forever sings,
And feels as light as it had wings.
A well of peace within it springs.

I. Williams

Trust in God – among wild animals

I did not use to believe the story of Daniel in the lions' den until I had to take some of these awful marches, and then I knew it was true, and that it was written for my comfort. Many a time I walked along praying, 'O God of Daniel shut their mouths,' and he did.

Mary Slessor, who had once been afraid to cross a field with a cow in it and now had to go alone through African countryside full of dangerous animals

Trust in God – and God's promises

Trust him. The more you trust him the better you will love him. If you ask farther: 'What should I do to trust him?' I answer: Try him: the more you make trial of him, the more your trust in him will be strengthened. Venture upon his promises; carry them to him, and see if he will not be as good as his word.

John Newton, Cardiphonia

Trust in God – at life's end

While I draw this fleeting breath
When mine eyelids close in death,
When I soar through tracts unknown,
See thee on thy judgement throne,
  Rock of ages cleft for me,
  Let me hide myself in thee.
                            Augustus Toplady

Trust in God – at sea

Eternal Father, strong to save,
Whose arm hath bound the restless
    wave,
Who bid'st the mighty ocean deep
Its own appointed limits keep;
  O hear us when we cry to thee
  For all in peril on the sea.
                            William Whiting

**Trust in God – because of his past
mercies**

All I have seen teaches me to trust the
Creator for all I have not seen.
                        Ralph Waldo Emerson

Our God, our help in ages past,
  Our hope for years to come,
Be thou our guard while troubles last,
  And our eternal home.
                            Isaac Watts

Trust in God – in battle

Captain, my religious belief teaches
me to feel as safe in battle as in bed.
God has fixed the time for my death. I
do not concern myself about that, but
to always be ready, no matter when it
may overtake me.
                        'Stonewall' Jackson

I know in whose powerful hands I am,
and on him I rely, and feel that in all
our life we are upheld and sustained by
divine providence, and that providence requires us to use the means he
has put under our control.
                            Robert E. Lee

You can get horses ready for battle,
but it is the Lord who gives victory.
                    The Bible, Proverbs 21:31

Trust in God – for the church

We tell our Lord plainly that if he will
have his church then he must look to
and maintain and defend it, for we can
neither uphold nor protect it; and if we
could, then we should become the
proudest asses under heaven.
                            Martin Luther

Trust in God – for the future

Trust the past to God's mercy,
the present to his love,
and the future to his providence.
                        Augustine of Hippo

O Lord, forgive what I have been,
sanctify what I am, and order what I
shall be.
                            Thomas Wilson

Never boast about tomorrow. You
don't know what will happen between
now and then.
                    The Bible, Proverbs 27:1

All will be will, and all will be well, and
all manner of things will be well.
                *Julian of Norwich, Revelations of
                                Divine Love*

Trust in God – when daunted by work

The very vastness of the work raises
one's thoughts to God, as the only one
by whom it can be done. That is the
solid comfort – *he knows*.
                        Florence Nightingale

Trust in God – when deserted

Then, as now, in the hands of God.
                *Martin Luther's reply when asked
                    where he would be when all his
                            supporters deserted him*

**Trust in God – when we seem
abandoned by him**

It is when God appears to have abandoned us that we must abandon ourselves most wholly to God.
                        François Fénelon

Judge not the Lord by feeble sense,
  But trust him for his grace;
Behind a frowning providence
  He hides a smiling face.
                            William Cowper

Be it ours, when we cannot see the face
of God, to trust under the shadow of
his wings.
                            C.H. Spurgeon

Truth see also REASON

Devotion to truth is the first and last
thing we demand of genius.
                                Goethe

Truth that is not experienced is no
better than error and may be fully as
dangerous. The scribes who sat in
Moses' seat were not the victims of
error; they were the victims of their failure to experience the truth they taught.
                            A.W. Tozer

If you are out to tell the truth, leave elegance to the tailor.

Albert Einstein

Everything should be made as simple as possible, but not simpler.

Albert Einstein

My way of joking is to tell the truth. It's the funniest joke in the world.

George Bernard Shaw

We know the truth not only by reason but by the heart.

Blaise Pascal, Pensées

A love which violates or even merely neutralises truth is an 'accursed love'.

Martin Luther

When you want to fool the world, tell the truth.

Bismarck

But there are seven sisters ever serving Truth,
Porters of the Posterns, one called Abstinence,
Humility, Charity, Chastity be the chief maidens there;
Patience and Peace help many a one;
Lady Almsgiving lets in full many.

William Langland, Piers Plowman

Mr Lely, I desire you would use all your skill to paint my picture truly like me, and not flatter me at all; but remark all these roughnesses, pimples, warts, and everything as you see me, otherwise I will never pay a farthing for it.

Oliver Cromwell

Truth, Absolute

Plato is my friend, Socrates is my friend, but truth is greater.

Latin proverb

There are no eternal facts as there are no absolute truths.

Friedrich Nietzsche

Truth and error

Truth overstated leads to error.

Author unknown

Whatever is only almost true is quite false, and among the most dangerous of errors, because being so near truth, it is the more likely to lead astray.

Henry Ward Beecher

Truth and God

Where truth is, there is God.

Cervantes

Truth is the daughter of God.

Thomas Fuller, Gnomologia

I thirst for truth,
But shall not reach it till I reach the source.

Robert Browning

If God were to hold out enclosed in his right hand all truth, and in his left hand just the active search for truth, though with the condition that I should ever err therein, and should say to me: Choose! I should humbly take his left hand and say: Father! Give me this one; absolute truth belongs to thee alone.

G.E. Lessing, Wolfenbüttler Fragmente

Truth and Jesus Christ

Pilate asked, 'Quid est Veritas?' ('What is truth?') In Latin the answer is an anagram, 'Est Vir qui Adest' ('It is the Man who is before you').

Author unknown

Truth and mankind

Man is ice to truth and fire to falsehood.

La Fontaine

He who begins by loving Christianity better than truth will proceed by loving his own sect or church better than Christianity and end in loving himself better than all.

Samuel Taylor Coleridge

Truth often suffers more by the heat of its defenders than from the arguments of its opposers.

William Penn

It is not truth that makes man great, but man who makes truth great.

Confucius

A thing is not necessarily true because badly uttered, nor false because spoken magnificently.

Augustine of Hippo

Truth and martyrdom

I am very fond of truth, but not at all of martyrdom.

Voltaire

To kill a man is not to defend a doctrine, but to kill a man.

Sebastien Castello

If anyone disagrees with us on any point of religion we condemn him and pursue him to the ends of the earth with dart and pen. We exercise cruelty with the sword, fire and water, and we exterminate the destitute and defence-less.

Sebastien Castello

A thing is not necessarily true because a man dies for it.

Oscar Wilde

Truth and novelty

We do not run after the new; we do not run after the unknown; we do not run after the extraordinary; we seek what is right and fitting, and much that is right and fitting was said before us much better than we know how to say it ourselves.

Charles Péguy, Men and Saints, The Humanities

It is the customary fate of new truths to begin as heresies and to end as supers-titions.

T.H. Huxley, The Coming of Age of the Origin of Species

An old error is always more popular than a new truth.

German proverb

Truth and the church

The history of the church ought properly to be called the history of truth.

Blaise Pascal, Pensées

Truth and the devil

Say the truth and shame the devil.

Hugh Latimer

Truth and the dying

Truth sits upon the lips of dying men.

Matthew Arnold, Sohrab and Rustum

Truth examined

Truth fears nothing but concealment.

Latin proverb

To become properly acquainted with a truth we must first have disbelieved it, and disputed against it.

Bismarck

Fraud and falsehood only dread examination. Truth invites it.

Thomas Cooper

One unerring mark of the love of truth is not entertaining any proposition with greater assurance than the proofs it is built upon will warrant.

John Locke

Truth in relationships

Be so true to thyself as thou be not false to others.

Francis Bacon, Essays, Of Wisdom for a Man's Self

Truth triumphant

The dictum that truth always triumphs over persecution is one of those pleas-ant falsehoods which men repeat after one another till they pass into com-monplace, but which all experience refutes.

John Stuart Mill

I believe that in the end the truth will conquer.

John Wycliffe, to the Duke of Lancaster

Truth wherever it is found

All truth, wherever it is found, belongs to us as Christians.

Justin Martyr

Wherever Truth may be, were it in a Turk or Tartar, it must be cherished. . . . Let us seek the honeycomb even within the lion's mouth.

Johan de Brune

Let us rejoice in the Truth, wherever we find its lamp burning.

Albert Schweitzer

Tyranny

Resistance to tyrants is obedience to God.

Thomas Jefferson, Epigrams

Tyranny is the wish to have in one way what cannot be had in another.

Blaise Pascal

Wherever law ends, tyranny begins.

John Locke

Taxation without representation is tyranny.

James Otis

U

Understanding

I am the master of everything I can explain.

Theodor Haecker

Thou art my hiding place and my shield: I hope in thy word.

The Bible, Psalm 119:114 (AV)

Unhappiness

Irresolution on the schemes of life which offer themselves to our choice, and inconstancy in pursuing them, are the greatest causes of all our unhappiness.

Joseph Addison

Union with God

Obey the Spirit's teaching, then, and remain in union with Christ.

The Bible, 1 John 2:29

God is love, and whoever lives in love lives in union with God and God lives in union with him.

The Bible, 1 John 4:16

True religion is an union of God with the soul, a real participation of the divine nature, the very image of God drawn upon the soul, or in the Apostle's phrase, it is Christ formed in us.

Henry Scougal, The Life of God in the Soul of Man

The heart of Paul's religion is union with Christ. This, more than any other conception – more than justification, more than sanctification, more even than reconciliation – is the key which unlocks the secrets of his soul.

James Stewart, A Man in Christ

Unity

Unity is strength.

French proverb

The French will only be united under the threat of danger. Nobody can simply bring together a country that has 265 kinds of cheese.

Charles de Gaulle

Consensus gives strength.

Latin proverb

Usefulness

O Lord, let me not live to be useless!

Bishop Stratford

V

Vanity

Vanity is so secure in the heart of man that everyone wants to be admired: even I who write this, and you who read this.

Blaise Pascal

Variety

Variety is pleasing.

Greek proverb

Vices

The leader should understand how often vices pass themselves off as virtues. Stinginess often excuses itself under the name of frugality while, on the other hand, extravagance hides itself under the name of generosity. Often inordinate laxity is mistaken for loving kindness, while unbridled wrath is seen as the virtue of spiritual zeal.

Gregory the Great

Victory

You can fight with confidence where you are sure of victory. With Christ and for Christ victory is certain.

Bernard of Clairvaux

It often happens that our passions lie dormant. If, during that time, we do not lay up provision of strength with which to combat them when they wake up, we shall be vanquished.

Francis de Sales

Another such victory and we are lost.

Pyrrhus, who was victorious over the Romans but at great expense

He conquers who overcomes himself.

Latin proverb

Even victors are by victory undone.

John Dryden

Who overcomes
By force, hath overcome but half his foe.

John Milton, Paradise Lost

Vigilance

The way to be safe is never to be secure.

Thomas Fuller, Gnomologia

Eternal vigilance is the price of liberty.

Wendell Phillips

Violence   see also NON-VIOLENCE

Robbery always claims the life of the robber – this is what happens to anyone who lives by violence.

The Bible, Proverbs 1:19

All they that take the sword shall perish with the sword.

The Bible, Jesus Christ, Matthew 26:52 (av)

Violence is an involuntary quest for identity.

Marshall McLuhan

Virgin birth

This is how the birth of Jesus Christ took place. His mother Mary was engaged to Joseph, but before they were married, she found out that she was going to have a baby by the Holy Spirit. . . . Now all this happened in order to make what the Lord had said through the prophet come true, 'A virgin will become pregnant and have a son, and he will be called Immanuel' (which means, 'God is with us').

The Bible, Matthew 1:18, 22–23

He came from God, all the apostles believed, in a *sense* in which no other came; does it not follow that he came in a *way* in which no other came?

*James Denney, Studies in
Theology*

Virtue

Virtue dwells not in the tongue but in the heart.

Thomas Fuller, Gnomologia

Sweet day, so cool, so calm, so bright,
The bridal of the earth and skie:
The dew shall weep thy fall tonight;
    For thou must die.

Only a sweet and virtuous soul,
Like season'd timber, never gives;
But though the whole world turn to
    coal,
    Then chiefly lives.

George Herbert

Virtue is stronger than a battering ram.

Latin proverb

Be virtuous and you will be eccentric.

Mark Twain

To be better than the worst, is not goodness.

Seneca

Silver is inferior to gold, gold to virtue.

Horace

Virtue is the safest helmet.

Latin proverb

Virtue is its own reward.

John Dryden

It is not enough to know about virtue, then, but we must endeavour to possess it, and to use it, or to take any other steps that may make us good.

Aristotle

Vision   see also REVELATIONS

Everything begins in mysticism and ends in politics.

Charles Péguy

Dream the impossible dream. Dreaming it may make it possible. It often has.

Author unknown

The subconscious mind tends to actualise what we visualise. So even when the roof is caving in, picture yourself as a giant success.

Author unknown

Go confidently in the direction of your dreams! Live the life you've imagined.

Henry David Thoreau

If you have a dream, you have everything that matters. If you have no dream, it's later than you think. Better get one.

Author unknown

Where there is no vision, the people perish.

The Bible, Proverbs 29:18 (AV)

The real voyage of discovery consists not in seeking new landscapes but in having new eyes.

Marcel Proust

Vocation   see CALL

W

War   see also NON-VIOLENCE

It is lawful for Christian men, at the commandment of the magistrate, to wear weapons, and serve in the wars.

*Book of Common Prayer,
Article 37*

In War: Resolution. In Defeat: Defiance. In Victory: Magnanimity. In Peace: Goodwill.

*Winston Churchill, The Second
World War, vol. i, Moral*

If I should die think only this of me
That there's some corner of a foreign
    field
That is for ever England. . . .

Rupert Brooke

In war, whichever side may call itself the victor, there are no winners, but all are losers.

*Neville Chamberlain, Speech at
Kettering, 3 July 1938*

If you want to stop war in the world, stop war in the home.

A ten-year-old boy

Waste of Muscle, waste of Brain,
Waste of Patience, waste of Pain,
Waste of Manhood, waste of Health,
Waste of Beauty, waste of Wealth,
Waste of Blood, and waste of Tears,
Waste of Youth's most precious years,
Waste of ways the Saints have trod,
Waste of Glory, waste of God – War!

G.A. Studdert-Kennedy

The lamps are going out all over Europe; we shall not see them lit again in our lifetime.

*Viscount Grey of Fallodon,
3 August 1914*

Never in the field of human conflict was so much owed by so many to so few.

*Winston Churchill, speech in the
House of Commons, 20 August
1940 on the RAF in the Battle of
Britain*

Weakness

My mind and my body may grow weak,
    but God is my strength;
    he is all I ever need.

The Bible, Psalm 73:26

I have two planks for a bed, two stools, two cups and a basin. On my broken wall is a small card which says, 'God hath chosen the weak things – I can do all things through Christ who strengthens me.' It is true I have passed through fire.

Gladys Aylward

When God delivered Israel out of Egypt, he didn't send an army. We would have sent an army or an orator! But God sent a man who had been in the desert for forty years, and had an impediment in his speech. It is weakness that God wants! Nothing is small when God handles it.

Dwight L. Moody

A proud and self-reliant man rightly fears to undertake anything, but a humble man becomes all the braver as he realises his own powerlessness; all the bolder as he sees his own weakness; for all his confidence is in God, who delights to reveal his almighty power in our infirmity and his mercy in our misery.

Francis de Sales

Wealth   see also MILLIONAIRES; MONEY; POVERTY

When a wicked man dies, his hope dies with him. Confidence placed in riches comes to nothing.

The Bible, Proverbs 11:7

Golden shackles are far worse than iron ones.

Mahatma Gandhi

The more easily you get your wealth, the sooner you will lose it. The harder it is to earn, the more you will have.

The Bible, Proverbs 13:11

It is much harder for a rich person to enter the Kingdom of God than for a camel to go through the eye of a needle.

*The Bible, Jesus Christ,
Matthew 19:24*

The fourth *Sunday Times* list of Britain's 300 richest people, on 10 May 1992, revealed that they have assets worth £50 billion.

In all time of our wealth, good Lord deliver us.

*Book of Common Prayer, The
Litany*

Whoever craves wealth is like a man who drinks sea water; the more he drinks, the more he increases his thirst, and he does not cease to drink until he perishes.

*Jesus Christ, according to Muslim
tradition*

No one, not even his neighbour, likes a poor man, but the rich have many friends.

The Bible, Proverbs 14:20

Rich people have many relations.

Latin proverb

Wealth has wings.

Sophocles

The mind grows wanton in prosperity, for it is hard to endure good fortune with calmness.

Ovid

We measure great men by their virtue, not by their success.

Cornelius Nepos

Frugality is a great revenue.

Cicero

Our Lord God commonly gives riches to those gross asses to whom he gives nothing else.

Martin Luther

It is better to live rich than to die rich.

Samuel Johnson

Wealth and happiness

I have made many millions, but they have brought me no happiness. I would barter them all for the days I sat on an office stool in Cleveland and counted myself rich on three dollars a week.

John D. Rockefeller

Wealth and its use

Surplus wealth is a sacred trust which its possessor is bound to administer in his lifetime for the good of the community.

Andrew Carnegie, The Gospel of Wealth

If a rich man is proud of his wealth, he should not be praised until it is known how he employs it.

Socrates

Wealth and pride

Prosperity and luxury gradually extinguish sympathy, and by inflating with pride, harden and debase the soul.

William Wilberforce, A Practical View

Command those who are rich in the things of this life not to be proud, but to place their hope, not in such an uncertain thing as riches, but in God, who generously gives us everything for our enjoyment.

The Bible, The apostle Paul, 1 Timothy 6:17

Wealth and slavery

Riches are a good handmaid, but the worst mistress.

Francis Bacon, The Advancement of Learning

Chains of gold are no less chains than chains of iron.

François Fénelon, Christian Perfection, letter to a lady at court

Banks and riches are chains of gold, but still chains.

Edmund Ruffin

A great fortune is a great slavery.

Seneca

Few rich men own their property. The property owns them.

Robert G. Ingersoll

Weariness

Art thou weary, art thou languid, Art thou sore distressed?
'Come to me,' saith One, 'and coming, Be at rest.'

J.M. Neale

Weddings

The Lord sanctify and bless you, the Lord pour the riches of his grace upon you,
that you may please him
and live together in holy love
to your lives' end.
So be it.

John Knox

Weeping   see MOURNING; TEARS

Wholeheartedness

God will put up with a great many things in the human heart, but there is one thing he will not put up with . . . a second place.

John Ruskin

Will

I knew Jesus, and he was very precious to my soul: but I found something in me that would not keep sweet and patient and kind. I did what I could to keep it down, but it was there. I besought Jesus to do something for me and when I gave him my will, he came to my heart, and took out all that would not be patient, and then he shut the door.

George Fox

Will-power   see also DISCIPLINE; FREE WILL

Will is to grace as the horse is to the rider.

Augustine of Hippo, De Libero Arbitrio

An ounce of will-power is worth a pound of learning.

Nicholas Murry Butler, President of Columbia University

True will-power and courage are not on the battlefield, but in everyday conquests over our inertia, laziness, boredom.

Dwight L. Moody

Too many develop every talent except the most vital one of all, the talent to use their talents . . . will-power.

Francis Bacon

Do one thing every day for no other reason than that you don't feel like doing it: the will is the man. Will makes giants.

William James

Wills

I testify and declare that I trust to no other security for my salvation than this alone, that as God is the Father of mercy, so he will show himself such a Father to me, who acknowledge myself to be a miserable sinner.

From John Calvin's will

Wisdom   see also LEARNING; PROVERBS

It is the Lord who gives wisdom.

The Bible, Proverbs 2:6

Wisdom offers you long life, as well as wealth and honour.

The Bible, Proverbs 3:16

Getting wisdom is the most important thing you can do. Whatever else you do, get insight.

The Bible, Proverbs 4:7

Wisdom will add years to your life.

The Bible, Proverbs 9:11

Being wise is better than being strong.

The Bible, Proverbs 24:5

Wisdom does more for a person than ten rulers can do for a city.

The Bible, Ecclesiastes 7:19

If any of you lacks wisdom, he should pray to God, who will give it to him.

The Bible, James 1:5

Wisdom from above is pure first of all; it is also peaceful, gentle, and friendly; it is full of compassion and produces a harvest of good deeds; it is free from prejudice and hypocrisy.

The Bible, James 3:17

Wisdom is nine-tenths a matter of being wise in time.

Theodore Roosevelt

A man may learn wisdom even from a foe.

Aristophanes, The Birds

The man of the present acts prudently from the example of the past, so as not to imperil the future.

Titian, in his allegorical painting of Prudence showing the heads of a youth, a mature man and an old man

Wisdom and happiness

Though a man had all the wisdom of the world and by his wit could compass upon earth what his heart could wish, yet if he fail in providing for true happiness all his wisdom is but madness.

Edward Dering

Only a wise man knows what things really mean. Wisdom makes him smile and makes his frowns disappear.

The Bible, Ecclesiastes 8:1

Wisdom and humility

Knowledge is proud that he has learn'd so much;
If you listen to advice and are willing to learn, one day you will be wise.

The Bible, Proverbs 19:20

Wisdom is humble that he knows no more.

William Cowper

Great wisdom is generous; petty wisdom is contentious. Great speech is impassioned, small speech cantankerous.

Chuang Tzu

Who is the wise man? He who learns from all men.

William Ewart Gladstone

Wisdom and knowledge

Knowledge comes, but wisdom lingers.

Alfred, Lord Tennyson

Wisdom by its very name implies an eminent abundance of knowledge, which enables a man to judge of all things, for everyone can judge well what he fully knows. Some have this abundance of knowledge as a result of learning and study, added to a native quickness of intelligence; and this is the wisdom Aristotle counts among the intellectual virtues. But others have wisdom as a result of the kinship which they have with the things of God; it is of such the apostle says, 'The spiritual man judges all things.' The gift of wisdom gives a man this eminent knowledge as a result of his union with God, and this union can only be his by love, for 'he who cleaves to God is one spirit with him'. And therefore the gift of wisdom leads to a godlike and explicit gaze at revealed truth, which mere faith holds in a manner as it were disguised.

Thomas Aquinas

Wisdom is the right use of knowledge. To know is not to be wise. Many men know a great deal, and are all the greater fools for it. There is no fool so great as the knowing fool. But to know how to use knowledge is to have wisdom.

C.H. Spurgeon

Wisdom and riches

Wisdom is often found under a shabby cloak.

Cicero

I am Wisdom, I am better than jewels; nothing you want can compare with me.

The Bible, Proverbs 8:11

It is better – much better – to have wisdom and knowledge than gold and silver.

The Bible, Proverbs 16:16

Wise people

The wise man draws more advantages from his enemies than a fool from his friends.

Thomas Fuller, Gnomologia

He is the wisest man who knows himself to be very ill-qualified for the attainment of wisdom.

Plato

Wise sayings   see also PROVERBS; QUOTATION

Wise sayings are like great men talking to us. It's the closest most of us can get to greatness. They are the cheapest teachers, consultants, advisers, guidelines, pilots, signposts, guardians and counsellors. They make us wise in one hundredth of the time of any other sources of knowledge or wisdom. Get closely acquainted with them. They're short cuts to wisdom. Yes, they're just common sense, but common sense ten feet high. Few young people accept such simple truths as found in them. No glamour, no hocus-pocus, no dramatics, no magic; just old-fashioned words, but power found nowhere else.

Author unknown

Wishful thinking

The mind is always prone to believe what it wishes to be true.

Heliodorus

Nothing is so easy as to deceive oneself; for everyone readily believes what he wishes to be true, even though the truth is far otherwise.

Demosthenes

Wit

Wit without discretion is a fool with a sword.

Spanish proverb

Witchcraft

Thou shalt not suffer a witch to live.

The Bible, Exodus 22:18 (AV)

Witness   see also EXAMPLE; TESTIMONIES TO CHRIST

Gentlemen, I am nothing; you are nothing; Beethoven is everything.

Arturo Toscanini to the orchestra when rehearsing a Beethoven symphony

He who does not bellow the truth, when he knows the truth, makes himself the accomplice of liars and forgers.

Charles Péguy, Basic Verities

Fear God, and where you go men will think they walk in hallowed cathedrals.

Ralph Waldo Emerson

If you want his monument, look around you.

Monument to Christopher Wren, in St Paul's Cathedral

One loving soul sets another on fire.

Augustine of Hippo

Every atom in the universe can act on every other atom, but only through the atom next to it. And if a man would act upon every other man, he can do so best by acting, one at a time, upon those beside him.

Henry Drummond

I spent the evening praying incessantly for divine assistance and that I might not be self-dependent. What I passed through was remarkable, and there appeared to be nothing of any importance to me but holiness of heart and life, and the conversion of the heathen to God. I cared not where or how I lived, or what hardships I went through so that I could but gain souls to Christ.

David Brainerd, diary, 21 July 1744

He buries gold who hides the truth.

Pythagoras

A candle lights others and consumes itself.

Jewish proverb

Witness through behaviour

Lord, make me like crystal, that your light may shine through me.

Katherine Mansfield

I have seen Christianity and it doesn't work.

Mahatma Gandhi

You Christians must begin to live like Jesus Christ. You must practise your religion without adulterating it or toning it down. You must put your emphasis on love; for love is the centre and soul of Christianity.

*Mahatma Gandhi, when Sadhu
Sundar Singh asked him how
Christianity could capture India*

Show me that you are redeemed and then I will believe in your redeemer.

Friedrich Nietzsche

To try too hard to make people good is one way to make them worse; the only way to make them good is to be good.

George Macdonald

I commend cheerfulness to all who would win souls; not levity and frothiness, but a genial, happy spirit. There are more flies caught with honey than with vinegar, and there will be more souls led to heaven by a man who wears heaven in his face than by one who bears Tartarus in his looks.

*C.H. Spurgeon, Lectures to my
Students*

Among the weak in faith I become weak like one of them, in order to win them. So I become all things to all men, that I may save some of them by whatever means are possible.

*The Bible, The apostle Paul,
1 Corinthians 9:22*

Let your light so shine before men, that they may see your good works.

*The Bible, Jesus Christ,
Matthew 5:16 (AV)*

Witness through speaking

There are some people who would never have fallen in love if they had never heard love talked about.

La Rochefoucauld

If anyone declares publicly that he belongs to me, I will do the same for him before my Father in heaven. But if anyone rejects me publicly, I will reject him before my Father in heaven.

*The Bible, Jesus Christ,
Matthew 10:32*

Go ye into all the world, and preach the gospel to every creature.

*The Bible, Jesus Christ,
Mark 16:15 (AV)*

Be ready at all times to answer anyone who asks you to explain the hope you have in you.

The Bible, 1 Peter 3:15

If he has faith, the believer cannot be restrained. He betrays himself. He breaks out. He confesses and teaches this gospel to the people at the risk of life itself.

*Martin Luther, preface to his
translation of the New Testament*

Wives

Find a wife and you find a good thing; it shows that the Lord is good to you.

The Bible, Proverbs 18:22

Man's best possession is a sympathetic wife.

Euripides, Antigone

Women   see also EVE

Each time that a man prolongs converse with a woman he causes evil to himself, and desists from the law, and in the end inherits Gehinnom.

Rabbinic saying

Woman was God's second blunder.

*Friedrich Nietzsche,
Antichrist*

I'm not denyin' the women are foolish: God Almighty made 'em to match the men.

George Eliot, Adam Bede, ch. 53

I consider the woman who has lost her modesty, lost indeed.

Plautus

Being a woman is a terribly difficult trade, since it consists principally of dealing with men.

Joseph Conrad

The great question . . . which I have not been able to answer, despite my thirty years of research into the feminine soul, is 'What does a woman want?'

Sigmund Freud

Women, Education of

To make women learned and foxes tame hath the same effect – to make them cunning.

James I

That learning belongs not to the female character, and that the female mind is not capable of a degree of improvement equal to that of the other sex, are narrow and unphilosophical prejudices.

Vicesimus Knox, Essays

Women, Inferiority of

Men have authority over women because Allah has made the one superior to the other. . . . As for those from whom you fear disobedience, admonish them and send them to beds apart and beat them.

Qur'ān, Sura 4

Once made equal to man, woman becomes his superior.

Socrates

[Wives are] in servitude to their husbands, a servitude . . . promoting obedience in all things.

Philo

The woman is inferior to the man in every way.

Josephus, Against Apion

Females are imperfect males, accidently produced by the father's inadequacy or by the malign influence of a moist south wind.

Aristotle, The Generation of Animals

Women, Leadership of

Still?

Winston Churchill, when told that people were saying women would be ruling the world by the year 2010

Women, Superiority of

Woman is a transitional creature between men and angels.

Honoré de Balzac

There is a woman at the origin of everything great.

Lamartine

Women, Wisdom of

No one knows like a woman how to say things that are at once gentle and deep.

Victor Hugo

A woman's guess is much more accurate than a man's certainty.

Rudyard Kipling, Plain Tales from the Hills

Women and religion

The weaker sex, to piety more prone.

William Alexander, Doomsday, V.lv

Better that the words of the law should be burned than delivered to women.

Rabbinic saying

Women and the fall of man

You are the devil's gateway; you are the unsealer of that (forbidden) tree; you are the first deserter of the divine law; you are she who persuaded him

whom the devil was not valiant enough to attack. You destroyed so easily God's image, man. On account of your desert – that is, death – even the Son of God had to die.

Tertullian, On the Apparel of Women, 1.1

Women and the home

Women are best suited to the indoor life which never strays from the house.

Philo

Homes are made by the wisdom of women, but are destroyed by foolishness.

The Bible, Proverbs 14:1

Women's rights

The extension of women's rights is the basic principle of all social progress.

Charles Fourier, Théorie des Quatre Mouvements

Women are not altogether in the wrong when they refuse the rules of life laid down for the world, for it is only men who have laid them down, and without women's consent.

Montaigne

Women are supposed to be very calm generally: but women feel just as men feel; they need exercise for their faculties, and a field for their efforts as much as their brothers do; they suffer from too rigid a constraint, too absolute a stagnation, precisely as men would suffer; and it is narrow-minded in their more privileged fellow-creatures to say that they ought to confine themselves to making puddings and knitting stockings, to playing on the piano and embroidering bags. It is thoughtless to condemn them, or laugh at them, if they seek to do more or learn more than custom has pronounced necessary for their sex.

Charlotte Brontë

Respect for women is the test of national progress in social life.

Grégoire

Whatever it is morally right for a man to do it is morally right for a woman to do.

Sarah Grimké, Letters on the Equality of the Sexes and the Condition of Women, Boston, 1838

Votes for women and purity for men

Early suffragette slogan

Wonder   see also MYSTERY

Two things fill the mind with ever-increasing wonder and awe, the more often and the more intensely the mind is drawn to them: the starry heavens above me and the moral law within me.
Immanuel Kant

Wonder is the basis of worship.
Thomas Carlyle

Men love to wonder, and that is the seed of science.
Ralph Waldo Emerson

Wonder is the feeling of a philosopher, and philosophy begins in wonder.
Socrates

Word of God

The Word of God is not a sounding but a piercing word, not pronounceable by the tongue but efficacious in the mind, not sensible to the ear but fascinating to the affection.
Bernard of Clairvaux, Sermons on the Canticles

The Word is the face, the countenance, the representation of God, in whom he is brought to light and made known.
Clement of Alexandria, Paedagogus

Words

'When *I* use a word,' Humpty Dumpty said in a rather scornful tone, 'it means just what I choose it to mean – neither more nor less.'
Lewis Carroll, Through the Looking Glass, ch. 6

Our words are a faithful index of the state of our souls.
Francis de Sales

Words and deeds   see also ACTION; SPEECH

Words and deeds are quite indifferent modes of the divine energy. Words are also actions, and actions are a kind of words.
Ralph Waldo Emerson

Work   see also GENIUS

Love of bustle is not work.
Seneca, Epistles

Man at work can be happy and spiritually healthy only if he feels that he is working in God's world for God's glory through doing what is God's will.
Arnold J. Toynbee

Monsieur de Balzac is requested not to come to work today as there is a great deal of work to be done.
Message reputed to have been sent to the novelist by the firm of lawyers for whom he once worked

Work hard at whatever you do, because there will be no action, no thought, no knowledge, no wisdom in the world of the dead – and that is where you are going.
The Bible, Ecclesiastes 9:10

Work is the refuge of people who have nothing better to do.
Oscar Wilde

Do what you can, with what you have, where you are.
Theodore Roosevelt

Honour lies in honest toil.
Grover Cleveland

Patience and ability for the work is not given before the work, but only through the work.
Andrew Murray

My father taught me to work; he did not teach me to love it.
Abraham Lincoln

Whatsoever we beg of God, let us also work for it.
Jeremy Taylor

To travel hopefully is a better thing than to arrive, and the true success is to work.
Robert Louis Stevenson

Work is the only pleasure. It is only work that keeps me alive and makes life worth living. I was happier when doing a mechanic's job.
Henry Ford

In all labour there is profit: but the talk of the lips tendeth only to penury.
The Bible, Proverbs 14:23 (AV)

Work, Limitations of

Lo! Men have become the tools of their tools.
Henry David Thoreau

To do great work a man must be very idle as well as very industrious.
Samuel Butler

I dressed the wound, but God healed him.
Ambroise Paré; inscription on wall of the École de Médicine, Paris

It is the Lord's blessing that makes you wealthy. Hard work can make you no richer.

The Bible, Proverbs 10:22

Work, Need for

If you do not wish God's kingdom, don't pray for it. But if you do, you must do more than pray for it; you must work for it.

John Ruskin

A thing worth having is never obtained without hard work.

Demophilus

Unless the clay be well pounded, no pitcher can be made.

Latin proverb

The only place where success comes before work is in the dictionary.

Author unknown

No athlete is crowned except in the sweat of his brow.

Jerome, Letters

If any would not work, neither should he eat.

The Bible, The apostle Paul, 2 Thessalonians 5:17 (AV)

Work, Perfection in

It's not good enough for Josiah Wedgewood!

Josiah Wedgewood's assertion every time he inspected one of his company's pots that was slightly imperfect, and which he would smash

Work, Reluctance to

What is everybody's work is nobody's.

Spanish proverb

I like work; it fascinates me; I can sit and look at it for hours.

Jerome K. Jerome, Three Men in a Boat

Everyone wants to harvest. Nobody wants to plough.

Author unknown

Work and overwork

Don't let Satan make you overwork and then put you out of action for a long period.

Charles Simeon

It requires more deeply-rooted zeal for God to keep within our strength for his sake, than to exceed it. Look at all the young ministers: they run themselves out of breath in a year or two and in many instances never recover it. Is this wise?

Charles Simeon, writing to Daniel Wilson, Bishop of Calcutta

Work at ordinary things

. . . Let us be content, in work,
To do the thing we can, and not presume
To fret because it's little.

Elizabeth Barrett Browning

Christians should do common things uncommonly well.

From the film And Now Miguel

Work for God's sake

A servant with this clause
Makes drudgery divine;
Who sweeps a room as for thy laws
Makes that and th'action fine.

George Herbert

All work must be done very simply and quietly because God puts it into our hands to do.

J.S.B. Monsell

God is a busy worker, but he loves help.

Basque proverb

O God, help us to perform our duties with laughter and kind faces; and let cheerfulness abound with industry. Give us to go blithely on our business all this day, and bring us to our resting beds weary and content and undishonoured; for Jesus Christ's sake.

Robert Louis Stevenson

Let us work as if success depended upon ourselves alone; but with heartfelt conviction that we are doing nothing and God everything.

Ignatius Loyola

Forth in thy name, O Lord, I go,
My daily labour to pursue,
Thee, only thee, resolved to know,
In all I think, or speak, or do.

Charles Wesley

O Lord, temper with tranquillity
Our manifold activity,
That we may do our work for thee
With very great simplicity.

Author unknown

O Lord, you sell us all good things at the price of work.

Leonardo da Vinci

Do all your work in love.

The Bible, The apostle Paul, 1 Corinthians 16:14

Working class

The workers have nothing to lose but their chains. They have a world to gain. Workers of the world, unite.

Karl Marx, Manifesto of the Communist Party, 4

World

The world and all that is in it belong to the Lord;
the earth and all who live on it are his.

The Bible, Psalm 24:1

The world has become a global village.

Marshall McLuhan

How swiftly the glory of the world passes!

Thomas à Kempis, The Imitation of Christ

Call the world if you please 'The Vale of Soul-Making'. Then you will find out the use of the world.

John Keats

World, Concern for   see also SOCIAL REFORM; SOCIETY AND THE CHRISTIAN

The least pain in our little finger gives us more concern and uneasiness than the destruction of our fellow-beings.

William Hazlitt

My brothers and sisters, the evangelical tradition is free salvation, scriptural holiness and social righteousness.

John Wesley, in the last letter he ever wrote, encouraging Wilberforce to continue the fight against slavery

Our sympathy is cold to the relation of distant misery.

Edward Gibbon

Those who do not feel pain seldom think that it is felt.

Samuel Johnson

World, Love of

We can love the world, or love God. If we love the world, there will be no room in our heart for the love of God. We cannot love both God, who is eternal, and the world, which is transitory.

Augustine of Hippo, Treatise on the First Letter of St John

Worldliness

'The world' is an enemy to the Christian's soul, and there is an utter opposition between the friendship of the world and the friendship of Christ.

J.C. Ryle, Practical Religion

Worry   see also ANXIETY

Don't give in to worry or anger;
it only leads to trouble.

The Bible, Psalm 37:8

'Don't you worry and don't you hurry.' I know that phrase by heart, and if all the other music perish out of the world it would still sing to me.

Mark Twain

Worry can rob you of happiness, but kind words will cheer you up.

The Bible, Proverbs 12:25

It takes 45 muscles of the face to frown but only 17 to smile.

Author unknown

Don't worry about anything, but in all your prayers ask God for what you need, always praising him with a thankful heart.

The Bible, The apostle Paul, Philippians 4:6

Do not worry.

The Bible, 1 Peter 3:14

No man ever sank under the burden of the day. It is when tomorrow's burden is added to the burden of today that the weight is more than a man can bear. Never load yourself so. If you find yourself so loaded, at least remember this: it is your own doing, not God's. He begs you to leave the future to him, and mind the present.

George Macdonald

We know nothing of tomorrow; our business is to be good and happy today.

Sydney Smith

Good morning, theologians! You wake and sing. But I, old fool, know less than you and worry over everything, instead of simply trusting in the heavenly Father's care.

Martin Luther, addressing the birds as he walked through the woods

The worried cow would have lived till now
If she had saved her breath;
But she feared her hay wouldn't last all day,
And she mooed herself to death.

Taylor Smith

Tomorrow makes today's whole head sick, its whole heart faint. When we should be still, sleeping or dreaming, we are fretting about an hour that lies a half sun's journey away! Not so doest thou, Lord.

George Macdonald

A hundred years' fret will not pay a penny of debt.

French proverb

Worship   see also PRAISE OF GOD

One day spent in your Temple
is better than a thousand anywhere
else;
I would rather stand at the gate of the
house of my God
than live in the homes of the wicked.

The Bible, Psalm 84:10

God is spirit, and his worshippers must worship in spirit and in truth.

*The Bible, Jesus Christ,
John 4:24 (NIV)*

To worship is to quicken the conscience by the holiness of God, to feed the mind with the truth of God, to purge the imagination by the beauty of God, to open the heart to the love of God, to devote the will to the purpose of God.

William Temple

I saw the heavens opened, and the Great White God sitting on the throne.

*Handel, telling how he wrote the
Hallelujah chorus*

We hold our general meeting on the Sun's Day because it is the first day, when God sent darkness and chaos packing and made the world; and on the same day Jesus Christ our Saviour rose from the dead.

Justin Martyr, Apologia

All hail the power of Jesus' name;
Let angels prostrate fall;
Bring forth the royal diadem
To crown him Lord of all.

Edward Perronet

The holy time is quiet as a nun
Breathless with adoration.

*William Wordsworth,
Miscellaneous Sonnets*

To believe God is to worship God.

Martin Luther

A triangle with one side left out.

*Friedrich von Hügel on religion
which ignores the adoration of God*

Till you can sing and rejoice and delight in God as misers do in gold, and kings in sceptres, you can never enjoy the world.

Thomas Traherne

'Sing to the Lord a new song,' the psalm tells us.
'I do sing!' you may reply.
You sing, of course you sing. I can hear you. But make sure that your life sings the same tune as your mouth. Sing with your voices. Sing with your hearts. Sing with your lips. Sing with your lives. Be yourselves what the words are about! If you live good lives, you yourselves are the songs of new life.

Augustine of Hippo

No one gives himself freely and willingly to God's service unless, having tasted his fatherly love, he is drawn to love and worship him in return.

John Calvin

The capital of heaven is the heart in which Jesus Christ is enthroned as king.

Sundar Singh

Wonder is the basis of worship.

Thomas Carlyle

Worship is transcendent wonder.

Thomas Carlyle

God be in my head,
And in my understanding;

God be in my eyes,
And in my looking;

God be in my mouth
And in my speaking;

God be in my heart,
And in my thinking;

God be at my end,
And at my departing.

Sarum Missal

The glory of God is a living man; and the life of man consists in beholding God.

Irenaeus, Against Heresies

Worth

The tiniest hair casts a shadow.

Goethe

Wrath of God   see GOD'S WRATH

Writing

Reading maketh a full man; conference a ready man; and writing an exact man.

Francis Bacon, Essays, Of Studies

Words fly, writing remains.
Spanish proverb

The ink of the scholar is more sacred than the blood of the martyr.
Muhammad

Without books God is silent.
Thomas Bartholin

Books are fatal: they are the curse of the human race. Nine-tenths of existing books are nonsense, and the clever books are the refutation of that nonsense. The greatest misfortune that ever befell man was the invention of printing.
Benjamin Disraeli

I penetrate the soul without neglecting the body.
Honoré de Balzac, on his novels depicting the whole of French life

This morning I took out a comma and this afternoon I put it in again.
Oscar Wilde

Give me twenty-six lead soldiers and I will conquer the world!
Karl Marx, referring to the letters of the alphabet in printer's type

I never desire to converse with a man who has written more than he has read.
Samuel Johnson

The spoken word perishes, but the written letter abides.
Latin proverb

Use the eraser frequently if you want to write anything worth reading twice.
Latin proverb

The pen is mightier than the sword.
Medieval proverb

The two most engaging powers of an author are to make new things familiar and familiar things new.
William Makepeace Thackeray

Y

Yawning

A yawn is a silent shout.
G.K. Chesterton

Young people

The young people of today think of nothing but themselves. They have no reverence for parents or old age. They are impatient of all restraint. They talk as if they know everything, and what passes for wisdom with us is foolishness to them.
Peter, a monk, AD 1274

How can a young man keep his life pure?
By obeying your commands.
The Bible, Psalm 119:9

When I look at the younger generation, I despair of the future of civilisation.
Aristotle

Youth

There is a feeling of eternity in youth.
William Hazlitt

Z

Zeal

Zeal is fit only for wise men, but is found mostly in fools.
Thomas Fuller, Gnomologia

Zeal without knowledge is fire without light.
Thomas Fuller, Gnomologia

We are sometimes moved by passion and suppose it zeal.
Thomas à Kempis

Dear Crito, your zeal is invaluable, if a right one; but if wrong, the greater the zeal the greater the danger.
Socrates

I could bear to be torn in pieces, if I could but hear the sobs of penitence – if I could but see the eyes of faith directed to the Redeemer!
Henry Martyn

Zeal, Thoughtless

[Some] can sin more from thoughtless zeal than pride. When they see that, after people have heard the Gospel, their lives do not match up to their beliefs, they conclude that no Church exists at all.
John Calvin, The Institutes of Christian Religion, 4.1.13

Index of Sources

Abelard, Peter   *1079–1142*
French philosopher and theologian
  Questions
Acton, John
1st Baron Acton; English historian
and politician
  Power
Acts of John
Greek apocryphal work
  Sex
Acts of Paul and Thecla   *2nd century*
Greek apocryphal work
  Paul, The apostle
Adams, Henry Brooks   *1838–1918*
US historian
  Education
  Experience
  Humility
  Philosophy
  Teachers
Adams, John   *1735–1826*
Second president of the US; one of the
writers of the Declaration of
Independence
  Bereavement
  Knowledge, Means to
  Roman Catholic Church
Addison, Joseph   *1672–1719*
English essayist and poet
  Advice
  Hope
  Last words
  Music
  Sunday
  Tradition
  Unhappiness
Æschines   *389?–314? BC*
Athenian orator
  Accusation, False

Aeschylus   *525?–456? BC*
Greek tragic dramatist
  Death, Non-Christian views of
  Error
  Evil
  Old age and maturing
  Promises of God
  Suffering, Learning from
Æsop   *620?–564 BC*
Greek writer of fables
  Kindness
  Perseverance
  Reality
Aggrey, Dr   *–1927*
of the Gold Coast (now Ghana)
  Race
Albert I   *1255?–1308*
King of Germany
  God's love, Response to
Alcuin   *735–804*
English scholar and theologian
  People
Alexander, Mrs Cecil Frances
1823–1895
Irish hymn-writer
  Cross
Alexander, Sir William   *1567?–1640*
Earl of Stirling; Scottish politician
and poet
  Women and religion
Alfonso the Wise   *1221–1284*
King of Castile
  Creation
Alfred   *849–899*
King of Wessex
  Self-discipline
Alleine, Mrs Joseph   *17th century*
wife of the Puritan minister
  Prayer, People of

Allilueva, Svetlana *20th-century*
Daughter of Joseph Stalin
Testimonies to Christ
Allshorn, Florence
Ideals
Ambrose *340?–397*
Bishop of Milan; composer and
hymn-writer
Behaviour
Christian life as following Jesus
Christians
Temptation, Purpose of
Amiel, Henri Frédéric *1821–1881*
Swiss diarist
Action
Mankind
Old age and maturing
Thinking and action
Anacreon *572?–488? BC*
Greek poet
God's love
Andrewes, Lancelot *1555–1626*
Bishop of Chichester and then Ely and
then Winchester; one of the translators
of the Authorised Version of the Bible
Church
Angot *1581–16??*
French poet
Money
Anselm *1033?–1109*
Archbishop of Canterbury; Scholastic
theologian who defended the faith by
the use of reason
Christ, Divinity of
God's existence
Perseverance to the end
Prayer, Method of
Salvation
Antiphanes *4th century BC*
Greek comic poet
Inner life
Antony *251?–356?*
of Egypt; one of the desert fathers;
reputed to have fought with demons in
the form of wild beasts
Self
Archias *2nd–1st century BC*
Greek poet
Procrastination
Aristides, Marcus *5th century BC*
Athenian statesman and soldier
Christians, Early
God's nature
Aristophanes *448?–380? BC*
Greek comic poet
Enemies

Thinking and action
Wisdom
Aristotle *384–322 BC*
Greek philosopher who studied under
Plato and was the dominant influence
on medieval thought
Affection
Anger
Art
Beauty
Democracy
Disability
Education
Gentleness
Good deeds
Government
Happiness
Humour
Hope
Laughter
Learning
Mankind, compared with animals
Nature
Politics
Revolutions
Virtue
Women, Inferiority of
Young people
Arnold, George *1834–1865*
Charity
Arnold, Matthew *1822–1888*
English poet and inspector of schools;
also wrote essays on literature and
religion
Last words
Miracles
Religion
Truth and the dying
Astley, Jacob *1579–1652*
English soldier in the Civil War
Busyness
Athanasius *296?–373*
patriarch of Alexandria; defended
Christian orthodoxy against Arianism
Christ, Mission of
Holy Spirit
Incarnation
Athenagoras *2nd century*
Christian apologist
Christians, Early
Auden, Wystan Hugh *1907–1973*
English poet
Sacrifice
Augsburg Confession *1530*
Lutheran confession of faith
Free will

Augustine *354–430*
Bishop of Hippo in North Africa; one
of the most influential theologians in
the Christian church
  Abstinence
  Action
  Adversity
  Anger, Positive views of
  Beauty
  Boasting
  Bible, Obedience to
  Bible, Reading the
  Blindness
  Boasting
  Change
  Christ
  Christian unity
  Christmas
  Church
  Church visible
  Compassion
  Despair
  Detachment
  Doubt
  Endurance
  Error
  Eternal life
  Faith
  Faith and reason
  Fear
  Forgiveness
  Forgiving others
  Free will
  Fulfilment
  God and mankind
  God, as Creator
  God's care
  God's love
  God's mercy
  God's nature
  God's presence in the believer's heart
  God's will
  Good deeds
  Grace
  Grace and human will
  Growth, Spiritual
  Heaven, Nature of
  Heresy
  Humility, Importance of, in
    Christianity
  Humility, Nature of
  Idols defined
  Illness
  Knowledge
  Knowledge of God
  Law of God
  Little things

  Longing for God
  Lord's Supper to be received worthily
  Lordship of Christ
  Love, Learning
  Love and God's nature
  Love for God
  Mankind, Insignificance of
  Mankind, potential with God
  Mankind, Social aspects of
  Martyrdom
  Martyrdom, Effects of
  Maturity
  Miracles
  Motherhood
  Neighbour, Love for, and love for God
  Old Testament
  Peace of God desired
  Perfection
  Praise of God
  Prayer and the heart's desire
  Prayer, Definitions of
  Preaching and practice
  Pride
  Pride and what it leads to
  Procrastination
  Punishment
  Repentance
  Rest
  Reward
  Roman Catholic Church
  Sacraments
  Salvation
  Salvation, as God's gift
  Searching for God
  Searching for God in one's interior
  Second coming of Christ
  Service, Prayers dedicating the self to
  Sex
  Sin
  Sin, Definition of
  Sorrow
  Tears
  Trinity
  Trust in God – for the future
  Truth and mankind
  Will-power
  Witness
  World, Love of
  Worship
Ausonius, Decimus Magnus *309?–390*
Roman poet and tutor to the Emperor
Gratian
  Beginning
Austen, Jane *1775–1817*
English novelist
  Ministers of religion

Aylward, Gladys *1902–1970*
English missionary in China
  Weakness
Bacon, Francis *1561–1626*
1st Baron Verulam; English
philosopher and essayist
  Adversity
  Anger
  Beauty
  Behaviour
  Boasting
  Careers
  Cheerfulness
  Doubt
  Fear
  Friendship
  Gardens
  God, Belief in
  Hospitality
  Hypocrisy
  Knowledge
  Learning
  Mankind, Nature of
  Mankind, potential with God
  Miracles
  Misery
  Money
  Nature
  Opportunity
  Peace of God and the death of Jesus
  Preaching, Purposes of
  Questions
  Reading
  Revenge
  Self
  Truth in relationships
  Wealth and slavery
  Will-power
  Writing
Bagehot, Walter *1826–1877*
English literary critic and political
theorist and editor of *The Economist*
  Ideas
  Marriage
Baillie, D.M.
theologian
  God's wrath
Baker, H.W. *1821–1877*
English clergyman and hymn-writer
  Bible, as the Word of God
Balzac, Honoré de *1799–1850*
French novelist who attempted a
realistic portrayal of all of French
society
  Action
  Envy

  Husbands
  Women, Superiority of
  Writing
Barclay, William
Scottish theologian
  Humility
Barnardo, Thomas John *1845–1905*
Irish doctor and founder of
orphanages; specially known for his
work in London's East End
  Character
  Conversion of Barnardo
  God's provision
  Missionary call
  Stewardship
Barnardo's Homes
  Mottoes
Barrie, J.M. *1860–1937*
Scottish dramatist and novelist
  Courage
  Humility, Learning
Barth, Karl *1886–1959*
German Protestant theologian
  Christ
  Faith
  Hope
  Theology
Barthélemy, *1796–1867*
French poet
  Change
Bartholin, Thomas *1616–1680*
  Writing
Basil *330–379*
the Great; founder of the ideal of
monastic community life
  Holy Spirit and free will
Baudelaire, Charles *1821–1867*
French poet
  Prayer, Occasions and times of
Baxter, J.S.
  Holy Spirit
Baxter, Richard *1615–1691*
English Puritan minister and religious
writer
  Families
  Humility, Importance of in
    Christianity
  Last words
  Prayer, Intercessory
  Preaching, Manner of
  Preaching, Skill in
  Preaching and practice
  Regeneration
  Resurrection
Bayly, Lewis
  Sabbath

Beattie
Martyrdom
Beckett, Thomas   *1118–1170*
Archbishop of Canterbury
Martyrdom welcomed
Becon, Thomas   *1511?–1567*
English Reformation theologian; a
follower of Zwingli
Faith
Becque, Henri   *1837–1899*
French dramatist
Equality
Bede   *673?–735*
English biblical scholar and church
historian; a monk at Wearmouth and
Jarrow
Last words
Neighbour, Love for, and love for God
Beecher, Henry Ward   *1813–1887*
US preacher and journalist
Anger
Anger, Righteous
Christian life
Compassion
Forgiving others
Giving
Greatness
Motherhood
Predestination
Proverbs
Reformation, Personal
Success
Theology
Truth and error
Beethoven, Ludwig van   *1770–1827*
German composer
Last words
Bell, Alexander Graham   *1847–1922*
US inventor
Proverbs
Benedict   *480?–547?*
Italian monk who founded the
Benedictine order and wrote the Rule
which formed the basis of all Western
Christian monasticism
Illness
Obedience
Bengel, J.A.   *1687–1752*
Lutheran New Testament scholar
Bible, Reading the
Joy
Mary
Bennett, Arnold   *1867–1931*
English writer
Dignity
Husbands

Benson, R.H.   *1871–1914*
Faith and reason
Love and humility
Berdyaev, Nicholas   *1874–1948*
Russian philosopher who wrote about
Christianity as the life of the spirit
Attitude
Evangelism
God and mankind
Bernard, Claude   *1813–1878*
French physiologist
Art
Bernard   *1090–1153*
Abbot of Clairvaux; author of a
monastic Rule and several mystical
works
Confession
Forgiveness
Freedom
Grace and nature
Growth, Spiritual
Holiness
Knowledge
Love for God
Name of Jesus
Nature
Neighbour, Love for, and love for God
Perseverance
Pride and what it leads to
Sanctification
Sight, Spiritual
Spirituality
Victory
Word of God
Bernard
early Franciscan brother
Last words
Berridge, John   *1716–1793*
English clergyman
Epitaphs
Preaching and the gospel message
Bewes, Richard   *1934–*
English clergyman
Religions, Non-Christian
Bhagavad Gita   *c.200 BC*
sacred text of Hinduism
Desire
Bias   *6th-century BC*
Greek philosopher
Beginning
Good deeds
Bible *(Authorised Version)*
Abundance
Adam and Eve
Adversity
Advice

Anger
Appearances
Atheism
Atonement
Backsliding
Belief
Charity
Children
Christ, as Mediator
Christ, as Shepherd
Christ, Mission of
Christ, Strength of
Christmas
Church
Comfort
Communal living
Conversion
Counselling
Creation
Cross
Death destroyed by God's power
Deceit
Discoveries
Duty
Enoch
Evil
Faith
Faith, Power of
Faith and action
Fear
Forgiveness
Forgiving others
Friends of God
Giving
Giving and getting
Giving willingly
God and mankind
God, as Creator
God, as Refuge
God, as Shepherd
God, as Sustainer
Godliness
God's care
God's holiness
God's invitation
God's love, Response to
God's nature
Good news
Grace
Happiness
Happiness, Sources of
Healing
Heaven
Holy Spirit, Fruit of the
Holy Spirit, Gifts of the
Home

Humility, Rewards of
Idleness
Instruction
Jealousy
Judging others
Kingdom of God
Kingdom of heaven
Knowledge, Warnings concerning
Life
Life after death
Love
Love and fear
Love and suffering
Mankind, Depravity of
Marriage
Meaninglessness
Meditation
Money, Love of
Mothers-in-law
Mottoes, Personal and family
Mourning
Nature as revealing God
Neighbour, Love for
Peace, False
Peace of God
Peace of God foretold
Pilgrimage
Positive thinking
Prayer, Persistence in
Preaching and the gospel message
Pride
Rebuke
Rejoicing
Renewal
Repentance
Rest
Restoration
Resurrection
Resurrection of Jesus
Righteousness
Sacrifice
Salvation
Salvation, as God's gift
Searching for God
Sin
Sin, Awareness of
Sin, Defeat of
Sin, Effects of
Sin, Seriousness of
Speech and self-control
Strangers
Temptation, Purpose of
Temptation, Ways to escape
Thinking and speech
Understanding
Violence

Vision
Witchcraft
Witness through behaviour
Witness through speaking
Work
Work, Need for
Bible *(Geneva Version)*
Adam and Eve
Bible, Translation of
Bible *(Good News Bible)*
Abandonment
Accepting God
Adultery
Advice
Ambition
Angels
Anger
Animals
Appearances
Argument
Arrogance
Atheism
Atonement
Authority
Beatitudes
Beauty
Beauty, Spiritual
Behaviour
Bible, Reading the
Bribery
Broken-heartedness
Call
Caring
Character
Children
Children of God
Christ
Christ, Baptism of
Christ, Birth of
Christ, Divinity of
Christ, Knocking
Christ, Life of
Christ, Mission of
Christ, Power of
Christ, Sinlessness of
Christian message
Christian unity
Christian upbringing
Christians
Christians, Early
Christians and the State
Christmas
Comfort
Compassion
Confession
Conscience

Consequences of evil
Contentment
Correction
Counselling
Covenant
Crises
Criticism
Cross
Dance
Dead, Christian
Death
Death, as leveller
Death destroyed by God's power
Death, Non-Christian views of
Decisions
Despair
Devil
Devil, Fighting the
Discipline
Divorce
Doctors
Drink
Duty
Eternal life
Evil
Example
Faith
Faith, Power of
Faith and action
Faithfulness
Falling away
Families
Family, The Christian
Farming
Fasting
Fathers in God
Fear
Food
Foolishness
Forgiveness
Forgiving others
Freedom, Christian
Friends of God
Friendship, in times of need
Friendship, Learning from
Future
Garrulity
Gentleness
Gifts
Giving
Giving and getting
Gloating
Goals
God, as Shepherd
God, greater than mankind
God's actions

God's image
God's judgement
God's love
God's love, Response to
God's nature
God's presence
God's protection
God's will
Good and evil
Good deeds
Gospel
Gossip
Grace
Grace and its effect on the believer
Grumbling
Guidance
Happiness, Sources of
Hate
Heaven
Heaven, Nature of
Hell
Heresy
Holy Spirit
Honesty
Hospitality
Humility
Humility, Rewards of
Husbands
Hypocrisy
Idleness
Idols
Insults
Jealousy
Joy
Judging others
Kindness
Law of God
Lies
Life, Spiritual
Listening
Living
Longing for God
Lord's Prayer
Lord's Supper
Lord's Supper to be received worthily
Love, Christian
Love, Sexual
Love and the faults of the beloved
Love for Christians
Love for enemies
Love for God
Loyalty
Lukewarmness
Mankind
Mankind, Inhumanity to man
Mankind, Insignificance of

Marriage
Marriage, Christian
Marriage and celibacy
Marriage and faithfulness
Marriage and heaven
Mary
Meaninglessness
Miracles
Missionary call
Mistakes
Money, Dissatisfaction with
Money, Love of
Money and the service of God
Morality
Motives
Nations
Nature, Redeemed
Neighbour, Love for
Neighbours
New creation
Obedience
Old age and maturing
Opinions, Other people's
Parenthood
Parents, Respect for
Passion
Patience
Peace
Peace and growth
Peace of God and the death of Jesus
Peace of God foretold
Pentecost
Perfection
Persecution
Perseverance
Poverty
Poverty, Relief of
Prayer
Prayer, Effects of on person praying
Preaching by God's command
Predestination
Prejudice
Pride and what it leads to
Promises of God
Prophecy
Prophets
Proverbs
Providence of God
Redemption
Rejection
Religion
Religions, Non-Christian
Remuneration
Respect of persons
Resurrection
Resurrection appearances

Resurrection of Jesus
Resurrection of the body
Revelations
Revenge
Reverence for God
Reward
Righteousness
Righteousness from God
Salvation
Science and Christianity
Second coming of Christ
Secrets
Security
Self-control
Self-examination
Sex
Sexual intercourse
Sin
Sin, Dealing with
Sin, Defeat of
Sin, Unforgivable
Smiling
Social action
Sowing
Speech, Thoughtless
Speech and self-control
Stumbling-blocks
Stupidity
Suffering
Suffering, Learning from
Swearing
Taxes
Teachers
Teamwork
Temptation, Resisting
Thinking, Maturity in
Thinking and character
Thinking and speech
Time
Tongues
Trouble
Trust in God
Trust in God – in battle
Trust in God – for the future
Union with God
Violence
Virgin birth
Weakness
Wealth and pride
Wisdom
Wisdom and happiness
Wisdom and humility
Wisdom and riches
Witness through behaviour
Witness through speaking
Wives

Women and the home
Work
Work, Need for
Work for God's sake
World
Worry
Worship
Young people
Bible *(New International Version)*
Worship
Bickerstaffe, Isaac   *1735?–1812?*
Irish dramatist
Contentment
Bickersteth, E.H.   *1825–1906*
Bishop of Exeter; hymn-writer
Peace of God and the death of Jesus
Prayer
Bierce, Ambrose   *1842–1914?*
US journalist and short story writer
Caution
Christians
Clairvoyance
Convents
Curiosity
Cynics
Diplomacy
Egotism
Faith
Fashion
Gossip
History
Knowledge
Marriage
Saints
Specialists
Speech and listening
Success
Billings, Josh   *1818–1885*
pseudonym of Henry Wheeler Shaw;
American comic essayist, philosopher
and wit
Money, Limits to the usefulness of
Bilney, Thomas   *–1537*
English Protestant martyr
Salvation, as experienced by Bilney
Binyon, Laurence   *1869–1943*
English poet
Death
Bion   *325?–255? BC*
Greek philosopher
Hell, Ways to
Bismarck, Otto von   *1915–1898*
German politician
Agreement
Education
Power

Truth
Truth examined
Blake, William   *1757–1827*
English engraver and visionary poet
  Action
  Animals
  Change
  Good deeds
  Gratitude
  Joy
  Love and self
  Mankind
  Mercy
  Morality
  Peace
Bliss, Philipp   *1838–1876*
US hymn-writer
  Cross, Personal response to
Bodin, Jean   *1530–1596*
  History
Boerhaave, Herman   *1668–1738*
Dutch professor of medicine and
chemistry
  Mankind
Bohler, Peter   *18th century*
Moravian pastor who helped John
Wesley come to his experience of
salvation
  Conversion
Bohn, H.G.   *1796–1884*
English publisher
  Morality
Boileau, Nicolas   *1636–1711*
French poet and critic who helped form
French literary taste
  Foolishness
Bolingbroke, Henry   *1678–1751*
1st Viscount Bolingbroke; English
politician
  Christianity
Bolsec, Hermes   *16th-century*
Carmelite monk from Paris; an
opponent of Calvin
  Election, Divine
Bonar, Horatius   *1808–1889*
Scottish clergyman and hymn-writer
  Patience
Bonaventure   *1221–1274*
Italian Franciscan theologian
  Cross
Bonhoeffer, Dietrich   *1906–1945*
German Lutheran theologian
  Christian life
  Christian life as following Jesus
Book of Common Prayer
  Bible

Bible, Sufficiency of
Charity
Death
Death in the midst of life
Death, Readiness for
Freedom, Christian
Government
Liturgy
Mankind, Depravity of
Mankind, Insignificance of
Marriage and celibacy
Mass
Possessions
Predestination
Purgatory
Reading
Reformation, Church
Resurrection of the body
War
Wealth
Booth, William   *1829–1912*
English evangelist; founder of the
Salvation Army
  Conversion of Booth
  Evangelism
  Goals, Examples of
  Last words
  Mottoes, Personal and family
  Music, Effects of
  Poverty, Relief of
  Power, Spiritual
  Social action
  Society
  Society and the Christian
  Sorrow
  Surrender
Bossuet, Jacques Benigne   *1627–1704*
French orator, philosopher and bishop
  Neighbour, Love for, and love for God
Boswell, James   *1740–1795*
Scottish and English lawyer;
biographer of Samuel Johnson
  Self
Bounds, E.M.
  Prayer, People of
  Prayer, Persistence in
  Preaching
Boyle, Robert   *1627–1691*
Irish chemist noted for his work on
gases and his separation of chemistry
from alchemy
  Difficulties in science
Bradford, John   *1510?–1555*
Anglican clergyman and English
Protestant martyr
  Grace and its effect on the believer

Bradshaw, John   *1602–1659*
English lawyer who passed the death
sentence on Charles I
  Revolutions
Bradstreet, Anne   *1612?–1672*
English poet who emigrated to
Massachusetts in 1630 and was one of
the earliest New England writers
  Death of a child
Brainerd, David   *18th-century*
US evangelist to American Indians
  Consecration
  Last words
  Prayer, Length of
  Witness
Brann, William Cowper   *1855–1898*
  Heresy
Braunstein, Richard
  Love and giving
Bray, Billy   *1794–1868*
Cornish tin-miner and evangelist
  Death, Readiness for
Brengle, Samuel
  Leadership
Bridges, Robert   *1844–1930*
English poet
  Spirituality
  Trust in God
Brillat-Savarin, Anthelme   *1755–1826*
French politician and gourmet
  Food
Brontë, Anne   *1820–1849*
English novelist
  Talents
Brontë, Charlotte   *1816–1855*
English novelist
  Women's rights
Brontë, Emily   *1818–1848*
English poet and novelist; sister of the
novelists Charlotte and Anne
  Death
Brooke, A.E.   *1863–1939*
English biblical scholar
  Love and giving
  Love for Christians
  Obedience
Brooke, Rupert   *1887–1915*
English poet
  War
Brooks, Phillips   *1835–1893*
Bishop of Massachusetts in the
Protestant Episcopal Church; noted
preacher
  Biography
  Prayer, Method of
  Preaching and practice

Broome, E.W.
  Music and the devil
Brown, Archibald G.
  Devil, Existence of
Brown, John
  Last words
Brown, T.E.   *1830–1897*
English minor poet
  God's presence in gardens
Browne, Thomas   *1605–1682*
English doctor and writer; author of
Religio Medici
  Fear of God
  Music, Effects of
Browning, Elizabeth Barrett
1806–1861
English poet; wife of Robert Browning
  God's gifts
  Marriage and love
  Peace of God
  Results
  Suffering, Learning from
  Work at ordinary things
Browning, Robert   *1812–1889*
English poet
  Beauty
  Change
  Conscience
  Darkness
  God's love, Response to
  Growth, Personal
  Ignorance
  Love
  Martyrdom
  Old age
  Service in small things
  Singleness of mind
  Truth and God
Bruce, A.B.
  Service
Bruce, F.F.   *20th century*
English theologian
  Perseverance to the end
  Sanctification
Brunner, Emil   *1889–1966*
Swiss theologian
  Mission
Buber, Martin   *1878–1965*
Jewish philosopher
  Food
  Love
Buchan, John   *1875–1940*
1st Baron Tweedsmuir; Scottish
novelist and statesman
  Atheism
  Humility

Buchanan, George   *1506–1582*
tutor to James VI of Scotland
  Humility, Examples of
  Last words
Buddha   *563?–483 BC*
Gautama Siddhartha; Indian prince
and religious teacher; founder of
Buddhism
  Compassion
  Hate
  Self
  Thinking, Buddhist view of
  Thinking and character
Buffon, Georges   *1707–1788*
Comte de; French naturalist
  Genius
Bulwer-Lytton, Edward   *1803–1873*
1st Baron Lytton; English novelist and
statesman
  Friendship, Learning from
Bunyan, John   *1628–1688*
English nonconformist minister and
writer; author of *The Pilgrim's Progress*
  Charity
  Christ, as our righteousness
  Contentment
  Conversion of Bunyan
  Death
  Death, Readiness for
  Decision for Christ
  Diffidence
  Employers
  Eternity
  Faith
  Families
  Giving and getting
  Heaven, Ways to
  Hell, Ways to
  Morality
  Persecution
  Pilgrimage
  Prayer and the heart's desire
  Prayer, Occasions and times of
  Pride
  Quietness
  Sin, Seriousness of
Burke, Edmund   *1729–1797*
Irish Protestant politician and orator;
he married a Catholic and championed
Catholic emancipation
  Action
  Ambition
  Ambition, Warnings against
  Change
  Custom
  Fear

  Flattery
  Grumbling
  Indifference
  Law
  Mankind, Nature of
  Morality
  Order
  Patience
  Persecution in the early church
  Perseverance
  Power
  Reading
  Reform
  Religion
  Superstition
  Sympathy
  Toleration
Burns, Robert   *1759–1796*
Scottish poet
  Life
  Mourning
  Self-knowledge
Burton, Henry   *1840–1930*
English Methodist minister
  Kindness, Response to
Burton, Robert   *1577–1640*
English clergyman
  Religion
Busenbaum, Hermann   *1600–1668*
German theologian
  Behaviour
Bushnell, Horace   *1802–1876*
US Congregationalist theologian
  Propitiation
Bussy-Rabutin, Roger   *1618–1693*
Comte de; French writer
  Friendship, and sincerity
Butler, Joseph   *1692–1752*
English bishop; author of *The Analogy
of Religion*
  Divorce
  Holy Spirit, Gifts of the
  Last words
Butler, Nicholas Murray   *1862–1947*
US educationalist
  Will-power
Butler, Samuel   *1835–1902*
English satirist who tried to make his
readers think more and question
conventional wisdom; author
of *Erewhon* and *The Way of All Flesh*
  Friendship, Acquiring
  Meaninglessness
  Money, Love of
  Tiredness
  Work, Limitations of

Buxton, Thomas
  Ambition
  Prayer
Byron, George   *1788–1824*
6th Baron Byron; English poet
  Bereavement
  Love, Learning
  Meaninglessness
  Persecution
Cairns, Hugh   *1819–1885*
1st Earl; British lord chancellor
  Prayer, Occasions and times of
Calvin, John   *1509–1564*
Leading Reformation theologian; born
in France settled in Geneva as political
and religious leader
  Ascension
  Awareness of God
  Baptism
  Bereavement, Individuals' reaction to
  Bible, Authority of
  Bible, Interpretation of
  Bible, Reading the
  Blood
  Christ, as Mediator
  Christ, as our Sin-bearer
  Christian life
  Christian unity
  Christianity
  Christians and the State
  Church
  Church, as Mother
  Church, Leaving the
  Church, True
  Church invisible
  Church membership
  Condemnation
  Cross
  Doctrine
  Election, Divine
  Enjoyment
  Evangelism
  Faith
  Falling away
  Freedom, Christian
  Godliness
  God's love
  God's nature
  Happiness
  Holy Spirit, Indwelling of the
  Hope
  Hypocrisy
  Idleness
  Ignorance
  Infant baptism
  Knowledge of God

  Last words
  Law of God
  Lord's Supper
  Lord's Supper, Physical elements in
  Love and the faults of the beloved
  Mankind, Depravity of
  Mottoes, Personal and family
  Neighbour, Love for
  Original sin
  Perfection in the church
  Persecution
  Prayer and faith
  Prayer, Definition of
  Prayer, Intercessory
  Prayer, Method of
  Preaching and the Holy Spirit
  Predestination
  Promises of God
  Reason, Limitations of
  Resurrection
  Revelations
  Righteousness
  Sacraments
  Self-denial
  Service
  Sin and sins
  Toleration
  Tribulations
  Wills
  Worship
  Zeal, Thoughtless
Camden, William   *1551–1623*
English antiquary
  Conversion
  Law
Campion, Thomas   *1567–1620*
English composer and poet
  Grace
Campoamor, Ramon de   *1817–18??*
Spanish philosopher
  Creation
  Friendship
Camus, Albert   *1913–1960*
French writer
  Old age
Carey, William   *1761–1834*
English Baptist missionary to India,
and Bible translator
  Christian life
  Mission
  Perseverance
Carey's Brotherhood, Serampore
  Prayer, Effects of on person praying
Carlyle, Thomas   *1795–1881*
Scottish historian
  Action and the present moment

Beginning
Belief
Careers
Christ, Divinity of
Dogma
Evil
Experience
History
Holiness
Humour
Job, Book of
Laughter
Mankind
Mistakes
Mockery
Motherhood
Pride
Prosperity
Proverbs
Public opinion
Science
Thinking and action
Wonder
Worship
Carmichael, Amy   *1867–1951*
Irish missionary to India, noted for her
work among women at Dohnavur
Love for God
Self
Carnegie, Andrew   *1835–1919*
US steel manufacturer and
philanthropist
Millionaires
Wealth and its use
Carroll, Lewis   *1832–1898*
pen-name for nonsense verse and
children's books of Charles Dodgson,
English mathematician
Busybodies
Faith
Words
Carver, George Washington
1861?–1943
US agricultural adviser, largely
responsible for creating an industrial
market for peanuts and sweet potatoes
Discoveries
Nature as revealing God
Casals, Pablo   *1876–1973*
Spanish cellist
Praise
Cassiodorus, Flavius   *490?–585?*
Roman monk, writer and statesman
Faithfulness
Castello, Sebastien   *16th-century*
French humanist scholar and Bible

translator; opponent of Calvin
Truth and martyrdom
Catherine of Siena   *1347–1380*
Italian mystic noted for her ecstatic
prayer and gift of reconciliation
Endurance
Heaven, Ways to
Love for God
Cato, Marcus Porcius   *234–149 BC*
Roman statesman and writer
Foolishness
Forgiveness
Luxury
Catullus, Gaius Valerius   *84?–54? BC*
Roman poet
Death, Non-Christian views of
Cavell, Edith   *1865–1915*
English nurse executed by the
Germans in World War I
Last words
Cecil, Richard   *1748–1810*
Anglican preacher
Bible, Interpretation of
Holy Spirit
Prayer, Lack of
Preaching and love
Cerf, Bennet
Proverbs
Cervantes, Miguel de   *1547–1616*
Spanish novelist; author of the satirical
novel *Don Quixote*
Death, as leveller
Friendship
God's mercy
Truth and God
Chadwick, Samuel
Judging others
Prayer and the devil
Prayer, Lack of
Success
Chamberlain, Neville   *1869–1940*
British prime minister at the outbreak
of World War II
War
Chambers, Oswald
English spiritual writer
Obedience
Service and love for God
Chamfort, Nicholas-Sébastien
1741–1794
French writer
Laughter
Chapman, George   *1559?–1634?*
English poet and playwright and
translator of Homer
Danger

Charles   *1433–1477*
the Bold; Duke of Burgundy
  Hope
Charles, Elizabeth   *1826?–*
  Nature as revealing God
Chateaubriand, François   *1768–1848*
Vicomte de; French writer and
politician; pioneer of Romanticism
  French people
Chaucer, Geoffrey   *1340?–1400*
English poet
  Christian life as following Jesus
  Fasting
  Peace
Chekhov, Anton   *1860–1904*
Russian dramatist and writer of
short stories
  Hate
  Learning
Chesterfield, Philip Stanhope
1694–1773
4th Earl; English statesman and writer
of letters on morality
  Action
  Behaviour
  Gossip
  Insults
  Relationships
  Time
Chesterton, Gilbert Keith   *1874–1936*
English Roman Catholic essayist
  Adventure
  Apologies
  Belief
  Boasting
  Christian life
  Christianity
  Commuters
  Cross
  Drink
  Encouragement
  Equality
  Evil
  Fall, The
  Gratitude
  Happiness
  Health
  Humility, False
  Judging others
  Justice
  Last words
  Mankind, potential with God
  Miracles
  Money, Love of
  Mysticism
  Neighbour, Love for

  Original sin
  Pleasure
  Praise
  Psychoanalysis
  Reason, Limitations of
  Self-confidence
  Silence in society
  Sin, Awareness of
  Soul
  Ten Commandments
  Thinking
  Toleration
  Tradition
  Yawning
Chevalier, Maurice   *1888–1972*
French popular singer and film actor
  Old age
Chillingworth, William   *1602–1644*
English theologian
  Bible, Sufficiency of
Christie, Agatha   *1891–1976*
English writer of detective stories
  Marriage
Chuang Tzu   *369–286 BC*
Chinese philosopher
  Wisdom and humility
Churchill, Charles   *1731–1754*
English poet and satirist who was a
friend of John Wilkes
  Excess
Churchill, Winston Spencer
1874–1965
English historian and prime minister
who led Britain's war effort from 1940
to 1945
  Anger, Positive views of
  Behaviour
  Challenge
  Church membership
  Death, Readiness for
  Determination
  Fanaticism
  Foolishness
  Foreigners
  Genius
  Giving
  Indecision
  Motherhood
  Proverbs
  Quotation
  War
  Women, Leadership of
Cicero, Marcus Tullius   *106–43 BC*
Roman orator who led the republican
party after Caesar's assassination
  Crucifixion

Debate
Environment
Freedom
Gluttony
Inspiration
Pleasure
Poverty
Slavery
Thinking
Wealth
Wisdom and riches
Clare, John   *1793–1864*
English poet
Home
Regeneration
Clark, Henry
Conversion of children
Clarke, W.N.
Knowledge of God, Possibility of
Clark   *17th century*
Travel
Claudius, Matthias   *1743–1815*
German poet
Good deeds, Motive of
Clement   *150?–215?*
of Alexandria (head of the Catechical
School there); Greek theologian
Christian life
Christianity, Spread of
Growth, Personal
Happiness
Holy Spirit
Hope
Resurrection
Trinity
Word of God
Clement I   *30?–101?*
Bishop of Rome; possibly the Clement
referred to in Philippians 4:13
Christ, Divinity of
Christianity, Historicity of
Endurance
God's nature
Humility
Persecution in the early church
Resurrection
Teamwork
Cleobulus
Excess
Cleveland, Grover   *1837–1908*
US president
Work
Cloud of Unknowing   *14th-century*
Anonymous English mystical treatise
Charity
Darkness

Humility, Learning
Sickness
Coggan, Donald   *1909–*
Archbishop of Canterbury
Abortion
Coleridge, Hartley   *1796–1849*
English poet and essayist; son of
S.T. Coleridge
Freedom
Prayer, Persistence in
Coleridge, Samuel Taylor   *1772–1834*
English poet and literary critic who
introduced German philosophy to
English thinkers
Christ
Common sense
Cross
Doctrine
Ephesians, Paul's letter to the
Freedom
Intolerance
Motives
Prayer
Progress
Romans, Paul's letter to the
Truth and mankind
Colet, John   *1467?–1519*
English humanist scholar and
theologian
Children, Advice to
Colton, Charles Caleb   *1780–1832*
English clergyman and poet
Examinations
Pride
Religion
Silence in society
Speech and observation
Columba   *521?–597*
Irish missionary
God's presence
Concord Formula   *1577*
Lutheran statement of faith
Conversion, Holy Spirit's work in
Confucius,   *551–479 BC*
Chinese philosopher and ethical
teacher
Failure
Forgiving others
Hearts
History
Home
Judging others
Modesty
Neighbour, Love for, and the
  'Golden Rule'
Respect

Speech and action
Thinking, Avoiding
Truth and mankind
Congreve, William   *1670–1729*
English dramatist
Ambition
Love, Sexual
Conrad, Joseph   *1857–1924*
English novelist
Women
Coolidge, Calvin   *1872–1933*
US president
Creativity
Cooper, James Fenimore   *1789–1851*
US novelist
Public opinion
Cooper, Thomas   *1759–1840*
English philosopher and lawyer
Truth examined
Copley, John Singleton   *1772–1863*
English lawyer and Chancellor
Resurrection of Jesus, Evidence for
Cosin, John   *1594–1672*
Bishop of Durham
Peace of God
Coubertin, Pierre de   *1863–1937*
French baron, who revived the
Olympic Games
Living
Cousin, Victor   *1792–1867*
French philosopher
Art
Coverdale, Miles   *1488–1569*
English Bible translator and Bishop of
Exeter
Bible, Translation of
Coward, Noel   *1899–1973*
English dramatist and actor
Careers
Cowley, Abraham   *1618–1667*
English poet and essayist
Lukewarmness
Cowper, William   *1731–1800*
English poet whose friend John
Newton got him to contribute to a
collection of Olney Hymns
Abiding in God
Comfort
Conceit
Falling away
Fanaticism
Grief
Hell
Holy Spirit and the Bible
Idols
Knowledge of God, Means of

Knowledge of God, Possibility of
Life after death
Nature
Prayer and the devil
Pride
Providence of God
Trust in God – when we seem
  abandoned by him
Wisdom and humility
Crabbe, George   *1754–1832*
English poet and clergyman
Habits
Cranmer, Thomas   *1489–1556*
Archbishop of Canterbury under
Henry VIII – main compiler of the
Book of Common Prayer
Last words
Marriage
Crates   *365?–285 BC*
Greek Cynic philosopher
Ignorance
Creighton, Mandell   *1843–1901*
English historian and Bishop of London
Good deeds, Motive of
Cromwell, Oliver   *1599–1658*
English revolutionary soldier and
statesman
Faith and action
Justice
Last words
Mistakes
Truth
Cumberland, Richard   *1631–1718*
Bishop of Peterborough and founder of
English Utilitarianism
Living
Cyprian, Thascius   *200?–258*
Bishop of Carthage; a practical
theologian and the first martyr-bishop
of the North African churches
Church, as Mother
God's protection
Ministers of religion, Choice of
Pope, The
Regeneration
Reverence for God
Dada, Bara
Holiness
Daishonin, Nichiren   *1222–1282*
Abuse
Difficulties in Life
Dale, R.W.
English congregationalist preacher
Preaching, Purpose of
Dalrymple, J.
Prayer, Occasions and times of

Dante Alighieri   *1265–1321*
Italian poet; author of the
Divine Comedy
  God's will
  Hell
  Tears
Darwin, Charles   *1809–1882*
English naturalist who proposed the
theory of evolution by natural selection
  Evolution
  Mankind, compared with animals
  Poetry
Das, Ram   *1524?–1581*
  Searching for God
De Brune, Johan
Calvinist poet
  Truth wherever it is found
Declaration of Independence   *1776*
  Human rights
Deffand, Mme du   *1697–1780*
French literary hostess
  Beginning
Defoe, Daniel   *1660?–1731*
English novelist and pamphleteer
  Church
  Devil
  Marriage
  Pleasure
De Gaulle, Charles   *1890–1970*
French soldier and statesman
  Unity
De la Salle   *1772–1855*
French writer
  Love, Sexual
Demades,   *4th century BC*
Greek orator
  Law
  Modesty
Demetrius
  Letter-writing
Democritus   *460?–370? BC*
of Abdera; Greek philosopher
  Festivals
  Friendship, Value of
  Ignorance
Demophilus
  Work, Need for
Demosthenes   *383?–322 BC*
Greek orator and politician
  Self-deception
  Success
  Wishful thinking
Denney, James   *1856–1917*
Scottish theologian
  Christ
  Christ, Mission of

  Christian life
  Preaching, Simplicity in
  Searching for God
  Virgin birth
Derby
Earl of
  Guidance
Descartes, René   *1596–1650*
French philosopher
  Mind
  Thinking
Dering, Edward   *1540?–1576*
English puritan clergyman
  Sin, Seriousness of
  Wisdom and happiness
Dewey, John   *1859–1952*
US philosopher and educator
  Belonging
  Christianity
Dickens, Charles   *1812–1870*
English novelist
  Accidents
  Behaviour
  Happiness, Effects of
  Humility, False
  Knowledge
  Mankind, Nature of
  Motherhood
  Neighbour, Love for
  New Testament
  Sacrifice
  Self
  Service
  Tears
Dickinson, Emily   *1830–1886*
US poet
  Death
  Last words
  Service
Didache   *1st or 2nd century*
Christian manual of morals and church
practice regarding baptism, the Lord's
Supper etc.
  Last Supper to be received worthily
  Ministers of religion, Choice of
  Prophets
Diderot, Denis   *1713–1784*
French philosopher
  Philosophy
Dinur   *20th-century*
Survivor of the Auschwitz
concentration camp
  Mankind, Depravity of
Diogenes   *412?–323? BC*
Greek Cynic philosopher
  Offence, Giving

Dionysius of Halicarnassus
1st-century BC
Greek literary critic and author of a
history of Rome
  History
Dionysius the Areopagite
1st century AD
Athenian mentioned in Acts 17:34
  Evil
Diphilus   *4th–3rd centuries BC*
Greek comic poet
  Sorrow, Remedies for
Disraeli, Benjamin   *1804–1881*
English prime minister and novelist
  Ages of man
  Agreement
  Biography
  Circumstances
  Despair
  Faith, Power of
  Grief
  Hopelessness
  Knowledge
  Mankind, compared with animals
  Mankind, Nature of
  Quotation
  Self
  Writing
Dobbie, Sir William
English soldier
  Prayer, Definitions of
Donne, John   *1571–1631*
English poet and preacher; Dean of St
Paul's Cathedral in London
  Accepting God
  Action
  Bereavement
  Death destroyed by God's power
  Faith and reason
  God's image
  Heaven, Nature of
  Heaven, Ways to
  Meditation
  Need of God
  Repentance
Doré, Gustave   *1832–1883*
French illustrator
  Love for God
Dormer, Lord
  Mottoes, Personal and family
Dort, Synod of   *1618–1619*
Dutch Reformed church synod which
condemned Arminianism
  Election, Divine
  God, Belief in
  Predestination

  Regeneration
Dostoevsky, Fyodor   *1821–1881*
Russian novelist who advocated
Russian mystical Christianity as against
socialism
  Belief
  Brotherhood
  Despair
  Faith
  God, Belief in
  Gratitude and ingratitude
  Hope
  Ideas
  Love, Consistency of
  Prayer, Persistence in
Drake, Sir Francis   *1540?–1596*
English admiral
  Perseverance to the end
Drummond, Henry   *1851–1897*
Explorer and evangelist associated
with Moody and Sankey
  Anger
  Christ, Power of
  Christian life
  Families
  Goals, Absence of
  God's will
  Knowledge of God, Means of
  Life
  Mission
  Motherhood
  Witness
Drummond, William   *1585–1649*
of Hawthornden; Scottish royalist
pamphleteer and poet
  Reason
Dryden, John   *1631–1700*
English poet and dramatist
  Ambition, Warnings against
  Compassion
  Patience
  Victory
  Virtue
Dumas, Alexandre   *1824–1895*
French novelist and dramatist
  Mottoes
  Respect
Duncan, George   *1884–1965*
Scottish New Testament scholar
  Christ, Divinity of
Eckhart, Meister   *1260?–1327*
German mystic and Dominican
preacher
  Being
  Closeness to God
  Consecration

Contentment
Detachment
Evil
Forgiveness
God, as Sustainer
God's love, inescapable
God's nature
God's presence
Good deeds, Motive of
Growth, Spiritual
Knowledge of God, Possibility of
Peace of mind
Purity
Searching for God
Self-denial
Self-knowledge
Success
Suffering, Causes of
Edersheim, Alfred
Crucifixion
Edison, Thomas Alva   *1847–1931*
US inventor
Determination
Disaster
Genius
Thinking
Thinking and action
Edward   *1004–1066*
the Confessor; King of the English
Last words
Edwards, Jonathan   *1703–1758*
US Calvinist philosopher and revival
preacher who wrote about conversions
which took place in religious revivals
Consecration
Conversion
Conversion of Edwards
Death, as leveller
Devil
God, as Creator
God's holiness
Grace defined
Humility, Importance of in
    Christianity
Learning from all sources
Living
Reading, Devotional
Reason
Religious practice
Revival
Searching for God in one's emptiness
Self-denial
Self-righteousness
Sin, Awareness of
Social action
Stillness

Einstein, Albert   *1879–1955*
US physicist who formulated theories
of relativity and worked for world peace
Ambition
Chance
Discoveries
Evil
Imagination
Mankind, Depravity of
Questions
Science
Truth
Eleazar   *1st–2nd centuries*
Jewish rabbi
Evangelism
Eliot, George   *1819–1880*
English novelist who translated
Strauss' *Life of Jesus* into English
Animals
Conceit
Creativity
Duty
Friendship
Gossip
Hate
Judging others
Pride
Speech and self-control
Women
Eliot, Thomas Stearns   *1888–1965*
English poet, dramatist and essayist
Humility
Elizabeth I   *1533–1603*
Queen of England
Lord's Supper, Physical elements in
Elliot, Jim   *20th-century*
missionary to Ecuador; killed by Auca
Indians
Death
Service
Elliott, Charlotte   *1789–1871*
English hymn-writer
Acceptance
Consecration
Elliott, Ebenezer   *1781–1849*
English minor poet
Facts
Elliott, Emily E.S.   *1836–1897*
English supporter of mission work
Christmas
Emerson, Ralph Waldo   *1803–1882*
US essayist
Achievement
Action
Ambition
Anglican Church

Beauty
Being
Civilisation
Common sense
Democracy
Discipline
Education
Enthusiasm
Fear
Friendship
Friendship, Acquiring
Friendship, and sincerity
Greatness
Happiness, Sources of
History
Home
Humility
Institutions
Living
Love, Sexual
Mankind
Money
Opportunity
Peace and its source in the self
Personality
Proverbs
Quotation
Science
Self-sacrifice
Sight
Simplicity
Sorrow
*Trust in God – because of his past
    mercies*
Witness
Wonder
Words
Enfantin, Barthélemy   *1796–1864*
French political theorist
Peace
Epictetus   *60?–140*
Greek Stoic philosopher who preached
endurance and abstinence
Confession
God's will
Imitation of God
Mankind, Insignificance of
Peace
Praise of God
Stoicism
Epicurus   *342?–270 BC*
Greek philosopher
Contentment
Epistle to Diognetus   *2nd/3rd century*
Neighbour, Love for
Persecution

Pilgrimage
Erasmus, Desiderius   *1467–1536*
Dutch humanist scholar who prepared
an accurate edition of the Greek New
Testament
Advice
Bible, Translation of
Preaching, Skill in
Self, Death of
Euripides   *480–406*
Greek dramatist whose plays show
people realistically but often bring in a
god at the end
Envy
Humility, Nature of
Mankind, Insignificance of
Meaninglessness
Sin, Effects of
Sorrow, Remedies for
Speech
Thinking deeply
Wives
Eusebius   *265?–340?*
Bishop of Caesarea; church historian
Living and human relationships
Perseuction in the early church
Evans, Mary *20th century*
English theologian
Marriage, Christian
Faber, Frederick William   *1814–1863*
English clergyman who became a
Roman Catholic and co-founder of the
London Oratory and wrote hymns and
devotional works
Action
Disappointment
God's love
God's mercy
Kindness, Response to
Little things
Patience
Perseverance
Fadiman, Clifton
Proverbs
Faraday, Michael   *1791–1867*
English chemist and physicist
Assurance
Farquhar, George   *1678–1707*
Irish dramatist
Poverty
Fénelon, François   *1651–1715*
Archbishop of Cambrai; author of
many letters of spiritual guidance
Failure
Faithfulness
Faults

Gratitude and trust
Growth, Spiritual
Humility, False
Humility, Learning
Knowledge, Warnings concerning
Kingdom of God
Love, Christian
Love and actions
Love and suffering
Love for God
Meditation
Prayer
Prayer, Definition of
Prayer, Method of
Pride and its source
Self-control
Suffering and prayer
Thinking, Humility in
Trust in God – when we seem
   abandoned by him
Wealth and slavery
Ferdinand I   *1503–1568*
King of Hungary and Bohemia
   Justice
Filene, E.A.   *1860–1937*
   Education
Finney, Charles Grandison
1792–1875
US evangelist
   Humility
   Revival
   Sin, Seriousness of
Fisher, Geoffrey   *1887–1972*
Archbishop of Canterbury
   Infallibility
Flavel, John   *1630?–1691*
English Presbyterian minister
   Bible
   Tribulations
Flecknoe, Richard   *1600?–1678?*
English poet and dramatist
   Silence
Ford, Henry   *1863–1947*
US car manufacturer who pioneered
mass production
   Experience
   History
   Learning throughout life
   Mottoes, Personal and family
   Thinking and action
   Work
Forsyth, P.T.   *1848–1969*
Scottish Congregationalist theologian
and teacher
   Prayer, Lack of
   Service and love for God

Fosdick, Harry Emerson   *1878–1969*
US liberal Baptist minister and author
   Faith and fear
   Mankind, potential with God
Fourier, Charles   *1772–1837*
French socialist reformer
   Women's rights
Fournier, Edouard   *1819–1880*
French writer
   Quotation
Fox, George   *1642–1691*
English preacher; founder of the
Quakers
   Conversion
   God's presence
   God's presence and the believer's
      response
   God's presence in the believer's heart
   Quakers
   Stillness
   Will
Foster, Richard
   Prayer, Persistence in
Francis   *1181–1226*
of Assisi; Italian founder of the
Franciscan order of friars
   Humility, Examples of
   Last words
   Living and human relationships
   Nature, Redeemed
   Original sin
   Peace of God
   Preaching and practice
Francis   *1567–1622*
de Sales; Bishop of Geneva; French
theologian who opposed Calvinism
   Anxiety
   Difficulties in life
   Gentleness
   Last words
   Love
   Love for God
   Meditation
   Mind
   Pleasing God
   Prayer, effects of on person praying
   Sin
   Suffering, Peace in
   Victory
   Weakness
François I   *1494–1547*
King of France
   Genius
Franklin, Benjamin   *1706–1790*
US printer and inventor; became
politically active in the movement for

independence, and was a signatory of the Constitution of the United States
Action and words
Christ, Verdict of non-Christians on
Christianity, Verdict of non-Christians on
Conscience
Conscientiousness
Contentment
Death, Inevitability of
Difficulties in life
Enemies
Example
Food
Forgiving others
Gluttony
Greed
Habits, Overcoming
Happiness, Sources of
Love, Response to
Mankind, compared with animals
Modesty
Parley
Peace
Praise of others
Preaching, Purpose of
Preaching and love
Selfishness
Success
Freud, Sigmund   *1856–1939*
Austrian neurologist who investigated the subconscious mind and effectively originated psychoanalysis
Belonging
God's existence
Meaning of life
Religion, Hostile views of
Women
Friedländer, M.
Prayer, Effects of on person praying
Friedrich, Caspar David   *1774–1840*
German painter
Art
Frith, John   *15th-century*
English Reformation scholar
Sunday
Froude, J.A.   *1818–1894*
English historian who started as a Tractarian under Newman's influence but later became a sceptic
Mankind, compared with animals
Fulgentius, Fabius   *5th–6th centuries*
African allegorical mythographer
Grace and its effect on the believer
Fuller, Edmund
Polygamy

Fuller, Thomas   *1608–1661*
English clergyman and popular historian; author of *Church History of Britain* and *Worthies of England*
Comfort
Miracles
Fuller, Thomas   *1654–1734*
English writer who published a collection of proverbs under the title *Gnomologia*
Anger
Anger, Positive views of
Conscience
Custom
Death, Readiness for
Enemies
Environment
Envy
Faults
Flattery
Forgiving others
Friendship, Learning from
Goals
Gratitude and friendship
Gratitude and ingratitude
Habits, Overcoming
Happiness, Sources of
Hope
Individuals
Inner life
Judging others
Kindness
Leadership
Life
Living and dying
Mind
Money, Spending
Poverty
Prayer, Occasions and times of
Punishment
Religion
Repentance
Ridicule
Shame
Speech, Thoughtless
Truth and God
Vigilance
Virtue
Wise people
Zeal
Furz, John   *18th-century*
Methodist preacher
Preaching, Open-air
Galileo   *1564–1642*
Italian astronomer and physicist
Bible, Interpretation of

Ignorance
Science and Christianity
Thinking
Gandhi, Mohandas K.   *1869–1948*
Mahatma; Indian lawyer and politician
who advocated non-violence, including
passive resistance to the British
  Living
  Non-violence
  Peace of mind
  Public opinion
  Sacrifice
  Weakness
  Witness through behaviour
Ganganelli, Giovanni   *1705–1774*
Pope Clement XIV
  Preaching
Garibaldi, Giuseppe   *1807–1882*
leader of the unification of Italy
  Challenge
Gascoigne, George   *1525?–1577*
English soldier and poet who wrote the
first English treatise on poetry
  Death, Readiness for
Gay, John   *1685–1732*
English poet and dramatist
  Love, Sexual
Gellert, C.F.   *1715–1769*
German poet
  Living and dying
George II   *1683–1760*
King of Great Britain 1727–1760
  Attack
Gerard family
  Mottoes, Personal and family
Gerhardt, P.   *1607–1676*
German hymn-writer
  Cross, Personal response to
Gesta Romanorum   *14th-century*
Collection of tales of romance and
legends of saints; compiled in Latin in
England
  Action
Gibbon, Edward   *1737–1794*
English historian; author of *The
Decline and Fall of the Roman Empire*
  Christianity, Spread of
  History and Jesus Christ
  Mankind
  World, Concern for
Gibran, Kahlil   *1883–1931*
Syro-Lebanese poet and mystic
  Friendship
Gide, André   *1869–1951*
French writer
  Quotation

Gildas   *6th-century*
British historian who upbraided the
princes and clergy of his day
  Abstinence
Gladstone, William Ewart   *1809–1898*
British prime minister
  Europe
  Justice
  Wisdom and humility
Glover, T.R.   *1869–1943*
English classical scholar
  Stoicism
Goering, Hermann   *1893–1946*
German Nazi leader
  Power
Goethe, Johann Wolfgang von
1749–1832
German poet and dramatist, and
student of science and the arts
  Beginning
  Belonging
  Encouragement
  Foolishness
  Genius
  Goals
  Growth, Personal
  Ideas
  Ignorance
  Judging others
  Knowledge
  Last words
  Life
  Love and humility
  Money, Spending
  Music, Effects of
  Originality
  Politeness
  Possessions
  Pride and what it leads to
  Procrastination
  Proverbs
  Relationships
  Sacrifice
  Self-discipline
  Self-knowledge
  Speech and listening
  Truth
  Worth
Goldsmith, Oliver   *1728–1774*
Irish poet, dramatist and novelist
  Law
Goodwin, Thomas   *1600–1680*
English puritan minister
  Spiritual coolness
Gordon, S.D.
  Prayer, Persistence in

Gracian   *1584–1658*
Spanish writer
  Reading
Gradin, Arvid   *18th century*
  Assurance
Graham, Billy   *1918–*
US evangelist
  Conversion
Grahame, Kenneth   *1859–1932*
Scottish writer
  Pleasure
Gray, Thomas   *1716–1771*
English poet
  Death
  Evening
Greek Anthology
  Envy
Greenham, Richard *1535?–1594?*
English puritan minister
  Death, Readiness for
  Faith and reason
  Pilgrimage
Grégoire   *1750–1831*
Bishop of Blois
  Women's rights
Gregory   *540–604*
the Great; Pope who organised the
papal estates so that help could be
given to starving people; founder of
monasteries and writer of the standard
textbook for medieval bishops
  Angels
  Counselling
  Faith and reason
  Good deeds
  Preaching and practice
  Vices
Gregory   *335?–394?*
of Nyssa; theologian and mystic
  Daily help from God
  Essentials
Gregory   *213?–270?*
Thaumaturgus; Greek bishop
  Love for God
  Teachers
Grenfell, Wilfred   *19th–20th centuries*
English medical missionary to
Labrador
  Living and human relationships
  Prayer, Power of
Grenville, Richard   *1541–1591*
English naval commander
  Last words
Greville, Fulke   *1554–1628*
English poet and politician
  Idols

Grey, Edward   *1862–1933*
1st Viscount Grey of Falloden; British
statesman
  War
Grimké, Sarah   *19th-century*
US pioneer of women's rights
  Women's rights
Grimshaw, William   *1708–1763*
English clergyman
  Bible, Reading the
Grotius, Hugo   *1583–1645*
Dutch jurist and statesman
  Freedom
Guarini, Battista   *1538–1612*
Italian poet
  Revenge
  Sorrow
Guevara, Che   *1928–1967*
Latin American guerrilla
  Revolutions
Guildford, Earl of
  Mottoes, Personal and family
Guinness, H.
  Sin, Seriousness of
Guiterman, Arthur   *1871–1943*
US poet and journalist
  Goals, Absence of
Guyon, Madame   *1648–1717*
French Quietist author
  Cross
  Follow-up
  Holiness
  Melancholy
  Prayer, Definitions of
  Prayer, effects of on person praying
  Prayer, Lack of
  Prayer, Method of
  Self, Death of
  Self-denial
  Silence
  Suffering
  Suffering, Patience in
Haecker, Theodore
  Understanding
Haile Selassie   *1892–1975*
Emperor of Ethiopia
  Bible
Hale, Everett   *1822–1904*
US Unitarian clergyman
  Little things
Halifax, George Savile   *1633–1695*
Marquis of; English essayist and
political pamphleteer who supported
Charles II
  Anger
  Punishment

Hall, Joseph   *1574–1656*
Bishop of Exeter and then of Norwich;
published poems and devotional and
theological works
  Formalism
  Moderation
  Prayer and the devil
  Superstition
Hall, Robert   *1764–1831*
English Baptist preacher
  Preaching and the Holy Spirit
Hall, Thomas   *17th century*
  Formalism
Hammarskjöld, Dag   *1905–1961*
Swedish Quaker statesman;
secretary-general of the United
Nations 1953–1961
  Self-knowledge
Handel, George Frederick   *1685–1759*
German-English composer who wrote
the oratorio *The Messiah*
  Worship
Hardy, Thomas   *1840–1928*
English novelist and poet
  Despair
  Heaven
  Progress
Harnack, Adolf   *1851–1930*
German church historian and
theologian
  Judaism
  Mission
Haskins, M. Louise
  New Year
Hazlitt, William   *1778–1830*
English essayist and literary critic
  Debate
  Friendship, Acquiring
  Mankind, compared with animals
  Monuments
  Nicknames
  Power
  Prejudice
  Public opinion
  Religious fanaticism
  World, Concern for
  Youth
Haywood, Eliza   *1693?–1756*
English writer
  Self-knowledge
Heidelberg Catechism   *1562*
Protestant confession of faith
  Trinity
Heine, Heinrich   *1799–1856*
German poet
  Last words

Heliodorus   *3rd century*
Greek novelist
  Wishful thinking
Helps, Sir Arthur   *1813–1875*
English writer and editor of Queen
Victoria's and Prince Albert's papers
  Kindness
Hendrix, Owen
  Change
  Goals, Absence of
  Old age
Henri IV   *1553–1610*
King of France
  Mottoes, Personal and family
Henry, Matthew   *1662–1714*
English nonconformist Bible
commentator
  Accepting God
  Eve
  Faith
  Grace defined
  Last words
Heraclitus   *535?–475? BC*
Greek philosopher
  Change
  Character
Herbert, Edward   *1583–1648*
1st Baron Cherbury; English poet and
historian; brother of George Herbert
  Action and words
  Deceit
  Duty
  Holiness
Herbert, George   *1593–1633*
Church of England clergyman and
religious poet; also wrote a book of
advice for country parsons
  Bible, Reading the
  Forgiving others
  Friendship, Learning from
  Giving and getting
  God's love
  God's love, Response to
  Gratitude
  Happiness, Effects of
  Healing
  Knowledge of God
  Lies
  Living for God
  Lord's Supper, Physical elements in
  Marriage and celibacy
  Money
  Nature, Redeemed
  Peace of God
  Poverty
  Prayer, Definitions of

Preaching and the gospel message
Religion
Respect
Rush
Service, Prayers dedicating the self to
Solitude
Sorrow
Tact
Virtue
Work for God's sake
Herman, Emma   *1874–1923*
English writer on mysticism
Listening
Herodotus   *480?–425? BC*
Greek historian who was the first to
collect his materials systematically;
wrote about the enmity between Asia
and Europe
Belief
Rush
Herrick, Robert   *1591–1674*
Church of England clergyman and poet
Prayer and the heart's desire
Repentance
Time
Hervey, James   *1714–1758*
English clergyman and devotional
poet; friend of early Methodism
Last words
Hesiod   *8th-century BC*
Greek poet
Beginning
Gossip
Idleness
Money
Procrastination
Heywood, John   *1497?–1580?*
English singer and epigrammatist
Faults
Hickson, William Edward   *1803–1870*
English educational writer
Perseverance
Hill, Rowland   *1744–1833*
English clergyman
Animals
Hillel   *60? B.C.–A.D. 9?*
Jewish rabbi who first formulated
principles of biblical interpretation
Law of God
Preaching
Hilton, Walter   *–1396*
English Augustinian canon and mystic;
author of *The Scale of Perfection*
God's love, Desire for
Possessions
Sin, Dealing with

Hippocrates   *460?–357? BC*
Greek doctor who gave his name to the
Hippocratic oath
Excess
Holiness
Hitler, Adolf   *1889–1945*
German dictator responsible for
anti-Jewish policies and World War 2
Lies
Power
Race
Hobbes, Thomas   *1588–1679*
English political philosopher whose
Leviathan upset both philosophers and
theologians when it was published
in 1651
Last words
Leisure
Mankind, Insignificance of
Public opinion
Hoffer, Eric
Freedom
Neighbour, Love for
Holmes, Oliver Wendell   *1809–1894*
US writer
Insight
Homer   *11th?–10th? centuries BC*
Greek epic poet; generally regarded as
the author of the *Iliad* and the *Odyssey*
Dreams
Hood, Thomas   *1799–1845*
English poet
Poverty
Hooker, Richard   *1554–1600*
English Anglican theologian
Bible, Interpretation of
Hooper, John   *–1555*
English Protestant martyr; Bishop and
Gloucester and Worcester
Last words
Martyrdom welcomed
Hope, Bob   *1904–*
US comedian
Mottoes, Personal and family
Hopkins, Gerard Manley   *1844–1889*
English poet who was a disciple of
Pusey and Liddon and Newman and
became a Jesuit after joining the
Roman Catholic church in 1866
Ascension
Beauty
Horace   *65–8 BC*
Roman poet
Adversity
Anger
Contentment

Death, Non-Christian views of
Disaster
Faults
Friendship, Value of
Gratitude and ingratitude
Greed
Judging others
Passion
Patience
Relatonships
Self-examination
Spirituality
Virtue
Horbery, Matthew *1707?–1773*
English clergyman
Purgatory
Horton, R.F. *1855–1934*
English Congregationalist minister
Conversion
Howe, Ed W. *1853–1937*
Friendship
Hubbard, Elbert *1956–1915*
Abiding in God
AIDS
Art
Committees
Conceit
Education
Failure
Gossip
Proverbs
Hubbard, F. McKinney *1868–1930*
Listening
Hugo, Victor *1802–1885*
French poet and novelist
Ages of man
Christ
God, Belief in
Happiness, Sources of
Ideas
Lies
Mistakes
Prayer
Women, Wisdom of
Huss, John *1372?–1415*
Bohemian theologian influenced by
Wycliffe; burnt for heresy
Last words
Hutcheson, Francis *1694–1746*
Scottish philosopher
Politics
Huxley, Aldous *1894–1963*
English novelist and essayist
Achievement
Technology

Huxley, Thomas Henry *1825–1895*
English surgeon and supporter of
Darwinism; the original 'agnostic'
Action
Science and Christianity
Truth and novelty
Ignatius *35?–107?*
third Bishop of Antioch in Syria;
author of letters to several of the early
churches; martyred by being thrown to
the lions in Rome
Apostolic doctrine
Bible, Christ in the
Bishops
Christ, Humanity of
Church government
Fellowship
Gentleness
God's presence in the believer's heart
Heresy
Lord's Supper
Marriage, Christian
Martyrdom welcomed
Ministers of religion, Authority of
Persecution in the early church
Resurrection of Jesus
Ignatius *1491/5–1556*
Loyola; Spanish founder of the Society
of Jesus
Predestination
Service, Prayers dedicating the self to
Work for God's sake
Inge, W.R. *1860–1954*
English writer and Dean of St Paul's
Cathedral, London
Christianity
Evangelism
Ingersoll, Robert G. *1833–1899*
Wealth and slavery
Irenaeus *130?–200?*
Bishop of Lyons; biblical theologian
Bible, Interpretation of
Cross
God, as Creator
God's nature
Holy Spirit, Gifts of the
Holy Spirit and the church
Knowledge of God, Limits of
Knowledge of God, Possibility of
Mankind, potential with God
Salvation
Trinity
Worship
Irving, Washington *1783–1859*
US essayist and short-story writer
Speech, Unkind

Isocrates   *436–338 BC*
Athenian rhetorician and teacher
  *Neighbour, Love for, and the
    'Golden Rule'*
Jackson, Thomas J.   *1824–1863*
known as Stonewall Jackson; US
Confederate army general
  Duty
  Last words
  Preaching and the gospel message
  Trust in God – in battle
James I   *1566–1625*
King of Great Britain
  Smoking
  Women, Education of
James, William   *1842–1910*
US philosopher and psychologist;
author of *The Varieties of Religious
Experience*
  Belonging
  Education
  Genius
  God's existence
  Indecision
  Prejudice
Jefferies, Richard   *1848–1887*
English naturalist and writer
  Hope
Jefferson, Thomas   *1743–1826*
US president; chief writer of the
Declaration of Independence
  Behaviour
  Caring
  Christianity, Message of
  Delay
  Faithfulness
  Honesty
  Justice
  Morality
  Principles
  Proverbs
  Thinking
  Tyranny
Jerome   *331–420*
ascetic monk; scholar; translator of the
Bible
  Affection
  Baptism
  Bible, Christ in the
  Christianity, Spread of
  Friendship, and sincerity
  Giving
  God's names
  Ignorance
  Inner life
  Love

  Persecution in the early church
  Soul
  Work, Need for
Jerome, Jerome K.   *1859–1927*
English humorous writer
  Work, Reluctance to
Jerrold, Douglas   *1803–1857*
  Kindness
Joan of Arc   *1412?–1431*
French heroine of the Hundred Years'
War
  Service, Prayers dedicating the self to
Johan de Bruce
  Truth wherever it is found
John   *347?–407*
Chrysostom; Bishop of Constantinople
noted for his preaching
  Action and words
  Anger
  Bible, Christ in the
  Bible, Reading the
  Charity
  Christian life as conflict
  Contemplation
  Cross
  Equality
  Example
  Exploitation
  Free will
  Little things
  Patience
  Prayer, Method of
  Prayer, Power of
  Preaching, Purpose of
  Predestination
  Sin
John   *570?–649*
Climacus; Abbot of Sinai
  Anger
John   *1542–1591*
of the Cross; Spanish Carmelite mystic,
who wrote on the Dark Night of the Soul
  Beauty
  God's love, Judgement and
  Good deeds, Motive of
  Gossip
  Gratitude
  Living for God
  Love, Purity of
  Meditation
  Peace of God
  Prayer, Lack of
  Purity
  Reading, Devotional
  Revelations
  Silence

Johnson, Samuel *1709–1784*
English writer and lexicographer
  Action
  Behaviour
  Caution
  Compassion
  Courage
  Criticism
  Death, Readiness for
  Friendship, Acquiring
  Friendship, Value of
  Greed
  Habits, Overcoming
  Happiness, Sources of
  Hope
  Idleness
  Justice
  Kindness
  Knowledge, Means to
  Knowledge, Warnings concerning
  Last words
  Living and dying
  Mottoes, Personal and family
  Pleasure
  Possessions
  Poverty, Relief of
  Praise
  Prayer, Persistence in
  Prejudice
  Remembering
  Shame
  Speech, Thoughtless
  Speech, Unkind
  Wealth
  World, Concern for
  Writing
Jones, E. Stanley
  Prayer
Jonson, Ben *1572?–1637*
English dramatist
  Heaven, Ways to
  Prayer, Occasions and times of
Josephus, Flavius *37?–100?*
Jewish priest, soldier and historian; the
chief source for 1st-century Jewish
history
  Christianity, Historicity of
  Leprosy
  Women, Inferiority of
Joubert, Joseph *1754–1824*
French moralist
  Change
  Life after death
  Living
  Politeness
  Positive thinking

Jowett, J.H. *1846–1923*
English Congregationalist preacher
and devotional writer
  Comfort
  Opinions, Other people's
  Prayer, Intercessory
Judson, Adoniram *1788–1850*
US missionary in Burma
  Prayer, Occasions and times of
Julian, of Norwich *1342?–*
English anchoress of Norwich whose
Revelations of Divine Love was the first
book to be written in English by a
woman
  Faith required
  God, as Creator
  God, as Sustainer
  God's goodness
  God's love
  God's love, Adversity and
  God's presence in the believer's heart
  Kindness
  Motherhood
  Peace of God
  Prayer
  Prayer, effects of on person praying
  Prayer, Persistence in
  Reverence for God
  Searching for God
  Sin, Effects of
  Trinity
  Trust in God – for the future
Julian *331–363*
Roman emperor
  Last words
Jung, Carl Gustav *1875–1961*
Swiss psychoanalyst, leading critic of
Freud
  Emptiness
  Goals
  Rush
  Self-sacrifice
Justin *100?–165?*
Martyr; the first Christian writer to try
to reconcile faith and reason
  Baptism
  Bible, and Reason
  Bible, Inspiration of
  Bible, Reading the
  Christ, Early witnesses to
  Conversion of Early Christians
  Evidences for Christianity
  Hospitality
  Lord's Supper to be received worthily
  Martyrdom
  Preaching by God's command

Juvenal, Decimus Junius *?60–?130*
Roman satirical poet who denounced
contemporary society and its vices
  Children
  Knowledge
  Poverty
  Revenge
  Symbolism
  Truth wherever it is found
  Worship
Kagawa, Toyohiko *1888–1960*
Japanese social reformer
  Good deeds
  Love, Lack of
  Meditation
  Miracles
  Mottoes, Personal and family
  Prayer, Lack of
  Service
  Service and God's plans
  Theology
Kant, Immanuel *1724–1804*
German idealist philosopher
  Freedom
  Mankind, Depravity of
  Wonder
Keats, John *1795–1821*
English poet
  Beauty
  Failure
  Genius
  World
Keble, John *1792–1866*
Oxford poetry professor and Tractarian
  Christian life
  Living, Day by day
  Longing for God
  Purity
Keller, Helen *1880–1968*
US deaf and blind writer
  Service
Kelvin, William *1824–1907*
1st Baron Kelvin; British physicist
  Testimonies to Christ
Ken, Thomas *1637–1711*
English bishop and hymn-writer
  Graces
  Living and dying
Kennedy, John F. *1917–1963*
US president
  Failure
  Revolutions
Kepler, Johan *1571–1630*
German astronomer
  Nature
  Patience

Keynes, John Maynard *1883–1946*
1st Baron Keynes; English economist
  Original sin
Kierkegaard, Søren *1813–1855*
Danish theologian and philosopher
  Martyrdom
  Obedience
  Prayer, Effects of on person praying
Khrushchev, Nikita *1894–1971*
Soviet premier
  Communism
King, Guy
  Old age
King, Martin Luther *1929–1968*
US Baptist pastor and leader of the
Black civil rights movement
  Evil
  Fear
  Justice
  Longevity
  Race
Kingsley, Charles *1819–1875*
English clergyman and social reformer
whose novels include *The Water Babies*
  Beauty
  Death, Readiness for
  Faith
  Freedom
  Friendship
  Prayer
  Preparation
Kipling, Rudyard *1865–1936*
English poet and novelist
  Mistakes
  Motherhood
  Questions
  Women, Wisdom of
Knox, John *1513–1572*
Chaplain to Edward VI of England;
main compiler of the Scottish prayer
book
  Bible, Interpretation of
  Last words
  Sin, Awareness of
  Weddings
Knox, Vicesimus *1752–1821*
English writer
  Women, Education of
Koestler, Arthur *1905–1983*
English writer
  Genius
Kuyper, Abraham *1837–1920*
Dutch Calvinist theologian and
politician
  Christians
  Sanctification

Lactantius   *240?–320?*
Christian apologist
  Christianity
  Slavery
La Fontaine, Jean de   *1621–1695*
French poet
  Action
  Gentleness
  Humility
  Service
  Truth and mankind
Lamartine, Alphonse de   *1792–1869*
French poet; historian and politician
  Old age
  Women, Superiority of
Lamb, Charles   *1775–1834*
English essayist
  Belief
  Good deeds
  Grace (prayer)
  Love
  Mankind, Nature of
Lamennais, F. de   *1782–1854*
French religious writer
  Poverty
Landon, Letitia Elizabeth   *1802–1838*
English poet
  Poverty, Understanding
Langland, William   *1332?–1400?*
English poet
  Truth
Langton, Stephen   *?–1228*
English Archbishop
  Service
Lao Tzu   *604?–531 BC*
Chinese philosopher
  Beginning
  Behaviour
  Being
  Boasting
  Enlightenment
  Kindness
  Leadership
  Living
  Trust
La Rochefoucauld   *1613–1680*
Duc de; French writer of maxims
  Abiding in God
  Comfort
  Detachment
  Faults
  Flattery
  Friendship, Value of
  Judging others
  Knowledge, Warnings concerning
  Listening
  Peace and its source in the self
  Praise of others
  Prayer, Definitions of
  Witness through speaking
Latimer, Hugh   *1485?–1555*
Bishop of Worcester; noted preacher
and Reformer, burnt at the stake
  Covetousness
  Perseverance
  Preaching
  Truth and the devil
Lavater, Johann Kaspar   *1741–1801*
Swiss poet and writer
  Action and the present moment
  Growth, Spiritual
Law, William   *1686–1761*
English clergyman and spiritual writer
  Chance
  Christian life
  Consecration
  Goals
  God's will
  Gratitude
  Gratitude and adversity
  Hell, Nature of
  Humility, Exhortations to
  Humility, Importance of in
    Christianity
  Last words
  Living for God
  Love and error
  Neighbour, Love for
  Praise of God
  Prayer
  Prayer, Effects of on person praying
  Prayer, Method of
  Prayer, Occasions and times of
  Pride
  Pride and what it leads to
  Repentance
  Rush
Lawrence   *1605–1691*
Brother; French Carmelite lay brother
and mystic; author of *The Practice of
the Presence of God*
  God's presence amid everyday
    activities
  God's presence and the believer's
    response
  Holy Spirit
  Perseverance
  Prayer, Method of
  Prayer, Persistence in
Lawrence, D.H.   *1885–1930*
English novelist and poet
  Peace

Lebowitz, Fran
Living
Lee, Robert E. *1807–1870*
US Confederate army general
Bible
Duty
Social sin
Trust in God
Trust in God – in battle
Lefèvre *1455?–1536*
French humanist
Christ, as our Sin-bearer
Legouvé, E. *1807–18..*
French writer
Music
Leland, John *1506?–1552*
English antiquary
Last words
Lenclos, Ninon de *1616–1706*
French courtesan
Love, Platonic
Leo XIII *1810–1903*
Pope
Toleration
Lessing, Gotthold *1729–1781*
German dramatist and critic
Prayer
Truth and God
Lewis, Clive Staples *1898–1963*
English literary critic and writer of
popular Christian apologetics
Atheism
Christianity
Conscience
Decisions
Discipline
Flippancy
Forgiveness
Free will
Giving and getting
God and mankind
God, as last resort
Hell
Hell, Ways to
Holiness
Individuals
Lies
Love
Mankind, Depravity of
Mankind, Inhumanity to man
Mistakes
Morality
Neighbour, Love for
Opinions, Other people's
Pain
Pride

Progress
Reality
Reason
Religions, Non-Christians
Repentance
Reverence for God
Shame
Sin, Seriousness of
Suffering
Li Hung Chang *1823–1901*
Chinese prime minister
Leadership
Lichtenberg *18th-century*
Guidance
Liddell, George *1811–1898*
English clergyman and scholar of Greek
Prayer, People of
Liddon, H.P. *1829–1890*
English Anglo-Catholic clergyman
Prayer
Lightfoot, J.B. *1828–1889*
English biblical scholar
Thanksgiving
Lincoln, Abraham *1809–1865*
US President
Atheism
Bible, Uniqueness of
Christian life
Christian upbringing
Consecration
Depression
Determination
Duty
Elections, Government
Families
Freedom
Government
Guidance
Immortality
Living and dying
Mankind, Nature of
Money and the service of God
Morality
People
Perseverance to the end
Progress
Public opinion
Silence, Reprehensible
Silence in society
Slavery
Thinking and happiness
Trust in God
Work
Lincoln, Thomas
father of Abraham Lincoln
Last words

Liszt, Franz *1811–1886*
Hungarian composer and pianist
  Music
Livingstone, David *1813–1873*
Scottish medical missionary and
explorer in Africa
  God's presence when there is no other
    help
  Mission
  Missionaries
  Mottoes, Personal and family
  Sacrifice
Lloyd-Jones, D. Martyn *1899–1981*
Welsh Nonconformist doctor and
minister noted for his expository
preaching at London's Westminster
Chapel
  Prayer, Humility in
Locke, John *1632–1704*
English philosopher
  Truth examined
  Tyranny
Lombard, Peter *1100?–1160*
Bishop of Paris; his *Sentences* was the
standard textbook of Catholic theology
until it was superseded by Thomas
Aquinas
  Eve
Longfellow, Henry Wadsworth
1807–1882
US poet who tried to reconcile religion
with modern thought
  Adversity
  Friendship
  Joy
  Life
  Living and dying
  Living and human relationships
Longstaff, W.D.
  Holiness
  Prayer, Method of
Loren, Sophia *1934–*
film actress
  Creativity
Louis XIV *1638–1715*
King of France
  Peacemaking
Lovelace, Richard *1618–1658*
English poet
  Prison
Lowell, James Russell *1819–1891*
US poet and critic
  Giving willingly
Lucan, Marcus Annaeus *39–65*
Roman poet
  Progress

Lucretius, Titus *?96–?52 BC*
Roman philosophical poet who
denounced religion
  Living
  Meaninglessness
  Nature
Ludendorff, Erich *1865–1937*
German Field Marshal
  Christianity
Lupset, Thomas *1498?–1530*
English clergyman
  Anger
Luther, Martin *1483–1546*
German monk and theologian who led
the Protestant Reformation and
translated the Bible into German
  Adversity
  Angels
  Annunciation
  Astrology
  Baptism
  Bereavement, Individuals' response to
  Bible, as the word of God
  Bible, Christ in the
  Bible, Obedience to
  Bible, Reading the
  Christ
  Christ, as our Sin-bearer
  Christ, Divinity of
  Christ, Humanity of
  Christian life
  Christian unity
  Christianity, Message of
  Church
  Church, as Mother
  Conscience
  Conversion, Holy Spirit's work in
  Conversion of Luther
  Conviction
  Courage
  Cross
  Darkness
  Denominations
  Dependence on God
  Devil
  Devil, Fighting the
  Doubt
  Duty
  Emotions
  Error
  Faith
  Faith and reason
  Faith required
  Forgiveness
  Free will
  Fruit, Spiritual

God, as Creator
God, as Father
God's love, Adversity and
God's wrath
Good deeds
Good deeds, Motive of
Grace
Grace and human will
Grace and its effect on the believer
Graces
Gratitude
Growth, Spiritual
Heresy
Holy Spirit and work
Hope
Idleness
Idols defined
Indulgences
Job, Book of
Justification by faith
Last words
Laughter
Law of God
Lies
Living for God
Lord's Supper
Lord's Supper, Physical elements in
Love for God
Mankind
Mankind, Depravity of
Ministers of religion
Ministers of religion, Authority of
Monks
Mottoes, Personal and family
Music
Music and the devil
Neighbour, Love for
Non-violence
Old age and maturing
Parenthood
Persecution
Pleasure
Pope, The
Prayer, Lack of
Prayer, Length of
Prayer, Power of
Preaching
Preaching, Manner of
Preaching, Simplicity in
Predestination
Pride and its correction
Promises of God
Prosperity
Reason, Limitations of
Reformation, Church
Repentance

Righteousness from God
Romans, Paul's letter to the
Salvation
Searching for God
Second coming of Christ
Self
Sin
Sin, Dealing with
Sin, Definition of
Speech, Godly
Stubbornness
Temperance
Temptation, Resisting
Ten Commandments
Theology
Tribulations
Trust in God – for the church
Trust in God – when deserted
Truth
Wealth
Witness through speaking
Worry
Worship
Lyte, Henry Francis   1793–1847
English clergyman
Abiding in God
God's presence when there is no other
    help
Heaven
Praise of God
Macarius   300?–390?
Egyptian who founded an important
monastery in the desert of Scetis
Prayer, Method of
Macaulay, Thomas Babington
1800–1859
English historian
Bible, Uniqueness of
M'Cheyne, Robert Murray
1813–1843
Scottish minister
Abiding in God
Christlike behaviour
Fear
God's judgement
Holiness
Humility, Examples of
Mottoes, Personal and family
Prayer, Occasions and times of
Speech, Godly
Macdonald, George   1824–1905
Scottish congregational minister; poet
and novelist and Christian writer
Adversity
Awareness of God
Beauty, Spiritual

Behaviour
Christian life
Death
Fellowship with God
Hate
Heaven, Nature of
Hell, Nature of
Humility, Examples of
Idleness, Sacred
Kindness, Response to
Last words
Laughter
Miracles of Jesus
Neighbour, Love for
Obedience
Old age and maturing
Resurrection of the body
Self
Selfishness
Suffering
Systematic theology
Witness through behaviour
Worry
Machen, J. Gresham *1881–1937*
US Presbyterian minister and
conservative biblical scholar who
founded the Orthodox Presbyterian
Church
Paul, The apostle
Machiavelli, Niccolo *1469–1527*
Italian political theorist; author of *The
Prince*
Fear of God
Forgiveness
Fortune
Maclaren, Alexander *1826–1910*
British Baptist preacher and expositor
Kindness
Maclaren, Ian *1850–1907*
pseudonym of John Watson, English
Presbyterian minister
Preaching, Purpose of
MacLeod, George
Meaning of life
McLuhan, Marshall *1911–*
Canadian author of works on the
sociology of mass media
Communication
Violence
World
Magna Carta *1215*
English charter which King John was
forced to sign, recognising the rights of
the people
Church government
Justice

Maimonides, Moses *1135–1204*
Jewish philosopher, physician and
jurist
Pride
Major, H.D.A.
Children and Jesus
Malvern Manifesto *1941*
statement issued by an Anglican
conference on Christianty and
economic life
Kingdom of God
Mann, Horace *1701–1786*
English diplomat
Affection
Mansfield, Katherine *1888–1923*
English writer of short stories
Witness through behaviour
Mao Tse-tung *1893–1976*
Chinese revolutionary leader
Power
Marcus Aurelius *121–180*
Roman emperor and Stoic
philosopher; author of *Meditations*,
written in Greek
Action
Behaviour
Happiness, Lack of
Leisure
Mankind, Exalted estimates of
Thinking and character
Thinking deeply
Maritain, Jacques *1882–1973*
French Roman Catholic philosopher
Social reform
Martial *43?–103?*
Latin writer of epigrams
Praise of others
Procrastination
Martyn, Henry *1781–1812*
English missionary to India who
worked on the translation of the Bible
into Asian languages
Mottoes, Personal and family
Prayer
Zeal
Marvell, Andrew *1621–1678*
English metaphysical poet
Death
Marx, Karl *1818–1883*
German political theorist
Communism
Philosophy
Race
Religion, Hostile views of
Working class
Writing

Mary   *1542–1587*
Queen of Scots
 Freedom
 Prayer, Power of
Masefield, John   *1878–1967*
English poet and novelist
 Ministers of religion
Massieu
a French deaf-mute
 Gratitude
Masterman, E.W.G.
 Leprosy
Matheson, George
 Disappointments
 God's love, Response to
Maurois, André   *1885–1967*
French writer
 Meaninglessness
Maximus   *580?–662*
the Confessor; Greek theologian
 Money, Love of
Meir
rabbi
 Praise of God
Melanchthon, Philip   *1497–1560*
German theologian and expert on
Greek; close colleague of Martin
Luther
 Salvation
Menander   *342–292 BC*
Greek dramatist
 Anger
 Blushing
 Conscience
 Conversation
 Debt
 Friendship
 Friendship, Learning from
 Justice
 Love and anger
 Old age
Mencius   *372?–289? BC*
Chinese Confucianist philosopher
 Childlikeness
 Duty
Mendelssohn, Moses   *1729–1786*
German Jewish philosopher
 Beauty, Spiritual
Merton, Thomas   *20th century*
US Trappist monk
 Belief
Meyer, F.B.   *1847–1929*
English Baptist minister
 Last words
Meyers, F.W.H.
 Biography

Michelangelo Buonarrotti   *1475–1564*
Italian artist
 Art
 *God's love, more important than
  anything else*
 Transformation
Mill, John Stuart   *1806–1873*
English logician and political
philosopher; early connected with
utilitarianism
 Automation
 Fulfilment
 Happiness
 Truth triumphant
Milton, John   *1608–1674*
English poet and Parliamentarian
pamphleteer; author of *Paradise Lost*
 Christmas
 Conscience
 Death
 Faithfulness
 Loneliness
 Mind
 Praise of God
 Service
 Victory
Moffat, Robert   *1795–1883*
British missionary in South Africa
 Prayer, Definitions of
Monsell, J.S.B.   *1811–1875*
English clergyman and hymn-writer
 Work for God's sake
Montaigne, Michel de   *1533–1592*
French essayist
 Judgement
 Mankind, Depravity of
 Prayer
 Proverbs
 Quotation
 Thinking deeply
 Women's rights
Montesquieu   *1689–1755*
Baron de; French political philosopher
 Happiness, Lack of
Montgomery, James   *1771–1854*
Scottish poet
 Prayer, Definitions of
Moody, Dwight L.   *1837–1899*
US evangelist; toured England and
America with Ira Sankey
 Bible, Interpretation of
 Bible, Reading the
 Character
 Conversion of Moody
 Evangelism
 Heaven

Holy Spirit
Holy Spirit, Fruit of the
Holy Spirit, Indwelling of the
Last words
Leadershp
Lies
Living
Peace of God and the death of Jesus
Prayer, Persistence in
Preaching and the gospel message
Pride
Refreshment, Spiritual
Salvation, Mankind's need of
Service and humility
Singleness of mind
Stewardship
Trust in God
Weakness
Will-power
Moon, Lottie   *1840–1912*
US teacher and missionary to China
Goals, Examples of
Loneliness
Morata, Olympia Fulvia
Last words
More, Hannah   *1745–1833*
English educationalist and religious
writer
Beauty, Spiritual
Idleness
More, Thomas   *1478–1535*
English statesman
Devil
Morgan, John Pierpont   *1837–1913*
US financier, philanthropist and art
collector
Discipline
Morley, John   *1838–1923*
English statesman and writer
Persuasion
Toleration
Morrison, Robert   *1782–1834*
first Protestant missionary to China
Mottoes, Personal and family
Teamwork
Morse, Samuel   *1791–1872*
US inventor
Discoveries
Moses ibn Ezra
Hate
Mote, Edward
Righteousness from God
Mott, John   *1865–1955*
US Methodist supporter of missions
and ecumenism
Call

Family, The Christian
Habits, Overcoming
Motteville, Madame de   *1621–1689*
French writer
Love, Sexual
Moule, C.F.D.   *1908–*
English theologian
Idols
Mount Edgcumbe, Earl of
Mottoes, Personal and family
Mowll, Mrs H.W.K.
Caution
Muhammad   *570?–632*
founder of Islam
Religions, Non-Christian
Writing
Müller, George   *1805–1898*
German-born English Brethren
preacher and founder of orphanage in
Bristol; renowned as a man of prayer
living by faith
Bible, Reading the
Difficulties in life
Faith and suffering
God's goodness
Old age
Self, Death of
Murray, Andrew   *19th-century*
preacher in Scotland and South Africa
Education
Faith
Family, The Christian
Humility
Lost souls
Perfection
Prayer, Intercessory
Prayer, Lack of
Pride
Salvation
Self
Self, Death of
Society
Work
Murray, John   *20th-century*
of the Orthodox Presbyterian Church
Divorce
Mursell, Arthur   *19th-century*
Bible, Criticism of
Musset, Alfred de   *1810–1857*
French poet
Prayer, Definitions of
Napoleon I, Buonaparte   *1769–1821*
French soldier and emperor
Ambition
Bible, Authority of
Character

Christ, Divinity of
Circumstances
Education
Feelings
History
Leadership
Love, Response to
Martyrdom
Power, Spiritual
Reading
Ridiculousness
Suffering
Neale, John Mason   *1818–1866*
English translator of Latin and Greek
hymns
Weakness
Nelson, John   *18th-century*
Early Methodist field preacher in
Yorkshire
Preaching, Open-air
Nepos, Cornelius   *100?–25? BC*
Roman historian and biographer
Wealth
Newman, F.W.
Teachers
Newman, John Henry   *1801–1890*
English clergyman who led the Oxford
revival of Anglican worship and later
became a Roman Catholic Cardinal
Cross, Personal response to
Daily help from God
Doubt
Faith and fear
Growth, Personal
Mottoes, Personal and family
Praise of God
Service in small things
Newton, Isaac   *1643–1727*
English mathematician, physicist,
astronomer and philosopher
Discoveries
Progress
Science and Christianity
Newton, John   *1725–1807*
English evangelical clergyman and
hymn-writer
Bible, Uniqueness of
Calvinism v. Arminianism
Comfort
God's love, Adversity and
Heaven
Name of Jesus
Prayer, Lack of
Prayer, Power of
Saviour
Trust in God – and God's promises

Nietzsche, Friedrich   *1844–1900*
German nihilist philosopher
Christianity, Verdict of non-Christians
on
Goals, Absence of
God, Belief in
Happiness, Sources of
Living, Purpose of
Music
New Testament
Punishment
Self-knowledge
Speech
Truth, Absolute
Witness through behaviour
Women
Nightingale, Florence   *1820–1910*
English nurse
Conscience
Consistency
Depression
Last words
Obedience
Prayer and the will of God
Service, Prayers dedicating the self to
Statistics
Trust in God – when daunted by work
Northampton, Marquis of
Mottoes, Personal and family
Northbrooke, John   *16th century*
English preacher and writer against
plays
Music in church services
Northumberland, Duke of
Mottoes, Personal and family
Ockenga, Harold John
Reading, Devotional
O'Malley, Austin   *1858–1932*
Revenge
Origen   *185?–254*
biblical scholar and theologian
Atonement
Baptism and salvation
Bible, Impact of
Bible, Interpretation of
Christ
Christianity, Spread of
Church
Debt to God
Gospel
Lord's Supper ineffective by itself
Orwell, George   *1903–1950*
English novelist and essayist
Equality
Otis, James   *1725–1783*
Tyranny

Ovid   *43 BC–18*
Latin poet
  Caring
  Habits, Overcoming
  Hope
  Prayer, Power of
  Sin, Definition of
  Tears
  Weakness
Owen, John   *1616–1683*
English Puritan theologian; chaplain
and adviser to Oliver Cromwell
  Conversion, Holy Spirit's work in
  Grace and its effect on the believer
  Holy Spirit, Gifts of the
  Holy Spirit and free will
  Knowledge of God
  Mankind, Christ's redemption of
  Mass
  Preaching and practice
  Sin
Oxenham, John   *1852–1941*
English novelist and poet
  Decisions
  Life in Jesus
  Prayer
Oxenstiern, Count Axel   *1583–1634*
Swedish chancellor
  Bible, Reading the
Paderewski, Ignace Jan   *1860–1941*
Polish pianist and prime minister
  Genius
  Practice
Paine, Thomas   *1737–1809*
US political pamphleteer
  Character
  Christ, Verdict of non-Christians on
  Fame
Palau, Luis   *20th century*
Latin American evangelist
  Bible, Obedience to
Paley, William   *1743–1805*
English philosopher and theologian
  Bible, Early scholars of
  Persecution in the early church
Palmerston, Henry   *1784–1865*
3rd Viscount Palmerston; English
foreign secretary and prime minister
  Death
Paré, Ambroise   *16th-century*
French surgeon; 'founder of modern
surgery'
  Work, Limitations of
Parkes, James   *1896–1981*
English historian and theologian
  Christianity, Message of

Pascal, Blaise   *1623–1662*
French mathematician and theologian
  Action
  Belief
  Christ
  Christ, as Mediator
  Comfort
  Custom
  Doubt
  Evil
  Faith
  Faith and fear
  Faith and reason
  Garden of Gethsemane
  God, as Creator
  God's power
  Gossip
  Habits
  Holiness
  Imagination
  Indifference
  Justice
  Knowledge of God
  Knowledge of God, Means of
  Little things
  Mankind
  Mankind, Christ's redemption of
  Mankind, compared with animals
  Mankind, Insignificance of
  Mankind, Middle state of
  Mankind, Nature of
  Meditation
  Nature as revealing God
  Originality
  Perfection
  Predestination
  Reason, Limitations of
  Religion
  Searching for God
  Self
  Self-denial
  Temperance
  Thinking
  Thinking and character
  Thinking deeply
  Truth
  Truth and the church
  Tyranny
  Vanity
Pasteur, Louis   *1822–1895*
French chemist and bacteriologist
  Nature
Patrick   *5th century*
English missionary in Ireland
  Conversion of Patrick
  Last words

Pausanias *2nd century*
Greek geographer and historian
  Conscience
Payson, Edward
  Prayer
Péguy, Charles *1873–1914*
French Roman Catholic socialist writer
  Dictators
  Friendship
  Habits
  Knowledge
  Love and the faults of the beloved
  Poverty, Understanding
  Truth and novelty
  Vision
  Witness
Penn, William *1644–1718*
English Quaker who founded Penn-
sylvania as a colony of religious liberty
  Christlike behaviour
  Good deeds
  Government
  Humility
  Kindness
  Love, Response to
  Meditation
  Pain
  Patience
  Prayer, People of
  Reading
  Temptation, Resisting
  Truth and mankind
Pepys, Samuel *1633–1703*
English diarist and naval administrator
  Music
  Pride
Percival, John *1843–1918*
Bishop of Hereford who invited
Nonconformists to take Communion in
his cathedral
  Politics
Perez, Antonio *1539–1611*
Italian politician
  Friendship, in times of need
  Love
Perot, H. Ross
  Discipline
Perronet, Edward *1725–1792*
English hymn-writer
  Worship
Peter *1007–1072*
Damian; Benedictine reformer
  Possessions
Peter *13th century*
a monk
  Young people

Phelps, Edward John
English businessman
  Mistakes
Phillips, Wendell *1811–1884*
  Vigilance
Philo *20? BC–AD 54?*
of Alexandria; Jewish philosopher
  Women, Inferiority of
  Women and the home
Philoctetes
  Money, Love of
Pierpoint, F.S. *1835–1917*
English classics teacher
  Nature as revealing God
Pierson, A.T.
  Habits
  Prayer, Prevailing
  Revival
Pittacus
  Power
Pius IX *1792–1878*
Pope who summoned the first Vatican
Council which declared the papacy
infallible
  Progress
Pius XI *1857–1939*
Pope
  Birth control
Plato *429–347 BC*
Greek philosopher
  Fulfilment
  Incarnation
  Mankind
  Self
  Suffering, Causes of
  Wise people
Platonius
ancient Greek literary critic
  Character
Plautus, Titus Maccius *254?–184 BC*
Roman comic poet whose plays were
imitated by Shakespeare and Molière
  Action
  Friendship, in times of need
  Modesty
  Money
  Preaching and practice
  Shame
  Women
Pliny *23–79*
the Elder; Roman naturalist
  Criticism
  Home
  Hope
  Novelty
  Perfection

Pliny *62?–113?*
the Younger; Roman writer and
administrator
  Persecution in the early church
Plummer, A.
  Christ, Life of
  Service
Polybius *204?–122 BC*
Greek historian
  Accidents
Polycarp *69?–155?*
Bishop of Smyrna, burnt for his faith
  Bible, Early witnesses to
  Christ, Divinity of
  Evangelism
  Martyrdom welcomed
  Persecution in the early church
Pompadour, Mme de *1721–1764*
mistress of Louis XV of France
  Ambition, Warnings against
  Happiness, Lack of
Pope, Alexander *1688–1744*
English poet
  Boasting
  Churchgoing
  Comfort
  Death, Readiness for
  Expectations
  Forgiveness
  Honesty
  Hope
  Mankind, Middle state of
  Order
  Peace
  Prejudice
  Repentance
  Self-deception
  Thinking, Maturity in
Powerscourt, Viscount
  Mottoes, Personal and family
Prior, Matthew *1664–1721*
English poet
  Garrulity
  Thinking and speech
Prodicus *5th-century BC*
Greek rhetorician
  Business
Protagoras *485–411 BC*
Greek philosopher
  Mankind
Proudhon, Pierre Joseph *1809–1865*
French socialist
  Marxism
Proust, Marcel *1871–1922*
French novelist
  Vision

Prynne, G.R. *1818–1903*
Cornish Anglo-Catholic clergyman and
hymn-writer
  Guidance
Publilius Syrus *1st-century BC*
Latin dramatist
  Debt
  Justice
  Learning from all sources
  Passion
Punch
British humorous magazine
  Procrastination
  Speech and listening
Pyrrhus *319–272 BC*
King of Epirus whose name is
preserved in the phrase 'Pyrrhic victory'
  Victory
Pythagoras *570–456 BC*
Greek philosopher
  Anger
  Mind
  Passion
  Speech
  Witness
Quarles, Francis *1592–1644*
English writer of religious poetry and
prose
  God and mankind
  Searching for God
Quintilian, Marcus Fabius *35?–96?*
Roman orator
  Contentment
  Hypocrisy
  Theology
Quintus Ennius *239–169 BC*
Roman epic poet
  Action
Qur'ān
Muslim holy book
  Women, Inferiority of
Racine, Jean *1639–1699*
French dramatic poet
  Mourning
Raleigh, Walter *1552?–1618*
English poet and soldier-explorer
  Last words
  Life after death
  Pilgrimage
Ramsay, William *1851–1939*
Scottish historian and archaeologist
  Bible, Trustworthiness of
Ramsey, Arthur Michael *1904–1988*
Anglican theologian and Archbishop
of Canterbury
  Resurrection

Rankin, J.E.   *1828–1904*
  God's protection
Rauschenbusch, Walter   *1861–1918*
Baptist pastor in poverty-stricken New
York and later Professor of church
history at Rochester Seminary
  Nature, Redeemed
  Society and the Christian
Ray, John   *1627–1705*
English naturalist and philologist
  Adversity
Reade, Charles   *1814–1884*
English novelist
  Habits
Reith, John   *1889–1971*
1st Baron Reith; first director general
of the BBC
  Opportunity
Rembrandt   *1606–1669*
Dutch painter
  Humour
Renan, Ernest   *1823–1892*
French critic; author of a *Life of Jesus*
  Agnosticism
  Christ, Verdict of non-Christians on
  History and Jesus Christ
Reynolds, Joshua   *1723–1792*
English painter
  Thinking, Avoiding
Richard   *1197–1253*
Bishop of Chichester
  Ambition
Richter, Jean Paul   *1763–1769*
German philosopher
  Art
  Forgiveness
  Music
Rilke, Rainer Maria   *1875–1926*
German poet
  Meditation
Robertson, F.W.   *1816–1853*
English preacher
  Love and suffering
Robertson, William   *18th-century*
English historian
  Christianity
Robeson, Paul   *1898–1976*
US singer and actor; leader in the Black
civil rights movement
  Freedom
Robinson, John   *16th–17th centuries*
Pastor to the Mayflower pilgrims
  Bible
Rochepèdre
French writer
  Ages of man

Rockefeller, John D.   *1874–1960*
US philanthropist
  Aid
  Wealth and happiness
Rogers, Will   *1879–1935*
US actor, newspaper writer and
humourist
  Gossip
  Ignorance
Rolle, Richard   *1300?–1349*
English mystic
  Meditation
Roosevelt, Eleanor   *1884–1962*
US diplomat
  Living
  Opinions, Other people's
  Proverbs
Roosevelt, Franklin Delano
1882–1945
US president during World War 2
  Expectations
  Fear
  Government
  Perseverance
  Spirituality
Roosevelt, Theodore   *1858–1919*
US president
  Bible
  Education
  Proverbs
  Selfishness
  Wisdom
  Work
Rossetti, Christina   *1830–1894*
English poet
  Christmas
  Failure
  Life in Jesus
  Mourning
  Obedience
  Repentance
  Self
  Sight
  Silence
  Sisters
Rossetti, Dante Gabriel   *1828–1882*
English artist and poet; leading figure
in the Pre-Raphaelite movement
  Atheism
  Love
Rousseau, J.B.   *1670–1741*
French poet
  Speech and self-control
Rousseau, Jean-Jacques   *1712–1778*
French philosopher who believed in the
natural goodness of man which he

thought had been warped by social
conditioning
  Bible, Uniqueness of
  Christ, Verdict of non-Christians on
  Conscience
  Freedom
  Giving and getting
  God, as Creator
  Last words
  Original sin
  Pride
  Self-sacrifice
Ruffin, Edmund   *1794–1865*
  Wealth and slavery
Ruskin, John   *1819–1900*
English social reformer and theorist
of art
  Architecture
  Art
  Conversion
  Funerals
  Humility
  Lies
  Mankind, Insignificance of
  Maturity
  Peacemaking
  Preaching, Purpose of
  Pride and what it leads to
  Rush
  Searching for God
  Travel
  Wholeheartedness
  Work, Need for
Russell, William   *1639–1683*
Lord; English politician executed for
plotting against Charles II
  Last words
Rutherford, Mark   *1831–1913*
pseudonym of William Hale White;
English civil servant and novelist of
religion
  Despising
Rutherford, Samuel   *1600?–1661*
Scottish Presbyterian minister;
member of the Westminster Assembly
  Adversity
  Feelings
  God's presence in prison
  Last words
  Prayer
  Prayer, People of
  Pride
  Suffering, Learning from
Ruysbroeck, John of   *1293–1381*
Flemish mystic
  Praise of God

Ryle, John Charles   *1816–1900*
first Anglican Bishop of Liverpool;
strongly evangelical theologian and
writer
  Abiding in God
  Bible
  Bible, Reading the
  Church
  Consecration
  Conversion
  Cross
  Death, as leveller
  Eternity
  Faith and prayer
  Formalism
  Grace and nature
  Hell
  Immortality
  Lord's Supper ineffective by itself
  Money and the service of God
  Prayer
  Prayer and faith
  Prayer, Lack of
  Prayer, People of
  Prayer, Persistence in
  Preaching, Simplicity in
  Preaching and the gospel message
  Purgatory
  Sin, Seriousness of
  Sin forsaken
  Thief on the cross
  Worldliness
Saki   *1870–1916*
pseudonym of H.H. Munro, Scottish
journalist and writer of humorous short
stories
  Pioneers
Sallust, Gaius   *86–34 BC*
Roman historian
  Fear
  Friendship
  Prosperity
Sand, Georges   *1804–1876*
French novelist
  Aid
Sangster, W.E.   *20th century*
English Methodist minister
  Prayer, Method of
Santayana, George   *1863–19252*
US philosopher, poet and critic
  History
Sarcey   *1828–1899*
French critic
  Sin
Sargent, J.
  Prayer, Lack of

Sartre, Jean-Paul   *1905–1980*
French philosopher
  Meaninglessness
Sarum Missal
medieval modification of Roman rite
  Worship
Sayers, Dorothy Leigh   *1893–1957*
English writer
  Cross
Schimmeleninck, M.A.
  God's gifts
Schopenhauer, Arthur   *1788–1860*
German pessimistic philosopher;
author of *The World as Will and Idea*
  Character
  Compassion
  Individuals
  Politeness
Schumacher, Ernst   *1911–1977*
British economist
  Environment
Schweitzer, Albert   *1875–1965*
German organist and theologian and
medical missionary to Africa who
especially emphasised 'reverence for
life'
  Decline
  Environment
  Example
  Preaching
  Race
  Thinking
  Thinking, Avoiding
  Truth wherever it is found
Scofield, C.I.
Bible annotator
  Aid
Scott, C.P.   *1846–1932*
Editor of the *Manchester Guardian*
newspaper
  Facts
Scott, Walter   *1771–1832*
Scottish historical novelist
  Aid
  Courage
  Love
  Motivation
  Mottoes, Personal and family
Scottish Confession   *1560*
first confession of the Scottish
Reformed church
  Conversion, Holy Spirit's work in
Scougal, Henry   *1650–1678*
Scottish theologian
  Christian life
  Union with God

Scriven, J.M.   *1820–1886*
English hymn-writer
  Prayer, Lack of
Seeley, John
  Evangelism
Selden, John   *1584–1654*
English antiquary
  Bible, Uniqueness of
  Preaching and practice
Seneca   *4?* BC–AD *65*
Roman Stoic philosopher, dramatist
and statesman; tutor to the future
emperor Nero
  Anger
  Art
  Behaviour
  Courage
  Cruelty
  Death in the midst of life
  Death, Non-Christian views of
  Disability
  Divorce
  Drink
  God's will
  Greed
  Judging others
  Laughter
  Living
  Living and human relationships
  Love and fear
  Mankind, Insignificance of
  Modesty
  Persecution
  Plagiarism
  Public opinion
  Quietness
  Revenge
  Secrets
  Sensuality
  Virtue
  Wealth and slavery
  Work
Shaftesbury, Anthony Ashley Cooper
1801–1885
7th Earl of Shaftesbury; politician and
social reformer
  Careers
  Courage
  Cruelty
  Friendship
  *God's love, more important than
    anything else*
  Mottoes, Personal and family
  Perseverance in politics
  Politics
  Retirement

Shakespeare, William *1565–1616*
English playwright and poet
  Ambition, Warnings against
  Angels
  Bible
  Christmas
  Conscience
  Devil
  Doubt
  Fashion
  Fortune
  Gratitude
  Gratitude and ingratitude
  Greatness
  Greed
  Honesty
  Humility
  Hypocrisy
  Jealousy
  Leisure
  Mankind, Depravity of
  Meaninglessness
  Mercy
  Music
  Nature
  Old age and action
  Self, Value of
  Sin, Awareness of
  Sorrow
  Speech and action
  Tears
  Temptation, Resisting
Shaw, George Bernard *1856–1950*
Anglo-Irish dramatist and wit
  Bible, Interpretation of
  Economists
  Flattery
  Goals
  Humility
  Mistakes
  Paul, The apostle
  Reformers
  Responsibility
  Saints
  Self-denial
  Teachers
  Thinking
  Truth
Shelley, Percy Bysshe *1792–1822*
English poet
  Power
  Sorrow
Shepard, Thomas
  Revival
Shepherd, Thomas
  Poverty, Spiritual

Sidney, Philip *1554–1586*
English poet and soldier
  Last words
  Love
Silvester, Hugh *20th century*
Christian writer
  Philosophy
Simeon, Charles *1759–1836*
Vicar of Holy Trinity church in
Cambridge where his evangelical
ministry influenced large numbers of
undergraduates
  Bible, Reading the
  Calvinism v. Arminianism
  Christian writing
  Holy Spirit and work
  Last words
  Persecution
  Preaching, Purpose of
  Preaching and the Holy Spirit
  Punctuality
  Regeneration
  Repentance
  Study
  Systematic theology
  Theology
  Work and overwork
Simon, Jules *1814–1896*
French philosopher and writer
  Teachers
Simpson, Carnegie
  Christ
Simpson, David *?–1799*
English Anglican theologian
  Bishops
  Christianity
  Creeds
Simpson, James *1811–1870*
Scottish physician and pioneer of
anaesthetics
  Testimonies to Christ
Singh, Sundar *1889–1929?*
Indian Christian mystic who wore the
robe of a Sadhu (Hindu holy man)
  Christ, as King
  Christian life as following Jesus
  Christianity
  Persecution
  Prayer and the will of God
  Prayer, Definitions of
  Prayer, Effects of on person praying
  Self-denial
  Service
  Service and love for God
  Sin, Definition of
  Worship

Slessor, Mary   *1848–1915*
Scottish missionary to West Africa;
responsible for the ending of human
sacrifice there
  Evangelism
  Trust in God – among wild animals
Smart, Christopher   *1722–1771*
English poet
  Christmas
Smiles, Samuel   *1812–1904*
English writer on social reform and
self-help
  Mistakes
Smith, Adam   *1723–1790*
Scottish economist
  Poverty
Smith, Alexander   *1830–1867*
Scottish poet and essayist
  Environment
Smith, Gypsy
  Revival
Smith, Preserved
  Bible and science
Smith, Sydney   *1771–1845*
English clergyman and wit; defended
Catholic emancipation and helped
found *The Edinburgh Review*
  Apostolic succession
  Caring
  Christian life
  Courage
  Home
  Learning
  Ministers of religion
  Worry
Smith, Taylor
  Worry
Socrates   *470?–399 BC*
Athenian philosopher
  Beauty, Spiritual
  Children, Upbringing
  Discipline
  Ignorance
  Last words
  Learning from all sources
  Self-examination
  Wealth and its use
  Women, Inferiority of
  Wonder
  Zeal
Sophocles   *496?–406 BC*
Greek tragic poet
  Causes, Righteous
  Last words
  Mankind, Exalted estimates of
  Prison

  Reason
  Wealth
Spenser, Edmund   *1552?–1599*
English poet
  Love
Spinoza, Benedict de   *1632–1677*
Dutch philosopher
  Life after death
  Speech and self-control
Spurgeon, Charles Haddon
1834–1892
English Baptist preacher
  Adversity
  Anxiety
  Appearances
  Bereavement
  Bible
  Bible, as the Word of God
  Bible, Authority of
  Charity
  Christian life
  Church
  Civilisation
  Cross
  Depression
  Evangelism
  Faith, Power of
  Faith and obedience
  Gambling
  History and Jesus Christ
  Humility, Nature of
  Ministers of religion
  Ministers of religion, Choice of
  Missionary call
  Parenthood
  Perseverance
  Prayer, Effects of on person praying
  Prayer, Method of
  Preaching, Manner of
  Preaching, Open-air
  Preaching, Purpose of
  Preaching, Simplicity in
  Preaching and the gospel message
  Preaching and the Holy Spirit
  Pride
  Pride and its correction
  Progress
  Promises of God
  Reading
  Silence
  Singing
  Suffering
  Teamwork
  Theology
  Trust in God – when we seem
    abandoned by him

Wisdom and knowledge
Witness through behaviour
Stalin, Josef   *1879–1953*
Soviet head of state
  Death
  Education
Stanley, Henry Morton   *1841–1904*
British explorer and journalist who
sought out David Livingstone, who was
missing in Africa
  Example
Statius, Caecilius   *220–168 BC*
  Environment
Steele, Anne   *1717–1778*
English hymn-writer
  Bible
Steele, Richard   *1672–1729*
English essayist and dramatist
  Flattery
  Reading
Stendhal   *1783–1842*
French writer
  Quotation
Stevenson, Adlai   *1900–1968*
US statesman
  Ignorance
  Poverty
Stevenson, Robert Louis   *1850–1894*
Scottish travel writer and novelist who
rebelled against a strict Calvinist
upbringing but retained a deep faith in
God
  Busyness
  Church buildings
  Death, Inevitability of
  Friendship, Value of
  God's provision
  Grace
  Gratitude
  Happiness
  Joy
  Life after death
  Mankind, Social aspects of
  Morality
  Perseverance
  Politics
  Prayer, Power of
  Sharing
  Silence, Reprehensible
  Work
  Work for God's sake
Stewart, James
  Union with God
Stobaeus   *5th century AD*
Greek anthologist
  Murder

Stone, Lucy   *19th-century*
Educated Massachusetts girl who
joined the abolitionists and pioneered
women's rights
  Slavery
Stowe, Harriet Beecher   *1811–1896*
US writer
  Bereavement
Strachey, Lytton   *1880–1932*
English biographer
  Discipline
Stratford, Nicholas   *1633–1707*
Bishop of Chester
  Usefulness
Studd, C.T.   *1860–1931*
English cricketer and missionary to
India and Africa
  Christian life as conflict
  Consecration
  Conversion
  Evangelism
  Sacrifice
Studdert-Kennedy, Geoffrey Anketell
1883–1929
English World War I army chaplain
and campaigner for the poor
  Church
  Cross
  Indifference
  Mankind, Nature of
  Service
  War
Summerfield
American preacher
  Last words
Sung, John
  Renunciation
Swift, Jonathan   *1667–1745*
English poet and satirist and Dean of St
Patrick's in Dublin
  Ambition, Warnings against
  Argument
  Conservation
  Doctors
  Garrulity
  Hate
  Law
  Living
  Mankind, compared with animals
  Manners
  Mistakes
  Religion
  Shame
Tacitus   *55–117*
Roman historian
  Caution

Christ, Early witnesses to
Hate
Judgement
Persecution in the early church
Tagore, Rabindranath   *1861–1941*
Indian poet and philosopher
Pain
Singing
Talbot, Neville
Depression
Talmud   *5th century* AD
Jewish compilation of law and tradition
Ambition, Warnings against
Duty
Egypt
Gluttony
Hearts
Kindness
Mankind
Neighbour, Love for, and the
*   'Golden Rule'*
Slander
Tanhuma
Title of a Rabbinic homily on the Bible;
part of the Midrash
Caring
Tate, Nahum   *1652–1715*
Irish clergyman and hymn-writer
Peace of God
Tauler, Johann   *1300–1361*
German mystic and Dominican friar
Free will
God's love
Tawney, R.H.   *1880–1962*
English economic historian
Searching for God
Taylor, Bert Leston   *1866–1921*
Speech
Taylor, James Hudson   *1832–1905*
English medical missionary who
founded the China Inland Mission
Difficulties in life
Fund-raising
Last words
Living for God
Loneliness
Missionaries
Patience
Prayer, Power of
Promises of God
Service and God's plans
Service and humility
Taylor, Jeremy   *1613–1667*
Anglican Bishop of Down and Connor;
author of *Holy Living* and *Holy Dying*
Christ, Divinity of

Despair
Eternity
Families
Friendship
Husbands
Mankind, Nature of
Marriage
Mystery
Prayer, Occasions and times of
Taylor, Thomas   *1576–1633*
English puritan theologian
Reading
Teilhard de Chardin, Pierre
1881–1955
French priest and scientist
God's presence
Temple, William   *1887–1944*
Archbishop of Canterbury; theologian
concerned with doctrine and social
issues
Bible, Reading the
Careers
Church
Forgiveness
God's wrath
Hell, Nature of
Knowledge of God
Love
Nature as revealing God
Prayer
Prayer, Method of
Sin
Theology
Worship
Tennyson, Alfred   *1809–1892*
1st Baron Tennyson; English poet
Christ
Christ, Life of
Doubt
Job, Book of
Mankind, Exalted estimates of
Mankind, potential with God
Nature
Prayer, Power of
Purity
Self
Service
Wisdom and knowledge
Terence, Publius   *190?–159* BC
Roman comic dramatist
Love
Teresa   *1515–1582*
of Avila; Spanish Carmelite mystic
Endurance
God's presence amid everyday
*   activities*

Good deeds, Motive of
Habits
Love and actions
Love and prayer
Neighbour, Love for
Prayer
Service in small things
Teresa *1910–*
of Calcutta; missionary nun noted for
her work with the dying
Abortion
Tertullian *150?–212?*
North African theologian
Apostolic doctrine
Baptism
Bible, Reading the
Caring
Christ, Early witnesses to
Christian life
Christianity, Spread of
Confession
Cross
Lord's Supper
Martyrdom, Effects of
Money, Limits to the usefulness of
Persecution in the early church
Philosophy, Pagan
Prayer, Extempore
Selfishness
Society and the Christian
Women and the fall of man
Thackeray, William Makepeace
1811–1863
English novelist
Laughter
Old age
Writing
Thales *624?–546? BC*
Greek philosopher
Idleness
Neighbour, Love for
Theocritus *310?–250? BC*
Greek pastoral poet imitated by Virgil
Death, Non-Christian views of
Theodoret *393?–466?*
Bishop of Cyrrhus in Syria
Sacraments
Theodorus
Prayer, People of
Theognis *6th century BC*
Greek elegiac poet
Meaninglessness
Thomas à Kempis *1380?–1471*
German devotional theologian; author
of *The Imitation of Christ*
Abiding in God

Action
Behaviour
Busyness
Christian life
Cross
Difficult people
Eternal life
Faith required
Friendship, in times of need
Goals, Examples of
God's love, more important than
anything else
God's presence
God's presence and the believer's
response
Good deeds
Government
Grace
Habits, Overcoming
Humility, Exhortations to
Humility, Nature of
Idleness
Judging others
Knowledge, Warnings concerning
Living
Living and dying
Love and actions
Love and self
Love for God
Obedience
Peace and its source in the self
Peace of God
Peace of mind
Peacemaking
Procrastination
Providence of God
Prudence
Reading, Devotional
Self-examination
Simplicity
Singleness of mind
Suffering
Suffering, Patience in
Temptation
Temptation, Purpose of
Trust in God
World
Zeal
Thomas Aquinas *1127–1274*
Theologian whose *Summa Theologiae*
remains the foundation stone of
Roman Catholic theology
Ascension
Beauty, Spiritual
Faithfulness
God's will

Grace and nature
Living
Living, God's help for
Salvation
Thinking, Maturity in
Wisdom and knowledge
Thompson, Francis   *1859–1907*
English poet
 Atheism
 Knowledge of God
 Nature as revealing God
Thoreau, Henry David   *1817–1862*
US mystical writer and nature-lover
 Friendship
 Immortality
 Listening
 Meaninglessness
 Prejudice
 Simplicity
 Solitude
 Vision
 Work, Limitations of
Thring, Edward
 Death
Thucydides   *460?–395? BC*
Greek historian and politician
 Courage
 Poverty, Relief of
Tillotson, John   *1630–1694*
Archbishop of Canterbury
 Purgatory
Titian   *1490?–1576*
Italian painter
 Wisdom
Tolstoy, Alexei Konstantinovich
1817–1875
Russian writer
 Happiness
Tolstoy, Leo   *1828–1910*
Russian novelist and thinker
 Change
 Families
 Self-control
 Service
Toplady, Augustus Montague
1740–1778
English Calvinist clergyman and
hymn-writer; author of 'Rock of Ages
Cleft for Me'
 Forgiveness
 Last words
 Salvation, Mankind's need of
 Trust in God – at life's end
Torrey, Reuben A.
US evangelist
 Bible

Torrey, Mrs Reuben A.
 Death of a child
Toscanini, Arturo   *1867–1957*
Italian conductor
 Witness
Tournier, Paul   *1898–1986*
Swiss doctor and counsellor
 Relationships
Toynbee, Arnold   *1889–1975*
English historian
 Proverbs
 Work
Tozer, A.W.
 Truth
Traherne, Thomas   *1636?–1674*
English clergyman and poet; noted for
his sense of the divine in nature and his
overwhelming sense of thanksgiving
 Cross
 God's wrath
 Worship
Trench, Richard Chevenix   *1807–1886*
Anglican Archbishop of Dublin; wrote
books on the Parables and Miracles
 Gentleness
 Humility
 Prayer and the will of God
Trueblood, Elton
 Faith
Twain, Mark   *1835–1910*
US writer and wit
 Bankers
 Bible, Obedience to
 Blushing
 Civilisation
 Courage
 Death
 Debate
 Devil
 Education
 Experience
 Fun
 Gambling
 Growing up
 Heaven
 Honour
 Humour
 Ideas
 Individuals
 Language
 Lies
 Living and dying
 Mankind, compared with animals
 Mankind, Insignificance of
 Manners
 Old age

Prayer, Method of
Procrastination
Public opinion
Reading
Respect
Sharing
Statistics
Temperance
Temptation, Resisting
Thinking
Tradition
Training
Virtue
Worry
Twells, Henry
Service and humility
Tyndale, William *1492?–1536*
English Reformer and Bible translator,
burnt for heresy
Bible, Translation of
Marriage
Study
Unamuno, Miguel de *1864–1936*
Spanish philosopher and writer
Doubt
Underhill, Evelyn *1875–1941*
English spiritual director and writer on
mysticism
Martyrdom
Upanishads *c.400–200 BC*
Hindu sacred writings
Light
Valéry, Paul *1871–1945*
French poet
Mankind
Van Gogh, Vincent *1853–1890*
Dutch painter
Comfort
God, Belief in
Varro, Marcus Terentius *116–27 BC*
Roman scholar and satirist
Nature, Redeemed
Vaughan, C.J. *1816–1897*
Dean of Llandaff; English clergyman
who trained many ordinands
Bible, Christ in the
Prayer, Lack of
Vauvenargues *1715–1747*
French writer of maxims
Behaviour
Praise of others
Solitude
Verdi, Giuseppe *1813–1901*
Italian composer
Individuals
Music, Effects of

Victoria *1819–1901*
Queen of Great Britain and Ireland
Bible
Second coming of Christ
Vincent de Paul *1581?–1660*
French Roman Catholic priest
Humility, Nature of
Virgil, Publius *70–19 BC*
Roman poet
Belief in self
Death, Non-Christian views of
Scandal
Voltaire, François de *1694–1778*
French philosopher and writer
Appreciation
Burden-sharing
Common sense
Doubt
Excellence
God's existence
Last words
Meaninglessness
Ministers of religion
Obedience
Opportunity
Philosophy
Questions
Speech
Toleration
Truth and martyrdom
Von Hügel, Friedrich *1852–1925*
English Roman Catholic who wrote
books about mysticism and the
philosophy of religion
Adoration
Caring
Fellowship
Suffering
Worship
Von Knebel, Karl
Advice
Walsh, Chad
Preaching, Purpose of
Waring, Anna Letitia *1820–1910*
Welsh hymn-writer
God, as Shepherd
Walton, Izaak *1593–1683*
English writer
God's presence in the believer's heart
Washington, Booker T. *1856–1915*
US negro educationalist and writer
Dignity
Washington, George *1732–1799*
First US president
Conscience
Duty

God's provision
Government
Watkyns, Rowland   *1610?–1664*
Rector of Llanfrynach in Breconshire
Friendship
Watts, Isaac   *1674–1748*
English Independent pastor and
hymn-writer
Christmas
Cross, Personal response to
Heaven, Nature of
Hope
Trust in God – because of his past
   mercies
Webster, Daniel   *1782–1852*
US politician
Goals
Wedgewood, Josiah
English industrial potter
Work, Perfection in
Weil, Simone   *1909–1943*
French philosopher and mystic
Hope
Love
Wellington, Arthur Wellesley
1769–1852
1st Duke of; British general who
defeated Napoleon at Waterloo and
later became prime minister
Education
Fear
Hopelessness
Lord's Prayer
Wells, H.G.   *1866–1946*
English novelist and historian
Atheism
Christ, Verdict of non-Christians on
Wesley, Charles   *1707–1788*
English clergyman and writer of many
famous hymns; brother of John Wesley
Ascension
Birthdays
Courtship
Death of a child
Faith, Power of
Fellowship
Forgiveness
God's love, Desire for
Faith, Power of
Fellowship
Forgiveness
God's love, Desire for
God's love, Response to
God's work
Heaven
Incarnation

Last words
Living for God
Purity
Righteousness from God
Work for God's sake
Wesley, John   *1703–1791*
English clergyman, travelling preacher
and founder of Methodism by his
organising of the new believers who
had responded to his preaching
Action and the present moment
Adversity
Ambition, Warnings against
Behaviour
Bible
Bible, Sufficiency of
Christian life
Christian upbringing
Church
Cleanliness
Courage
Doctrine
Evangelism
Families
Follow-up
Forgiveness
Fretting
Giving
Good deeds, Motive of
Holiness
Humility, Importance of in
   Christianity
Humility, Nature of
Knowledge, Warnings concerning
Last words
Methodism
Missionary call
Money
Opposition
Perfection
Perseverance
Poverty, Spiritual
Prayer, Length of
Prayer, Power of
Preaching
Preaching, Open-air
Preaching, Simplicity in
Rush
Salvation
Salvation, as experienced by Wesley
Service in small things
Slavery
Speech and self-control
Spiritual guides
Temptation, Ways to escape
World, Concern for

Wesley, Susannah
mother of John and Charles Wesley
  Self-control
West, Gilbert *1703–1756*
English theological writer
  Christian upbringing
Westcott, B.F. *1825–1901*
Bishop of Durham; scholar of the
Greek New Testament
  Prayer
  Temptation
Westminster Shorter Catechism
statement of faith of the English church
in Parliamentary times and, more
permanently, of the Church of
Scotland and other Presbyterians
  God's names
  God's nature
Whateley, Richard *1787–1863*
Anglican Archbishop of Dublin
  Belief
  Preaching, Purpose of
Whitefield, George *1714–1770*
English clergyman who attracted huge
crowds to his open-air preaching in
both Britain and America
  Action
  Bible, Reading the
  Conversion of colliers at Kingswood
  Conversion of Whitefield
  Examinations
  Follow-up
  Friendship, and sincerity
  Humility, Examples of
  Last words
  Prayer, Length of
  Preaching, Simplicity in
  Service, Prayers dedicating the self to
Whiting, William *1825–1878*
  Trust in God – at sea
Whitman, Walt *1819–1892*
US poet
  Miracles
Whittier, John Greenleaf *1807–1892*
US poet
  Bible
  Christian life as following Jesus
  Forgiveness
  Future
  God's love, inescapable
  God's presence
  Peace of God
Whittingham, William *1524?–1579*
Calvinist minister who succeeded John
Knox as pastor in Geneva
  Reformation, Church

Whyte-Melville, George *1821–1878*
  Commandments
Wilberforce, William *1759–1833*
English politician and philanthropist
who worked for the abolition of slavery
  Difficulties in life
  Gratitude and ingratitude
  Holiness
  Perseverance in politics
  Politics
  Prayer, Lack of
  Rush
  Wealth and pride
Wilde, Oscar *1854–1900*
Anglo-Irish poet, dramatist and wit
  Art
  Mankind
  Temptation, Resisting
  Temptation, Ways to escape
  Truth and martyrdom
  Work
  Writing
Wilkes, P.
  Prayer and the heart's desire
  Revival
Williams, Isaac *1802–1865*
English theologian and poet who wrote
Tract LXXX on 'Reserve in
Communicating Religious Knowledge'
  Trust in God
Williams, Roger *1603?–1683*
Founder of Providence in New England
  Time
Wilson, Edward *1872–1912*
English explorer with Scott of the
Antarctic
  Love, Purity of
Wilson, Thomas *1663–1755*
Bishop of Sodor and Man
  Revenge
  Trust in God
  Trust in God – for the future
Wilson, Woodrow *1856–1924*
US president who helped found the
League of Nations
  Bible, and society
  Bible, as the word of God
  Duty
  Proverbs
  Service
Winchester, Marquis of
  Mottoes, Personal and family
Windsor *1894–1972*
Duke of; Britain's former King
Edward VIII, who abdicated
  Parenthood

Wishart, George   *1513?–1546*
Scottish Reformer
  Forgiving others
Wood, F.P.
  Opposition
Woolf, Virginia   *1882–1941*
English novelist and critic
  Self-control
Woolworth, F.W.   *1852–1919*
US retailer
  Delegation
Wootton, Henry
  Ambassadors
Wordsworth, Christopher   *1807–1885*
Bishop of Lincoln
  Devil, Existence of
Wordsworth, William   *1770–1850*
English poet
  Evening
  Prayer, Effects of on person praying
  Quietness
  Rainbows
  Service in small things
  Worship
Wyatt, Thomas   *1503–1542*
English poet
  Prayer
Wycliffe, John   *1330?–1384*
English clergyman and academic
philosopher who became a religious
reformer and Bible translator
  Government

Temptation
  Truth triumphant
Wylie, James Aitken
  Preaching, Open-air
Xavier, Francis   *1506–1552*
Jesuit teacher and pioneer missionary
in India
  Child evangelism
Xenophon   *444–354 BC*
Greek historian
  Praise
Yattendon Hymnal
  Cross, Personal response to
Young, Edward   *1683–1765*
English poet and dramatist
  Procrastination
Zeuxis   *5th century BC*
Greek painter
  Criticism
Zinzendorf, Nicolaus von   *1700–1760*
German religious reformer
  Mottoes, Personal and family
Zohar   *medieval*
Jewish mystical commentary on parts
of the Pentateuch and Hagiographa
  Pride and what it leads to
Zusya
rabbi
  Self, Value of
Zwingli, Huldrych   *1484–1531*
Swiss Reformation theologian
  Dress